MADELEINE KAMMAN'S SAVOIE

Books by Madeleine Kamman

Madeleine Cooks *(1986)*
In Madeleine's Kitchen *(1984)*
When French Women Cook *(1976)*
Dinner Against the Clock *(1973)*
The Making of a Cook *(1970)*

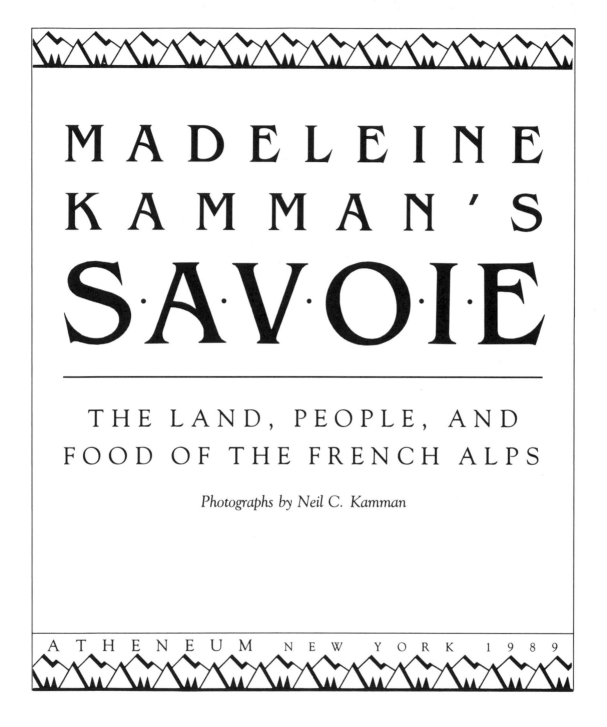

MADELEINE KAMMAN'S

SAV·OIE

THE LAND, PEOPLE, AND FOOD OF THE FRENCH ALPS

Photographs by Neil C. Kamman

ATHENEUM NEW YORK 1989

This book is dedicated to my mother,

SIMONE PIN

with my undying gratitude for putting
me on that train to Annecy on July 11, 1937.

Atheneum
Macmillan Publishing Company
866 Third Avenue, New York, N.Y. 10022
Collier Macmillan Canada, Inc.

Library of Congress Cataloging-in-Publication Data
Kamman, Madeleine.
    Madeleine Kamman's Savoie : the land, people, and food of the
French Alps / Madeleine Kamman ; photographs by Neil C. Kamman.
        p.   cm.
    Bibliography: p.
    Includes index.
    ISBN 0-689-11969-0
    1. Cookery, French.   2. Cookery—France—Savoie.   3. Savoie
(France)—Social life and customs.   4. Alps, French (France)—
Description and travel.   I. Title.
TX719.K263   1989
641.5944′48—dc20   89-6865   CIP

Printed in the United States of America

CONTENTS

INTRODUCTION

What a day! Fifty-one years later I still remember fondly July 11, 1937, the last day of my first serious school year. My very straight hair had been curled, I was wearing a blue organza dress made especially for me by my older cousin —a rated *première main* at Molyneux—and when my name was called, nervous, hot, and red-faced, I went to the podium to receive the *prix d'excellence* for the school year. It was one of those volumes bound in crimson with gold letters, which no French person who went to school in my generation could fail to remember; its title, *Loulou in Africa*, could not have been more typical in those days of diehard French colonialism.

The day of celebration included one of those huge French lunches, especially prepared by my grandmother, who, in the afternoon, took all of us grandchildren to the Fête at Neuilly. Ah, *la fête*, as we called it, was the biggest convention of merry-go-rounds you ever could think of, one after another lined up on both sides of the long avenue, which then ran from the Neuilly bridge to the *Défense*. *La fête* was fun and excitement made out of not much more than watery ice cream cones and multicolored twists of something sweet and cloying called *guimauve*, which in the American world would be roughly a cross between a marshmallow and a saltwater taffy, a few joyrides, and a few wheel games. On that day I was lucky and won several little Bengali lovebirds for which my mother had to find a cage, at the same time as she had to finish packing my suitcase, for that night I was to leave from the Gare de Lyon to spend the summer in the Savoie.

Electric trains did not yet exist, so it was in front of one of those frightening and smelly coal and steam engines that I was delivered into the hands of the counselors who would be my mentors for the summer. As it turned out, I did not remain with them only a few weeks; they remain with me to this day, taking such an important place in my education that I owe to their teaching at least some of the decisions I have made about my life. These ladies were lay sisters, dedicated to taking to the mountains children from the best and worst Paris suburbs. The home they made for us on a large remodeled Savoie farm was for some a rough summer camp, for others the most luxurious place they had ever known. It was a place where children could ask innocently, "What is that, Mozart?" and be answered by the superb soprano voice of a young woman singing equally well the *Ave Verum*, or the arias of Cherubino or Susanna.

The community we formed was a microcosm of pre–World War II French society (which, fundamentally, has not changed all that much), and the summer was one long and interesting blending of our lives with that of a very small Savoie village. This wonderful experience lasted for me through six summers and the whole somber war and school year of 1940. During all that time I received from *Mesdemoiselles* so much knowledge and kindness that I developed for the Savoie village in which we lived our summers, a nostalgia very much akin to what can be found in the first chapters of Jean Jacques Rousseau's *Confessions*.

What I can now, after many years, call a true love affair, started even before we arrived. The train had left around seven at night, and since I was the youngest and the smallest on a ten-hour trip, I had been put to sleep in the baggage rack; I proceeded to fall out of it around six o'clock in the morning, waking up all the other children in the train compartment. The window shades were opened to reveal the most amazing sight I had ever seen in all my not quite seven years. The train was gliding along a dark silvery lake on which the morning fog formed long, silky and translucent white sashes; here and there fishermen's boats appeared through the mist. On the other side of the lake I saw a large white building, not quite a castle, not quite a church, over which loomed a mountain looking very much like a gigantic tooth. I had discovered the lake made famous by Lamartine, and I started to cry. Asked what was wrong, I innocently declared as loud as I could, "Oh nothing, I just think it is beautiful." It certainly was beautiful, but I must have missed my mother and did not want to admit it, so I remained over the years the "kid who cries because she thinks mountains are beautiful." Since I have shed adult tears of aesthetic joy in front of the Parthenon and the Tetons many years later, there may have been some truth to my bombastic declaration, and I am still not too sure of what will happen when I finally can contemplate Everest. That first beautiful morning was a mere beginning. When we arrived in Annecy, it felt cold, the grayish mountains were flooded in morning light, and the lake was even more beautiful than Lamartine's had been. I sat on the edge of my bus seat very quiet and subdued. We arrived at our village, La Balme de Thuy, sleepy and exhausted, and tried to settle down to a routine. We were treated at night to one of those impressive mountain thunderstorms; in the mountains a storm will paint the end of a valley an unforgettable purple and send thunderclaps bouncing and resounding from mountain wall to mountain wall. Steady rain poured for three days. We were lost in clouds with only the smell of the cows and the constant noise of rushing water to remind us that we were in the mountains. And then, for July 14, the weather changed. It was cold; the dew slowly rose from the fields in large puffs of steam and slowly and playfully climbed up and along the steep rock faces that towered on all sides over the village. By noon it was searingly hot, and all the diamonds of rain that in the morning had dotted the beautiful carpets of field flowers had disappeared. A few days later, once the grass had dried, the villagers started mowing. What a sight at night! Big hay wagons brought huge loads of fresh-smelling grass topped with children our own age who thought nothing of letting themselves slide down to the ground and help attach the bales to large hooks; their father, who stood way up under the eaves of the family chalet, pulled the bales up and stored them as winter fodder.

Another interesting sight was offered every night by the few cows that were not spending the summer on the mountain. They came back to the village from their field, called *le champ les vaches*, and never but never failed to stop right in front of our house. At first my nose wrinkled, then I got used to it, and it became part of the life and scenery. So did our neighbor, a statuesque person in a white apron who collected the cows into her barn and, balanced on a three-legged stool, proceeded to hand-milk them. She was to introduce us little city girls to *lait bourru* straight from the cow, which tasted marvelous compared to the bottled products we got at home. She also made cheese every night, at just about the time the church bell rang the Angelus; she never failed to cross herself and say a quick Hail Mary before starting her work.

Breakfast was simple—none of the city croissants, *biscottes* with jams, and other delicacies some of us had been raised on. Here the table held large bowls of milk clabbered by Mélanie our cook, mountains of chewy dry and none-too-fresh bread, and colorful russet-colored pots full of our neighbor's milk, hot and foamy, and yellow pots full of weak coffee. The bread, served without butter, was democratically dipped into café au lait by many, daintily broken by others. For many of us, lessons in table manners started there, and so did our domestic arts education. No sooner were breakfast and morning prayers over than we had to execute our domestic "charges": cleaning dorms, peeling vegetables, or participating in the preparation and cooking of both meals for the day. The second part of the morning, *Mesdemoiselles* sat us in the grass in the *verger*, a large field filled with apple trees, and our education on the surrounding countryside and its life and customs followed. Looking back on what notes I took over the years, I was surprised at all that had been taught in that field about religious history, the geology of the Alps, the history of the Savoie, local music, and songs. The afternoons were spent running in the mountains and forests, and that for me was the best. What started as small walks when I was a young child ended up in tremendously interesting and challenging climbs when I became a teenager and young adult with backpack and ice pick. It was with *Mesdemoiselles* that, no older than nine, I climbed the 7000-foot peak of the Tournette that dominates the Annecy lake.

After the war, when climbing sports developed seriously in France, great mountain names such as Louis Lachenal, Lionel Terray, and Maurice Herzog were given to us as examples. It was Gaston Rebuffat who sent me scampering, hiking, and climbing all over the Alps, and Frison Roche who gave me my passion for the Mont Blanc massif. And it was with *Mesdemoiselles* that I found my first edelweiss and saw my first brown eagle and my first mountain goat through the antiquated binoculars that Monsieur le Curé had lent us.

These years marked my life so deeply that later, when I was working as reservations manager for Swissair in Paris, I would keep begging my supervisor for three days off here and there to hike up some peak. More often than not I was successful since he was Swiss and felt as separated from his Swiss mountains as I did from my Savoie ones.

Our cook Mélanie, of whom more will be said, prepared the very best dinners for kids who were ravenously hungry and whose first question upon arriving back from the mountain was, "Madame Mélanie, pray tell, what's for dessert?" After dinner we enjoyed going on the balcony because all the kids —at least, in those days, the boys of the village—gathered right there at the fountain, and whoever was interested in the life of the village—and I was intensely so—could listen, try to understand the patois, and learn a lot about one cow or another, or what the priest had said to some baaaaaad girl, etc. The best time came on Sunday when we filled the little church pews to the point of leaving no space for the village people. I had more fun in that church getting a stiff neck while trying to see what happened on the balcony, where the village boys formed the chorus. One of my greatest disappointments came in 1980 when, visiting the church, I realized that the balcony had been taken down. It had indeed been dangerously rickety!

When I came to the United States it looked as if I would never see the land of my love again, so I proceeded to indoctrinate my very willing husband, and four years later we spent a great vacation together with our first young son in Chamonix. Obviously, when the time came to choose a small dwelling in France, I went straight to Annecy, which is only a few miles from my beloved Balme. I do not own a car in France because I prefer to walk as much as possible; my greatest treat consists of walking the ten miles or so to La Balme and coming back by bus, or vice versa. Except for a few more houses along the narrow road, which is now paved, nothing much has changed; the same trees line the road, reminding me that on one day I stole pears here or walnuts there. The fields in the fall offer the same purple crocuses, and in the spring the same primulae.

Amazingly enough, although I have spent more time in the Touraine, where my father's family came from, than in the Savoie, it is the Savoie that is my elected home. I always dreamed of writing a book on the food of the Savoie, but not enough was known about it until very recently. Even Waverley

Root in his *The Food of France* describes the fare of this large part of France in only a few pages. Luckily, things changed in 1981; while I was living and teaching in Annecy, the only serious book on the food of the Savoie was published. There was already a good deal of geographical, historical, and ethnological material, and more recently a veritable torrent of fascinating data, as well written as it is well documented. Of all the French provinces, the Savoie is probably the most written about, at least in the French language. The announcement in 1987 that the 1992 Winter Olympic Games would take place in Savoie spurred me on to write a book in English and precipitated a project that I had had in mind for many years. The difficulty resided in the sifting of a huge amount of material to extract what was the essential information. I hope I have succeeded in offering the American reader a general picture of how a people lived, worked, and cooked, and how they have succeeded in transforming their lives and surroundings to live happily at the end of the twentieth century. Modern traveling is in a way terribly bad—one flies, one drives, and one sees and feels nothing but what is on the roadside; hotel rooms remain hotel rooms everywhere, and the true soul of a region or country remains unknown. What there is to see and understand in the Savoie is not in the modern cities; it is in the backcountry, in the villages, on the farms, with the people who work and produce small works of art on a daily basis not only in the form of arts and crafts but also in the form of cheeses, wines, herbs, vegetables, flowers, and liqueurs.

In the Savoie, it is close to impossible to separate the old from the new. Much of what one does for a living has been done for centuries, whether one makes cheese, fishes in the mountain lakes, or grows vines. Even if roads and cars make the mountains more accessible, cows remain cows and must be tended to today as they were always. The hay must still be mowed in the summer and the sky watched for storms that would make it wet. So if you visit the Northern Savoie today and reread Rousseau's *Confessions* as soon as you return home, his text will give you a definite impression of déjà vu.

This is not strictly a cookbook because it reflects my philosophy of teaching cookery. It has become apparent to me over the years that without geology, geography, and history as support disciplines, there is absolutely no way to understand the food of any region properly, so I have made this book a cookbook that also contains all the elements of geology, geography, and history necessary to understanding why in the Savoie the food is what it is, and where it is coming from geographically and ethnologically.

This book will help visitors to the 1992 Winter Olympic Games—or anyone else lucky enough to visit the area—to understand the intense sense of belonging that exists in the Savoie. It is not a guidebook to the best view on Mont Blanc, the best value in cheese or restaurant meals, or the best shopping places; it is a simple book (what is called in French *une synthèse de vulgarisation*) that hopes to make the reader want to visit the Savoie and, once there, understand life through the passing of the centuries. That I am not a historian, but only a cook interested in relating cooking, geography, and history, will be evident to all trained historians; there is no doubt that I will have missed a few connections, just as historians who write about the history of cooking or cuisine can on occasion miss a connection because they are not trained cooks. Eventually, through the efforts of cooks and historians combined, a broader truth will emerge.

One word on reaching the Savoie. The best way is to fly into Geneva directly from the United States or into Lyon, Annecy, or Chambéry through Paris; and if one drives, to take the expressways through to Chambéry or Annecy, Chambéry being the door to the Southern Savoie and Annecy to the Northern Savoie. By 1992, many more expressways will have been built to reach Albertville and Thonon, and to bypass what, so far, have been traffic jams between the ski resorts of the Upper Tarentaise and the Combe de Savoie. To see the true Savoie, you must go on the small country roads; even in the winter they are cleared very well of snow so that you can get to the countryside and not stay only in the larger city centers. Our American cities are so gigantic and spread out that even larger cities in the Savoie may appear like villages to the American eye. They are not, and it is essential to leave those small cities, to go into the true villages. There are still rural communities with little more than a hundred dwellers, and this is where the true spirit of the Savoie remains. Enjoy it!

Without all the people listed below, this book could never have been written, and to all of them I owe much gratitude for their love, understanding, education, erudition, and dedication. They are:

My father, Charles Pin, who recognized early my love for all things aesthetically pleasing and sat me in the jump seat of his 5HP Peugeot to see the Savoie valleys before World War II.

My mother, Simone Pin, who, as a widow, worked very hard so I could complete my education; without her efforts, I would not now have the background necessary to sift and relate the mass of information that came to me through living in the Savoie and reading many books.

My husband, Alan, who always shared my love for the Savoie mountains, and my two sons, Alan and Neil, who mastered so well skiing and mountain climbing. A special thank you goes to Neil, who took the pictures for this book.

Mesdemoiselles, the team of educators in La Balme de Thuy, among them Melle Madeleine Gaugué, who first realized that I could become a true teacher and started me on my career; Melle Madeleine Chevallier, who taught me both first aid and Christian charity; Melle Cécile Lévesque (appearing later in this book as *Mademoiselle*), the strict disciplinarian who instilled self-discipline in me; and Sister Jeanne Vidard (appearing later as *la metra*), who came from her convent of Carmelites and went back to it, leaving Mozart in my life.

Madame Déléan, the mother of my friend Mimi, with whom I constantly sat around just to talk and observe.

The American food writer Waverley Root, whose pioneering work in the United States on French provincial cuisines, *The Food of France*, sent me on all the research projects I have so far conducted on all the provincial and regional cuisines of France.

Monsieur l'Abbé Lucien Chavoutier and all the writers of the Société Savoisienne d'Histoire et d'Archéologie in Chambéry, Savoie. It is mostly in the immense wealth of knowledge and erudition included in all the books and pamphlets they published that I have found the formal information I needed to corroborate my own experiences.

Georgette Reygrobellet, my friend and neighbor in Annecy, who worked with me for several years and shared memories of her grandmother's cooking and baking in Annecy-le-Vieux during the first half of this century.

Monsieur Reymond, the bus driver of Crolard Voyages in Annecy, who for several years took my classes on tours through the Savoie and the Val d'Aosta and generously shared with me his wealth of knowledge about local customs and history.

The members of the Hermann family: Madame Marie Thérèse Hermann, author of the only Savoie farm cookbook, and her son and daughter-in-law, Monsieur and Madame Jean Christophe Hermann, who operate the most authentic Savoie pottery in Evires as well as a very well-documented museum. They all gave me generously of their time in talking about this book and their beloved country of birth.

Madame Marguerite Allemmoz, president of the Académie de la Val d'Isère, who gave me a personal and intensely documented tour of the small museum of Moûtiers.

Madame Allemmoz-Servanin, owner of the Moûtiers bookstore, for her advice on choosing major historical texts and for calling Monsieur l'Abbé Chavoutier for me.

Madame Bulloz, librarian at the Public Library in Annecy, who searched for all the texts I needed from the Annecy Library, and her colleagues at the Archives of the Haute Savoie who researched some texts buried in the archives of the old Annecy Seminary.

Monsieur Max Michoud of the Department of Fisheries of the Administration des Eaux et Forêts in Thonon, who took the time to explain to me the modern methods of pisciculture in the Alpine lakes.

Monsieur l'Abbé Milleret, Curé of Termignon, and his sister for opening his church so we could take extensive pictures of the baroque altars, statues, and wood carvings.

Monsieur le Curé Gros of Jarrier, who, among the many persons I contacted, was the only one to truly help me find a lady willing to dress up in one of the multiple Savoie local costumes so we could photograph her.

Madame Albert Viallet of Jarrier, who took the time to dress up in that costume and who looked like a vision of centuries past as she walked out of her house into the eternal Alpine scenery.

Monsieur Defollin, the extraordinary guide of the Abondance Abbey, who explains the restoration of fresco paintings with such enthusiasm that it becomes contagious.

Madame and Monsieur Bastard Rosset, owners of the perfect small Nouvel Hôtel du Commerce in Thônes, who prepared for me the *farcement* appearing in the picture in the color insert (between pages 176 and 177). When my parents visited me in La Balme, they used to stay at the hotel then run by the Rossets' grandparents. Madame Rosset was born in La Balme and has the same memories of it as I have.

Madame Marthe Schmidt, the soul of the Hôtel de l'Arveyron in Les Praz de Chamonix, whose bicycle I used and almost wore out over the years while investigating the Chamonix valley.

Madame Gagneux, last maker of the Vacherin cheese in the Abondance valley, who spoke to me at length of her profession.

Madame Deloche from Le Paradis in Thônes and Madame Marius Bastard Rosset of Le Bouchet in Le Grand Bornand, who both were kind and patient enough to show my students how the Reblochon is made; and Madame Patricia Burgat of Serraval, who makes my favorite goat cheese and sells it at the Annecy market.

Monsieur Maret, director in 1981 of the Fruitière of Frangy, who took a whole day to guide me and several friends through the making of Savoie Emmental and to explain the chemistry of proteins in cheese-making; and the directors of the Fruitières of Beaufort and Saint Jean d'Arve for the wonderful windows and balconies where one can comfortably observe the making of Beaufort cheese.

My editor, Judith Kern, who for years has made good English out of my Frenglish.

Carla Mayo, who drew for me the costumes and bonnets on pages 70 and 71.

THE LAY OF THE LAND AND THE NATURAL ENVIRONMENT

This will be the story of the Alps as they developed over millions of years. It will be a very general overview of all the geological and geographical traits of the Savoie that are absolutely essential if one is to appreciate the scenery, be able to find important valleys and cities, know which trees, flowers, and animals can be seen, understand how the pretty Alpine lakes happened to be, what the weather can be like, and how the geography and geology of an area determine which foods will be locally cultivated and consequently cooked.

I have drawn several charts that explain the geology of the French Alps visually and two maps that give the exact position of all locations and areas mentioned. May I suggest that readers who would like to visit the Savoie refer to Michelin map numbers 74 and 73, or to the French Institut National de Géographie's map number 12. If traveling by car, the two best maps to use are 74 Haute Savoie and 73 Savoie, *plans nets* (Editions Pauchet, Paris), which show all access roads to valleys existing at this date and which will surely be reprinted to include the new expressway extensions now being built in the Isère valley for the 1992 Olympic Games. I always carry the last three maps with me on study trips. The *plans nets* leave enough space to make notes about curiosities to be seen when preparing an itinerary.

GEOLOGICAL FORMATION OF THE FRENCH ALPS

The amount of material written on the formation of the Alps is absolutely staggering. As you read my story, you may want to go back to your high school days and try to recall what you learned about the four geological eras. The primary era was marked by the formation of mountain massifs that are now eroded but have left a considerable amount of crystalline rock on this planet. The secondary era was marked by millions of years of ocean invasion over the existing solid rock expanses and the formation of sedimentary rock layers over this crystalline base. The third era was marked by the upsurge of many crystalline mountain massifs, which are still only moderately eroded and quite high. The Alps are one of those in Europe, the Rocky Mountains one in America. The Quaternary period is the geological period in which we are now living. At its onset, it was characterized by a successive number of very important glaciations, remnants of which are still visible in the ice caps of both poles and the valley glaciers that cover many mountain massifs all over the world.

The Savoie is located in the westernmost part of the chain of the Alps, and within its limits the highest summit in Europe, Mont Blanc, sits in splendor. Many people assume that Mont Blanc is in Switzerland because it is so very visible from Geneva on clear days, but in reality it lies sixty miles within the French border. Mont Blanc is an old friend of mine. Not too far from my home in France, in the small city of Annecy, there is a relatively low Alpine pass called the Col des Aravis. When I have a car I love to drive up there after dinner on summer or early fall nights. The evenings up there are as quiet as a church, fragrant with the perfume of fresh grass and Alpine flowers. The tourists have all gone home for the day and the mountain returns to its eternal peace. If the weather is good Mont Blanc sits at the dead center of the pass like a huge diamond, and the sunset on its eternal snows is a treat for the eyes and the soul. In the palpable quiet, the big white rock changes from salmon pink to deep orange and gradually deepening purple before disappearing into the night. I usually head down for the valley as the last touch of light dies on the summit. But often I have stayed up there overnight, the guest of cheese-makers, to be awakened early by cowbells. At sunrise the play of the light goes in reverse order. If there is a full moon, it sits low on the horizon, accompanied by Venus, its faithful companion. As they both wane rapidly, the sun announces its arrival from the other side of the world by touching the snowy summit with the barest hint of green, followed by several shades of purple, rose, and peach, until finally the blinding whiteness of the snow heralds the arrival of another day on the ice castle that has been standing there for so many million years.

True-blue geologists may not like the way I explain the birth of the French Alps, because my story is very simplified, but they will know that the story is horribly complex and that anyone truly fascinated by the subject can find many interesting theories explained in any number of European and American texts. I read many books and was fascinated, but quickly realized that geology is such a technical subject that my readers would be likely to fall asleep on me if I did

Figure 1

The African plate juts into the Eurasian plate through the Alps to form the SUB-ALPINE PLATE.

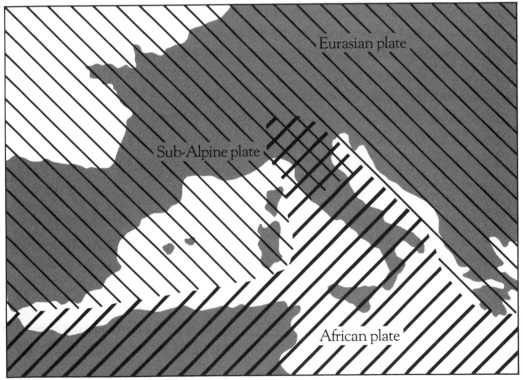

not keep things as simple as possible. For help in simplification I went to the Annecy museum, where I found the latest theories explained in the light of continental plate tectonics.

Just so you remember what happened in the mind-boggling length of time that our planet has existed, our Earth was at one time a single huge mass of land called Pangea. Pangea started separating into pieces: Eurasia went one way while what became Africa, India, and Australia went the other, slowly separated by a large sea called Thethys. As the movements of the continents continued, Thethys became a large channel that took the name of Mesogea. Mesogea has become continually smaller and smaller, and one of its tiny remnants is our bright blue Mediterranean. Eventually Africa separated from the Indo-Australian plate to leave the following arrangement: Eurasian plate, African plate, and Indo-Australian plate. It might be logical to assume that the line of separation between the African and Eurasian plates would be straight and pass right through the Mediterranean, but it does not. The African plate extends a large excrescence into the Mediterranean that passes to the right of Sardinia and Corsica, goes up through the Gulf of Genoa, makes a right turn above the Po River in Italy and another right turn down into the Adriatic Sea, thus enclosing Italy in a small extension of the African plate called the SUB-ALPINE plate (see Figure 1).

The formation of the Alps started 200 million years ago while Pangea still existed as a single mass. On a bottom of oceanic crust there already existed a continental crust of crystalline rock formed during the primary era. This crystalline crust was covered by a shallow sea that deposited sediment called Triassic

Figure 2

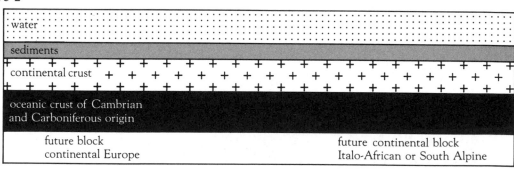

water	
sediments	
continental crust	
oceanic crust of Cambrian and Carboniferous origin	
future block continental Europe	future continental block Italo-African or South Alpine

rock, which was made of limestone, dolomite, and gypsum, over the primary rock. A schema of what the plate looked like is shown in Figure 2.

Still during the secondary era, during the Jurassic or Lias period, which is approximately 180 million years ago, stretching and buckling movements occurred in the crust, which made the primary core of continental crust elevate and come out of the sea, building what is known as two geosynclines on either side of the elevated core. Geologists named the western geosyncline Dauphiné geosyncline and the eastern geosyncline Piemontese geosyncline. Figure 3 illustrates what happened; note the direction of the pressure causing the deformation.

Figure 3

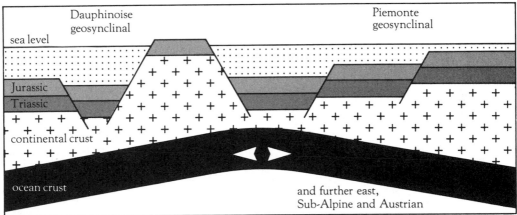

At the end of the Jurassic period, approximately 140 million years ago, a large ocean developed, the level of which rose so high that it once more covered the overelevated primary core. This resulted in further accumulation of sediment. Meanwhile the pressure on the rock base was increasing considerably from beneath (upward arrows in Figure 4) and continuing sideways (right and left arrows in ocean crust core). A break in the plate occurred. At this point the schema for the formation of the Western and Eastern Alps was completed. The French and Northern Italian Alps are situated on the western edge of the Eurasian plate; the Mediterranean chains find themselves inside the delimitations of the Sub-Alpine plate, and the Austrian and Eastern Alps rest on the Eurasian plate at the eastern margin of the Sub-Alpine plate.

Figure 4

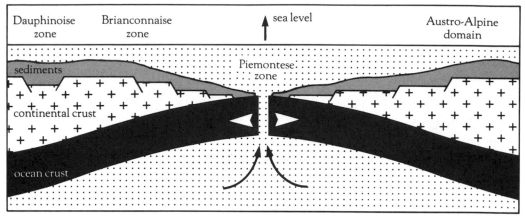

Figure 5

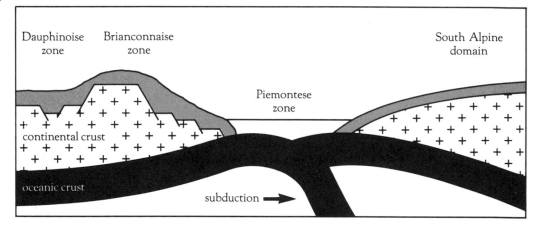

Figure 6

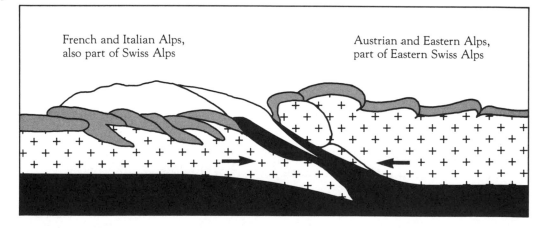

After 90 million years distension movements had stopped and been replaced by contraction movements, as the Eurasian plate progressively plunged under the Sub-Alpine plate. At the end of that part of the secondary era called the Cretaceous period, the heavily sedimented Piemontese zone had almost disappeared under the Sub-Alpine plate, and this shortening of the Piemontese area provoked the first mountain folds in a northwestern direction as well as the first ripples on the Sub-Alpine margin (see Figure 6). Every chain or massif of mountains in formation reaches a paroxysm of folding activity. For the Alps it happened between the Eocene—60 million years ago—and the Miocene—27 to 25 million years ago—epochs. By this time the subduction of the European plate under the Sub-Alpine plate was completed; the enormous pressures involved gave birth to the chain.

A look at Figure 7 on page 8 will make it easy to recognize the arrangement of plates. The portion at the bottom right of the map is made of stones called green lustered schists that are part of the Sub-Alpine plate. Its fusion line with the western edge of the Eurasian plate is marked by a sawtooth pencil line.

The Western Alps are now arranged as can be seen on the same map: Just west of the zone of fusion of the two plates are the internal crystalline massifs of the VANOISE and MONT POURRI, which are surrounded by large masses, or nappes, of materials carried westward over those crystalline massifs by the folding pressure; these mountains, when you see them, will show a black or gray soil made of materials related to coal, or even coal itself.

One step more to the west, one can see the chains that form the external crystalline massifs of the Alps: Mont Blanc, Aiguilles Rouges, Beaufortain, Belledone, and the Grandes Rousses. Some of their granite is of primary origin, some of Tertiary, the two being distinguishable by their different colors.

Yet another step to the west one reaches an area where the mountains are made of sedimentary material that originally covered the external massifs; it took these sedimentary terrains millennia to slide down and form what are called the Pre-Alps.

There remain on the map three mountainous areas made of sedimentary material capable of retaining a lot of water, which was pushed violently westward by the upsurge of the eastern blocks of mountains. The largest of these

Figure 7 THE MOUNTAINS AND THEIR GEOLOGICAL ARRANGEMENTS

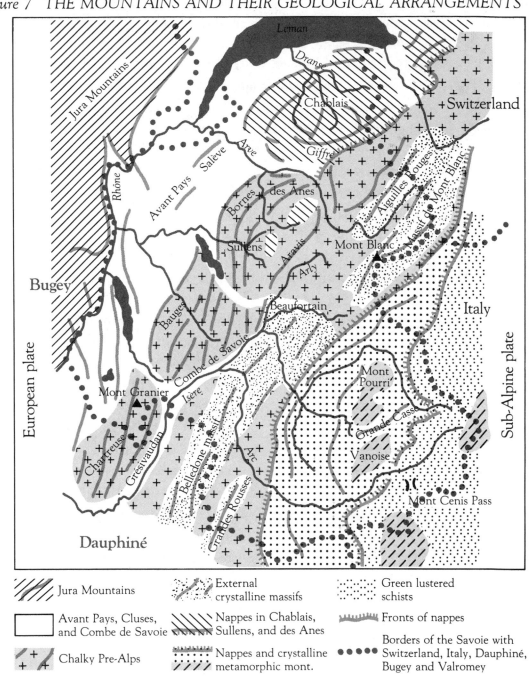

Jura Mountains

Avant Pays, Cluses, and Combe de Savoie

Chalky Pre-Alps

External crystalline massifs

Nappes in Chablais, Sullens, and des Anes

Nappes and crystalline metamorphic mont.

Green lustered schists

Fronts of nappes

Borders of the Savoie with Switzerland, Italy, Dauphiné, Bugey and Valromey is the Chablais (the geological name there is nappes), the smaller two the Montagnes des Anes and de Sullens (geological name, klippes).

Before going on a trip through the Alps it is a good idea to understand some special terms that will recur in this text:

A CLUSE is more or less a narrow cut almost perpendicular to a mountain fold through which two depressions situated on each side of the fold communicate.

A COMBE is a longitudinal depression dug by erosion at the hollow of a mountain fold.

Nowadays both erection and erosion are occurring simultaneously as the Alps slowly continue developing faults. Once in a while there is a great catastrophe, a big rockslide or an earthquake, just to remind the mountain population that the earth mantle is constantly moving. On November 24, 1248, Mont Granier, the main summit of the Chartreuse Massif in the Pre-Alps, lost a great big slice of its face, transforming a pretty little plain full of farms and cultivated fields into a boulder desert. The Savoie people have learned how to reuse the area, as you will see later. Also, in much more recent times, early one morning in 1980 in Annecy, Mozart's Jupiter Symphony lasted exactly three minutes as a small earthquake pushed the diamond from the beginning of the record to the end while lights flickered madly. It was a small aftershock of the huge earthquake that had recently shaken the Benevento area in Italy, at the other end of the Sub-Alpine plate.

Glaciers have been waxing and waning in the Alps since the beginning of our Quaternary period. At one point the glaciers extended way way down into the flatter lands of the foothills. For example, the glacier out of which the Rhône River flows came very close to Lyon and left, as it retreated, large ice holes northeast of the city in an area called Les Dombes; these ice holes are now used for cultivating sturgeon. What small parts of these huge glaciers are left nowadays add a great deal of attraction to the countryside, which can literally be read like a living manual of geology. Glaciers dug gigantic valleys, very recognizable by their U profiles, as opposed to the sharp V profiles of valleys crafted by rivers.

THE REGIONS OF THE SAVOIE AND THEIR GEOLOGICAL LANDMARKS

When I travel I like to be able to read the countryside. So that you will be able to do just that if you come to the Savoie, I am going to draw your attention to some of the most important geological features by taking you on a few interesting trips.

CHABLAIS TRIP

If you start from Geneva and drive to Thonon and Evian along Lake Leman through route N5, you will be passing through the areas of the Savoie called the Bas Chablais and the Chablais. The major geological landmark here is Lake Leman itself, which, in its small, narrow western end is called Lake Geneva because of the presence of the big city. Lake Leman is more than one quarter of a mile deep, some sixty miles long, and ten miles across, exactly where the thickest part of the Rhône glacier was embedded; it was formed by glacial ice sinking deep into the floor and melting there, and it stays filled because the Rhône River flows right through it.

On your left-hand side, the roadbed on which you are driving has been dug on the moraine of the glacier, and you can see quite a number of vineyards around the little town of Douvaine. In the mountains, vineyards grow well on old moraines. On your right-hand side, the moraine was so considerable that it has disappeared under the forest covering its stones and forming the hills on which modern villages sit.

After Thonon, as you continue toward Evian, you will see the mountains gradually start falling into the water until you reach the Swiss border at Saint Gingolph. You are in the Chablais, which is covered by beautiful lush green forests. If from Evian you make a right turn onto road D21, you will be headed toward the Abondance valley and you will know what those Pre-Alps made of nappes look like: green rolling mountains with slowly sloping sides covered by peaceful forests and fat green cow pastures, with occasional sharp summits sitting on the horizon; the striking Dent d'Oche and Cornettes de Bise are such summits.

CHABLAIS TO FAUCIGNY TRIP

If you go back to Thonon and again turn south into D902, you will be traveling through the gorges of the Dranse, a large wild torrent that brings its waters to Lake Leman; the road passes through the heart of the Chablais, turning and twisting through small attractive cheese and ski communities until, after passing Les Gets, one arrives in the Faucigny region and the little town of Taninges.

It is a must, for your enjoyment of the natural beauty to drive on to Samoëns and Sixt, where you will reach what many people feel is the end of the world. At the end of the Giffre valley, a long mile beyond Sixt, you will come to a series of steep gray walls out of which multiple cascades fall from thousands of feet to form a famous sight called le Cirque du Fer à Cheval. These mountains look so very vertical because they did not fold; they could not—they could only jut upward, squeezed as they were between the Mont Blanc–Aiguilles Rouges group and the blocking nappes of the Chablais. They stand there like a fortress, best seen in the fall, when the crowds have gone home, golden light filters through the foliage, and the only noise is that of rushing water. The sight is so impressive that one can feel the presence of the creative force, and, personally, I always ache when I have to come down.

But since eventually one has to come down, the best thing to do now is to drive to Cluses, a small semi-industrial town, situated both on the A41 Autoroute Blanche going toward Italy and the old National road N205, called the vacation road by my family when I was growing up. Cluses could not be more accurately named, for it is surrounded by small transversal valleys called cluses that are crisscrossed with small torrents bringing their waters to the large irregular Arve River on its way to meet the Rhône. From Cluses you will be tempted to go in many directions, all of them beautiful: You can choose between Megève and the Aravis Pass, two different ways through the Bornes Pre-Alps; please refer to Figure 8.

GENEVOIS TRIP

When, from Cluses, one heads back toward Geneva either on the National road or on the expressway, one drives on the bed of the huge Arve glacier, which used to flow down from the Mont Blanc massif, and, again, on both sides of the road around Bonneville you can see traces of moraines with pretty vineyards sitting on them. After you arrive in Saint-Julien-en-Genevois via Annemasse, the best road to take for education is the N201 toward Annecy.

Geologically this is a depression between the Jura, which you can see in the distance on your right, and the Pre-Alps, called here the Bornes, which will soon appear on your left. Here and there you can still see large chunks of the Jura, such as Le Salève, which dominates Geneva. The whole area, a sort of hilly piedmont dedicated to the polyculture of vegetables, fruits, and flowers, and the making of cheeses, is named the Avant Pays. The maximum altitude there is 4200 feet, and rivers crisscross the countryside in deeply interesting gorges. You will pass over Les Usses, the gorges of which are spanned by striking bridges known as the Ponts de la Caille; the old bridge, impressive in my young days, now just looks cute and quaint.

Let us hope that you are enjoying a brilliant day, because right in front of you the Pre-Alps of the Bornes and Bauges are about to appear with their typical rock summits that take all kinds of different shapes: a fortress for Le Parmelan, an upturned ship for Le Semnoz, and lovely peaks in the cordillera of the Aravis, which you will only catch a glimpse of. The altitude of these mountains is between 6000 and 9000 feet. The secondary limestone of which they are mostly made appears white and shiny as snow in the bright sunshine. The two Pre-Alpine massifs of the Bornes and Bauges are clearly visible as one arrives in the Cluse d'Annecy, one on the eastern shore of the lovely lake and the other on the western.

The Annecy lake is roughly ten miles long and forms a narrow waist between the little towns of Talloires and Duingt. It was originally a large ice hole made by the pressure of an ice block that stood there three quarters of a mile thick and sank into the ground. When it finally melted, there was a lake now fed by small torrents and underground springs. Annecy is larger than a village, since 60,000 plus people live there; it is built on a huge morainic deposit around which the large torrential river Le Fier bends. Although the smallest of the three major Savoie lakes, Annecy is by far the prettiest. To read the geology there, one pleasant little hike or drive to the Super Panorama restaurant will do just fine. One can sit with a bottle of wine or a great cup

Figure 8 REGIONS AND MAIN CITIES, RIVERS, AND LAKES

of coffee while gazing at the most impressive summits of the Bornes massif, the Tournette, and the famous Dents de Lanfon.

The next direction to take would be the D909 toward the little town of Thônes. You will pass along the Annecy lake through Veyrier and up the Col de Bluffy for a beautiful sight of the Castle of Saint Bernard de Menthon and a view of the Bauges. As you reach the small Morette bridge just about ten and a half miles from Annecy, there stands the famous Montagne de Sullens, lush green in the summer and powdered with white snow that remains virgin through the winter. This is one of the famous klippes described on page 9. Beyond Thônes, on your way to La Clusaz, you will see the Aravis chain slowly appear, a true cordillera made of successive peaks culminating at approximately 9000 feet and separated by ancient glacier beds, now paradises for Alpine botanists. La Clusaz is at the foot of the cluse that cuts the Aravis chain into the Northern and Southern Aravis chains. At the top of the cluse lies the famous Aravis Pass that I have already mentioned as a choice place from which to see Mont Blanc. The pass marks the end of the Genevois region.

HAUT FAUCIGNY TRIP

Driving down the eastern slope of the Aravis through sharp hairpin curves, you will reach the two villages of La Giettaz and Flumet. At Flumet, turn left toward Megève and you will reenter the Faucigny region through its southern end. You are approximately twelve miles from Cluses, which now lies to the west. From where you are now driving, between Megève and Saint Gervais, the fortresslike mountains across the Arve valley are the Aiguilles de Warens, Platée, and the Aiguilles Rouges; tucked immediately behind them is Le Cirque du Fer à Cheval, which was mentioned on page 11. Almost directly in front of you is the white mass of Mont Blanc, some of its glaciers clearly visible. A good twenty miles still separates you from the foot of the mountain. As you arrive in Saint Gervais and climb the magnificent viaduct "des Essarts," it will disappear, to surge again in front of you, so close that you feel you can touch it. Minutes after passing the village of Les Houches you level off in the Chamonix valley and have reached the region called Haut Faucigny. From Chamonix you can go to Italy through the Mont Blanc tunnel or to Switzerland through the Col de Balme.

Driving through the Chamonix valley is a great lesson in glaciology, especially if you can take the cable car that goes up to the mountain called Le Brévent where the view is striking. The whole massif is in front of you. The Aiguilles de Chamonix and just behind them the Grandes Jorasses are right there, all between 10,000 and 12,000 feet high. They are part of the old reelevated primary rocks; topping them in height by another 2500 to 2800 feet are the snow-covered and dark gray summits of Mont Blanc, Mont Maudit, and the Dôme du Goûter, which were born later during the Tertiary period. The difference in color between the primary and Tertiary rocks is clearly visible on days when the sun shines and it is nice and dry.

The ultimate summit of Mont Blanc, as is well known, sits at 14,430 feet and is fascinating to watch; it changes almost each minute. It can smoke fine plumes of powder snow if there are high winds; it can shimmer as the ice melts under the sun and refreezes at night; and when bad weather announces itself, a huge almondlike cloud sits up there. Known to all mountain people as a "donkey back," it tells every mountaineer to stop the climb in good time, not to be caught in a storm.

The glaciers are stunningly beautiful. Three are particularly interesting. Les Bossons is the archetypal valley glacier. It hugs the sides of Mont Blanc and, as it follows its curves, spills several falls of glacial ice, which you can see towering above Chamonix. I have observed this glacier since I was a child; the way it has waxed and waned has been fascinating. Its side moraines, bare and slate gray during the forties, are now overgrown with young forest; the ice tongues come much lower down than they did in the fifties. Nothing as drastic as the advance of the seventeenth century, when Les Bossons had to be exorcised by a bishop because its tongue threatened to block the path heading out of the valley.

All the glaciers that flow from the southeastern side of Mont Blanc and the surrounding summits gather into a large bowl called the Vallée Blanche; the ice makes its way to the Chamonix valley through the valley glacier of the Mer de Glace. A funny little train as black and sooty as our Mt. Washington marvel in New Hampshire still is, has now been replaced by a clean electric one that goes up to the glacier hugging the slopes of the Montenvers, bringing the tourists in masses to a platform overlooking the glacier. Try to go on a September day just before the season ends and you will have a splendid view of the stern mineral world up there; it is an exciting study trip for children, a trip that I have taken with the very same pleasure a number of times in my life. If you were to plan it on foot, make it in late June, before large groups of hikers that frighten the marmots start going up. The Alpine flowers in June are a joy. In winter the Vallée Blanche is opened to experienced skiers under the mandatory leadership of a mountain guide who takes them through the maze of glacial crevasses.

The third interesting glacier is at the little village of Le Tour, a tiny place that stubbornly refuses to overmodernize; the front tongue of the Le Tour glacier came crashing down in the early 1900s, and every so often heavy blocks of glacial ice known as seracs fly across the face of the cliff over which the now-suspended glacier front looms; the play of light through the ice of the seracs is a striking example of the famous glacier blue. You will, as you do when you pass any glacier, notice the famous *roches moutonnées*, those rounded, polished rocks streaked and gashed abundantly by centuries of erosion caused by the ice on the rock bed.

If you are a passionate hiker, more so than an experienced one, the hiking tour known as Le Tour du Mont Blanc follows the huge massif and requires a whole week to accomplish, leaving you with memories of an unforgettable experience.

BEAUFORTAIN, UPPER TARENTAISE TRIP

Until now we have been traveling in the department of the Haute Savoie, and we are going to pass into that of the Savoie. You should choose late June to visit this part of the Savoie; you can either retrace your steps down the Chamonix valley toward Megève and through the gorges of the Arly to reach Ugine, or you can come back to Annecy via the expressway and go to Ugine and through to Albertville in a matter of half an hour. Both are interesting, but I tend to favor the Arly route because it gives a good view of the "Sillon Alpin" at its narrowest point. The Sillon Alpin is a combe that formed after the sedimentary layers covering Mont Blanc and the Belledone mountains slid forward and surged up again to form the Pre-Alps. It remains very narrow between Megève and Ugine because the Beaufortain mountains never lost their sedimentary covering, but as one reaches Ugine, then Albertville, it starts to widen considerably.

Before going any further, we will take a left turn on the D925 to climb toward Beaufort. You will be struck by the quality of the forests and the amazing quantity of water. Towns in this area, called the Beaufortain, sit high at the limit of forest and Alpine meadows, and I recommend that for true Savoie atmosphere you stop at Beaufort, Hauteluce, and Arèches, and then continue on to the Cormet de Roselend. You will notice water falling all around and that the Electricité de France has built, very intelligently, a large electric plant with an artificial lake to gather the waters.

The mountains you are driving through receive a lot of precipitation during the winter. You cannot pass here between mid-October and mid-June because snow blocks the way. Then in mid-June, it can melt in a matter of hours if there is a warm snow-eating southern wind called the foehn. On pages 163 through 165 you will be able to read about other Beaufortain attractions, such as cows, cheeses, and Alpine flowers. Right now, concentrate on the physical features. The mountains are high but not nearly so high as the neighboring Mont Blanc, which is just over the line of summits on your left. The sedimentary rock covering that has remained on these mountains absorbs the water from the melting snow and produces a riot of green grass on the ground. Although quite vertical, the summits have none of the élan they had in the Upper Faucigny. Nature has made this more human world, a symphony of green in which man has put cattle to graze to produce cheese of first quality.

As you continue on your way through the Cormet, you will undoubtably meet these lovely little cows called *Tarines* and enter the narrow valley of the Chapieux. Somewhere along the way, toward the upper left, you will catch a glimpse of the last outpost of the Mont Blanc massif, the beautiful Aiguille des Glaciers. Rather rapidly you will arrive at Le Châtelard, in full view of the large metamorphic internal massif of the Alps: the Vanoise.

It certainly is beautiful, but notice how blunt the summits appear compared to the pure granitic needles of Mont Blanc. What you see is actually a combination of metamorphic mountains (Mont Pourri and Vanoise) with different nappes. You will immediately notice the Grande Casse, which is a gigantic isolated chip of limestone. The area is generally made of rippled nappes covering metamorphic cores; notice also how much shorter the glaciers are. They tend to remain in upper basins; only a few on the Mont Pourri and the Dôme de la Sache still attempt to stretch a lazy tongue. You are now at the entrance of the Upper Tarentaise, almost in the upper valley of the Isère; you can see the river, on its way to the lower Tarentaise and the Rhône valley.

Go down to Bourg Saint Maurice, the next town, and there you will have two options: You can take the road to Italy through the Petit Saint Bernard pass and see the cromlech (see page 35) and the ruined hospice. If you do so, do not miss observing the black schists uncovered by the—in geological time—recently melted glacier. They are so strikingly dark because no growth has yet had time to cover them. If you prefer, you can take a spin in the Terra Santa, the very upper valley of the baby Isère, where famous Val d'Isère and Tignes are located.

Right now I would like to go down toward the Middle Tarentaise following one of the most frequented roads in France. The N90 is built on the bed of the ancient Roman way that joined ancient Rome to Ganava, now Geneva. On your right is the Beaufortain and on your left some peaceful villages hanging literally on the sides of mountains made of geological nappes, which hide the Vanoise from your sight. Just before the city of Moûtiers, you will pass the very narrow Etroit du Saix, which has given civil engineers many thoughts. Some of the mines visible on the left bank of the Isère have been there since the Stone Age. The entrance to what is known as the Trois Vallées, where some of the Olympic Games competitions will take place in 1992, is at Moûtiers. You will find the lower Isère valley between Moûtiers and Albertville quite narrow and quite industrialized, but many of the villages remain lovely and with a historical background that is extremely impressive. A book as large as this one could be written on each of these small communities.

MAURIENNE TRIP

The Maurienne is the valley of the Arc River. To reach it you must drive to Aiguebelle from Albertville and thread your way through the Lower Maurienne to try to escape the nightmare of its chemical industries as fast as possible. The mountains on your right are those of the Belledone and the Grandes Rousses.

Drive through Saint Jean de Maurienne toward the Arvan valley road, and immediately climb up to Jarrier. Jarrier is such a wonderful village that I shall write about it several times, but right now concentrate on the geology, which will offer you a magnificent view of the Aiguilles d'Arves as they jut majestically out of the bottom of a nappe.

If, continuing to investigate the Arc valley, you go back down to Saint Jean and drive on toward Saint Michel de Maurienne and Modane, you will pass through nappe after nappe. At Modane the front of the Sub-Alpine plate will appear on your right-hand side and the eastern rim of the European will be on your left. The famous lustered schists begin at the village of Lanslebourg, and as you reach the next community of Lanslevillard you will see the scenery change radically, for between this village and Bonneval-sur-Arc the two continental plates have fused together; please refer to Figure 4 (page 6). There is, of course, much more to the Maurienne than this fascinating geology, and we shall come back to it several times in the pages that follow.

COMBE DE SAVOIE TRIP

There are three ways to leave the Maurienne: One can go to Italy over Mont Cenis or through the Fréjus Tunnel; one can pass back into the Terra Santa to go through Bonneval-sur-Arc up the Iseran Pass toward Val d'Isère; or one can retrace one's steps and go back down the Arc valley toward the Combe de Savoie through Aiguebelle.

The Combe de Savoie is the lower part of the Isère valley, where it receives successively the rivers Arly at Albertville and Arc at Chamousset. Relatively narrow between Albertville and Chamousset, the Combe de Savoie widens considerably toward Montmélian and Chambéry. On the right side of the Isère, the southern exposure of the Bauges shows their limestone faces. Their narrow foothills harbor lovely villages and many vines and fruit trees; the grapes for some of the best Savoie wines are grown there. On the left-hand side of the Isère, the plain is wider and dedicated to varied cultivation as well as to many vines.

At Montmélian, you will feel the road take a bend toward the right, for should you continue straight south, you would leave the Savoie and enter the Dauphiné part of the Sillon Alpin, the Grésivaudan, which leads straight to

Grenoble. As you head rapidly toward Chambéry, you will see the face of the Granier with its different colors, the slide of 1248 very visible. The Granier is the highest summit of the Chartreuse mountains, half of which are located in the Savoie and half in the Dauphiné. It is in the Chartreuse that one truly senses that the Savoie was once an independent nation; at the ancient border, the village of Saint Pierre d'Entremonts is a double village, complete with two churches and two town halls separated by the torrent of the Guiers. The Chartreuse massif is absolutely charming, quiet, and only minimally disturbed by modernism.

Chambéry is the capital of the Savoie, dominating the life of its own cluse with its university and multiple industries; the scenery remains very attractive, however, and the city remains surrounded by thermal spas such as Challes-les-Eaux and Aix les Bains, which sits at the edge of Le Bourget Lake. Le Bourget is far from being as attractive as Annecy's lake, mostly because it is surrounded by severe, dark mountains that give a dark reflection to the water. The lake is attached to the Rhône by the Canal de Savières and the area between the lake and the Rhône is a pleasant, restful, almost idyllic little region called Le Petit Bugey. Between the Cluse de Chambéry and that of Annecy are two important regions:

The Chautagne is squeezed at the foot of the last Jura folds and has wonderful vines, while the Albanais is like a little Provence with a lovely climate that brings fresh vegetables and fruit as *primeurs*—the first of the season—to the markets of Savoie cities.

THE IMPORTANT INTRA-ALPINE VALLEYS

The Alps are a very pleasant chain of mountains because of the diversity of the river valleys that crisscross its layers of folds. The many valleys opened to the penetration of diverse winds keep the chain well aerated, and each valley has its own microclimate and its own individual mini-civilization. Every valley is worth a visit; some, however, will be more striking than others.

I have already mentioned several of the most interesting northern valleys—that of the Abondance, the Dranse, the Giffre, and the upper Arve—but there are others in Southern Savoie that tend to be neglected because they are out of the mainstream of civilization; it is precisely for that reason that they should be visited and investigated. Some of the old civilizations of the Alps are still alive in these upper valleys; the human rhythm has been preserved there, at least during the non-tourist season.

Still in Northern Savoie, the valley of the Bon Nant beyond Saint Gervais toward the Contamines Montjoie is a heaven of peace during the summer and very easily accessible by the small Mont Blanc tramway that starts from Saint Gervais. The Arly valley, ensconced in its impressive gorge, offers some lovely villages on the way to the famous Col des Saisies, and one can still see there some of the best-preserved ancient houses I know.

The word for river or torrent in Northern Savoie is *nant*, which is Celtic, and in Southern Savoie and the Beaufortain it is *doron*, which is probably Ligurian, but both have the same meaning. There are many *dorons*, and many of them take on the name of the main village of a valley, such as the Doron de Beaufort or the Doron de Bozel.

Besides the wild valley of the Chapieux, which I have already mentioned, you should take a ride in the valley of Peisey-Nancroix; especially if you are a lover of baroque Church art, you will not regret it. There is a small measure of modernization, but it has been done well and intelligently, without incurring too much damage.

The valleys of the Doron de Pralognan and the Doron de Champagny each represent a very beautiful entranceway into the National Park of the Vanoise. Not to be missed, not only for their skiing in winter but also for the immense peace of the summer months, are Saint Bon-Courchevel, Méribel-les-Allues, and especially the valley of the Bellevilles. In the Bellevilles, life started very early, in prehistoric times, and there exist antiquities and monuments that have played a major role in the history of the Savoie. In essence, anytime you see a little road branch off a major one, you can almost be certain that something quite lovely is tucked away there, something that has not been damaged and will be totally regenerating for your tired mind and heart. There is only one exception, the lower Arc valley. It is essential to leave it as soon as possible to investigate the wonderful intra-Alpine valleys of the left bank of the Arc, or else the industry will discourage you quickly. During the good months of the year one can reach the Lower Maurienne from the Lower

Tarentaise through the pass known as Col de la Madeleine, thus avoiding the big hook through Aiguebelle. As you arrive into the Arc valley, cross the river at the first available bridge and immediately take the D927; you will find yourself in the valley of the Villards, green, peaceful, and lovely, well known fifty years ago for its striking costumes and not to be missed if you find yourself in Savoie around August 15, the day that everyone dresses up as Great Grandmother would have.

Saint Jean de Maurienne marks the opening of the remarkable Valley of the Arvan, the road to which is just below Jarrier. Go in June, when the wildflowers are just peeking from under the snow, and do not miss the cheese-making *fruitière* of Saint Jean d'Arves or the amazing old church and cemetery of Saint Sorlin d'Arves.

Baroque church lovers should make a point of driving up the valley that leads to Valloire, where the church is quite a treat. The Upper Maurienne, which starts at Modane, is a kingdom of splendid baroque architecture, at least as interesting as the Italian Val Sesia. Bonneval-sur-Arc, the last village of the Upper Maurienne before the Iseran Pass, is a classified historical monument —yes, the whole village. Nothing can be changed; the village has been fixed in time and must be preserved as it is. Enjoy it after the summer hordes have gone home or before they arrive; it is a treat.

As for the Val d'Isère and Tignes areas, you will have to decide for yourself whether you would like it best in winter or in summer. The concrete villages built in box style during the late sixties and early seventies are not pretty, and one must definitely climb above them. "Val," as all French people call it, and Tignes, together with Courchevel, probably provide the most beautiful skiing in the whole chain of the Alps. This *is* skiing, off the marked trails as well as on, provided you stand secure on your boards, are experienced enough, and know your mountain weather well enough to realize when you should get back to civilization quickly. If you are not sure, stay on the trails. If the first sentence of this paragraph does not sound all that enthusiastic, it is because, like many Savoie lovers who have known the area before the Chevril dam, when the women up there were still making lace by hand, I cannot see the changes without the most cruel nostalgia taking hold of me.

Do, by all means, investigate all the villages of the Terra Santa, located between Bourg Saint Maurice and Val d'Isère; such peace you will have trouble finding anywhere else in the world.

WEATHER AND VEGETATION

Generally speaking, the Savoie climate is determined by depressions coming from the west and southwest and/or the high pressures of Central Europe; it is a semi-continental climate very much influenced by the altitude.

While the large cluses and combes are mild in the winter—although snow can be plentiful there—they can be very hot in the summer. Those cluses with lakes, like Annecy, benefit from the warmer mass of their lake and are more temperate than the intra-Alpine valleys.

Still, it rains quite a bit in the Savoie, especially in the Avant Pays and the Northern Savoie; when it rains in the lower altitudes, it snows in the upper ones, unless one is above 3000 feet, tucked behind a mass of mountains such as Mont Blanc or the Vanoise. It is not unusual to arrive in Chamonix or Val d'Isère and find a deep blue sky and only light clouds, the stations sitting high above the atmospheric depressions.

The weather is also a matter of microclimates. Annecy, on a clear day everywhere else, may sit in dense fog until noon because the warm mass of the lake provokes a temperature inversion, while in the Thônes valley twelve miles up the road, the air is bright and clear.

Summer weather is mostly bright and clear, but thunderstorms, attracted by the higher summits, often build by nighttime. And then there is the effect of precise winds. The *Foehn*, called *Bohju* in Annecy patois because it comes from the south right over the Bauges, is the snow eater; warm and mellow, it melts snow in no time, makes young people fall in love, and fills older ones with vague or even precise regrets. The *Johre* passes over the Jura to bring in wild western storms, and *La Bise Noire* blows in from frigid Russia chasing everybody inside remarking, "Ah, c'est la Bise, la bise noire." *La Bise Noire* is a black wind, taking its name probably from the ancestral and instinctive fear of all things black.

And then there is also the all-important question of exposure. Each valley has a side exposed to the sun and one that remains in shadow. The sunny side is the *adret* or *endroit*, the shadowy side the *envers* or *ubac*. Two examples of the *adret/ubac* arrangement are quite noticeable when you travel on main roads: In the Chamonix valley, the Aiguilles Rouges, where there is little snow and lots of sun, is on the *endroit*, while Mont Blanc, on the *ubac*, is covered with glaciers. When one passes into Italy through the Mont Blanc Tunnel or over Mont Cenis, the difference is striking; the glaciers on the Italian slope, the southern one, are half the size of those on the northern exposure. Apparently the exposure of whole villages must also have a lot to do with the emotional dispositions of their inhabitants; up in the Terra Santa the saying goes "*Zain de rever, zain de traver*" ("people of the *envers* are contrary people").

There is quite a visible stratification of the vegetation. Between 2500 and 3000 feet, fields of corn, tobacco, cereals, and fresh vegetables alternate with fruit trees and, in the Combe de Savoie, well-ordered vineyards. In the Chablais and part of the Bauges, the fields are not as extensive and forest and meadows take over.

The next stratum is the domain of the forest between 2500 and 5500 feet. Forests are well tended and without too many signs of acid rain damage; wood is an important source of income as it is the material used to make most work instruments. In the lower forests grow hazel, wild cherry, field maple, oak, sycamore, maple, alder, birch, ash, and walnut trees; these mix as the altitude gradually increases with larch, pine, spruce, and aspen. One most important and delightful flower grows in the northern forests with large amounts of precipitation—the wild dwarf Alpine cyclamen—so fragrant that one knows if flowering has started just as soon as one goes under tree cover. The cyclamen grow in masses in the Bauges and the Bornes in old moss-covered moraines. It is prudent to teach children to wash their hands very well after picking them because their sap contains the powerful poison cyclamin. Hopefully the cyclamen will soon be protected, for it has been wildly overpicked for the last forty years. In the northern mountains, spruce dominates while in the Tarentaise and Maurienne a wonderful mixture of spruce, larch, and pinion pine filters the sometimes almost Mediterranean light.

Above 5000 feet is the Sub-Alpine stratum, a beautiful lawn of grass dotted here and there with rhododendron, juniper bushes, bilberry bushes, and dwarf trees, which must be kept under control lest they invade the Alpine lawn used for grazing animals. This beautiful rug of grass reaches all the way up to the piles of stones at the foot of mountain cliffs and pushes against the moraines of still-active glaciers. I know very few feelings as exhilarating as hiking up a mountain and coming out of the forest at the timberline; the magnificence of the summits against the sky, the smells and perfumes of the alp, the silence, the peace, and the colors of all Alpine flowers can mend any part of the soul or body. This level of the mountain is snow-covered from mid-October until early June, and by June 15 reaches its peak of beauty. I know I shall have reached old age when I finally renounce my slow hiking rhythm and stop going up the alp to look at the multicolored rugs of wildflowers. Let me indicate a few wonderful places most easily accessible where one can see and admire the flowers in full bloom:

Easy to reach on foot is the Plateau de Beauregard in La Clusaz, Haute Savoie, just in front of the Aravis.

Easy to reach by car are the Cormet de Roselend in the Beaufortain, and the valley of the Arvan above Saint Sorlin d'Arves, both in the Savoie. The Col des Montets at the very top of the Chamonix valley offers a mint of wild bilberries, abundant flowers, and a breathtaking view of the glaciers of Mont Blanc.

The flowers you will find in the spring are red primulae and yellow auriculae in the crags and clefts of rocks. The tiny, amazing *Primula minima*, deep pink and most delicate, sits in bunches among the taller blades of grass; so do the blue fringed bells of the *Soldanellae*. The Christmas rose (*Helleborus niger*) grows close to the moraines of active glaciers, and many have been transplanted to Savoie gardens, where they bloom around Christmas and the beginning of the New Year. Growing in April, as soon as the snow disappears, are tiny white and purple crocuses, which build colorful patches beside the areas of melting snow in the upper valleys. Orange lilies remain easy to find, but the gorgeous lily of Saint Bruno has become rare. In their deep blue corollas, the small spring gentians and the big purple-blue stemless gentians have not once failed to make my heart jump with pleasure as I discovered their first flower of each spring. In July comes the blooming of the huge yellow and purple gentians (the pannonian).

If you are an orchid lover, go to the summit of the Semnoz in late June or to the Vallée des Fins above La Clusaz toward the end of July. The old beds of the glaciers there are full of dwarf orchids with as many as thirty tiny yellow, purple, and deep blue blossoms to a stem.

For the most gorgeous rugs of Alpine pansies in all variations of size and color, the Cormet de Roselend again has very little competition, but I am certain that at around 6000 feet you will find the same flowers anywhere in the Savoie.

In the fall, all the Alpine meadows around 6500 feet will bloom with the gorgeous light purple *Colchicum autumnale*, as lovely to look at as it is poisonous. Its toxin, colchicine, was used in ancient days for the mercy killing of fatally injured patients suffering unbearable pains.

The famous edelweiss, said by legend to be a fallen star, can be found easily in the Col des Aravis, if one climbs toward the rocks. Wild edelweiss is protected, and good pictures of its flowers last longer in any case than a poor plucked flower; the edelweiss sold everywhere as a good luck charm is cultivated. Edelweiss grows at the limit of the last Alpine stratum of rock, ice, and snow, which many climb with elation in paroxysms of concentration and effort. I have for many years been among those climbers coming down with burned nose and cheeks, callused hands and feet. I have passed on to my two sons some of my passion for Alpine sports and secretly hope to be the first one to guide my first grandchild up the slopes on his or her first Alpine hike.

A word of warning for hikers and climbers: The Electricité de France taps energy from the bottom waters of all glaciers, and you *must heed* all warning panels along rivers carefully; a trickle of water one minute might become raging white water the next. The posted signs are deep yellow with black letters, plentiful and very visible.

CONSERVATION AND THE FAUNA

As I have already said, it is in June and September that one can see the Savoie at its best. But the good weather in the fall can last to the end of November. This is when the best sights for photographs just happen. There is always valley fog at this late date, and as one climbs out of it snowy summits framed by the green and gold branches of spruce and larch slowly unveil or abruptly appear.

It is also the good time for hunting. I remember fondly going hunting with a classmate and her grandfather. The gentleman had dreamed of shooting a *grand tétras* (a gorgeous ptarmigan) and took us two girls along, positively keeping us in unnerving religious silence the whole day. We drove for hours in a cold car to reach a certain forest reputed to be full of ptarmigans, and we waited from much too late morning till almost late afternoon, for nothing. We heard the bird; Porthos the golden retriever sniffed it without being able to flush it; the *tétras* remained elusive. Around four o'clock Grandfather unloaded his gun, whistled for his dog, gathered his two little girls, and as we were crossing a path to go home the *grand tétras* literally flew into our faces, narrowly missing Grandfather's plumed hat. The dog went wild for nothing, Grandfather swore as one swears when one is born, as he was, with a title of nobility, and all I can remember was a flash of dark green and brown with a big red dot and that was it—and it has been it and probably will be it, for the species is getting rarer and rarer in the Alps.

Rather than hunt, I much prefer to look for animals, and I have been blessed with several wonderful encounters: a family of brown squirrels which were so tame that I stayed there looking at them for half an hour; a grouse and her tiny baby; and then there was my adventure with a mother fox. I mentally sing operatic arias when I hike and I was in Cherubino's company when I caught a whiff of a telltale smell; on the right of my path was a mother fox and on the left three little cubs, ever so cute, their paws fat and their fur short and fluffy; I quickly abandoned Cherubino, retreated approximately a hundred feet, and sat down motionless. The cubs eventually rejoined their mother and I continued on my way up. That day was truly blessed with wildlife, for later, as I came out of the timberline, I met a family of marmots carousing around a meadow. They remained undisturbed by my presence, but rolled out of sight rapidly as a great big hawk started to circle overhead.

Outside a few brown rabbits, it is not always easy to sight wild animals in the Alps. Occasionally one hears about a solitary skier flushing a snow hare or ptarmigan in winter plumage while sliding at the edge of a forest, but if you want to sight animals in more serious numbers there is only one direction to take, that of the national parks and reserves. City people who, like me, came to the Alps to find peace and nature, thought of creating a national park in the Vanoise. In 1922 King Victor Emmanuel III of Italy, then head of the house of Savoie, established the Italian National Park of the Gran Paradiso, which borders on France just above Val d'Isère for a stretch of roughly ten miles. Books are full of stories of Val d'Isère hunters sneaking into the Italian park to give the guards a hard time and bringing back home a couple of Alpine ibex. The king, through his personal efforts, had been successful in bringing a nearly extinct ibex population back to 4000 by 1939 (the Chamonix ibex was extinct by 1890).

During World War II when all park guards were away fighting, the ibex population dwindled again. The ibex is a great big peaceful sheep with a huge pair of horns that are ribbed and exaggeratedly bent backward; it is hunted for these trophies, which you will see displayed in many private homes or country restaurants. The slaughter would have gone on had it not been for the efforts of a number of very enthusiastic hunters, climbers, and nature lovers, among them the writer and artist Samivel and many private citizens, members of the French Alpine Club, and French hunting societies.

After many discussions and meetings with local Savoie people, the concept of a national park was presented to the French government, and in 1960 a law was signed by General De Gaulle allowing the creation of the National Park of the Vanoise. It came perhaps a century late compared to America, but many people worked hard at establishing the statutes, calming the anguish of those on whose property the park would be established, creating a network of tracks and paths through the park, and establishing huts in which people could stay overnight. Sixteen communities in the Tarentaise were involved and twelve in the Maurienne.

By American standards, the park is small, but in proportion with the surface of France's national territory, it is quite considerable. The average altitude of the park is 6000 feet, with the highest summit, La Grande Casse, at 10,456 feet. The park encloses 107 summits and 34 mountain passes above 9000 feet, with 60 square miles of glaciers. The national park is surrounded by natural reserves. On some of these there are ski installations that had to be tolerated because they preexisted the creation of the park. All around the park is a so-called peripheral zone in which the local populations present interesting programs explaining the ancestral Savoie culture and way of life, and its artistic and artisanal expressions.

When in 1969 a promoter tried to have thousands of acres reclassified for the building of more ski installations, public protest all over France was so strong that in 1971 a law was passed that ended forever all efforts at further reclassification.

If I had to say something not quite positive about the park, it would be that from July 1 through August 31 it is wildly overutilized. The park contains twenty-two huts (compared to the seven of New Hampshire's White Mountains) and some of quite a capacity. Being familiar with huts and mountains through my family activities, I tend to feel that too many people come through in those two summer months and that, as was done in Yosemite, the number of reservations should be limited. The entrances to the park are many, both from the Tarentaise and the Maurienne sides. The park is well marked on all maps and the little towns at its entrances all have tourist offices eager to give out information.

Do go by all means, but go early or late, before or after the crowds have arrived or left; you will have a better feel for the beauty of the place. For those who cannot hike extensively there is an interesting *sentier-nature*, or classroom trail (at the location known as the Orgère), accessible through the Modane entrance. No longer than one and a half miles, it is solidly documented with extensive information on the surrounding vegetal, mineral, and animal worlds. For true hikers the nicest trails are between Val d'Isère and Bonneval-sur-Arc. There one can see eagles and chamois if one gets up early enough. As in United States huts, one must carry one's supplies in and one's trash out since there is no place at which it can be discarded within the park.

The chamois around Val d'Isère are quite plentiful. When there are such heavy layers of snow after winter storms that they cannot find the slightest bit of food at their natural altitude, they will come down very close to civilization, not disdaining sometimes the hay in barns. It is in the spring that one stands the best chance of sighting some young kid following its mother, and very closely at that. In the winter, if you ski within the park, look for large oval indentations in the snow; they are the *baignoires* in which the animals rest. Chamois are just as skittish and shy as the ibex are placid; they scamper easily and very quickly. Because their brown fur blends easily into the colors of the surrounding terrain, it is easier to spot chamois in the winter. A solid pair of binoculars is very much recommended.

Besides eagles, which have survived the trigger-happy nineteenth century, there are all kinds of hawks in the French Alps. During the last few years a great big campaign has been successful in saving the *Gypaetus*, or lammergeier, which came back from the brink of extinction. The *chocards*, which you will hear called *choucas* by everyone, are high-altitude blackbirds that I swear must live on what crumbs fall from Alpinists' sandwiches; they are fast to come down to the valley, however, when the weather closes down, and flock to roofs when a major storm menaces.

Marmots are wonderful little animals that live in underground dens called *tapias*, hidden at the end of a fifteen- to thirty-foot-long and narrow tunnel. They hibernate, and it has always been one of the great distractions of children to ferret them out come the winter. One of my Chamonix friends, like all upper valley people, used to make a fine stew with marmot—which really needed a lot of skimming of the poor animal's fat. But when one does not have too much money, a nice little marmot looks good on a plate with some polenta beside it; from this point of view, American pioneers knew as much about marmots as the Savoyards. A friend of mine had his comeuppance. Having spent a summer taming one of the little guys, he found his garden, come the fall, so badly dug out that the marmot quickly won its release back to nature.

With the exception of the natural reserve of the Bauges, deer are no longer plentiful in the Savoie. No more bears, no more wildcats, no more wolves, although when winters get tough, an occasional tale of an old fellow prowling around eventually haunts some village, but these are tales. Those of you who love rock climbing should know that there are small vipers in the Alps that love to sun on the ledges of limestone rock faces, and it is preferable to investigate rather than trust that wonderful wide and inviting ledge.

Lakes and rivers still have a lot of fish, such as trout, pike, and char. More details will be given later in the food section, but I have to warn all fishermen that all the large rivers have been fished for thousands and thousands of years and contain some of the smartest fish I have ever met. So many rises you never saw, but just cast a fly into the water and nothing happens, however many hours you may try. These are educated trout! Mercifullly, the fish population of the lakes is not so wary.

KEEPERS OF THE ALPINE PASSES

A QUICK OVERVIEW OF THE HISTORY OF THE SAVOIE

La Province, in French, means "every part of the country that is not located within thirty miles of Paris." *Vivre en Province* simply means "living outside the big city," in a place where one cannot get a glimpse of the now-tentacular Paris suburbs' concrete blocks.

During the pre-1789 monarchy, which the French call *l'ancien régime*, France was divided into provinces governed by intendants, a system of government initiated in the sixteenth century and formalized by Louis XIV a century later. Some provinces represented very definite ethnicities, such as the pure Celtic Bretons or the Alemannic Alsatians, who to this day remain, respectively, Breton- and Alemannic-German-speaking; others were ancient English possessions, still others had always been French, because they had been settled by the Franks. Provence, with the syllable *en* not *in*, which takes its name from the Latin and Roman Provincia Romana, was one of the French provinces. Often in the United States the two terms *provençal* and *provincial* are confused. The Savoie was never an *ancien régime* province of France, since it entered the French community for the first time, and for a period of about twenty years, in 1792, when the provinces were no longer designated administrative units, and permanently not until 1860.

A somewhat identical confusion occurs when it comes to the modern *régions* of France. If I were to write a book on the region in which the Savoie is now located and which is called Rhône-Alpes, I would have quite a problem, for I would find work in this endeavor for ten years to come. Lyon, the Bresse, the Savoie, and the Dauphiné, plus a few other smaller entities, are all included in Rhône-Alpes and all were part of different provinces or even, as the Savoie, part of a state in its own right. So, when you think about a region in France nowadays, it can be in the modern administrative sense of *région de programme*, which is a concept of convenience from the commercial and economic point of view; or it can be in the older geographical sense, as a subdivision of a province. You will see this second concept used in this chapter.

The Savoie is divided within our French Republic into the two *départments* of Haute Savoie in the north and Savoie in the south. What follows is a succinct synthesis of the long history of the Savoie before it finally became part of France in 1860.

Human habitation of the Savoie began as soon as the first Quaternary glaciers receded. If you want to imagine what the scenery must have been like, think of the valley that is now the Denali National Park in Alaska. The upper valley of the Rhône River at the Furka in Switzerland would also be a good comparison: small and multiple rivers flowing in disorder through many channels on the very flat bottom of a gigantic U-shaped valley; it looks bare and slate gray because no vegetation has yet had time to grow; the ground is saturated with water.

The Savoie of these wild valleys was already inhabited in 70,000 B.C. Traces of Neanderthal man have been found; Neanderthal disappeared around 40,000 B.C., giving way to a succession of representatives of *Homo sapiens*. Twelve different layers of civilization have been found in the rock shelter of Saint Thibaud de Cou; one of them, dated about 7000 B.C., contained the oldest dog fossil in Europe. The people represented in these many layers of civilization came from many directions. Anyone deeply interested in these ancient times will find an excellent chronology in the book *La Savoie des Origines à l'An Mil* (see Selected Bibliography).

There exist many archeological sites in the Savoie, but special permissions are required to visit them. The village of La Balme de Thuy in Haute Savoie has such a site. From Annecy, take the D909 to the Morette bridge, turn left onto D216; barely one mile up you will find an Our Lady of Lourdes shrine and a waterfall. Go up the very small road that branches off to the right immediately after the waterfall and you will very soon come to a patch of green with a large cross in the center. If you raise your eyes toward the rock face, you will see it build a sloping overhang. Among the bushes, there is a rock shelter that has been excavated; it has been established with certainty that it was occupied as early as 7000 B.C., maybe even earlier. The site is classified and surrounded by a fence, but it is easy to see how smart those early Savoyards were. The site dominates the valley of the Fier River, and from the entrance of the shelter one surveys the east and west passages; at the time the Fier offered a large supply of fish, and a few steps above the cascade that you saw rush down the hill, there is a delightful water hole for a cool bath in the summertime. The excellent little museum in the small town of Thônes two miles down the road offers extensive explanation on the excavations. The village developed where the cross now stands. People just came down fifty yards to build houses, and the cross marks the place of their former necropolis. The first village was destroyed by a rockslide still very visible and rebuilt on the same sunny southern slope one mile farther to the west.

During the late Bronze Age a number of villages existed along the Savoie and Swiss lakes (such as Chindrieux on Lake Le Bourget and Sevrier and Duingt on the Annecy lake). Their settlers were involved in extensive pottery-making and bronze-smithing, the wood for their fires being floated directly into the lakes from the mountainside. The name *Chablais* (from the Latin *de capulum*) indicates that this region of the Savoie practiced woodcutting in the forests. It has now been established that their dwellings were not built on the water but on firm land and that they were destroyed by a sudden change of climate, which, at the beginning of the Sub-Atlantic period, raised the water level considerably. Other historical sources suggest that impressive, equestrian, pre-Celtic invaders of the Iron Age may have been responsible for that destruction.

The intra-Alpine valleys above the Isère and the Arc rivers were also rich in settlements, as witness the numerous archeological finds in the Arvan and

Belleville valleys, where many ancient burial sites were found while digging to build foundations for modern houses. Little is known about these early layers of population. Some left megaliths such as the menhir at Regnier in the Lower Faucigny and the cromlech through which one drives when one now passes from France into Italy at the Little Saint Bernard Pass. If you have the "antique roving eye," stop there: The foundations of Roman buildings and a Celtic *fanum* (temple) are clearly visible. All over the mountains one finds those curious round and oval stones indented with holes for hands or feet and called *pierres à cupules*; their dating has proved difficult; some go back to 2500 B.C., others are more recent, from between 450 B.C. and 15 B.C., and their role in early civilization has not yet been finally established.

In the hamlet of Le Villaret des Brévières, two miles or so from the ski resort of Tignes in the Savoie, one can see chiseled on a block of stone the figure of a man some four feet high. He is known as the Ceutron des Brévières and is supposed to be a member of those Ligurian populations, the Ceutron or Centrons, which inhabited the upper valleys of the Arve and of the Isère. The Ceutrons' neighbors, the Salasses, occupied what is now the Val d'Aosta (the upper valley of the Dora Baltea, now in Italy), while yet other tribes by the name of Medulles and Graioceles were established south of them in the Maurienne and the Susa valley. It is believed that these Ligurian tribes had arrived through the Rhône valley from the south and were originally settled much more to the west, until they were pushed toward the east by the invading Celts.

The Celts of the Savoie were the Allobroges, their capital city was what is now French Vienna, twenty miles or so south of Lyon, on the Rhône. The Celtic migrations took place first as a trickle, then as powerful waves between 500 and 400 B.C.; the Celts came from Bavaria through the Alps at Mont Cenis, Mont Genèvre, and probably the Julier passes. Happy with lower altitudes, they finally settled down into what is now the Avant Pays and the middle mountains of the Pre-Alps. They did not penetrate the high valleys held by the Ligurian tribes.

The date 218 B.C. is historically important because this was the year, during the Second Punic War, when Hannibal crossed the Alps with his 48,000 foot soldiers, 8000 horsemen, and fifteen elephants. Rivers of ink have been spent on Hannibal's feat. The enigma of where exactly he crossed the mountains is by no means resolved, but the latest thesis suggests the pass at Savine-Coche, which joins Bramans in the Maurienne to Giaglione in the Piemonte. Two Americans, Jack Wheeler and Jackie Vial King, brought a couple of elephants successfully over the Alps through that pass. If you want to see where Hannibal passed, take the D100 from Bramans to Le Planay and inquire whether the pass is open because the French army does a lot of shooting exercises in the area; also be well equipped for hiking and against hypothermia.

In 125 B.C., when Greek Massilia, now Marseille, called the Romans to help defend against the pesky attacks of yet another tribe of Ligurians, the Salyens, Consul Sextius Calvinus came to the rescue and in 124 destroyed the Salyens' *oppidum* (fortress) of Entremont; they installed and conveniently left a garrison just below the former *oppidum*, which was to become Aix-en-Provence. Gaul was calling the Romans irresistibly! In 122 B.C. another Roman legion advanced into the Rhône valley and defeated a coalition of Allobroges and Arvernes (another Celtic tribe from the Central Mountains). Quintus Fabius Maximus won his surname, Allobrogicus, by defeating the Allobroges in 121 in another area. The Allobroges finally submitted to the "Roman peace," which among other very noble things included heavy taxation. Like all Celts, these Allobroges were not a pliant people; they sent a delegation to Rome with the hope of having their taxes revoked or at least lightened. The whole affair could be compared to a modern Mafia deal: Cicero himself and his old foe Catiline, to whose conspiracy the poor Allobroges found themselves drawn, were both members of the cast. But the plan was to no avail: Heavy taxation remained. So another revolt brewed and exploded in 61 B.C. Our mountain men, under the direction of their chief Catugat, caused quite a bit of damage but were still powerless to resist three Roman legions.

Almost at that same time Julius Caesar was making his way to Allobrogia through the Little Saint Bernard Pass, crossing it, says the chronicle, while reading a treatise on grammar, so as not to see the "horrible abysses" that bordered the path. His "official" mission was to prevent the Helvetii Celts, who were on their way to relocate on the Atlantic Coast, from passing through

Allobrogia. This was a very noble goal, the results of which are a part of history described by Caesar himself in his *De Bello Gallico*. The only part of trans-Alpine Gaul Caesar did not invade was the center core of the Alps where the Ligurian tribes were still holding the passes. Ligurians were to the Alps then what Sherpas are to the Himalayas now; they were not ready to surrender their source of income as guides over the mountains, and it was not until the reign of Caesar's nephew Augustus that the Alpine passes fell into Roman hands. Augustus was busy with plans for invading Germany, and since he needed the passes he simply came and took them between the 30s and the 20s B.C.

The Gallo-Roman world is still very visible in the Alps: Roman arches of triumph still stand in Susa and Aosta, and on the road to the Little Saint Bernard Pass a number of segments of the old Roman road still exist; on the French side, it is very visible at the Creux des Morts, where the path is so rough that the name is self-explanatory. Close to Annecy there is part of the Roman road that joined the Little Saint Bernard Pass to Geneva through Axima (now Aime), Darentasia (now Moûtiers), Ad Publicanos (now Conflans-Albertville), Casuaria (modern Faverges), and Boutae (Annecy). The road, as were many Latin Alpine roads, is cut through the rock in which one can read this inscription:

L. TINCUS PACULUS PERVIUM FECIT

This passage has been made by L. Tincus Paculus. The inscription is now protected by a transparent plastic shield. Best to look for it on foot; it is only a few feet off a road that to this day retains its Roman-style narrowness (to reach it, take the D16 through Annecy-le-Vieux, turn left at the Fier bridge, and left again from the bridge onto the D216).

All the cities I have mentioned here saw a substantial development throughout the Roman period. They were centers of commerce and administration, and points of passage between Rome, Lyon, and Geneva. While digging up a street in order to repair it, the city of Geneva recently uncovered some parts of the Roman port of Geneva, which now lie open for everyone to see. It is quite an experience to stand in the midst of late-twentieth-century traffic and be able to look at a perfectly excavated and preserved Roman waterwall. Many of the artifacts excavated from the Roman period of the Savoie can be seen in the Chambéry museum, as well as in the spare but well-organized little museum at Moûtiers.

Germanic incursions, turning over time into true invasions, did not spare the Savoie. In A.D 260, then again in 277, the Alamanni came; a few people in the Savoie still go by the patronym Allemand or Alaman. Hoards of coins dating back to these invasions have been found. People took refuge behind the walls of cities or the larger country estates. Around 450 the Burgundians, chased by the Huns from not-too-well-defined holdings in what is now Switzerland and the French Franche Comté, were "invited" by the Romans to relocate in Savoie. By then, Allobrogia had been renamed Sapaudia, which became Savoie in French. The origin of the name may be Sapindia (country of the fir trees), or it may have been a person's name, no one knows for sure. The Burgundians were a genial people who readily assimilated into the local population. They made their capital in Geneva and crowned their kings there. They were not invaders, they were refugees who had left half of their nation enslaved by the Huns on the Rhine. Sidonius Apollinarius, writer, poet, and bishop of the early Catholic Church, described them around 430: "Tall, the Burgundians are brave soldiers and good, but heavy and coarse people; they consume a lot of garlic and smell mightily since they are in the habit of greasing their hair with rancid butter."

Through battles and agreements, the Burgundians retained their domination over what is now Burgundy and Provence. We owe to their King Gondebaud the famous and important Gombette law, well known to all historians. In 534 the sons of Frankish King Clovis attacked the Burgundian kingdom and conquered it within two years. For approximately four centuries the Savoie, included in that Frankish kingdom, sank into total and complete anarchy with very few periods of respite.

On the better side of the picture, slow but deep Christianization took place. Because of the isolation of the intra-Alpine valleys, the faith did not spread as fast in the Savoie as it did in other parts of the Roman world; Christianity reached first Geneva, Aix les Bains, and Aime, coming both from the Po and the Rhône valleys. In 286 it reached what is now the Swiss Valais, once part of the Savoie, in a spectacular manner: Some of the legionnaires of

Emperor Maximinus refused to swear fidelity to the Roman gods in Agaunensis, now Saint Maurice d'Agaune. The legionnaires and their leader Maurice were executed and buried on the spot. Saint Maurice became one of the most revered saints of the Savoie, and the beautiful abbey developed there over the centuries.

After the advent of Pepin the Short and his son Charlemagne the Savoie became part of the huge European empire governed from Aachen in Germany. In 843 the Verdun treaty, the first document written in early French, gave the Savoie to Lothar I. Fights between lords monotonously followed one another until the vicious incursions of the Saracens. Established in Provence just above the Mediterranean, those followers of Mohammed jumped on their wild horses, galloped up the Rhône valley, and entered the Alpine valleys, causing desolation. They left farms burning and women violated, appearing in the Tarentaise in 906, in the Maurienne in 916, and pillaging the Abbey at Saint Maurice d'Agaune in 939, as well as that at Novalaise. It is often said that the Moors gave their name to the Maurienne, but this is an error since the term already existed in the 400s and possibly comes from Mau Rian (bad river), the Arc having indeed to this day its moments of madness.

The Saracen incursions in a way served to cement the feudal system in the Savoie, as every lord secular or spiritual tried to protect his people. With the arrival of Hungarian hordes from the east, one lord, named Conrad the Pacific, managed to pit the Moors against them and cleaned up the whole lot in 954 after the two invaders had exhausted themselves fighting each other. It is possible that Saint Bernard de Menthon, then a priest in Aosta, saw his name given to both the Little and Great Saint Bernard passes because he took a major part in the fights to liberate these passes from the Saracens.

The Saracens were followed by a long line of inept Frankish/Merovingian kings, who were succeeded by the line of sovereigns known as the Bossons in Provence and the Rodolphes in Savoie. In 974, Provence and Savoie were united. In 1032, the last Rodolphe having passed away without an heir, the place was open for the true founder of the house of Savoie, Humbert aux Blanches Mains—in English, Humbert of the White Hands—who set the scene for Savoie to become a political power.

Probably from the smart Burgundian line, Humbert had quite a political sense and was intelligent enough to realize that his being situated on the passes between Savoie and the Piemonte gave him a unique opportunity. The Alps were then considered an impassable barrier with a wonderful sunny land tucked behind them. In the beginning Humbert was a minor lord, but well connected and with a good understanding of worldly affairs. We do not even know which language he spoke, whether Low Latin or early German, but it was probably both since he communicated so well with the German emperor. Through his finely honed political acumen, he acquired control over four of the six main Alpine passes: Mont Genèvre, Mont Cenis, and both Saint Bernards. Humbert died master over the Maurienne, the Combe de Savoie, the Val d'Aosta, the Lower Chablais, and part of the Faucigny, carrying proudly the title of Count of Savoie.

His successors continued the favorite game of medieval sovereigns—the acquisition of new lands. The Piemonte and the Tarentaise, along with the Upper Chablais, came to Humbert's sons through diplomacy or marriage, and to his grandson came what is now the Swiss Valais. The Humbertians, as they came to be called, possessed a fine sense of unity, and all acquired new territories on both sides of the Alpine chain. Some were serious organizers, others true warlords, such as Amadeus III, who developed important fortresses in the Piemonte and the Combe de Savoie; Montmélian was built then to guard the border with France through the Dauphiné.

Problems with the emperors of Germany were ever-present, especially for Humbert III, called the Saint, who would have liked nothing better than to be a monk. As it turned out, the poor man had a major problem for a king: It took him four wives to produce a son. In spite of reverses and wars the counts of Savoie continued their patient work of piecing together the largest possible county on both sides of the Alps, and on the northern side of Lake Leman in what is now part of the southern Jura areas of France. It was during the reign of Thomas I (1189–1233) that Chambéry was acquired and made the capital of the ever-extending county. A few of the Savoie counts did not hesitate to put their whole brood of brothers and sisters to work in many European courts to further the holdings and politics of the county. Pierre II and his son Philip V added to their already huge county all of the present Canton de Vaud in

Switzerland, the Chablais (both the present-day French and Swiss parts), and the small Pays de Gex close to Geneva.

Then came the all-important Amadeuses, well remembered in the Savoie because they extended the county to its farthest boundaries. Amadeus VI, known as the Green Count, brought in the Faucigny; Amadeus VII, his son, known as the Red Count, brought in Nice, which for a landlocked county represented a most important window on the sea. Amadeus VIII, his successor, was probably one of the greatest Savoie sovereigns. After acquiring the Genevois, he welcomed the Emperor of Germany, Sigismund, with such political flair that his title of count was changed to duke in 1416. By 1430 the Duchy of Savoie extended from the Sâone River to the Pays de Vaud on the northern shore of Lake Leman, down into Lombardia and Piemonte, and way down to the opening on the sea at Nice.

The next most important historic figure was a woman, Yolande de France, sister of the crafty and smart Louis XI of France. She became regent after the illness and death of her husband and during the childhood of her son. The princess was charming, but in alliance with Charles the Bold of Burgundy, she became involved in a nasty conflict for domination of some of the Swiss possessions. Louis XI of France helped put an end to it and had the Savoie made a protectorate under his authority. This was to be the first of many French interventions in the Savoie. Following Yolande's regency came a number of dukes who were politically unimportant until the reign of Charles III, which began in 1504. A parent of the powerful Charles V of Spain, later also Emperor of Austria, Charles III of Savoie found himself caught in the net of intrigues passing between the Spanish king and Francis I, King of France. This involvement eventually led to the invasion of the Duchy of Savoie by the troops of Francis I in 1536. When Charles III passed away in 1553, all he had to leave to his heir Emmanuel Philibert was Nice and a few cities in the Piemonte.

Going by the principle that *Spoliati arma supersunt* ("To those who have lost everything arms are everything"), Emmanuel Philibert set out to regain his rights by winning a few battles for Philip II of Spain in Flanders; when Philip died his adversary Henry II of France made peace with the Savoie at Cateau-Cambrésis in 1559. Not only was Emmanuel Philibert given his duchy back but he also received in marriage Madame Marguerite de France, Henry's sister, who sustained him emotionally while he was rebuilding his duchy. During his reign the capital was transferred to the Piemontese city of Turin, a step that would become most important in the nineteenth century.

In the constant fluctuations of history that seem to bring a successful generation then a completely unsuccessful one, Charles Emmanuel I, son of Emmanuel Philibert, brought on disaster again by becoming enmeshed in the wars of Henry IV of France, who thought nothing of once more bringing French armies into the Savoie and taking a few bites out of the territory.

The dawn of the seventeenth century was not much more peaceful. Dukes Victor Amadeus I, Charles Emmanuel II, and Victor Amadeus II saw their territories invaded three times by the French: in 1639 by Louis XIII and his tough minister Richelieu, and again by Louis XIV in 1690 and 1703. These last two invasions coincided with famines (see the Bread chapter, page 124) and epidemics that brought the duchy to the verge of total collapse.

The 1715 Treaty of Utrecht put an end to the wars of Louis XIV, and as a compensation the Duke of Savoie was given Sicily. In 1718, when Sicily was exchanged for Sardinia, he became king of Piemonte-Sardinia. Significant fact: The Savoie became a province of that kingdom. King Victor Amadeus II was to become a great sovereign; very down to earth, always modestly dressed, he rebuilt his armies and published in 1721 the Royal Constitutions that reunified the kingdom as a Catholic country. Customs, taxes, the mapping of the kingdom (in which Jean Jacques Rousseau participated) were reviewed and/ or instituted, respectively. In every way as despotic as Louis XIV of France had been, Victor Amadeus II abdicated in his sixty-fourth year in favor of his son Charles Emmanuel III, who completed his father's administrative work. Charles Emmanuel's long reign was to see the kingdom involved again in two major wars.

During the first, France and Sardinia being allies, the mountain people enjoyed seeing the impressive armies of Louis XV cross the Alps (the uniforms were indeed very colorful and beautiful in those charming eighteenth-century days when everything serious was done lightly and everything light was considered serious). During the second war, Louis XV remained neutral, perhaps out of respect for his mother who had been Adelaide of Savoie, but he did "send" instead the troops of his nephews and cousins from Spain, a total of 18,000 soldiers at once pious and violent, who occupied the Savoie for seven trying years. Their Spanish arrogances levied extremely heavy taxes, ate and drank everything in sight, and left the country totally depleted when they finally departed early in 1749.

Peace finally settled in until the French Revolution. Everyone went back to work, the borders with France were once more set, war debts were paid, and intelligent laws were enacted to resolve the problems of land ownership without breaking the social hierarchy. By 1771 a whole organization had been set up to allow the lower classes to purchase back all feudal rights still in existence across the duchy—this exactly eighteen years before the famous French Abolition of Privileges of August 4, 1789.

That great French Revolution happened during the reign of Victor Amadeus III and was to be another disaster for the Savoie. In 1792 France declared war on Austria; during the night that followed the key victory of the French armies at Valmy (September 21, 1792), a second French army massed at Grenoble and marched into the Savoie. This was a battleless invasion: The Sardinian troops folded back to the Alpine passes, giving the Savoyards the impression that all the taxes they had paid to support a Sardinian army were eminently wasted. The well-known writer Joseph de Maistre recorded in his diary: "This will be an eternal shame for the government."

In October an Assembly of the Allobroges opened in Chambéry, and in eight days it demolished the Sardinian regime with as much gusto as the French had destroyed their ancestral monarchy in 1789. The Savoie became the "département du Mont Blanc" of the First French Republic: Every bit of superior authority was destroyed; complete decentralization ended up in complete tragedy. The currency was unstable, famine was around the bend, and looming large on the horizon was the dictatorship of the French Convention, which, in Paris, was about to send thousands of people to the guillotine. By 1793, exacerbated by the stupidity of men like Simond and Hérault de Seychelles, the Savoie population was ready to start a counterrevolution. Revolts occurred in many places and, sin of sins in that very Catholic country, the Bishop of Chambéry was arrested.

Victor Amadeus III, who had taken refuge in the Piemonte, was trying without success to move into Savoie through the Alpine passes. As its representative, to complete the revolutionary work, the French Convention sent Albitte, who was the incarnation of terror as well as of stupidity and cruelty; he developed a fixation about priests, who, of course, were in open rebellion against the regime. But life eased up a bit after Albitte was replaced by various other *commissioners* of the Republic. Soon after the Italian wars of Bonaparte, Victor Amadeus died, leaving his son Charles Emmanuel IV a state in complete disarray; there was nothing left for him to do but to rejoin the island of Sardinia under the protection of the British fleet. The poor king finished his passage on earth as a Jesuit mendicant in Rome. His brother and heir, Victor Emmanuel I, had to wait for the collapse of France after the Napoleonic Wars to recover his country.

For the Savoie people, Napoleon Bonaparte was synonymous with the return of order: Religious rights and mass every Sunday were reinstated as the priests were called back from the French penitentiaries. During the ten years of Napoleon's empire the road of the Mont Cenis Pass was built, as were a number of other roads; industrial spinning mills, faïence factories, and a school of mines were opened; school resumed in villages and cities, and the religious orders were allowed to reintegrate their convents.

The defeat of Napoleon saw the Savoie divided in half by the 1814 treaty of Paris: Chambéry and Annecy remained in France, while the remainder of the Savoie went back to the king of Piemonte-Sardinia. This decision was so unpopular at all levels of society that the Congress of Vienna in 1815 returned the entire Savoie to the king of Piemonte-Sardinia. The king, who looked older when he came back in his eighteenth-century clothing and wig, made all heads turn in some kind of amazement, but he was welcomed and the kingdom went back to routine except for the famines of the years 1816–17. There was one significant difference in the political atmosphere, however: The kingdom's center of gravity was definitely in the Piemonte, and the Savoie had become only a bastion of western protection for its Italian part. The Hapsburgs were taking over the rest of Italy, with Milan, Venice, Verona, Vicenza, Parma, and Padua all in the hands of various archdukes and archduchesses.

From then on, the attention of the kings of Piemonte-Sardinia turned eastward, to try to wrench Italy out of Austrian hands. Victor Emmanuel made peace with his nobility and clergy, and Catholicism was again declared the official religion. The countryside sank into deep piety. Helped by its Italian-speaking *carabinieri*, the government was given the ironical name of *buon governo* as the systematic suppression of all literary and artistic expression emanating from Paris brought on criticism and mockery. Nevertheless, it was not the Savoie that revolted; it was the Piemonte that clamored for a constitution. The political situation turning rapidly difficult, Victor Emmanuel I abdicated!

In the absence of his heir and brother, Charles Felix, it was his nephew, young Charles Albert, twenty-two years old, who took the regency and rashly accepted the constitution. Upon his return, Charles Felix promptly repealed it. Honest but not extremely smart in a time when politically one had to be extremely cunning, Charles Felix took refuge in the past and adopted a laissez-faire attitude sustained by the faith that things would take care of themselves. He finished whatever public works he had started, visited the Savoie four times, died, and was buried in 1831 at the Hautecombe Abbey on Lake Le Bourget, which he had rebuilt.

The year 1830 had been less than quiet in Europe, with the wind of revolution blowing hard again in France, Belgium, Poland, and the duchies of Modena and Parma. As Charles Albert returned to succeed his father, his eyes were decidedly set upon the eastern horizon, not the Savoie; he truly believed that he had been entrusted with the divine mission of delivering Italy from the Austrians. In 1848 he followed with enthusiasm an initiative of Pope Pius IX, who announced reforms in his government and had found a lot of followers for his ideas. Thus infused, Charles Albert granted a constitution to his people, inaugurated a new flag with green, white, and red bands, and went off to war against Austria. This war was extremely unpopular with the Savoyards, who could not see why they should fight for the benefit of the Italians.

The concept of separating the Savoie from the Kingdom of Piemonte-Sardinia began to take hold. The twenty-two deputies sent by the Savoie to the Parliament in Turin felt isolated by the difference in their language; meanwhile the war with the Austrians went awry as Charles Albert was defeated at the Battle of Novara. In his turn, he abdicated in favor of his son, Victor Emmanuel II.

Victor Emmanuel maintained the constitution, refused to comply with Austrian demands, and quickly became the incarnation of free Italy; Cavour became his minister, and the meeting of the two minds and personalities culminated in the creation of modern Italy and the so-called annexation of the Savoie to France. I say to, rather than by, since the Savoie people had their own word to say in such a momentous step.

In 1858, Cavour met with Napoleon III in Plombières and there very secretly cooked up a fantastic plot that would put the Savoie into the French basket and make the Pope, of all people, president of an Italian confederation. Soon after that Cavour and Napoleon III decided to go to war against Austria again, to try to implement their plans. The war was like Napoleon III: indecisive. The French emperor would take the Savoie and Nice one minute, but the next he thought that maybe after all he should not.

It was the people of the Savoie themselves who took things into their own hands and wrote their king a celebrated letter in which they politely but strongly stated that they did not feel and had no desire to be Italian. This step, taken not by the deputies to the Parliament but by plain intelligent citizens, made a lot of sense in Chambéry but was not extremely popular in Turin. Even the Swiss entered the picture, demanding that Northern Savoie become part of their confederation. Protests were sent both to Turin and Paris, since the Swiss do not happen—even now—to be very popular in Northern Savoie. Cavour went back to work, and on March 24, 1860, a treaty legalized the final arrival of the Savoie into the French community; the people were consulted and, on April 22, 1860, overwhelmingly voted themselves French.

France divided the Savoie into two *départements* now still existing: The Haute Savoie contains the Genevois, Faucigny, and Chablais; and the Savoie comprises the Combe de Savoie, Val d'Arly, Beaufortain, Tarentaise, and Maurienne.

The two departments sent their men to war against Prussia in 1870 and in 1914 as distinguished French soldiers. A deep political and economic revolution started after World War I when people who for centuries had scratched a difficult living out of a difficult soil in autonomous family units found themselves becoming "peasant-workers" as they took employment in the newly established industries.

The two world wars saw the loss of a lot of men, and women left alone to survive, run the farms, and raise the children. In 1941, after Mussolini's Italy had declared war on France, the Italians invaded the upper valleys, to be replaced in 1943 by ferocious German SS units. The Resistance in Savoie and the intense work to save Jewish people were, with all due respect to the criticisms of the French Resistance by a number of British historians, as valiant as the Battle of Britain. I happened to be there as the conflict ended: It was the Savoie Resistance task force that liberated Annecy and Chambéry, not the Allies, and the Free French troops that cleaned up the Alpine passes of their stubbornly vicious nests of Axis forces.

The mountains nowadays blatantly show the interference of modern civilization: Roads as wide as the slopes will allow, huge electrical and chemical plants, sophisticated ski equipment, snow fences to prevent avalanches, concrete block constructions, all have slowly climbed the high Alps, opening wide the passages through which Hannibal and the Romans struggled. Nevertheless, very few parts of France have kept their identity as well as the Savoie. Because the Savoie was for such a long time a proud, independent country, its people remain very conscious of their heritage and keep it superbly documented.

PEOPLE OF THE MOUNTAINS: LIFE IN THE TRADITIONAL AND IN THE MODERN SAVOIE

In the Savoie as everywhere else in countries that have known many population movements and wars, the original ethnic groups are so mixed that it is almost impossible to guess who is descended from pre-Celtic or Celtic populations, who from Burgundians or Alemanni, Romans or Saracens. But once in a great while, one very typical person just stands there in the middle of a village and you wonder whether the centuries did not get all mixed up! I had just such an experience in a very remote hamlet that sits almost 3000 feet up on the side of a mountain. I arrived with my camera, and three generations of women were chatting on benches in the tiny village square. All but the youngest of them, possibly in her early twenties, had their heads covered, which nowadays has become uncommon, and all of them were wearing the wonderful traditional dangling Savoie earrings of warm pink gold. Slightly embarrassed in my modern pantsuit, I politely said hello and tried to start a conversation. I so would have liked to take just that particular picture! But the matriarch, somewhere in her middle eighties, fiery eyes darting above her very Saracen nose, and earrings flashing light, spoke. Before I could utter a word, she boomed No! with an almost savage passion. She did not want her picture taken, it was not in the custom of this village, no one here would even think of having her picture taken! Too bad! The arduous trip on foot was not useless, though; houses cannot speak or protest, and they were the best-looking Tarentaise houses I had ever seen.

Savoie people are quiet; they speak little, but they speak wisely; it is hard to be accepted by them as a friend, but once you have been accepted you are a friend for life, a bit like in some parts of New England. I think that living and working in the mountains brings on economy of words, which does not mean that one is sad; far from it. One is just very very careful until one knows people well.

LANGUAGE

When Montaigne, the great French Renaissance writer, arrived in the Savoie over the Mont Cenis Pass on his way back from Italy, he noted in his book: "*Ici on parle francès.*" While some people in the Savoie can speak Italian, as many people in France also speak English or German, the official language of the Savoie has never been Italian because the Savoie has never been Italian, a fact that is not always clear. Great writers of the French language have come from the Savoie, from the thirteenth to the nineteenth century, their names familiar to all students of literature. Best known are Claude Favre de Vaugelas, the grammarian, and Saint Francis de Sales, patron saint of all journalists, preacher of the Counter-Reformation, and superb writer of the *Introduction to the Devout Life* in the seventeenth century. Jean Jacques Rousseau, although born in Geneva at a time when the city was not Savoyard anymore but already independent and Calvinist, came to the Savoie and lived there the ten formative years of his writer's life. The text of the first chapters of his *Confessions* remains a delightful memoir; a walk in the Thônes valley has changed very little since Rousseau wrote about it, and I have often gathered plums where he gathered cherries. Joseph de Maistre, at the close of the eighteenth century, was another great Savoyard writer concerned with religion and monarchy at a time when both were under threat of the French Revolution. The modern Savoie has inspired many writers, the most Savoyard of all being Henri Bordeaux, who loved his mountains, and the very modern Frison Roche, whose novels inspired my youth. I used to listen to Beethoven's Pastoral Symphony as I read Frison Roche. The Chamonix valley he wrote about was mine, pure, its air crystal-clear; that of my sons has been changed by the Mont Blanc Tunnel.

People of my generation and even some much younger still speak patois. There are as many patois as there are valleys and sometimes villages. If you are at a market stand and hear a fast idiom spoken that definitely does not sound French, you are hearing patois. I am slowly getting to the point of understanding it and having the best time, for conversations in patois are more often than not happy, even hilarious. The patois all belong to the group of Franco-Provençal languages—that is, those languages where the usage of consonants follows the rules of the *Langue d'oïl* (spoken in northern France) and the usage of vowels follows the rules of *Langue d'oc* (spoken in southern France). The patois are interesting because they show roots coming from all the different ethnic groups that ever lived in the Savoie: the pre-Latin Celto-Ligurian and Celtic roots, some Greek roots acquired during the first century A.D. when Lyon, the main city of the Rhône sphere of influence, was a mostly Greek metropolis, and of course lots of Germanic roots, through the Burgundians, a large number of immigrants returning from the Germanic countries, and the peddlers of the eighteenth and nineteenth centuries.

SOCIETY

Savoie society around the time of the annexation was structured pretty much like French society. The upper nobility, the old solid one going back to feudal times, was still in existence, although very diminished by the effects of the French Revolution. In the middle—be it the upper- or lower-middle—were the impoverished lesser nobility and all the layers of the bourgeoisie; the common folks made up the remainder and the majority. Although generalities on the matter would be, as usual, vastly inaccurate, it is not unreasonable to say that the upper nobility remained idealistic, and not too well oriented toward commerce and industry, living mostly from their land and leaving to their impecunious members and to the bourgeoisie the duties of truly keeping commerce and industry going. The bourgeoisie made up the bulk of magistrates, politicians, and business people. The common folks' lot was to survive and produce from their environment what was needed to survive; they did this either on their own land or as tenant farmers for the bourgeoisie and the gentry. In the nineteenth century, the concept of "the lord" had disappeared, but *le monsieur* or *le maître* was still an important person. Everything was produced at home in a perfect example of economic autonomy. Many traces of that old Savoie are still visible throughout the countryside.

HOUSES AND DWELLINGS

The houses in the Savoie, as everywhere in the world, reflect the ethnic origins and professions of their inhabitants, the climatic conditions, and the agricultural vocation of the surrounding countryside. There are definitely several easily recognizable types of houses. The best preserved are always in the upper valleys. The fronts of all houses everywhere seem to open predominantly toward the south to catch as much sun as possible; since most dwellings are built on mountain slopes, the northern exposure is very reduced, the northern wind, *la Bise*, being feared by everyone. The descriptions that follow are short, but any architect interested can find thousands and thousands of very precise and articulate studies published mostly in French, but complete with such detailed diagrams that they can be understood by people of any linguistic expression.

The Annecy and Chambéry museums offer several exquisite models. One of the most modern texts among many excellent ones is H. Raulin's *L'Architecture Rurale Française: La Savoie* published in 1977.

All the houses I shall describe here are of the traditional type. So many are still standing and in good shape that they are extremely visible and should be understood. They stand in the middle of new, very modern little houses and villas built by developers in the last thirty years. Developers have done both poor and good jobs. In the thirties the construction of villas in the "French Ile de France type" that looked totally silly in the middle of the mountains was more or less the rule, and unfortunately too many of those are there, built to last and healthy, mostly puny and poorly organized inside. Modern developers recognized, after the "concrete" disasters of the 1960s and 70s in modern ski resorts, that something more attractive, modern, but in the Savoie style could be done; after that, most new houses were given a style that resembles in some ways that of the old traditional homes. It is not hard as one looks at the scenery to immediately recognize which buildings belong to which category.

When one talks strictly about traditional houses, the more south one goes, the more stone there is in the construction. So if you are in the Chablais, the Faucigny, and the mountainous parts of the Genevois, you will see houses of the chalet style with stone foundations only, and upper floors made entirely of wood.

Many families own two "chalets," one for winter use in the valley and a smaller one on the alp. In front of each house is a small paved area called the *portina*, where in the summer one sits to chat with members of the family or friends, all the while keeping busy with needlework or a pipe. The private *bachal*, or water fountain, if one has one, is also there, with a couple of benches and sometimes a flight of stairs to allow access in and out of rooms that open onto an upstairs wood gallery; the gallery is always embellished in the growing season with vividly colored flowers. Quite a few of the houses are two-family dwellings separated into equal parts under the point of the roof.

There are differences among the houses of all regions of the Northern Savoie. From my observations, the Giffre valley in the little town of Sixt offers the best-preserved examples of wood houses still existing. The larch wood turns a lovely deep red as it weathers. All kinds of intriguing carvings are used as decoration just under the eaves, and even barn walls have aerating vents for the hay cut into various decorative patterns. These openings may be carved

Figure 9

The ying-yang pattern combinations in which the aeration vents of barns were cut in the Giffre valley between Samoëns and Sixt

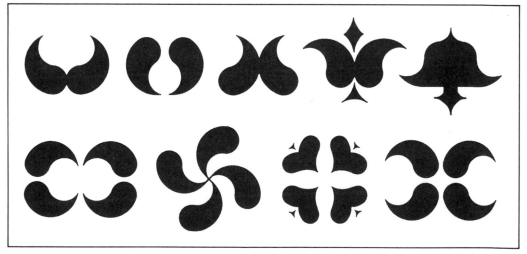

into the aces of card games or oriental-looking comas which can be arranged ying-yang fashion, or in many other patterns (see Figure 9). Several barns showing these patterns can still be seen between Samoëns and Sixt.

Next to each house one can see what looks like a smaller version of the house, the *grenier*, or storage shed. Since the houses were made entirely of wood, fire was a great hazard, and to prevent losing all of one's precious possessions in a fire, one would store them in one of those charming little buildings. The most delightful one I have ever seen is in Sixt, just at the entrance to the path that goes to the church. The original paint is still visible on it and it is signed "Jacques Allaman 1791." If one had a lot of possessions to store, the *grenier* might have two floors. Some of these two-story *greniers* have now been purchased by Parisians and transformed into tiny summer homes. The doors are thick, rounded at the top, and so low that one must bend to enter. When I spent the winter at La Balme, our Sunday clothes were hung in one of those *greniers*. As we went to fetch them for Christmas, the key looked so interesting, and kids being kids, we argued a bit about who was to carry it. It measured ten inches or so and was of commensurate weight; each of us finally "got to hold it to see." It must have weighed in the vicinity of three pounds or more.

In the Lower and Upper Faucigny, it is a bit different; the rooms in which one lives are solid masonry and only the top floor in which the hayloft is located is of wood. It is not unusual to see a collection of pastel-colored beehives on the sunny side of the house. The roofs, instead of forming a plane angle, often show a broken front and are then called *à l'allemande*, since indeed in all the Alemannic parts of Europe such roofs are prevalent. This style roof breaks the wind and may have been brought by the immigrations of Alemannic populations both in the Chablais and the Faucigny during the twelfth and thirteenth centuries.

The Genevois presents an interesting collection of houses, especially in the Thônes valley, in the areas of Manigod, Le Grand Bornand, and La Clusaz. It is in this area that you can see the most interesting galleries of beautifully carved wood and those large chimneys in which one could smoke hams; they can be partly closed by a mechanically controlled slab of stone to prevent the abundant winter snows from blocking the flow of air and smoke.

The roofs are made of *tavaillons* or *ancelles*, the names of the wood tiles that fit tightly into each other. Over the tiles run on each side of the roof at least two long, thin larch or pine trunks, which are affixed there to retain the snow during the winter and prevent it from falling onto the porch and blocking the front door. In spite of other, more modern roofing procedures, some houses are still covered this way. In this area, the same little *greniers* can be seen, perfectly organized, with special storage bins for wheat and other cereals, and racks for all the *toupines*, or large stoneware vases, in which one stored the clarified butter and the lard necessary for use during the winter. The Thônes museum offers wonderful exhibition rooms in which one can see and understand the way of life at the beginning of this century, as well as an exceptionally beautiful hand-carved beehive, representing a primitive seventeenth-century woman complete with hat and hoop skirt.

The Combe de Savoie and the Avant Pays have stately large gray houses, square looking with overhanging roofs. Generally called *maisons dauphinoises*, they exist all over France and in the Savoie present some definite local characteristics. The best example of this type of dwelling is, in almost every village, the very large and comfortable home of the village priest known as *le presbytère*, very easy to locate since it is rarely more than a few steps away from the church. In each village to this day there may be two or three of these houses, occupied by bourgeois such as the local lawyer and physician.

The Avant Pays homes of people involved in agriculture, cattle-raising for milk, and vineyard cultivation show the differences in the occupations of their owners, not only in the disposition of the buildings but also in the surrounding smells. Cows and wine cellars cannot ever remain undetected by the passerby.

The Beaufortain, placed as it is exactly halfway between the Mont Blanc country and the Tarentaise, offers types of houses that vary between the Faucigny and the Genevois types, but remain definitely northern houses with a preponderance of wooden structures.

Tarentaise houses are almost all made of stone covered by masonry, with wooden balconies. The upper part under the eaves is all wood, and the roof is covered with large flagstone slabs known as *lauzes*. Some of these houses, around Bourg Saint Maurice, Sainte Foy, and Séez, have their eaves resting on huge columns of stone, very much as can be seen in some of the houses of the Val d'Aosta, where the *lauzes* are known as *tegole* and have by extension given their name to a type of shortbread cookie. The houses with columns are now protected by the Beaux Arts; they are so attractive that the community of Val d'Isère is rebuilding the whole center of its ski station in this style. In front of some Tarentaise houses one can often see a small courtyard complete with a door that can be locked, or even more often, as in the beautiful Moris house again in Val d'Isère, two huge sidewalls reaching from eaves to ground and protecting the entrance from accumulating snow.

That leaves us with the Maurienne. Types of houses there vary between the Lower and Upper Maurienne. The geographical limit of change usually accepted by the specialists is the little town of Saint Michel de Maurienne. Many Maurienne houses have their first floor level with the ground and built in vault shapes. But there are many variations. The Arvan valley presents interesting wooden walls made of young tree trunks between which alder branches have been woven; in the same valley, one can still also see a few thatched roofs, if one knows about them and looks carefully.

The most typical houses of the Upper Maurienne are way up at the beginning of the Arc valley, in full view of the severe glacial country that goes up the Iseran Pass to rejoin the Tarentaise at Val d'Isère. There is the wonderful little "museum village" of Bonneval-sur-Arc and the even more typical hamlet of L'Ecot, where every stone is protected by the Beaux Arts and constantly shored up from inside so the look remains as original as possible. Other villages (Bessans, Termignon) built on the same patterns were destroyed by Axis bombings during World War II and have as a consequence lost a lot of their original charm. When you drive between Modane and Bonneval, notice all the stone constructions still remaining. Complete houses are made of stones piled up tightly on top of one another and are very reminiscent of the *bories* of Provence. The building techniques here were, without doubt, inherited millennia ago from the Ligurians. The roofs are made of *lauzes*, and the use of wood is minimal because there is just not very much wood in the Maurienne. Wood appears only in light balconies, which to this day remain chock-full of the bundles of wood or *fascines*, strictly reserved to light the bread oven. Historically, the dried-out *grebons*, or mutton droppings, used to heat the house were also stored on these balconies, but they disappeared with the advent of fuel and electricity as sources of heat.

CASTLES

Castles are rare in the upper valleys, but plentiful in the Genevois especially and the Combe de Savoie, where the feudal system was highly developed. Some of those dating from ancient times are now in ruins, and you can see them in the Combe de Savoie and the Lower Tarentaise, lining the hills above the modern roads. These "eagle nests" were strategically built on the foundations of former Celtic and/or Roman fortresses to guard the approaches; there was in the Combe de Savoie a whole system of communication from castle to castle that sent news back and forth to and from the capital city of Chambéry. One of these fifteenth-century fortresses, the Château de Miolans, is still standing and can be visited. Not all castles date back to these ancient times; many were built as country dwellings after the seventeenth century and are not so visible from the road since they are at the end of those wonderful lanes shaded with trees that lead in Europe to most private estates. Many of these castles have been repaired as necessary and look quite good. Many are still private properties, some better kept than others in these modern times of heavy taxation. You may want to visit the large museum castles at Chambéry and Annecy.

One of the jewels of the Northern Savoie is the Château de Menthon Saint Bernard, where the saint is said to have been born, although it is not a totally historically established fact; the beautifully preserved castle is still occupied by the de Menthon family, and its view over the Bauges mountains and the Annecy lake is breathtaking. The château at Ripaille (see Wine section, page 108) is worth the trip, preferably in the spring or after September 10; and the Château of Montrottier in the Fier valley, at Lovagny, is known for its wonderful collections of just about everything interesting, and fascinating to visit, also preferably in September. There are many more castles, and if you are interested in architecture, classification by style, or other technical data, there is a large catalogue, with millions of details, available in all public libraries entitled *Châteaux et Maisons Fortes de Savoie*.

Maisons fortes are much less well known, although they are very visible in many villages and small towns. They often have a tower, which houses the flight of stairs, and are a little higher than the best bourgeois houses of the community. They housed the lesser nobility and the bourgeoisie of means, or even large agricultural enterprises. One of the best towns in which to investigate *maisons fortes* is probably Megève, which had eleven of them plus a priory. Basically, just open your eyes; they are plentiful and easy to recognize, since they are too big to be missed.

VILLAGES AND HAMLETS, TOWNS AND CITIES

It is relatively easy to figure out how individual villages have formed. Sometimes it is the name of the village itself that gives the clue, sometimes the buildings in the village, sometimes its geographical location.

The most ancient villages are probably those with a name including the word *balme* or *barme*, which indicates that in the area is a cave or several caves that were occupied as early as the Neolithic period. The occupants simply left the cave to build shelters in its vicinity.

In the same line of thinking, whenever the word *villard* is included or stands alone as the name of a village, the origin of the village is Roman, *villard* being the local spelling of the Old Latin *villa*. If you travel in the countryside, you will see many of these *villards* or *villars* pass by. The Thônes valley seems a microcosm of good examples: There is Les Villards-sur-Thônes where in Roman times one could most probably find several villas; a little higher up the mountain is the Villard-Dessous, indicating a group of chalets in the middle mountain at an altitude of between 2400 and 3600 feet; and higher, in the vicinity of 4800 feet, is the Villard-Dessus, the two words *dessous* and *dessus* meaning in French "below" and "above," respectively. But a little farther up the road there is also Le Villaret, which means that in Roman days an annex to the larger villa was there.

Some villages have developed around castles. Such is the case of Menthon Saint Bernard, which sits at the foot of the hill just below the castle, from which it can be surveyed easily. Around the castle at Miolans is the most wonderfully preserved little village of very humble houses where, it is obvious, the domestic help or soldiers who were employed at the castle must have been living. This is such a very lovely, tiny village that one wonders how something as sweet and peaceful can have survived to the end of our inhuman twentieth century.

Other villages grew around abbeys, their houses literally climbing onto and hugging the sides of the church; such is the case at Abondance, where the beautiful cloister of Notre Dame is being slowly and patiently restored by the Beaux Arts. Abondance is lucky to have Monsieur Depollin, a retired history teacher, to guide visitors through the mysteries of the restoration process for the fourteenth-century frescoes that adorn the cloister. The revived pictures show that life occupations in this upper valley have not changed all that much in six centuries.

The traveler who comes to the Savoie only to ski and enjoy the snow is likely to miss completely the traditional Savoie that can be found in the remote villages. No village nowadays is so remote that it cannot be reached by car or even by bus. So drive, walk, or ski to the next hamlet; what I have just described is so apparent and visible that you will be taken back sometimes into the eighteenth century.

In the Chablais, go to the end of the Giffre valley, to the Cirque du Fer à Cheval; one hamlet there, Le Frétenay, is still in its original state. Dingy Saint Clair, is only four miles from the center of Annecy, La Balme de Thuy, no more than eight. La Balme has it all, a prehistoric cave and a *maison forte*. From Le Grand Bornand, Le Bouchet is only a mile away; it is a typical middle-altitude cheese-producing community. In the Chamonix valley, Le Tour, the last village in the valley, has refused to modernize too much, and in the summer it is empty but for a few "crazy" climbers; the birthplace of Michel Croz, first climber of the Matterhorn with Whimper, who died on it on the same day he climbed it, is there, its windows hidden behind cascades of flowers. In the Lower Faucigny, Mont Saxonnex is still unspoiled, although developers are arriving with their "boxes to put people in." In the Beaufortain, most villages are well preserved. The pearl of the Tarentaise in the vicinity of the big ski centers around Courchevel is Le Laisonnay, the typical Tarentaise hamlet, complete with its bread oven and its chapel, no longer in use but still standing. In the Upper Tarentaise, there are several jewels: La Gurra, Villaroger, and especially Le Miroir. The whole Peisey-Nancroix valley is unspoiled and peaceful. The jewels of all Maurienne villages are Jarrier and Bonneval-sur-Arc. Jarrier, which sits on an eastern slope facing the whole Maurienne valley, is dominated by the almost incomparably beautiful Aiguilles d'Arves, while Bonneval, in its morainic environment, with nothing but a bunch of cute marmots whistling around, regains, just after the last snow and just before the first one, the peace of the unspoiled mountain (in between, it is busy since it sits at the southern end of the Iseran Pass).

Most cities with a saint's name grew around an important church and eventually became the seat of bishoprics; such is the case of Saint Jean de Maurienne.

Larger cities have developed at important points along the Roman roads that led from Rome to Lugdunum and Ganava, now the modern cities of Lyon and Geneva, respectively. Along the road from the Little Saint Bernard Pass, Bourg Saint Maurice is the typical *bourg*, which means "place of market," where early on people came to sell and buy, in these mountainous surroundings, mostly bovines and their products, butter and cheese. The word *bourg* is found in many places; one other good example is Lanslevillard and Lanslebourg, both on the road from the Mont Cenis Pass, which before the building of the Fréjus Tunnel was the main access to the lower Maurienne, Chambéry, and Lyon. The city of Moûtiers, called Darentasia in Roman times, owes its name to ancient monasteries and was the seat of a bishopric. Darentasia, by the way, gave its name to the valley of the Isère, which became the Tarentaise.

Albertville, where the 1992 Olympic Games will take place, is the most modern Savoie city, but on the other side of the Arly, up on the hill, sits the old city of Conflans, which you should not miss visiting, not only for its museum but also because of its medieval buildings and its sweeping view over the Lower Tarentaise and the Combe de Savoie. The site on which Albertville stands was, however, already well known to the Romans, who, in the vicinity of the modern city at a place called Ad Publicanos, kept, what else, but a tax collection center!

And then there are those cities that have grown remarkably into the twentieth century. Chambéry, built around the castle of the dukes of Savoie, was the capital for centuries; it is now a sprawling metropolis that houses the progressive University of Savoie and a number of industries. A trip to Chambéry will bring you to a small "old town" in which three or four streets have been preserved as they probably were in the sixteenth century, complete with one little money-changing shop. In the "Sainte Chapelle" at Chambéry you will see where the Mandelion was originally displayed before it was sent to the Turin Cathedral; Chambéry has only a reproduction of it now. If while you are in Chambéry you feel in the mood for visiting with the spirit of Jean Jacques Rousseau, by all means go to Les Charmettes, which he describes so vividly in *Les Confessions*. The house has been restored and provides a typical example of a lovely eighteenth-century *maison bourgeoise*. I visited there on a bright and sunny November day when the mountains were clear and "smoking" with plumes of snow carried by high-altitude winds, and I came back totally inspired, happy, and probably for the first time in my life in complete unison with Rousseau.

Annecy started as the Roman town Boutae. In 1980, I saw some Roman excavations being plowed under during the building of yet another "box to put people in." Between the old village of Annecy-le-Vieux, developed from what had been the port of Boutae, and huddled around its abbey and Annecy-le-Neuf, now simply called Annecy, a few Roman stones still can be seen, only a stone's throw from the city center. Annecy grew up around the castle of the dukes of Genevois, where one of the towers has walls twelve feet thick; it was a walled city, and like all walled cities its buildings are tightly squeezed against one another. The old medieval streets, the *traboules*, are simple corridors between buildings. Most of the sixteenth-century buildings still stand and are kept in their original state, always repainted in pastel colors, the formulas for which come straight from the eighteenth century; the old buildings are piled along canals where the swift water of the lake runs out. Since people mostly keep their windows open through the summer, some of the beautifully beamed French ceilings can easily be seen from the outside. The streets are lined with low arcades under which one can walk easily, should the weather be bad. The rainfall in the Annecy lake basin can be serious, but on the other hand, it contributes to the deep green of the foliage in the area. The best time to avoid carrying an umbrella is September through November.

Annecy is now a modern city complete with a nuclear research plant, one of the Gillette plants, mechanized industries, flour mills, and Paccard, the largest bell manufacturer in France, which sends its bells all over the world; all replicas of the Liberty Bell are made by the house of Paccard, as are many of the bells that ring in university chapels in the United States.

By the seventeenth century, Annecy had many churches and monasteries and two saints of its own. Saint Francis de Sales, whom I mentioned on p. 49 was Bishop of Geneva but lived in Annecy, where his beautiful house still stands; he was canonized for wrenching the Chablais and Thonon from the hands of the Calvinists and to this day lies in state in the modern Basilica of the Visitation in the company of Sainte Jeanne de Chantal, founder of the order of the same name. I have the pleasure of living just below the Visitation; its bells ring my time every fifteen minutes and on High Holidays, sitting at home, I can listen to the concert of its wonderful carillon.

And then there are the "water" cities, which grew out of the Roman and eighteenth-century fondness for "taking the waters." Always skeptical of drinking water since I have vintners' blood, I have to admit that a little stay at Evian, Aix les Bains, Thonon, or Brides-les-Bains takes a great deal of weight off my person. There are other water cures in Challes-les-Eaux, Saint Gervais les Bains, and La Léchère, which among them can cure a great percentage of all human ills. After being worked over fifteen whole mornings by masseurs and water pumps at a cost of approximately half that of any spa in the United States, one feels absolutely grand.

AT HOME IN THE SAVOIE

I am lucky enough to have lived through both Savoies, the old-fashioned one that existed until 1950 and the modern one that started with the 1960s. It took approximately a century for the old customs to fade away and the modern French ones to replace them.

In each Savoie village, there were three important meeting places: the public *bachal*, or water fountain, in the middle of the village or town; the bread oven, or *four banal*; and in some but not all villages, the *fruitière*, where the cheese was made.

Since not everyone had a private source of water, one fetched one's water at the public *bachal* that, beautifully carved or simple, was always the most popular meeting place for the young. Some women, not having their own source of water, came there to do their wash; lively conversations flowed in all directions every Monday morning.

In La Balme, the use of the bread oven had already almost stopped when I arrived, and bread was purchased from the *épicier*, who had large, round sixteen-inch loaves called *meules* delivered from the Thônes baker, but the *fruitière*, over a mile down the road, was still active; all important notices were posted there, and it is where I first saw the mobilization posters for World War II and admired the first young men in the blue Alpine uniform with the famous slanted beret ready to leave for the 27th Regiment of Alpine Rangers in Annecy. Later, during the following spring, they fought in Narvik.

Our children's home was a huge farm-style house that had been remodeled. By thinking hard and looking at the plans of other local homes, I was able to reconstruct the internal arrangement of the rooms, which you can see in Figure 10. The hay had been stored upstairs in a huge hayloft that covered the whole area of the house and that had been transformed into our dormitories. One of our dormitories, called Paradise, had taken the place previously occupied by the large rack in which the bread loaves were stacked during the winter (see page 124); the pulley system was still intact.

What most interested the first tourists at the beginning of the century, especially British author Estella Canziani (see Selected Bibliography), was the cohabitation in many areas of men and animals. In the intra-Alpine valleys of the Maurienne (Arvan and Villards), and especially in the Upper Maurienne and the Upper Tarentaise around Bessans, Tignes, and Val d'Isère, men and animals cohabited for the duration of the winter, which was a good six months. The reasons were simple: More bodies produced more heat, there was little wood—only the malodorous *grebons*—to burn, and it was easier to have direct

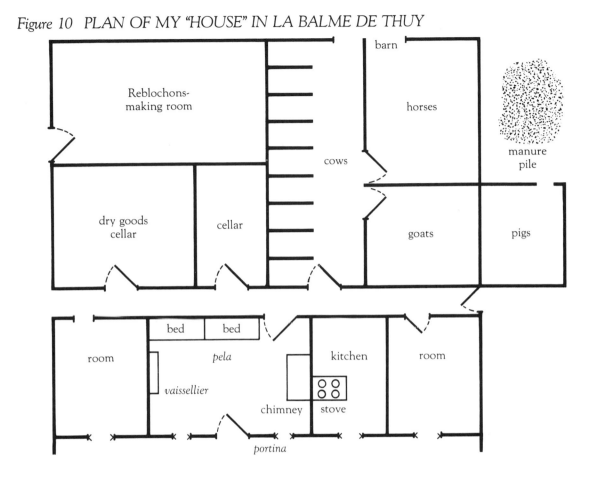

Figure 10 PLAN OF MY "HOUSE" IN LA BALME DE THUY

access to the animals in locations where a snowstorm might easily deposit a cover of four to five feet in one night. The storms of these upper valleys are awesome and so were the avalanches, until in the last twenty-five years high altitude avalanche fences were installed above important avalanche channels. In the summer, the family moved from the ground-floor winter quarters to the upstairs summer quarters.

Fifteenth-century inventories of furniture show that even the upper classes were not exactly living in luxury; the furniture was sparse and made mostly from the resinous woods of the area. But in the seventeenth and eighteenth centuries, wills and inventories show an improvement in amenities, the quality of furniture and appointments. By the eighteenth century, much of the nobility had left their castles to come to the cities and settle in apartments where one established a home in "city" style, complete with exotic wood furniture, beautiful libraries, and the latest in home decoration from Paris and Geneva. The old inherited pieces of furniture were left in the castles, which came to be used only as country dwellings. To this day many of these castles are full of treasures in which their owners sometimes show interest, sometimes not. As I was complimenting one lovely young lady on her precious, big, beautiful Lyon faïence pieces, she very casually answered, "Oh, they come from some lady in our past. I wonder whether they are expensive because if they are, I should probably start worrying about them." In many bourgeois households, better woods such as walnut appeared, and an instrument of bliss: the faïence coffeepot.

There was an abysmal disparity between the standard of living among the two upper classes and that of the peasantry. Here is the description of a farmhouse that would have been standard and is still to be found on many farms all over the Savoie:

One enters a farmhouse from the courtyard directly into the *pela*, also called *outa* in several areas. This is the larger room of the house, which most often contains the large chimney; on its mantle are displayed a crucifix of ebony mounted on a little stand or a picture of the Sacred Heart and the Virgin Mother, together with the military distinctions of the grandfathers. I have seen a large number of Legion of Honor Crosses and Medals of the Liberation citations for fighting at Verdun, Narvik, or with the Free Forces during the Occupation.

The long table may be both a kneading trough and a table or simply a "farm" table with benches on both sides to welcome a large family. Before the twenties or thirties, along the longest wall were one or two cupboard beds closed either with sliding doors or colorful curtains. These have now disappeared and can be found decaying in the piles of old furniture sold at a premium price by antique dealers always ready for a fast franc; museums have some striking examples. Against the wall facing the chimney stands, even if one is not that well off, a beautiful *vaissellier*, or breakfront, on which cherished pretty plates are displayed. Many homes still display their grandmothers' wedding chests, beautifully carved wood coffers with a large key and an ornate lock, which in old times was expensive, since metal was so rare. In this chest went precious possessions and papers. I have been lucky enough to acquire a late-eighteenth-century two-door chest of pinion pine wood; the doors are decorated with simple symbols of the sun, and a huge ornate key to lock it. When one opens the chest, two inlaid hearts of darker reddish larch wood contrast with the honey-colored pine, to indicate where to put one's hands to open the long inner drawer; when I first slid my hands under the drawer, I discovered that the young man who made this chest for his bride had also carved a place for the fingers of each of her hands. The chest has found a loving home in mine; it is one of those pieces on which generations of young children have scratched their initials in several places. I have often wondered whether N, W, A, and C got the licking I did when, like them, all excited by my newfound writing ability, I used a pin to engrave my great grandmother's precious sewing machine with a majestic MP!

And then, in many homes, even sometimes in the poor ones, there was a wonderful clock. To save money, one bought only the movement, which came most of the time from Morbier in the Jura, and Father or Grandfather would build one of those simple and primitive high-standing cases with a window for the face. These can now be bought in flea markets, and if one redoes furniture they offer a nice opportunity to show one's talents. A few well-off farms and many bourgeois homes had this absolutely striking piece of furniture, the breakfront cupboard with a clock case built exactly in its middle. I dream of owning one, someday it will come my way. I already have the 1792 movement to put in it when the time comes. Mine is a royalist movement and this is how I know: Clocks built during the years of the constitutional monarchy in France had the top of their faces decorated by the three fleurs de lys of the monarchy on which stood the proud Gallic rooster. When, in January 1793, Louis XVI was guillotined, people all over France (Savoie was the French department du Mont Blanc at the time; see page 43) who remained royalist broke off the rooster; those who were republican erased the fleurs de lys. My clock has the three fleurs de lys, and, of all places, I saw a clock with the rooster in Tuscaloosa, Alabama.

Next to the *pela* is the kitchen, most of the time and not so long ago outfitted with the two- or four-burner wood or other burning material stove. Nowadays the kitchen still exists, but often its wall has been opened into the *pela*. The old sink made out of solid slabs of mountain stone and draining to the outside by a hand-carved channel has been replaced by the white modern convenience. The handmade wooden stand with three shelves called a *seiller*, which in Grandmother's home was filled sparingly with wooden spoons and bowls, a little coffee mill, a faïence or enameled metal coffeepot, and plates of local earthenware, glazed in bright colors and decorated with primitive themes, is now, more often than not, used to store an electric coffeepot and an electric mixer, and it is not unusual to see the old wooden shelf sit side by side with a clothes washer.

The other rooms in the house contained nothing more than a straw-mattressed bed, maybe another chest, and toward the middle of the nineteenth century maybe a chair, since chairs were a late luxury on farms. I have seen many chapel chairs end up in private homes as chapels on the alp were closed. The chairs were bought to provide funds for the church. These little chapel chairs are now also finding their way to flea markets and ending up in the new postage stamp–size apartments bought by Parisians starved for oxygen and ready to transform Savoie villages into suburbs of Paris during the ski and summer seasons.

All rooms were lit with the *croeju* or *croezu*, the little oil lamp inherited from the Romans, and not really that special to the Savoie. There were many lamps of this type in other parts of France; special to the Savoie was the habit of standing it on an upside-down cheese mold. The remote intra-Alpine valleys would light their homes with torches of evergreen wood. Now one lights rooms sparingly, with low-voltage electric bulbs, because one is still very conscious of the cost of electricity, much more so than we are in the United States.

In villages of the Upper Tarentaise and the Upper Maurienne, where cattle and people cohabited, there was one convenience, called the *beto* in the village of Bessans and the *tournavel* in Val d'Isère. It was a cupboard built into the wall, with a door opening into the *pela* through which one could pull the hay down from the upper-floor loft. Many a *tournavel* was used to hide people from the Germans or the Italians during the war.

Many families to this day still use for the making of smaller cheeses, especially the Reblochon, their grandmother's beautiful copper kettle. It will sit either in the *pela* or in the cheese room if there is one. It is scrubbed after every cheese-making session and shines bright and happy.

CUSTOMS AND COSTUMES

The two most important personalities of every community in the Savoie were the *curé*, or priest, and the *notaire*, or lawyer, since both were in charge of recording the important acts of life until the French annexation.

When a child was delivered by the midwife, the most important and immediate step was to have it baptized. In very Catholic Savoie, it was extremely important, so important that babies delivered stillborn were carried to the church of Notre Dame de la Vie in Saint Martin de Belleville with the hope that a miracle of the Virgin would infuse just enough breath into the poor mite so that it could be baptized right then and there and go to heaven, not to limbo.

Arnold van Gennep (see Selected Bibliography) offers a vast catalogue of all the customs pertaining to the main acts of life, and his description of baptism rituals covers pages and pages, out of which I have retained the following essential facts: The child was carried to church in a wooden crib to which ribbons of pink for boys and blue for girls were attached. The church bells sometimes replaced the ribbons to make the sex of the child known to the whole village: the largest church bell ringing for the boys and the smallest for the girls; but the variations of bell ringing were forever changing from village to village. Godfather and godmother were either the grandparents or uncles and aunts, or even faraway relatives emigrated to better positions. Their responsibility was important since they might eventually replace the child's parents and, in any case, they donated the beautiful new costume for his or her First Holy Communion.

The church forbade celebration with large meals for baptisms, and often one was content with offering a glass of walnut wine and a few homemade biscuits. Marie Thérèse Billard (see Selected Bibliography) has a wonderful description of the baptism of her youngest sister.

Childhood was busy; children helped with house and field work, the elder daughters taking care of the younger babies in families that were always relatively large. There existed a sort of wooden rack into which one slid tightly swaddled infants; the contraption was hung on a large hook on some wall or center roof pole, and the little soul could feel part of the family, survey the surrounding activities, and be chatted to constantly by older members of the clan. Boys and girls of a community would grow up together and came to know one another very well through the winter *veillées*, the after-dinner gatherings in the *pelas* of the village. Neighbors took turns receiving one another, and one knitted, spun hemp or wool, and made lace. Children and adults shelled walnuts, roasted chestnuts, shucked corn, sang, and told stories. A whole mythology of the mountain *sarvans* (domestic trolls) and *diables* (various forms and incarnations of the devil), malicious chastisers of bad boys and girls, was told by the older women. The *veillée* still exists in remote villages, and I am certain that there are still a few *raconteuses* around to entertain young children with stories of the fairies hiding on the alp. Estella Canziani, in her splendid book on customs and costumes, tells a few of these stories; they are naïve and always weird and chilling enough to raise a child's imagination. Various researchers have gathered a rather large amount of materials that offer all kinds of wonderful stories about fairies, proverbs, maxims, and all kinds of pseudo-magic formulas, which have been published in a number of booklets. There is often a confusion, however, between two words that sound alike: *fée*, which means "fairy," and *fée*, which means "ewe," so that when one sees a *grotte aux fées*, is it a cave where the fairies dwell or one where ewes were sheltered?

The *veillée* was one of the occasions when relationships were cemented, but meetings happened also at the *vogue*. The *vogue*, or village feast, was and in many places still is held generally on the feast day of the patron saint of the village or town. One or two old carousels would come and the children would enjoy themselves, stuffing their little faces with *rezuls* (see page 376). In the old days, young adults danced to the music made by two *violoneux*, or fiddlers, and a drum. Carnival and the celebration of the wheat or grain harvest were also good meeting places, but young people saw most of one another on the alp during the summer *inalpage* (see page 148). Van Gennep tells of the priests fulminating at what dens of iniquity the mountain chalets were in the summer! So a few weddings were celebrated in the fall. But the Church went on fulminating: "We forbid engaged persons of whatever condition or quality to live under the same roof until their marriage under the menace of excommunication" (cited in Verneilh, from *Statistique Générale de la France*, Départment du Mont Blanc, 1807). In spite of the early date of that declaration, admonitions in the same vein were still being issued when I was young, and like all people my age I fidgeted in the pew while the curé of Chamonix preached in the late fifties at the little chapel of the Praz de Chamonix.

With only a few exceptions, it was the young people who decided to get married. Next, the young man secured the informal acceptance of the young woman's family, then came the official request accompanied by the prospective groom's giving his bride-to-be a certain amount of money. The engagement was celebrated in church just a few days before the wedding, then the bridal couple and both sets of parents went to purchase the traditional jewelry: a beautiful cross and a pair of earrings in the shape of half-moons. Once the bride-to-be had her ears pierced and had received the jewelry, she was said to be *ferrée*, because often one was so poor that the jewelry was not made of gold or silver, but simply of polished tin. I have, after eight years of research, been able to locate one such cross from the village of Albiez in the Maurienne; it was authenticated as being a Croix Jeannette with a rare Saint Maurice cross on one side and a Holy Spirit symbol on the other. Inspection under a magnifying glass shows the rough etching of the local country jeweler. Such old crosses were often made from large melted coins.

The style and size of the crosses varied from one valley to another. The Arvan and the Villards valleys had two different styles, one flat and very large, the other with holes in each of the four ornate extremities, for which reason it was called a *Croix Grille*. In Bessans and the Upper Maurienne, one wore a thin cross on a ribbon, a rich piece of jewelry encrusted with stones was placed just above the cross.

The marriage always was accompanied by a "contract" listing what the young woman was bringing to the new family and what the young man was contributing. Everything was listed, from the amount of money involved to the number of handkerchiefs and petticoats. Customs varied considerably over the different valleys, but the concept of a white bridal gown to be worn only once in a lifetime has come only recently to the Savoie. In a society where one normally wore only functional black dresses and very rough and simple home-woven underwear made of hemp, young women were given the most beautiful costume of their lives for their wedding day. Each valley had a different style and presentation, and the wedding costume was then worn on all special occasions for the rest of one's life. It was given the very descriptive name of *le beau.*

These costumes are slowly disappearing, for, as one of the local priests told me recently, all the old women insist on being buried in them. Those remaining are mostly located in the Tarentaise and the Maurienne. The best day to see them come out of armoires is on the Feast of the Assumption, on the 15th of August.

Some of the styles are unforgettable, such as the beautiful costume that Madame Emma Viallet of Jarrier in the Maurienne was kind enough to wear, so we could photograph it (see page 71). The skirt is made of horizontal panels of material vertically pleated and gathered at the waist in such a way

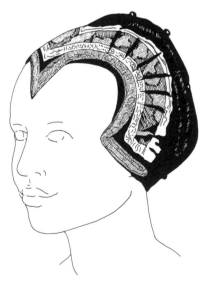

Figure 11 The coif of the Tarentaise: the frontière. The variations of colors were multiple.

that the skirt lifts elegantly above the heels. The headdresses vary from snow white and stiffly starched to a plain black laced bonnet called a beretta. In the villages of Bramans and Bessans in the Upper Maurienne, black lace is combined with striking pink or lilac ribbons. The best known, of course, is the famous Tarentaise *frontière*, which has so captivated the public imagination that it appears on every postcard, even though it is worn in only one small part of the Tarentaise, between Bourg Saint Maurice, Saint Foy, and Séez. I have known only one woman who wore her *frontière* daily until her death five years ago. Putting on this little headdress (which looks uncannily like the headdress worn by the subject of a Sofonisba Anguissola painting in 1570) was a whole ceremony. To maintain the *frontière*, the hair had to be both braided and twisted upward in such a complicated procedure that it was done only once a

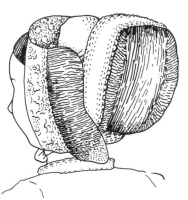

Figure 12 Coifs: from Bessans on the *bottom right*: the couiffa worn by the young girl for the procession of the 15th of August. *Top right*: the coif of Saint Jean d'Arves, Arvan valley. *Left*: the skirt of the Arvan valley made of heavy black wool material; cut into thirty bands of material sewn together and accordion-pleated.

week. Actually, one of the reasons the bonnets and coifs do not look as strikingly beautiful nowadays is that the loose modern hairdos are not as regal as the long, disciplined hair of our ancestors. What were once beautiful wedding and ceremonial costumes are nowadays kept alive mostly by folkloric groups who sing and dance the local ballads and dances. Their costumes are authentic: A few dressmakers have made a specialty of learning how to cut and sew them and how to starch the lace bonnets over wooden sticks to set their pleats properly (see the *couiffa* Figure 12 on page 71).

I have seen most of the costumes of the Savoie, since they started to disappear from the upper valleys only in the fifties. With their beautiful embroidered shawls and black skirts (there were dresses in blue, red, and brown, but they were worn exclusively by the bourgeoisie), their aprons tied by colorful ribbons, they evoked for me those of the Alsace, the Black Forest, Switzerland, and even Brittany. In Brittany the coif used for the baptism of infants is almost identical to that of the Savoie. Even though many experts believe the costumes do not go back further than the eighteenth century, I keep wondering whether all that love for color, handsome embroidery, and elegance is not a trait common to all people with an ancient Celtic background. I may be right, I may be wrong. There were many other influences that brought modifications in the costumes over the centuries, such as fashions from big cities copied from the upper classes or brought by the peddlers; the subject of costume development would fill a large volume in itself.

Men were never dressed with as much color as the women. In most cases, men wore a strict black suit, often with interesting buttons that were sometimes made in the village of Bessans, sometimes collected from military uniforms from around the world. Men also wore dashing hats. In some Maurienne villages such as Jarrier, the jacket was of a rough, stiff, natural off-white woolen material woven in the village itself.

The rites of wedding celebrations were many and included some customs going back probably to times as ancient as the Celtic and Roman occupations. At the end of each marriage ceremony, there was always some reminder of death, such as a visit to the tombs of ancestors of both families, to impress upon each partner the fact that he or she had become part of a new family unit. One came back home in a long procession led by the new couple, and there followed a long and elaborate meal including more than surely a *farci* or a *farcement* (see page 225).

Brides left their parents' home to live in that of their parents-in-law. Their entrance into that new dwelling gave rise to all sorts of customs, such as the mother-in-law's tying a beautifully embroidered apron around the bride's waist.

Then came *la soupe*, a sexually charged little ceremony in which the young couple were given a heavily spiced concoction to drink or eat before they went to bed. The concoction could be a potent onion soup or some hot spiced wine. The custom is retained in some country families even today, and the young people must accept a huge bowl of peppered cocoa, served in an unmentionable vessel such as a chamber pot! Second marriages gave rise to noisy celebrations called charivaris.

Funerals were characterized by huge offerings for the poor and the ecclesiastical authorities, who, in turn, would pray for the soul of the departed. The soul was always and until recently cared for with great love, which was expressed in several interesting customs. In Chamonix, as soon as someone had died the window of the room was opened to let the soul escape. And in the Tarentaise, where it was believed that the soul stayed on in a neighboring field, the straw of the deceased's bed was laid out against a wall and left to disperse in the wind so that the soul could come and rest on it. Huge meals were cooked in a special pot called *la marmite des morts*, which was kept in the church between funerals; each member of the community took some of that food home. The widow or widower was to distribute the clothing of the departed so the deceased would not come back in dreams and request the absolute observance of this custom. And in some valleys there were loud lamentations by the female members of the family. None of these customs are left nowadays; if a large meal still takes place, it is reserved for relatives only.

EMIGRATION

Until well into the nineteenth century the average income in most Savoie villages was so low that during the winter young men would emigrate to other parts of Europe to try to supplement their income and come back to their fields in the summer. That left the women alone to cope with young children and older parents and maintain the family holdings during their absence; some sociologists think that this situation has contributed to the conservatism of the Savoie.

If you are wondering about the silly little chimney sweep dolls that are sold in all the kitsch stores of tourist cities and villages, they are good luck charms and are a symbol of the poor little children who at a very tender age left their parents and mountain villages under the direction of shady masters to go to big cities and clean chimneys. This is no legend, this is a fact. Not only little boys were involved in these pitiful arrangements; some little girls were also pressed into service because their bodies were so thin that they could squeeze through very narrow chimneys. These children were exploited by their masters and lived in pitiful conditions all over the big cities, especially in Paris.

A Société Philanthropique was founded in Paris by well-established Savoie-born people who tried to help the recent immigrants. The King of Sardinia was the patron of the association until 1860, and the city of Paris took it over afterwards. At one time the name *Savoyard* was synonymous with itinerant worker and as such was considered a pejorative, so the term *Savoisien* was used instead. Nowadays, Savoyard is perfectly acceptable since the emigration problem no longer exists.

There are several historical causes for emigration. The large increase in population during the twelfth century, the necessity to save food for the mother and younger children who stayed home through the winter, a rise in the birthrate combined with the heavy taxes levied during the seventeenth and eighteenth centuries by invading armies, and the total poverty left in the villages by poor harvests during most of the eighteenth century. Contact with foreign armies was also important: Friendships were formed with French soldiers billeted in Savoyard homes who told of the wonderful life in France. During the small ice age of the late seventeenth to late eighteenth centuries, the Chamonix glaciers spilled so far into the valley that whole villages were destroyed by their advance (they have since been rebuilt). During that period the son of Jacques Balmat, who first climbed Mont Blanc, had to emigrate to Ohio. Anyone by the name of Balmat whose American ancestry is from Ohio and Kentucky, is almost certain to be a descendant of the great mountaineer; also families anywhere in the United States with the names Couttet, Claret, Tournier, Devouassoud, Savioz, and Payot would also be from the Chamonix valley; these facts are outlined in a very solidly documented book by M. Gay and M. F. Balmat published in 1986 for the celebration of the bicentenary of the ascension of Mont Blanc. The 1813 Mayor of New Orleans, Monsieur Nicolas Girod, was born in Cluses in the Faucigny and many New Orleanites must have Savoie ancestors who came from Samoëns and the Giffre valley.

Emigrants went in many different directions. As early as the twelfth century there was a substantial emigration of Savoyards to England, Pierre II of Savoie having been the preceptor to King Edward I. And until the thirteenth century Savoie prelates made up a large part of the canons of the Hereford chapter.

People from the Maurienne and the Tarentaise seemed to direct their steps toward the Piemonte, while Faucigny men went toward the German-speaking countries. This, and the fact that some brought back German-born wives, may explain the presence of several dishes of visibly Germanic origin in the food of some Faucigny villages. After the wars of Louis XIV there was a major emigration to Lyon. After 1850 people went to Spain, Burgundy, the north of France, Belgium, and various parts of Provence. It was not until after the annexation of the Savoie that the majority of people went to Paris, at which point the emigration went from seasonal to permanent as many families opened small businesses there. There is not one Savoie family that does not have "cousins from Paris" or "cousins from America." It was that final emigration which brought a lot of people from the lovely village of Jarrier to central Canada, where they still reside.

The emigration was not confined to poor people; a large part of the nobility, who found employ and protection with prominent European families, went to Austria, Württemberg, Russia, France, and Bavaria, and worked in the employ of both Kings Louis XV and Louis XVI of France and of King Frederick I of Prussia.

The professions practiced by the emigrants were very diverse: During the summer masons built castles, convents, and fortifications all over France.

Peddlers came from all over the Savoie selling specialized items such as rabbit skins, plants for medicinal compounds, matches, or barrels; most of the peddlers, however, sold small haberdashery items such as ribbons, shawls, stockings, and silks from Italy. There were also those who specialized in spices, pretty decorative items, rings and crosses of tin or silver, or even exotic fruit. While still young, these peddlers easily carried a large box weighing over a hundred pounds on their shoulders. The Germans had taken to calling them *Buckelkrämer*, "the humpback haberdashers." As they grew older they traveled with a donkey to carry their wares. Marie Thérèse Billard talks about the peddler who came every second or third year to buy her mother's hair. After years of roaming the roads of Europe, many peddlers saved enough money to be able to establish a permanent shop.

There were also those called *magnins*, makers and repairers of pots and pans. They carried pots and pans on their backs, selling, on time, the wares they themselves had bought on time from established city *magnins*. These colorful, mysterious people were ever so slightly frightening to children as they settled down in a field to melt tin and reline the pots and pans of the children's mothers.

Many *magnins* sold their services throughout the summer to help with the harvest or to pick grapes; some women made an income taking groups of young girls to work in the Lyon silk centers. There is a list of all the professions practiced by the immigrant Savoyards; they could be just about anything: physicians, surgeons, lawyers, professors, scientists, traveling salesmen, accountants, dealers in just about everything, country teachers, peddlers of different wares, day workers, unskilled workers in the first industrial plants, hurdy-gurdy players, knife sharpeners, chimney sweeps.

And, of course, there were the smart ones who knew enough to be hired as house servants and acquire a pleasant lifestyle with the nobility somewhere in Europe (see page 75).

THE SAVOIE COMMUNITY

EDUCATION

The community, which could contain a number of villages and hamlets, was well and quite strictly organized. After a family had resided and worked in a particular location for a number of years, the father could request the right to belong to the community; this right was granted with the curé's permission after the family contributed to the needs of the poor or to some repair for the church. Among the privileges allocated to members of the community were the right of the man and his family to be buried in the local cemetery and to have a family pew in church, and the duty to be present at all community meetings, which were held by the men in the cemetery after mass, a custom probably inherited from the Celts, who made their important decisions among the tombs of their ancestors. The archives of a community were often and for centuries sealed in one large coffer, stored in the church presbytery or even in the church itself.

In the early communities, members elected three or four syndics for three years. These men were responsible for the running of all important affairs; they had to render accounts at regular intervals and lead the population in solving any problem with their local lords. The system was changed in the eighteenth century after the feudal rights were bought back by the communities. But whatever the system, it was democratic and organized in such a way that the vast communal lands both in the valley and on the alp would be managed properly so that as much income as possible would be drawn out of the land, the cows, and the cheese-making into which most resources were locked. After the annexation and the fall of Napoleon III, the Savoie, as a part of France, was governed like the rest of the country. Nowadays, the mayor of a town or village is all-important, and he and his *conseillers* direct the affairs of the community. Some of these mayors are extremely down-to-earth people, familiar with their territory, aware of each member of the community and of their performance. Rustic though they may look, they are very much attuned to modernization and work efficiently so their administration brings as much benefit to the community as possible. To many of them, assisted by their deputies, senators, and the regional assemblies called *conseils généraux*, we owe the development of the splendid skiing establishments both in the Savoie and the Haute Savoie.

The community was responsible for the education of children, and as early as the eighteenth century many villages had private little one-room schools with a teacher paid by the community or an educated person donating his or her time. The schoolroom was in the presbytery, a barn, or a hayloft, and the windows were covered mostly by oil paper, not glass, but a school it was, and there was less illiteracy here than in other parts of Europe. The famous Loi Jules Ferry of 1882, which made public education free and mandatory in France, saw a lot of little buildings being built and used as *Mairie-Ecoles*. Many of them are still standing, by now empty and touching in their desuetude but still very visible; they have, of course, been replaced by large modern establishments. I remember well our one-room school at La Balme, where we sat at farm tables arranged in a U shape so none of us would acquire a stiff neck trying to see and hear *la metra*. *La metra*, the *maîtresse* in French or "teacher" in English, was a Carmelite sister released temporarily from her cloister by her Mother Superior and probably the most serene teacher I ever had. I loved to study with her. She had to borrow a map of France from the schoolmaster of the village school, who was an older, stern man, very republican to boot, and we felt sorry for la Metra because this old teacher always seemed ready to needle her with his political opinions. It was the rule, in general, be it under the Sardinian kings or under the French Republic, that men would teach in villages and young women in hamlets, which were isolated and almost desolate in the winter. Marie Thérèse Billard, in her charming book, gives a lively account of her years as a young schoolteacher. Skis arrived as a boon for children in isolated hamlets, allowing them to slide down to the main village school for an education, and this is how the fathers and mothers of some of our modern ski champions received their early education. In mountain areas, there has always been a complete and total respect for teachers; any other attitude would be unthinkable.

If one's parents could afford it, and if one had the intelligence, one was sent to a college run by the fathers or, later, to a normal school to become a teacher; villagers who could reach a university to become a professional were rare, but they existed. Higher education has become more and more prevalent since the 1960s, and Savoyards now hold a good share of French doctorates and professorial chairs.

PROFESSIONS, COMMERCE, AND INDUSTRY

From the fifteenth through the eighteenth century the trade guilds were organized in Savoie more or less as they were in other European countries. Apprenticeships were based on a contract between master and apprentice; the apprentice paid the master and also gave to the master's wife a certain sum known as *les épingles*, probably because the sum was not large enough to buy anything else but pins. In exchange for these payments, the apprentice lived in the master's house, where he was given room and board and taught all the secrets of the master's techniques. The apprenticeship was concluded by the presentation of a masterpiece. Tradesmen who arrived from foreign towns or cities to establish businesses of their own had to undergo the critical visit of their new city's authorities. Statistics show that 50 percent of confirmed apprentices stayed on in the master's atelier, 30 percent emigrated to France or the Piemonte to learn other techniques and points of view, and 20 percent solved all their problems by marrying one of the master's daughters.

Besides being controlled by the state and/or the city, professionals were organized into fraternities under the protection of their respective saints. Tailors and stocking weavers were under the protection of Saint Marie-Madeleine, shoemakers under Saint Crépin and Saint Crépinien, the swordmakers of Cran, next to Annecy, where there are still large active ironworks, under the protection of Saints Fabien and Sebastien. Some groups were extremely privileged, such as the silk weavers who established themselves in Chambéry and Annecy after the cultivation of the silkworm had become a favorite source of income in the eighteenth century. Members of these fraternities were exclusively Roman Catholic. Every day they had a low mass read for which the members took turns contributing the Communion bread. The fraternity offered assistance in difficult times, and delegated members were present at any administering of the last rites. The guilds disappeared with the French Revolution, (and the fraternities also went into decline. Some of them reappeared in the nineteenth century and still survive today; in the village of Morillon in the Giffre valley the fraternity of the Quatre Couronnés still offers Communion bread to the village on the last Sunday before Christmas. This small society is a remnant of a much larger fraternity that included masons, stonecutters, carpenters, and cabinetmakers, and each year held a big celebration banquet where sobriety was not necessarily observed.

Professional stonecutters came for the most part from the Giffre valley, especially Samoëns and Sixt. A look at the centers of both these little towns reveals some beautiful buildings and sculptures such as the public fountains. In both town cemeteries, one can see the most interesting tombstones filled with mysterious markings that experts believe to be signatures of contract fulfillment by the stonecutter.

The important professions throughout the nineteenth century were butchers, whose statutes were ancient, candlemakers, pot makers or *magnins*, nail makers or *cloutri*, shoe and saddlemakers, and the makers of barrels and fitted wood-plank containers who were called *boisseliers*. And then there were the painters of signs. In the old city of Annecy there are still at least three upholsterers and cabinetmakers and one wonderful couple who are artists painting on wool and silk and designing cloth that is unique; they all work in small "boutiques" dating back to the early 1800s.

Several professions were tied to agriculture. Millers often both milled flour and ground walnuts to make oil. The farrier could offer several services; while he was shoeing horses, his coworker might have been a *magnin* fixing pots and pans, a wheelwright, or an ironsmith. Metal was so expensive that beautiful hand-hammered door locks and hinges for furniture were used over and over by several generations, and from one century to the next. I own a lovely poplar *bonnetière*, a small cabinet in which one was supposed to keep coifs but which can be used for anything really; it was definitely made in the nineteenth century, but it has exquisite seventeenth-century hinges.

This brings me, of course, to woodworking. Furniture was usually made by the man of the house. If one had enough money one would hire a specialist, and the cabinetmaker/wood-carver would come to the house and build on the spot whatever piece of furniture one desired. So nowadays, when one wants to move a precious piece of furniture from an older home to a new one, it may be necessary to fetch a mason to dismantle and rebuild the front door or a window, because there is no opening in the house large enough to let a large, beautifully carved armoire pass through. Wood carving is quite extensive and beautiful throughout the Savoie, and some older homes offer amazing features such as roof-supporting beams, the ends of which are cut out as faces. Not only is the furniture quite beautifully decorated with rosettes and sun symbols, but all the small tools and objects of the pastoral life are also hand-carved, mostly with the help of the famous Opinel knife. In Bessans, probably the most artistically gifted village in the Savoie, the salt boxes took the shape of hens and were absolutely exquisite. And the famous Bessans devils, carved in wood to incite people to be good and virtuous, were true masterpieces. Baby cribs, in spite of being showpieces the godmother would carry to church, complete with the new little Savoyard to be baptized were not always luxurious; the best examples are in the Annecy museum and originally came from Morzine; the many that are still to be found would surely be used as planters in modern homes. Spinning wheels and distaffs were also remarkable and now sell for small fortunes; it is interesting to compare them with their very plain-looking American counterparts of the same period. And in this butter-producing area, butter molds and stamps could be masterpieces; the most beautiful ones are displayed in the Geneva and Annecy museums. A few relatively simple ones are still made nowadays and sold in the better gift shops. The village of La Magne in the Bauges mountains specialized in maple or sycamore serving dishes that were hand-turned and -polished; these pieces were given the name *Argenterie des Bauges*, or Bauges silver, and are now also collectors' items. Many can still be found at flea markets, and if you know how to refinish wood, some glorious results can be obtained. Sold by antique shops, smoothly refinished in the famous French manner, they can be pricey. The woods used for these serving dishes and kitchen tools were pine, larch, and pinion pine, the first two being Northern Savoie woods and the last one an Upper Tarentaise and Upper Maurienne wood.

And then there were, and still are, the potters. The village of Sevrier along the western shore of the Annecy lake yielded during excavations a small ceramic baking oven dating back to the Bronze Age, which can now be seen in the Annecy museum. The rustic pottery of the traditional Savoie is made of earthenware highly glazed in various colors: deep brown, deep yellow, deep green, and deep blue. They should not be confused with faïences; the few faïence factories that existed in the Savoie (La Forêt and Sainte Catherine) stopped activities near the beginning of the nineteenth century.

It is said that the potters took their inspiration from the Germanic pottery of Alsace, Germany, and Switzerland. There may be some similarities, but for the expert observer the individuality of the Savoie pottery is easy to discern.

There were traditional "themes" used for the decoration of pottery: Very simple polka dots decorate the milk pots, which come in two styles—the straight-sided, or Jura style; and the rounded, or Swiss style. These milk pots were also used to bring soup to field workers. There is an *à l'oiseau*, or bird decoration; an *à la biche*, or deer decoration, and also a tree of life, and all kinds of native flowers. One style, known as the *jaspé*, which was made by pouring brown, yellow, russet, and green on pieces with a mutiple funnel called a *barolet*, resulted in wild color patterns, which, considering that they were done between the early years of the century and the 1940s, look extremely modern, some would even say avant-garde. They now have become collectors' items and sell in England for small fortunes. Several ateliers still survive around the basin of the Annecy lake and in the Tarentaise, where wine pitchers known as *taras* sell rather well, probably because they often have decorations of edelweiss to which French tourists seem inordinately attached. If you are interested in pottery, and even if you are not but want to find an authentically Savoyard object that is elegant and really a very affordable work of art, you must visit the Poterie de la Côte in Evires, the Musée de la Poterie of Mr. and Mrs. Jean Christophe Hermann (see page xv). His work is outstanding and completely different from anything else to be found anywhere in the two departments. Evires is only ten minutes from Annecy by car. If you cannot go to the factory, many of the best gift shops all over the Haute Savoie carry Mr. Hermann's work.

There was quite a bit of local weaving of woolen material done in the traditional Savoie, but that has almost disappeared. The village of Jarrier used the wool of its lambs to weave the material for the costumes of its men. The last Jarrier weaver disappeared in the late sixties. There is only one small weaving mill left in the Tarentaise at Séez, but a popular one that manufactures a very thick woolen material known as *drap de Bonneval*; it is so thick and waterproof that mountain guides and polar explorers use it to this day; I have seen it on sale at several American sporting goods stores selling mountaineering equipment.

Lace-making was for a long time one of the winter sources of income for Savoie women. These activities have disappeared, but if you go to flea markets and have sharp eyes, you will find pieces of local lace that can be turned into pretty things. I have been lucky enough to find a small table covering and I keep collecting little pieces that I hope to assemble one day into something really lovely.

Whatever commerce existed in Savoie cities before the annexation was small, with only a few solid businesses that lasted over generations. It was the development of tourism and industry at the beginning of this century that brought the extension of commerce. In cities like Annecy especially, but also in Chambéry, whose upper classes had been purchasing their important goods from Geneva and even Paris, more local commercial enterprises started to open during the last years of the nineteenth century.

Although mineral and salt-extracting mines have existed in the Savoie since prehistoric times, the development of industry was slow until the late 1800s. For lack of roads and train connections, the Savoie did not experience the Industrial Revolution of the nineteenth century. It remained for a long time only a way station for goods and people traveling to different parts of Europe through the Alpine passes. When industry finally came, it came in successive huge waves. The first was in the 1880s and 90s, when the first hydroelectric plants appeared in the Maurienne and the Tarentaise, bringing on the development of aluminum and steel manufacturing. The little city of La Roche-sur-Foron oddly enough was, in 1885, the first completely electrified city in Europe. Then between 1919 and 1937 more huge installations were completed in the Arc and Doron de Beaufort valleys, to be followed after World

War II by the plants built by the Electricité de France. The development of modern industry provided salaries for Savoyards who needed a better income than what their toiling in high fields could bring them, but at what cost to the environment. Chedde, for example, where electricity was produced very early on is an eyesore that stands right at the entrance to the Chamonix valley. The same fate has befallen several parts of the Tarentaise and Maurienne, making one grateful just to pass through very fast and hurry to the fresh air of the upper Alpine resorts.

Although the Arve valley is also industrialized, the industry there is given more to small, private enterprises that do not necessitate huge installations of the type that have been built in the Southern Savoie. The politics of each department seem to reflect their respective type of industry: The Northern Haute Savoie is definitely conservative, the Savoie is more socialist. Some sociologists seem to think that, ultimately, the politics and economic development of the two departments reflect their old ethnic substrata: Germanic in the Haute Savoie and Mediterranean in the Savoie.

Tourism, still the Savoie's biggest industry, was started in the nineteenth century by the British, always ready for a good sporting experience, and developed along with the railroads and highway systems. Tourism *à la française* in the Savoie is not even a cousin to American-style tourism; individualism there reigns supreme. Certainly there are modern chain hotels, but even those are run by *gérants*, or managers, who have been trained the French way, which is always individualistic. The Savoie hôteliers and restaurateurs like to build a personal relationship with their guests. It is not rare for a family to find "a nice little hotel" in one village or another and go back there year after year for the famous French *congés payés* (the paid vacations of the Léon Blum government, and the very first political event that I can clearly remember). I did not escape that rule when I was living in France as a young adult, and now I go back again and again to the same little hotels and restaurants during each of my trips to France.

Again, there are two types of tourism, one in the Haute Savoie and one in the Savoie. The Haute Savoie started to develop its tourist trade much earlier than the Savoie; and towns and villages there developed slowly and almost methodically into local tourist centers run by the local people. It would be wrong to say that this type of enterprise does not exist at all in the Savoie, but the predominant conditions are those of Courchevel, Tignes, Les Arcs, and Val Thorens: huge complexes of modern construction more or less owned and operated by "out of Savoie" developers.

The Savoie is turning more and more into a vacation park with huge chaletlike buildings compartmentalized into tiny apartments, or nice little country houses where city folk pile up during vacation time. By the inception of the European open market, which will be just about the same time as the 1992 Olympic Games, the expressways into the center of the Savoie will be finished and the access to the upper regions as easy as they will ever be. The Savoie will turn more cosmopolitan, for many English, Swiss, German, and even American families are already purchasing vacation apartments or homes there.

CHURCHES, ART IN RELIGION

As the last major aspect of Savoie life, I have kept these few paragraphs for a discussion of the importance of religion in this part of the French Alps and of its influence on art.

Before Roman times there must have been intense religious activity if one believes the many engraved stones, or *pierres à cupules*, to be found everywhere, especially in the Tarentaise and the Maurienne. During the Roman period there is no doubt that the population was devoted to the many pagan gods existing at the time. There are remnants of *fana*, or Celto-Roman temples, in many places, and divinities coming from the Celtic pantheon were revered with as much fervor as the Latin *lares*. Many of the absolutely beautiful and simple statutes of the Virgin and Christ, as well as the crucifixes to be found in the homes of those whose parents have kept them, are small works of art and faith. If at a flea market you find, as I did, a beautiful Christ of pinion pine, try not to be broke as I was on that day . . . I have not found another one in the last seven years; they are rare, but once in a while good luck may be with you.

The Christianization of the Savoie was completed between the fourth and eighth centuries, and the building of the great monasteries by 1100. The most strikingly Savoyard monasteries still stand after many rebuildings, and to this day they are places of solemn pilgrimages; a visit to Saint Maurice d'Agaune in the Swiss Valais, Novalesa at the entrance of the Italian Val de Suza, the Great Saint Bernard, or the Grande Chartreuse, even at the end of the twentieth century, is an impressive experience.

For several reasons, the place of the Roman Catholic religion has been historically important in the life of the Savoie. The new saints of the Catholic religion replaced, sometimes very slowly, the former pagan divinities, taking over their therapeutic virtues and powers: The Saint John fires on June 24, the healing springs under the protection of a saint, are examples of this, and so, most probably, the statues of the Virgin at the several beautiful shrines of Notre Dame. In Notre Dame de la Vie, for example, what is believed by some to be a very ancient statue of the earth mother has been transformed into what she had always been—a fountain. But I am afraid that when Monsieur l'Inspecteur des Beaux Arts sees that she has been pierced and patched up with concrete to fit a spigot into her stomach, something terrible is going to happen to the contractor who committed such a terrible artistic sin.

Geneva, the Calvinist city, sits at the entrance of the Savoie and was once part of it, which inspired Saint Francis de Sales—a born Savoyard—to preach convincingly during the seventeenth-century Counter-Reformation. The anti-clerical excesses of the representative of the French Revolution, Albitte, mentioned in the History section (page 41), brought a renewed religious ardor to the villages. Priests were eagerly hidden in rooms with double ceilings (a brieviary was found complete with dates when modernizing the double ceiling of an old house in Jarrier) or protected by being dressed as local shepherds. After the reinstatement of the Sardinian monarchy in 1815, a strict Catholicism was made the state religion to encourage people to repent their lack of religion and the sins they had committed during the revolution. As everywhere else in France, during the revolution, while some were hiding priests, others made fortunes purchasing at low prices the properties more or less stolen from the nobility by the government. Most of the crosses and calvaries one can see throughout the countryside date back to that time, when bishops went on preaching missions there.

Places of worship abound in any Savoie village. There is always a beautiful church with main and side altars at the center of the village, and many hamlets have a quiet little chapel sometimes dating as far back as the twelfth century. Everywhere there are small oratories in various styles, simple or overdecorated; they punctuate the countryside at least as much as the calvaries and are never neglected except in bad weather, when they are buried in snow. Come spring the bouquet of flowers is replaced every few days until the frosts of November stop the supply. When I visit on farms I like to bring a potted flowering plant; more often than not, I am told that my gift will be placed in the chapel of the hamlet.

Like private homes, the churches of the Northern Savoie and those of the Maurienne look completely different from the outside. In Northern Savoie, the steeples tend to have bulbs, probably copied from the Tyrolian and South German edifices at the suggestion of returning emigrants, who often contributed heavily to the rebuilding of the churches during the Counter-Reformation. There is no end of variations to those bulbs, and they look ever so pretty covered, as they often are, with metal. In Southern Savoie, churches, like houses, are all of stone as they are in Provence, which is also partly Ligurian.

The outsides of the churches, however, are nothing compared to the baroque splendor that awaits you inside. Most churches were rebuilt between the last two decades of the seventeenth century and the first three of the eighteenth. They are typical examples of baroque religious art, which may not necessarily be in the taste of American visitors but are worth looking at by all means. Some very great artists have worked in cooperation with local craftsmen on these golden altars. The great altar designer was François Cuenot, who came from the Franche Comté, and the best local craftspeople were the men of the Clappier dynasty in Bessans—Jacques Clérant in Champagny, Claude and François Rey in Termignon, Etienne Fodéré in Peisey, Sainte Foy, and Séez. If you care deeply about baroque art, make an itinerary for yourself, being certain to include glorious Bessans, Termignon, Peisey, Champagny by all means, plus a few others mentioned at the end of this book. You will be rewarded both by the altars and by the *poutres de gloire*, those supporting beams at the center of the choir which often carry beautifully carved Calvary scenes. If you care at all for this type of architecture and art, do not go away without seeing either the pretty shrine at Notre Dame de la Vie in Saint Martin de Belleville or the splendid one at Notre Dames des Vernettes in Peisey, or simply the village church of the resort where you are staying. Shrines are mostly open, but "out of season" some churches may not be because many statues have been stolen since tourism has increased so dramatically. Nevertheless, do not hesitate to ring the bell of Monsieur le Curé, and if he is not there someone will open the church for you; all you have to do is leave a dollar or so for the restoration fund, which is always open for contributions. As you look at the faces of all those angels and golden statues, think that you are seeing most probably the faces of the Savoyards of two centuries ago, both adults and children. The local "painters," as they were called, knew only those faces, since most, except one of the Clappiers, had never traveled outside their native Savoie.

THE WINE, FOODS, AND COOKING OF THE ANCIENT AND MODERN SAVOIE

The last part of this book will be devoted to the traditional foods of the Savoie and the ways the fresh produce of the Savoie markets are used in modern cuisine.

To dig a bit into the past, I went to the large Public Library and the Archives of the Haute Savoie in Annecy. The oldest text I could find was a facsimile of Maître Chiquart's *Du Fait de Cuisine*. The original of this manuscript, dated 1420, was part of the library of Bishop Supersaxo and his son Georges, and is now resting in the Bibliothèque Cantonale du Valais in Sion, Switzerland.

The Valais was, at the time, part of the Duchy of Savoy under the leadership of Amadeus VIII, who had recently been made Duke of Savoie by the Emperor of Germany, Sigismund. Amadeus, having lived extensively at the Court of Burgundy where he waited for his Burgundian princess bride to be of marriageable age, had learned the great ways of the splendid Burgundian court and, taking it as a model, reorganized his dukedom, including his kitchens. He entrusted Maître Chiquart, a senior member of the battery of many *queux* (cooks) who ran his kitchen, with the writing of recipes and rules of good order to be applied by everyone in the preparation of banquets and foods.

One of the reasons for entrusting Maître Chiquart with this important work may have been that he had some measure of literacy; elements of Latin pop up all throughout the manuscript, but the question remains, did the Latin come from Maître Chiquart or from his clerk, Jehan de Dudens, who wrote the manuscript under his dictation? By the way, Jehan de Dudens may have been from Annessier. There was a Jehan de Dudens living in Annecy at the time, although no one can be certain whether it was the same person as Maître Chiquart's clerk. One thing remains certain, the text of the manual is a wonderful example of Franco-Provençal language.

Maître Chiquart insists that he did not own a cookbook, which in the second decade of the fifteenth century would make sense. Consequently, we can assume that his material is entirely original. At first sight the recipes look very much like those of Taillevent's Viandier and the Ménagier de Paris, but when one looks closer, important differences appear: The names of the dishes may be very similar to those of the two earlier works, but the contents of the dishes fail to correspond in many cases.

Maître Chiquart is said to have been the cook responsible for producing the huge cake—probably the *Gâteau de Savoie* in the shape of the duchy, complete with each mountain in correct relief—that was presented to Emperor Sigismund, and was therefore a tiny bit responsible for the Savoie becoming a duchy. Maître Chiquart must have been quite an executive chef, for he was certainly organized—always ready with two huge banquets for every day, one made mostly of meat and the other of fish. And from him we receive a good insight into the workings of a princely kitchen in the fifteenth century, complete with rules and recommendations to *bien faire*—that is, to work well and always carefully, and to observe the rules of good sanitation when washing one's pots and pans. Some of our twentieth-century cooks could learn a few very important facts from reading Maître Chiquart.

The types of meals presented in the book are typically long medieval menus that make a modern cook bemoan the scarcity of our modern food resources. Meats and fish abound, and even then this very good cook adapted his basic sauces to fat or lean fare, very much as Carême would do at the beginning of the nineteenth century.

I went carefully through the book to find the raw materials that are still very much in favor today. Mostly I found lake fish, leeks, and turnips—those good old turnips, or *raves*, of the Savoie, which, as you will see, are so dear to all Savoie people. And here also was that wonderful *pièce de résistance* of the Savoie woman in the late nineteenth and early twentieth centuries, the *jalle de chert*, or as they say in patois, *la zalia*, and in good modern English, meat in aspic. So it took at least four centuries for that dignified dish to come down from the table of the duke to that of the Savoie farmer.

What happened during the last four hundred and fifty years? To learn about this evolution, it is essential to go to the text of historian Jean Nicolas about eighteenth-century Savoie (see Bibliography). Nothing about the ways of the sixteenth and seventeenth centuries was available in any library or archive that I would discover. What can be found in Nicolas's text is a splendid analysis of what he calls the influences of the "Sky and the Arms," as reflected in the vagaries of the weather and of war. From the last decade of the seventeenth century until very close to the French Revolution of 1789, the production of wheat and other grains with which the Savoyards made their bread was extremely irregular, and the prices were subject to rates of inflation so enormous as to be almost unbelievable. For example, during the winter of 1693–94 the price of wheat went up 144 percent and that of rye 225 percent. This situation was not unique to the Savoie, for this is the time when Europe was passing through what has been called the small ice age. One froze in elegant salons and comfortable bourgeois households while the poor roamed cities in quest of just about anything to eat, and the bread of the poor farmers consisted of ground walnut shells. The situation did not improve much as large numbers of men emigrated to other European countries and whole villages were left in the hands of women and children who were at the mercy of roaming bands of the homeless, to say nothing of wolves. In 1756 the famine reached its peak in Europe, especially in Savoie, Lombardia, and Piemonte. Ten years later, things were not too much better and a magistrate said, "One sees everyday women bringing their crosses and rings for sale in an effort to buy bread." In Annecy in 1783, as the Prince of Piemonte visited the city, "two thousand souls fought over a bone," as the Church distributed whatever food could be located.

This penury of foods did not seem to be for everyone, however. If one believes a talk delivered by the president of the Savoie Academy, François Descotes, in 1899 to a meeting of the Learned Societies of Savoie, the table of the Savoie Senate in 1783 was not that poor. At a banquet given on June 22, fifty-four different dishes were served. It is indeed a wonderful meal, but if one looks very closely at the menu, the dishes are mostly vegetables and small barnyard and wild animals such as quail, duck, pigeon, turkey, chicken and rabbit, and lake fish. The large animals—calf, lamb, and beef—offer only their heads and sweetbreads, tail and cheek; so what happened to the large roasts? It is very possible that even the Senate of Savoie had not enough funds at the time to afford them.

The menu of this banquet, however, is interesting, for in the list one can already find a number of Savoie favorites such as two dishes of small turnips, pigs' ears with garnish, sausages in cream, quail with cabbage, chicken with crayfish butter, *Ombre* (see page 289; the correct name is Omble) *Chevalier*, quenelles, and *Gâteau de Savoie*, the modern versions of which you will find in the pages that follow.

The food of the Savoie, as it passed on to us, was radically changed and enriched during the eighteenth century by two new foods, corn and the potato. Corn was brought in from the Piemonte between 1730 and 1733 by a gentleman named Bonnafoux; by 1750 it was growing so well in the Chablais and the lower Isère valley that the Church started to think of levying on it the usual tax of one tenth of the production levied on other grains. By the end of the century, it was on all tables. As for potatoes, they arrived in 1742 and thrived in the cool climates of the Alpine valleys. After having appeared as "curiosities" on upper-classes tables for a few years, they became the basic nourishment of the lower classes as of 1768, heralding the end of the great famines.

There was to be another last great famine in the Savoie during the years 1816–17, when again poor weather and heavy rains conspired to ruin every single possible harvest of every possible fruit or vegetable all through the year.

It was in Marie Thérèse Hermann's book *La Cuisine Paysanne de Savoie, La Vie des Fermes et des Châlets Racontée par une Enfant du Pays*, published in 1981, that I learned about two other Savoie cooks of the late nineteenth century: Mique (Dominique) Grandchamp and François Descotes, apparently not the same François Descotes as the gentleman I mentioned on page 92. I have not been able to locate Descotes's text, entitled *Les Secrets d'un Bec Fin*, which is dated 1897, but from the few recipes of his and the small part of his text quoted in Mrs. Hermann's book, I am not certain that I like what he did and the person he was. Descotes could take a boned loin of deer and prepare some kind of quenelle paste from it, which he poached in small flat cakes in water; then, alternating the cakes of deer with slices of truffles, he served the whole thing with a sauce of reduced veal stock chock-full of cocks' combs and crayfish tails.

Who would eat anything like that? A lot of people of the best kind, among them Napoleon III; and I probably would have enjoyed it tremendously myself in 1945, just as we were coming out of the war years. Now I very much prefer a grilled filet of deer, the more so as they do not come so often. Truthfully, I may not be partial to the gentleman because he seems slightly chauvinistic—in the modern feminist sense—and boasts of having served his exalted guests baby chicken instead of woodcock and leg of fox instead of leg of deer. I truly do not think that any of the lords he claims to have fooled, were fooled; they were just awfully good-natured and tolerant! But this is only an opinion based on limited information until I can put my hands on the whole book.

Mique Grandchamp was completely different. He was a born enthusiast. I have read both the 1883 and 1897 editions of his *La Cuisine à la Bonne Franquette*. Some not too nice person wrote in pencil inside the cover of the 1883 edition: "he was a lazy bum and a . . . to boot"! Ah, there it is! My longtime experience in various professional kitchens allowed me to recognize the symptoms immediately. Mique must have been one of those good kitchen chefs who direct operations well but never put a finger on the food; as to the second part of the statement, if one reads carefully through the first pages of his advice to the bourgeois homemaker of his time, yes of course, it seems as if he could have been a bit heavy-handed. But he meant well, and his food, for being a bit on the not-so-light side, is absolutely delicious. On the cover of the book he was advertising some extract of meat and vegetables called "*Le Trésor de la Cuisinière*" for which he never gave a recipe, but which sounds really good to me, as one who likes well-rounded flavors. Mique used all his local ingredients with glee and style, and his advice to the housekeeper of the late nineteenth century, as comical as it may appear to the late-twentieth-century cook, is sound and interesting. Everything is covered, from cleaning the kitchen floor to preserving truffles for the length of the winter. We are, with Mique, far from the penurious if abundant food of the Senate of Savoie in 1783; exactly a century later the food for the middle bourgeoisie is far more opulent than that of the senators; there are plenty of good, rich dishes made with all kinds of meats, red and white. If I were to sum up his style, I would say that Mique is the perfect cook for a Savoyard practicing at the end of the nineteenth century. The influence of the Piemonte is apparent in his starch dishes, while at the same time the techniques of the Classic French cuisine appear already strongly established in many of his meat and dessert recipes. And, as you will see in his *Bouillon Démocratique* on page 182 he is thrifty, a Savoyard trait if there is one, and the major virtue of any chef.

The first half of the twentieth century brought forth a physician, contemporary to the famous Dr. Babinsky better known as Ali Bab, who hailed from Douvaine just above Lake Leman, at the center of the vineyards that produce the wonderful Crépy wine I shall describe later. He was Dr. Paul Ramain, a *chevalier de Tastevin* who besides being related to the celebrated French writer Henri Bordeaux, was said by many of his contemporaries to have been the "first wine taster" in France. He did indeed produce a volume called *Les Grands Vins de France*, and more important for the cooks than for the wine people, two small booklets on mycogastronomy, a term that he coined. The first booklet concentrates on educating the public about the proper identification of mushrooms. It appeared in 1941, a year that saw the beginning of starvation all over France. It was written after he had witnessed forty-eight deaths due to mushroom poisoning over the course of a single summer.

In this booklet, Dr. Ramain announced the forthcoming publication of a serious volume on mycogastronomy, which was to contain five hundred recipes, of which eighty were guaranteed to be original. That large book, as it turned out, was never published. Only five hundred copies of a small volume containing no more than fifty-four recipes were printed by the Bibliophiles Gastronomes. In 1952 this small volume received the most prized award for gastronomic literature, that of the Club des Cent, which was the most exalted gourmet society in France. Original copies of this book are impossible to locate; luckily, a facsimile published by Editions Jeanne Lafitte in Marseille is available.

Dr. Ramain, who wrote for *Cuisine et Vins de France* when Robert Courtine was at its helm, and for the famous newspaper *Crapouillot*, called himself a "provincial and independent gourmet." One of his articles, published in a special edition of *Savoie Française* commemorating the one hundredth anniversary of the Savoie's annexation to France, is most interesting because it concentrated on showing what the Savoie had brought to the lore of French Provincial foods; the list was impressive, and most of the dishes he mentioned appear in one form or another in the chapters that follow. One of his articles, in *La France à Table* of 1934, contained a succinct but most accurate description of the wines of the Savoie, which I shall use in the section on wines. Dr. Ramain's creations are those of a well-to-do person who can afford to spend healthy amounts on truffles and who says without ambiguity that a true gastronome never tastes truffles that are not fresh. Truffles appear generously in many of his mushroom creations, and so does foie gras. A dish of morels stuffed with foie gras left me panting at the library table, where I happened to be starving anyhow. His grandmother's morels, of which he seems very proud, were served in a *coulis* of *crevettes grises* (those tiny gray shrimp of the northern seas that, when cooked, become a most beautiful salmon color) and cream; in the Savoie of the late twenties, when farm people were still consuming starches and cheeses everyday, this recipe speaks volumes about her social status.

The recipes tend to be involved, even complicated, and typical of the already decadent Classic Cuisine of the pre- and immediate postwar years. But considering that he was writing for a public who to this day has not completely emerged from that classic culinary frame of mind, he was adventurous and original. Several of his soups are splendid: The *Velouté* of Watercress with *Mousserons* (*Marasmius oreades*), for example, or the *Potage* of Mussels and Boleti, both faithfully tried in my kitchen, are masterpieces. I faithfully re-created and also loved his Beefsteak Mushroom (*Fistulina hepatica*) with Horseradish and Coleman's Mustard, but much more, I enjoyed learning from him that the beefsteak mushroom must be leached in salt for three hours before being used. Dr. Ramain gives wonderful advice, such as using only day-old mushrooms, chopping herbs only with scissors or a knife, cooking mushrooms only in heat-resistant porcelain or heavy-enameled cast iron. Ah, Dr. Ramain, what would you say about our "wild-husbanded-supermarket-sold mushrooms" chopped in the food processor and cooked in a microwave oven—you, who like my great grandmother, cooked your boleti in walnut oil and, like her also, grilled your boleti caps upside down with a dab of butter in them? Now *that* we still can do with our barbecues and the wonderful boleti of our forests. Try it and you will thank the spirit of the doctor.

If one reads only one book, however, it should be Marie Thérèse Hermann's, for it is a perfect compendium of the traditional women's dishes of the Savoie as they were passed on to us by the last generation of cooks born in the nineteenth century. As the title of her book indicates, Madame Hermann is indeed a child of the Savoie, where she was born my contemporary, and one of Dr. Ramain's "babies" in Douvaine, Chablais. She is immensely proud of her heritage and clearly deeply taken with the art and folk art of her native, mountainous country. I had the pleasure of entertaining her at a Texas-style lunch, complete with barbecue sauce and pecan pie, during the winter of 1987–88. She is neither a trained historian nor a professional cook. She is a passionate Savoyarde who has put to work the splendid, old-fashioned, classic education our whole nation received before the 1960s. She has written several other fascinating books among which there is one on the Genevois and another two about traditional Savoie life and houses, which I have not yet read. She is currently writing a book on the Maurienne, which promises to be completely different from any existing text on the subject.

Mrs. Hermann's *La Cuisine Paysanne de Savoie* is different because she took the time to travel from farm to farm and home to home to gather her information. In addition, from reading her text, one can immediately understand several very important points—namely, what was inherited from the Ligurian and Celtic substrata of populations; a visibly Germanic influence in some of the food of Northern Savoie; the different names given, in different regions, to dishes belonging basically to the same category; the degree of individualism and the differences in final products due to microclimates and the isolation of the intra-Alpine valleys; the differences in availability of foods between the northern part of the Savoie and the more southern Maurienne; and, last but not least, the economic difficulties of women cooks trying to feed their families with nothing but the bare necessities.

The recipes in Mrs. Hermann's book are what we call in French *des recettes de bonne femme*, those recipes that brought on the derision of Paul Bocuse a few years ago. Of course, her recipes are not precise. It is up to you to adjust them so that they work with the ingredients available to you. Woe to you if you do it the way it is written; there are too many differences between the Savoie ingredients available in, let us say, the 1930s and yours for a recipe to ever work like magic. But that is of no importance; what counts is the concept. Understanding the concept and using good techniques, one gets there, and still respects the spirit of the book, which is to have the freedom to do it the way you like, so long as, in the long run, it tastes like the Savoie, not like the microwave at the end of the 1980s.

Another reason I like Mrs. Hermann's work so much is that it reflects the same feminist philosophy I have followed in my book *When French Women Cook*, published in 1976. Her women are at work putting all their creative effort into using their ingredients as well as they can.

In my previous book, I gave a portrait of a friend of my youth, built on some of my childhood memories. After reading enormous amounts of material over the last seven to eight years, I realized that some of my statements were not quite accurate; the going up to the alp, for example, does not take place in April but in late May at the earliest, and I finally was able to find out that a fondue is not a *berton*, as some of my former sources indicated, but a *berthoud* (page 172), although Dr. Ramain calls it a *berre-tout*. Such details aside, however, my friend Mimi is now retired in a little town not too far away from La Balme de Thuy, and her strikingly beautiful mother with the high smooth forehead rests in the cemetery outside the little St. Peter and St. Paul church.

Other people will enter this Savoie scene of mine, other cooks either born in the Savoie or attached to it by marriage, and you will find their names listed with each recipe idea. Let me introduce them to you:

First Mélanie, who will have to remain forever Mélanie, for I never knew her last name. She was the cook at the children's camp/home in which I spent several of my summers and one almost-whole year between 1937 and 1940 and again between 1945 and 1947. Not only did I observe Mélanie at work, but I also worked with her. Since it was known that I came from a family where kitchen work was a source of income, I more often than not had to perform my assigned domestic chores in the kitchen. I never gave much thought to Mélanie's food until I realized while I was putting all my thoughts together for *When French Women Cook* that she had cooked authentic Savoie food, not stereotyped mass-produced food for a kids' camp. I decided then to save her dishes for the time—now finally arrived—when I would write my own book on the Savoie. You will read about Mélanie often. It was, however, through the recipes described by Marie Thérèse Hermann that I have been able to pinpoint her as a native of the Tarentaise. Several of the women who assisted her and who also cooked were from the Thônes valley.

Madame Déléan, Mimi's mother, whom I have often observed as she worked in front of her house or, during the winter, in her kitchen or barn.

Georgette—Mademoiselle Reygrobellet—is my dear friend and neighbor in Annecy. She cooks very much like her grandmother, Madame Maillet from Annecy-le-Vieux. Both their dishes will be in this book.

Madame Marthe Schmidt cooked for me years ago when I was on vacation at her tiny Crèmerie du Bouchet next to Chamonix. She cooked me some memorable meals, especially some delicious little guinea hens. Marthe is now retired, and the tiny hotel is in the *Guide Michelin* as the larger Hôtel de l'Arveyron; her son Alain is in charge.

I observed Madame Folliguet, Marthe's cousin, whose family I had be-friended in Les Praz de Chamonix, cook several times. Madame Folliguet had a large family, so the meals were as plentiful as they were simple. I always left her home for my hotel table aching to taste what she had prepared.

Madame Berthod was the owner of Le Vieux Pommier in Courmayeur and in the old days cooked herself. She now has been replaced at the desk by her son and at the stove by an Italian chef. The food, however, remains in the old Savoie style.

Madame Arnaud Goddet, the spirited and jovial wife of my butcher in

Annecy, is now running a roadside restaurant on the road to La Roche-sur-Foron. I am desperately looking for her; every roadside restaurant I checked when I was able to rent a car has turned out to be the wrong one, but I know she is there somewhere. I shall find her yet, and if you do before me, try her sausages.

And then there was Madame Bossonaz, with whom I made a famous soup on a thundery evening (see page 191). She was very old already in the late 1950s, and she is probably now resting in the Vallorcine graveyard.

So must *la cuisinière des Bois*, as I always called her. She was an older woman from the Chamonix valley who was hired as a cook in the "Les Bois" summer home of one of my fancy friends. Her dinner was so good that I would have liked to tell her, but in those old-fashioned days this was just not done.

And Mademoiselle Riondet. She remains a mystery. I remember her definitely, moving through the woods with her basket and her stick unearthing mushrooms with great authority, something like a Druidic priestess. Recently I tried to find out who she was and when she died; Madame Bastard Rosset, who was born at La Balme, had no idea whom I was talking about. Was she really a Druidic priestess come back just so Madeleine could remember her and learn so much about mushrooms?

Marie Becker . . . dear Marie Becker, who seems to be with me in every one of my books. She was born in Lorraine, in Lunéville. As a twenty-year-old, she married in Paris a young man from the large village of Saint Pierre d'Albigny in the Savoie. After becoming widowed she married my grandfather and raised my mother. I often wondered why her food seemed to come from two different places. The solution is simple: Some of her dishes were from the Lorraine, others came from Saint Pierre d'Albigny, and she probably had learned them from her first mother-in-law or her first husband. Again without the information found in Marie Thérèse Hermann's book and my mother's faithful reproduction of Marie Becker's food, I would never have found out.

And, then there will be yours truly. I shall be the one in this book to use Savoie ingredients to create more modern recipes.

I am lucky enough to remember the old Savoie at the time just before World War II when the structure of the village was still old-fashioned. I distinctly remember the grocery store that existed in the corner of what is now an ugly bistro. It was a tiny store with a man behind the counter who was suffering from goiter. Were it not for his kindness never to say a word as I was snitching pieces of bread from the sides of the huge fresh loaves he sold, I might not remember his shop so fondly. He sold everything: smelly dried cod, tuna and sardines in cans, sugar and flour in barrels, candies of the worst colors in glass jars, raisins, dried prunes, rum and marc, midget Opinel knives that, as kids, we used to love carrying during our walks on the road to Dingy, just in case we found a fallen nut or a pear. And it smelled "funny" in that store. The cod smell and that of the spices, mixed with those of spilled vinegar, evaporating rum, and drying roasted coffee, filled the small space powerfully.

There were also for sale some of those jasper earthenware dishes that were made in Annecy, just around the corner from where I now live, and of which each year, faithfully, I bought my mother a sample. Ours disappeared during a bombing of my native Courbevoie during the war, and they are now great collectors' items. And then there were those absolutely lovely little *clarines*, midget copies of the bells that hang around the necks of the cows during the *inalpage*. I remember coming back with one around my neck in 1947 and getting in trouble with desiccated Mademoiselle Bergeron, my French literature professor, because its tiny ring disturbed her lecture on Voltaire at Ferney, as if Voltaire, who lived in full view of the Jura mountains, would ever have minded midget *clarines*.

Once in a while some smashingly whittled wooden birds, their wings spread wide, were for sale. I never had enough money to acquire one, and now they are more than collectors' items, they are true museum pieces; one young man is making them again, though, in the privacy of his barn.

I remember the women cooking. Some still cooked on the hearth, most on one of these funny little cast-iron stoves with four burners. They would cook just about everything in what is known as a *bronzin* around Annecy and a *bru* in other parts of the Savoie. Madame Folliguet's *bru* conveniently embedded itself into the hole of the little stove. Otherwise, one owned a frying pan, and that was about all there was for cooking implements. Most bowls and receptacles were still made out of wood and hand-carved by some ancestor. Recently, as we were taking the pictures for this book at Le Laisonnay, I saw one of those old stoves lying on its side, discarded in the middle of a patch of Bon Henri. My first thought was to load it into the back of our rental car, but reason prevailed.

It will be easy for you to figure out which ingredients were used most often: grains to make bread and polenta, green vegetables grown in the home plot or collected in the neighboring fields, cheese, milk and cream, very little meat, which came rarely or by accident (beef and lamb were extreme rarities and barnyard animals delicacies). Fresh fruit and dried fruit, eggs and honey made up the rare desserts. The basic philosophy was survival. One consumed what one produced in an almost perfect self-sufficiency, and one cooked it as well as one knew how. You will realize as you read that the variety achieved within any one category of food was amazing.

One fried in melted butter, of which one also used the sediments for other types of foods, and of course in lard, obtained from one's own porker. Modern types of oils arrived late in the nineteenth century, but the Maurienne could use hemp oil to make some starch products, although in all other areas this type of oil was reserved for the *croeju* (see page 66).

Marie Thérèse Hermann has listed the seasonings and aromatics most commonly used in the Savoie. They did not come from a fancy shop, but from the mountainsides, where they were collected together with berries and wild herbs for teas. I was always intrigued by the faint taste of celery dominating the old-fashioned Savoie dishes, very much akin to that of certain Swiss or Austrian foods; it turned out to be precisely the herb contained in Maggi seasoning, with which the Swiss to this day douse their foods and which is actually lovage. Both the dried roots and the stems were powdered and used as a spice while the leaves found their way into soups and sauces.

You will find caraway seeds to replace the wild cumin that grows all over the countryside, whole or powdered in many dishes, and also often dill, which grows wild and in dry terrain "climbs" rather high on the slopes of mountains. Juniper berries are much in use, especially for the wild meat preparations and in the preparation of the famous mountain smoked ham.

According to Marie Thérèse Hermann, saffron grew extensively in the Savoie as late as the sixteenth century; she discovered that as she studied the old *mappes* established in 1730. Saffron gradually disappeared from the Savoie cuisine, to remain only in some soups and pastries. The pastries themselves, such as the *Bescoin* (see page 142), disappeared after World War II. They are now reappearing slowly after the publication of Mrs. Hermann's book.

Slow changes in the traditional eating habits of the Savoie occurred first in the cities, because of the opening of roads and the relatively large number of tourists in some centers such as Annecy, Talloires, the Chamonix valley, and the Tarentaise.

For a very long time the villages, which have now become ski centers, were reachable only by small roads and were consequently not easily accessible to tourist penetration. Such was the case of Val d'Isère, which took off as a ski resort of importance only after 1945. Beautiful Tignes remained isolated in its splendor, with its old-fashioned food and its glorious lace-making until the Electricité de France decided to annihilate it. Young women who lived in the intra-Alpine valleys of the Tarentaise during the war were students in some of the itinerant cooking classes organized by the Vichy government to teach them better nutrition. It was only then that greens started to become salads as well as soups.

Some of the traditional foods that you will see here started to die out during the fifties, and by the sixties they had virtually disappeared. That is why Marie Thérèse Hermann's book is so important. Thanks to her volume many small local restaurants are now starting to prepare the true old specialties of the Savoie, not just the stereotyped polenta and the Swiss raclette and fondue. If you plan a trip to the Savoie, read this food section carefully so you can compare menus and know where the authentic food is; otherwise you will find yourself confronted with the same bistro food at any ski resort that you will find in a big city. Right now, only a few restaurants offer the traditional food, but more and more are appearing each year; do not be shy about asking the locals; they will know and tell you very gladly.

Traditional Savoie food is not food for the grill, except for a few completely modern dishes. It is food for slow ovens and nice heavy *cocottes* to replace the old *bronzins*. If you still have your mother's cast-iron pans, by all means use them to cook Savoie specialties.

Savoie food is rich in fats, which means two things for us: Make it rarely if we have to, but enjoy it as it should be when we make it. I cannot urge you enough, when you cook Savoie style, not to rush the process. If you hurry, you will not draw the wonderful flavors out of the food and you will be thoroughly disappointed. And most of all, if you are the type of person who absolutely abhors rich foods, stays on a diet as a matter of principle, and leaves two thirds of your food uneaten so you will always look thin, do not even bother to start cooking this food; it is just not for you. I have come to an age when I personally must consider such good things carefully, but I shall never stop stepping off the dietary path now and then. I am much too grateful that I can enjoy these foods every so often.

In well-to-do homes, meals, by the end of the nineteenth century or the beginning of the twentieth, were organized to follow the French timetable of a breakfast, a lunch (which in the Anglo-Saxon mind could be called a dinner and which was often called *dîner* to differentiate it from the evening meal), and a supper (or *souper*, since it always contained a soup). This nomenclature changed when I was a child, and it became a succession of a *petit déjeuner* of bread, butter, jam, and coffee or tea; *déjeuner*, which was a complete meal with a first course, meat or fish, vegetables, salad, cheese, and dessert, and finally dinner, which consisted of pretty much the same items. The variations, depending on the family, are multiple, and in the Savoie, people of true Savoie origin tend to keep soup, cheese, and fruit for the evening meal.

Up to 1940 meals on the farm were (and still may be in very remote areas) as follows:

At 5 A.M., just before milking the cows, there was coffee, bread, and often *la gota*, a drop or so of marc dribbled more or less generously into the black coffee. The habit still persists in many places, though only for the men.

At 9 A.M. was the true breakfast, consisting of soup, bacon, fresh cheese—mostly *Tomme blanche* (see page 160)—and bread. On holy days, there was always chocolate milk to drink.

At noon was the main meal, which consisted mostly of a *farcement* (see page 225), or a large gratin containing starchy vegetables, or polenta or pasta. If it was the growing season, this meal and the following one, prepared by the older women, were brought by the children to the fields where the younger men and women were busy working.

At 4 P.M. the *goûter* was *de rigueur*. To this day children come home from school to drink a large bowl of milk and eat some cake or batch of rustic cookies. Parents would have café au lait, bread, and an aged cheese such as tomme (see page 160) or sometimes those countryside pancakes known as *matafans* (see page 201).

Late afternoon, between four-thirty and five, it was time to milk the cows again and make the cheese, so it was not until 8 P.M. that one could enjoy the equivalent of our dinner, which consisted of soup, whatever leftover was still there from lunch, bread, and cheese.

Except in vineyard areas, wine was not always served with meals. Often it was replaced by the *maude*, a cider that, in the Savoie, is made half of pear and half of apple juice. One also drank whey, milk, and, of course, water. The taste of the water varied with the geological composition of the mountains it came from.

Now, of course, it is not unusual to see factory workers eating lunch in a small local restaurant with their "restaurant tickets" for a very reasonable prix fixe.

Since the Savoie has become such a popular tourist area, I have to say a few words about restaurants for tourists. Those considered good by Michelin will not have traditional Savoie food, and even if they try to make it, it comes out twice as rich as it should be because of the sempiternal additions of puff pastry or something even richer. Since I use my own firsthand knowledge to evaluate the food, often Michelin and I disagree, shall I say, radically?

I tend to talk a lot to local people to find out what they think is good, and cannot urge you enough to take this approach rather than following guidebooks that lump the restaurant's accommodations and amenities together with its food. Following the guidebooks blindly is about the same as drinking the label of a wine.

In spite of all the criticisms I hear all over the United States, I like to go at least once a year to l'Auberge du Père Bise in Talloires. The reason is probably that I understand the basis of its work. This restaurant is and will remain a bastion of enjoyment for the *grande bourgeoisie* and consequently will serve only what satisfies its guests. Madame Bise has always been the essence of graciousness and generosity to me, and I hope that having Sunday dinner on her terrace will remain one of my yearly luxuries for many years to come. If you want something special, order the simplest dishes: the true *Omble Chevalier* in noisette butter when it comes during the summer, and that wonderful *Poularde à l'Estragon*, the taste of its sauce remaining the absolute best of its kind in France. This is not a restaurant that, as a French person, one visits to be surprised by novelties, but rather to be reassured that one's country is still alive and well.

While I was not always partial to Mr. Collon's offerings when he was in Annecy at the Auberge de Savoie, his new Auberge de Letraz in Sevrier offers a very good table and is worth investigating. The dining room is most pleasant and one can, if one likes al fresco dining, sit on the pleasant terrace overlooking the eastern shore of the lake.

Otherwise, I like very much Le Marie-Jean in Amancy-Vozerier one mile outside La Roche-sur-Foron, where the chef and owner, Monsieur Signoux, has no stars but richly deserves one, and certainly cooks better and more interesting dishes than the only star in Annecy.

La Verniaz in Evian has always been a most pleasant experience for me. But if you like an experience that will be different, you can try the Savoie et Léman in Thonon les Bains, a state restaurant and hotel school. On each of my visits there I have felt like revamping the whole culinary program, which is something I feel like doing in any school I visit as soon as my plate is delivered. But if you are a fan of youth, as I am, because I am a mother and a teacher, you will get a kick out of it.

To continue in a more serious vein, the Hôtel Million in Albertville should not be missed. I have had some of the best meals in the whole French Alps there—interesting, modern, and always well-presented. Monsieur Million, like Paul Bocuse, is the descendant of a very long line of restaurateurs who have been practicing at the same location for almost two centuries.

Le Bateau Ivre, both in Courchevel and in Le Bourget du Lac, has been a true pleasure every time I have visited there; not only was the food interesting and personal, but the welcome was also perfect.

Two restaurants have been part of my everyday vacation life for as long as I have come to the Savoie, and that was fifty years in 1987—the Nouvel

Hôtel du Commerce in Thônes (see page 226) and the Hôtel de l'Arveyron in Les Praz de Chamonix (see page 98). Otherwise there are a number of wonderful little places such as l'Amandier and Le Grand Alexandre in Annecy, the *brasserie* Sapaudia, where the grillades are fine and not expensive at all.

With the exception of the Capucin Gourmand in Megève, which is most pleasant, the ski resorts offer very little "star" food; plain, honest, well-prepared fare is the general rule. And after exercising all day, the pizza places are, as my young men say, "super" for a good beer.

Now if, like me, you are a tea nanny, there are a few nice pastry shops from which to take out true Savoie pastries, well prepared and *pur beurre* (pure butter), which is most important. La Gâterie in the rue Sainte Claire in Annecy gets a triple A for quality. As a *salon de thé* to observe the town's bourgeoisie, the Fidèle Berger in Annecy and in Chambéry have very few equivalents in France, and their teas and coffees are superior; you can also try their Opéra and their Pistachio Opéra cakes. In Saint Jean de Maurienne, the pâtisserie Pignon is always open during lunch hour and has good savories and coffee. And when one arrives in Chamonix nice and tired either from skiing or simply because one feels like seeing "Cham" again, there is only one place: the Pâtisserie Confiserie Albert on Place Jacques Balmat; their hot chocolate is hot chocolate, not powder in water.

Before you start cooking, please read the following comments on basic ingredients; they will be useful to obtain the true Savoie taste.

Butter and cream as we find them in the United States will never have the nutty taste of the Savoie products, but they work. Using homemade *crème fraîche* will be useless since the Savoie people much prefer their cream sweet, with no hint of sourness. Madame Mugnier Pollet, my wonderful milk lady at the Laiterie Parisienne in the Faubourg Sainte Claire, will make quite a face if you ask her for ripened cream. I always blend a bit of sour cream into our American heavy cream, not enough for the taste to be frankly detectable. The butter is *always* unsalted and unpasteurized.

Milk in Savoie is so rich that often in desserts you will see me use light cream to replace it.

American store-bought bacon never seems quite smoky enough. It may be a good idea to use either Pennsylvania Dutch bacon or corncob-smoked Vermont bacon, unless you want to try preparing your own (see page 323).

For the cheeses, follow the directions given in the Cheese chapter. You can find Savoie cheeses in all the large cheese stores in big cities.

Vinegars in the Savoie are potent and homemade; a 6 percent acetic acid vinegar is average. Vinegars in modern Savoie food are apt to be flavored with berries.

For the wild mushrooms, I urge you to check all the varieties I mention in each recipe in a mycology book to ascertain that they are edible in your part of the United States. If your book is unclear, *ask* your local mycological society. It is better to use store-bought mushrooms than make a bad mistake. Checking on the mushrooms you collect is your responsibility.

Marc de Savoie is not readily available in the United States; use Marc de Champagne or Marc de Bourgogne, or even good old California brandy. This brings me, naturally, to the wines.

Wines and Liqueurs

Your first thought will probably be that in mountains as cold as the French Alps can be there might not be very much wine. But for millennia, some mighty fine vines have been growing just about anywhere they could grow— old moraines, the rocky slides of the Pre-Alps, and as high as an exceptional 3,003 feet in the little town of Orelle in Maurienne.

This was in the nineteenth century, however. The amount of acreage given to the cultivation of vines has diminished seriously since 1860. At that time wines from the Roussillon and Corbières were so inexpensive that they could almost be shipped to Savoie at a lesser cost than local wines could be produced. There were up to very recently wines in Talloires and in Veyrier around the Annecy lake. I remember in my childhood sitting in the back of my father's Peugeot 5HP as we were driving behind a rickety truck full of manure; at Talloires the truck turned into a small patch of vines where its cargo was used as fertilizer. In earlier times, the same cargo had been transported by boat on the lake, and the manure was produced by all the horses in the city of Annecy. Now, with very few exceptions, the Annecy lake vines have succumbed to the multiple summer homes built in the last fifteen years.

Any reader of French will be able to understand how important the vines were to the Savoyard by reading Jean Gaspard Perrier's delightful book *Le Petiou* (see Bibliography). There he recalls his uncle taking care of the family plot. "To reach those vines, a path climbed from the village straight across the side of the mountain. . . . Everything had to be carried up there on a man's back: the manure was carried in *bartelles* [baskets also called *casse-cou*. They now decorate many chalet walls], the sulphur in the sprayers, and . . . the buckets. . . . Filled with grapes, they were sent back down to the vats well tied on a sled, which itself had had to be carried up on a man's back." All through the book, Perrier laments the diminishing of the vines in his village of birth.

In the last few years, however, the decline of multi-crop cultivation in many small farming enterprises of the Savoie has brought a renewal of vine cultivation, and new wines are appearing on the market under the label Vins de Pays d'Allobrogie. They come from various parts of the Savoie and are most pleasant *vins de pays*.

To understand the location of the historic vineyard areas, please refer to the simple map on page 111; the numbers inscribed inside each area represent the grapes from which the wines are produced.

The best way to appreciate the wines of the Savoie is to take a two- or three-day wine tour, starting in the north by Lake Leman, then going down toward the Rhône valley through Seyssel, on toward Lake Le Bourget/Aix les Bains, and finally into the Combe de Savoie. The views in the vineyards can rival any of the better-known Provençal areas. There are bistros that serve the local wines and the welcome is absolutely wonderful. A delightful trip for wine people who are searching for something new. The best companion book would be Roger Girel's thorough volume *Le Vignoble Savoyard et Ses Vins*, (See Bibliography), which has been my guide for all the tours I took for writing this book.

RIPAILLE, MARIN, MARIGNAN, AND CRÉPY

These four vineyards, located close to the edge of Lake Leman, are planted in the Chasselas grape. The same grape is known on the Swiss side of Lake Leman as fendant, because the pressure of two fingers is enough to split the skin, which *se fend* but does not crush to pulp. The fendant comes in pale green and russet pink. Its exact origin is contested, and it was grafted on the roots existing in the Lemanic areas after the philloxera crisis of the late 1890s and early 1900s.

The wines made from Chasselas grapes are intensely diuretic. Someone even quipped—and it may have been Dr. Ramain—that they were "a lot more so than Evian."

Very fresh (please read my French mind, it means the tiniest bit acid), they ripen into well-rounded white wines that are great by themselves before a meal, or excellent with Leman fish and wild trout.

You may, if you understand French, have heard the expression *faire ripaille*, which is a favorite way of saying that one has participated in one huge and delicious meal in the most joyous of companies. Voltaire himself is supposed to have coined the expression. In reality, the word *ripaille* comes from the Germanic-Burgundian root *rippe*, which means that the area was torn apart and left as a heap of wild low growth after a battle. It is only a coincidence that Countess Bonne de Bourbon, wife of Count Amadeus VI, the Green Count, chose Ripaille as one of the favorite hunting lodges for her prince and entertained there with good, plentiful fare and happy people around.

In 1391, Count Amadeus VII, the Red Count, died in Ripaille, so fast that no historian has been able to establish with certainty the cause of his passing away. The castle was enlarged by Amadeus VIII and his spouse Marie de Bourgogne and from then on housed a monastery of monks of Saint Augustine. In 1434, after Marie passed away, Amadeus founded the order of the Chevaliers de Saint Maurice and the castle became a Carthusian monastery where he himself lived as a monk after renouncing his title of Pope in 1449.

It is at about the time of Amadeus VIII that vines started to be grown on the glacial moraines that line Lake Leman. Ripaille went through all kinds of changes between the fifteenth and nineteenth centuries. It is now private property and the seat of a foundation whose mission it is to preserve both the castle and its natural environment.

Good wines are produced at Ripaille, which has an AOC, (Appellation d'Origine Contrôlée), although connoisseurs do not quite agree whether its aroma is of peach, almonds, or hazelnuts. I am for peaches, and I must say that although it would never cross my mind to refuse a glass of Ripaille, I prefer other Savoie white wines.

The tiny village of Marin is just a few miles east of Thonon, in the hills

Figure 13 LOCATION OF SAVOIE VINEYARDS

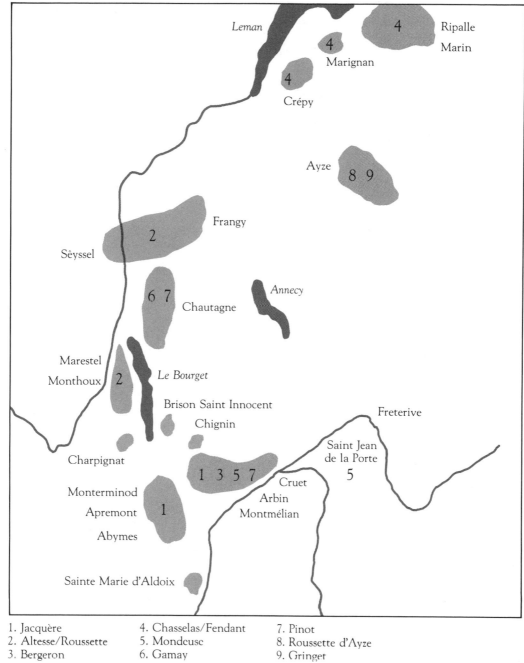

1. Jacquère
2. Altesse/Roussette
3. Bergeron
4. Chasselas/Fendant
5. Mondeuse
6. Gamay
7. Pinot
8. Roussette d'Ayze
9. Gringet

that overlook the lower Dranse. It produces mostly white wines and a bit of Mondeuse (see page 114) and Gamay. I had the pleasure of tasting some of the Mondeuse, which is deliciously fruity.

The quality of the white wines here depends on the vintner, but the few I tasted had more character than those produced at Ripaille. You must look for them around Thonon, for they are not so easy to come by.

I love Marignan, the more so as I have drunk it only twice, and both times it left me yearning for more. This wine was started by the monks of the nearby Abbey of Filly, which is renowned as the most ancient cellar in the Savoie and a wonderful wine museum. Young, the wine is *perlant*, which means *spritzig* and older; it can keep very well, according to Dr. Ramain. Both wines have an AOC.

Should you find your way to the Lemanic area of the Savoie around the last Sunday of August, do not miss making a little time for the pilgrimage to Notre-Dame-des-Vignes in Ballaison. The statue of the Virgin has been there since the philloxera crisis, and in this very Catholic country, the pilgrimage was never discontinued after the crisis was over. The lovely vineyard of Crépy, which takes its name from a little mountain called Mont Crépy, has existed since the late 1300s when it was started by the same monks of the Filly Abbey. The AOC wine is bottled *sur lies* (the lees are left to deposit on the bottom of the barrel and the wine is drawn from above the lees without being clarified) and crackles, crystal clear when poured. Furthermore, it is probably the best cooking wine of all the Savoie wines, since it reduces with a lot of the bouquet left in and almost no acidity. It is the best companion to féra and lake trout (see pages 290–291). For what it is worth, it is one of my two favorites. Dr. Ramain wrote in one of his articles that dining in 1924 with Austin de Crozes, they had enjoyed an 1895 Crépy that showed no trace of madeirization. I never had the pleasure of such an old one!

AYSE

If you drive through the Northern Savoie to go from Annecy to Chamonix on the *autoroute blanche*, at the Bonneville interchange you will see in the hills on your left a beautiful rug of vineyards that climbs up the slope of a mountain called Le Môle. This vineyard is six centuries old. It extended to its maximum at the end of the last century and has been regressing seriously ever since. But the present owners and growers are so attached to it that they have sworn to keep producing. The grapes used in Ayse and two other villages, Marignier and La Côte d'Hyot, are the Roussette d'Ayse for 70 percent of the volume and the Gringet for the remaining 30 percent, the Gringet being a very close relative of the Alsatian Traminer.

The vinification is done two ways. In the traditional manner, a little over one third of an ounce of sugar per liter is added to the still wine to start a second fermentation. Crystals form and drop to the bottom of the bottle; the wine is not decanted; one just pours it carefully when serving. The second method is slightly more modern; over a half ounce of sugar is added per liter, and the bottles are put in *lattes* as is done in the making of champagne, but only for eight months; during the last three weeks, when the bottles near the upside-down position, the wine is rilled to bring the sediment into the neck of the bottle, then disgorged in the old *à la volée* (by hand) manner as in the old-fashioned champagne. What is obtained is called *brut de brut*, and no *liqueur de dosage* (or additional sweetening syrup) is ever added.

I used to be able to buy a great little Ayse in Annecy, and by mistake a case of it found itself buried under several cases of Bordeaux. When I found out it was over four years old; it had turned deep golden, was as sparkling as ever, and was so pleasantly rounded to the palate that I have voluntarily renewed the experience. Ayse cooks very well and is excellent when making a fondue, or with any of the local fish dishes.

FRANGY AND SEYSSEL

There will be no way for the reader ever to taste a Roussette de Frangy or a Roussette de Seyssel in its natural state in the United States since it does not travel well. The only version we can find is the Royal Seyssel, its *mousseux* version, which is pleasant but in no way the same as the natural wine. Both the Roussette de Frangy and that of Seyssel are grapes derived from the Altesse grape, which came originally from the island of Cyprus.

The red wines are made from the Gamay grape, with which we are all very familiar, and another grape, very local and indigenous to the Savoie, the Mondeuse. Mondeuse is so ancient that it was mentioned by Caesar in the *De Bello Gallico*. Loved by all vintners of the Savoie, the Mondeuse was given the name *la princesse*; it is difficult to vinify: Pressed with the small stalks still attached, it may, if some of the small grape stems are left on a little too long, turn slightly astringent and even in the worst cases raspy.

Frangy wines are very old; their existence goes back perhaps as far as the eleventh century. Frangy vintners had great customers in the bourgeoisie of the city of Geneva until around the middle of the eighteenth century when Swiss physicians launched a strong campaign against alcohol. The philloxera and the First World War were another two enemies that contributed to the reduction of the vineyards. After World War II, however, the vintners were successful in redeveloping most of the formerly planted land. Dr. Ramain found almond and linden flavors to the white wines.

Seyssel was, before 1860, separated into two little towns, Seyssel Savoie and Seyssel France, on either side of the Rhône River. The Roussette de Seyssel is very different from that in Frangy because the soils are in no way identical, but the same golden color and a wonderful nose characterize them both.

CHAUTAGNE

The Chautagne is a small area northeast of Lake Le Bourget/Aix les Bains, protected by a low ridge of chalky mountains. Chautagne has produced wines since the eleventh century and, like Frangy, sold them mostly to Geneva. During the eighteenth century the vintages issued from the Chautagne became the official wines of the Sardinian court.

Several grapes are used: Gamay for 45 percent of the vintage, 12½ percent each of Pinot and Mondeuse, the remainder being in white grapes such as Jacquère, Roussette, and even a bit of Aligoté. Although some of the white wines are very pleasant, I think that the reds in this area have more character, especially the Gamay. It's ruby red in color, and the powerfully floral taste of the wine when young is a true pleasure that should not be missed. At the risk of being considered a philistine, I like to drink it after strawberries in the summer; I enjoy the way the two aromas seem to lock into each other. This

Gamay is long-lived and retains a lot of its fruit for over two-and-one-half years.

MARESTEL AND MONTHOUX

The Marestel and Monthoux wines come from a small area squeezed between the Rhône and the Lake Le Bourget/Aix les Bains. The name Marestel (to be pronounced Marêtel, without the *s*) comes from the early owners of the land, the Comtes de Mareste. In decline since the late 1800s, the vineyard started to grow again around 1970. Both the red and white wines are simply elegant, the whites being in some instances very sweet and liquorous. Sixty percent of the production is in reds made from Pinot, Gamay, and Mondeuse grapes, some of it also vinified in rosés; both the reds and rosés are perfect for *saucissons*, hams, and terrines. The Roussette de Savoie here is wonderful, says one eighteenth-century expert: "with mixed nuances of hazelnuts, violets, honey, and almonds." I can vouch only for the honey and a hint of violet once in a while. I recommend that, to drink these wines, you have lunch in a pleasant little restaurant.

BRISON SAINT INNOCENT AND MONTERMINOD

Brison wines have been a rarity in my Savoie life, since I have tasted only one white in all the years I have been here; the vineyard is very small, but still has an AOC; it is often associated in older books with another small vineyard, which has now succumbed to new construction and which was called Charpignat. But in wine circles Brison is still important enough to be mentioned.

Monterminod is almost at the entrance of the city of Chambéry; its vines surround a castle, which stands very proud upon a hill, at the exact position where the Burgundians had built one of their fortresses. Here both Roussette and Gamay grapes are turned into delicious wines that have an AOC. The Mondeuse there has been exceptionally good.

APREMONT AND ABYMES

What a story! What a sight! Please come, do come, to the Combe de Savoie and take a look for yourself at the splendor of the vines growing under the stern face of Mont Granier. Late September is the best time, when the fog drifts across the mountain, the gold of the turned vine leaves reflects the sunlight, and the first snows powder the distant summits of the high Alps.

Before 1248 this area was a peaceful plain producing wheat. The area and the mountain now called Granier took their name from the Latin *Granarium*; it is said that Caesar fed his legions on the grain grown there. But on the night of November 24, 1248, the face of the mountain slid down into a gigantic cataclysm and created the landscape now existing. Here and there you can still see huge boulders dotting the countryside. Seen from the road of the Granier Pass, which climbs into the Chartreuse, the countryside is made up of small hillocks billowing one after another and dotted here and there with tiny lakes. Below this lie a number of villages sleeping forever in their shroud of stone and mud. People coming from the Bauges mountains across the Isère valley gradually established the vineyards of Apremont and Abymes on these apocalyptic slopes.

After seven centuries, what you see there is a typical Savoyard scene of vineyards and *sartos*, those tiny vineyard houses in which one ate and slept while taking care of the vines, celebrated the end of the vintage, and often prepared the famous sausages called *diots* (see page 317). Many of the houses were built from the end of the nineteenth century on, and many bread ovens are there, although they are not as striking as some to be found in the mountain communities.

The Apremont and Abymes wines are always flinty, sometimes smelling very much like the flowers that grow wild all around the vine plots. I find them the most thirst-quenching wines I know of all over France. Very pale yellow and fresh, in the French sense of the word (see page 115), they are very diuretic and amazingly light to the stomach. I have been known to dispose of a whole bottle myself without the slightest damage. They must be tried in the winter when oysters and all shellfish are in season; but cheese fondue and Apremont and Abymes seem to be made for one another. Do not hesitate to stop; in all the vineyards located around the little towns of Apremont, Saint André, Myans, and Les Marches, you will receive a wonderful welcome and feel compelled to leave with a bottle for the road. Several bottles crossed the Atlantic with me, and after sitting in my New Hampshire cellar survived very well.

It is a possibility that the grape which makes up all these wines, the Jacquère, is indigenous to this area, since it is also called Plant des Abymes. Extremely subject to black rot, it has given the growers more than passing headaches, which now seem under control, thanks to the modern fungicides.

CHIGNIN

I should add as subtitle: the pearl of the crown. First, the scenery is intriguing—towers and castles everywhere, some so ancient that archeologists are not yet quite sure of their exact dating. The high Alps and the Granier face you across the valley of the Isère, and then, of course, there are the vines. The grapes climb up the hills and are being replanted higher and higher every year for better exposure to the sun.

Besides the Jacquère, another grape, the wonderful Bergeron is used here to make some of the least-known, best-vinified and best-tasting white wines in France. There are many good producers, but go directly to Monsieur Yves Quenard, who, in the small village of Tormery, produces what I consider the very best wine in the Savoie, his Chignin de Bergeron. You can definitely find it in the better restaurants all over the Savoie, but it is at a premium since only about 50,000 liters are produced each year. The grape was grafted from the Roussanne (one of the components of the Côtes du Rhône); also called Barbin, it is probable that the two names are those of the people who brought the original plants into the Savoie. In great years, the alcohol reaches between 13 and 14 percent. I can always discern the taste of hazelnut in this wine, which rolls on the palate like velvet. It is one of the greatest white wines in France, comparable for me, given the differences of grape, soil, and exposure, with the best Condrieu.

The Mondeuse reaches in Chignin, and also under the signature of Yves Quenard, its height of quality and varietal distinction, with a color to its robe, a perfume to the nose, and a fruitiness to the palate that are unsurpassable. Now, of course, this is a personal opinion.

MONTMÉLIAN AND ARBIN

These two vineyards are the oldest in the Savoie, already in existence in Roman times. Medieval texts mention very favorably the wines of Mons Amelioratus, which, of course, became Montmélian. A book on Montmélian and its wine history would cover many pages and never stop being interesting. Montmélian and the neighboring little town of Arbin formed a complex that, at the time, defended the entrance to the Savoie from the French Dauphiné. In the early 1600s, 1500 souls lived in both communities with forty-five pubs ready to sell them wine.

This is Mondeuse country *par excellence*, and many a Savoyard brings his or her *bosson*, a small barrel of approximately 25 liters, to be filled as soon as a vintage becomes available. True Savoyards seem to think that the Mondeuse d'Arbin is the very best. The wines at Montmélian are all made in a cooperative cellar from the must collected from all the vinters of the district.

CRUET, SAINT JEAN DE LA PORTE ET SAINT PIERRE D'ALBIGNY

The vineyards are at the foot of the southern slopes of the Bauges mountains. These vineyards produce only a little Roussette, but a lot of excellent Mondeuse, and a lovely Gamay. The wines are made by a cooperative and sold in large quantities to *négociants* all over the Savoie.

FRETERIVE

This is a lovely succession of small hamlets that has specialized in very difficult work: the production of young vine plants. Freterive is the second largest producer of young vines in France. This type of work was started after the First World War, and considerably extended and improved in 1945 by the installation of machines to perform the grafting.

The roots are purchased from the southern departments in Provence and Languedoc. Once assembled, the root stock and the sprout are dipped into a bath of cool but still liquid paraffin to achieve a more solid structure. They are laid in wood chip–filled containers and placed in a warm room for a month or so, to allow the grafting procedure to take place.

The small plants are then transferred to the lower fields of the plain rather than to the hills and allowed to grow in plastic-covered ground through the summer. It is very interesting to see all these little plants looking very much like asparagus peeking out of the plastic. The treatments against mildew and other fungi are numerous. In the fall, the young plants are pulled out of the soil and packed in bundles of twenty-five or one hundred. They will be sold during the winter for planting the next spring.

Each vineyard area of France purchases from Freterive the young vines that are traditional to its particular wine production. Some of the plants also go to other European countries and overseas.

VERMOUT

No, I did not make a mistake, the spelling in the Savoie goes without the final *h*. A Chambéry gentleman by the name of Joseph Chavasse started vermout-making after a long stay in some Turin cellar. What he ended up with, however, was a very dry wine quite different from its sweetish Italian cousin and containing a lot more mountain herbs. Vermout was "officialized" in France in 1930 by a court order, of all things. When I was growing up in Paris, it was called Chambéry because several houses from Chambéry, the oldest one now way over a century old, were preparing it.

The dry vermout is a French preparation and the Italian a sweeter one. This does not keep the Italians from making French vermout and the French from preparing Italian vermouth. The herbs and flowers entering the composition of French vermout are basically *Artemisia absinthium* flowers (not the leaves, which would be too potent), bitter orange zest, chamomile, aloe vera, cardamom, and anise. Knowing that, try to find the artemisia and you are in business. I found some in the mountains, brought it back, and made myself a bottle with part alcohol and cooked white wine. I could not say that it was pure nectar, but I was pleased. The way to drink it in Chambéry is with a trace of strawberry syrup.

A SPECIAL LIQUEUR: LA CHARTREUSE

As you will see from the Dessert chapter that starts on page 358, many liqueurs in the Savoie are prepared at home. A few pure spirits are distilled in specialized areas, such as the Kirschwasser from Evian and the Eau de Vie de Poires from Brenthonne.

A few small houses prepare some pleasant liqueurs, such as the liqueur des Aravis and the Génepi, hazelnut, bilberry, and raspberry liqueurs by the house of Routin, all very pleasant when poured over ice cubes.

The world-renowned product is the Chartreuse, which is prepared by the Carthusian monks of the monastery in the Chartreuse mountains. There should be no reason for me to discuss this liqueur in a book on the Savoie, since the monastery is in the French Dauphiné, but originally, when the fathers started to make the liqueur, the flowers and herbs must have been collected in the Savoie parts of the mountains as well, and the Savoie peddlers, who after 1850 sold the liqueur from their boxes to all the farms and towns of the Savoie and Europe, did a lot for what we call today its distribution.

The monastery is but a few miles into the Dauphiné. The Carthusian Order became nine hundred years old in 1984: The Bishop of Grenoble, who was later canonized as Saint Hugues, had had a dream. He had seen God building a large dwelling in the Chartreuse mountains, with seven stars showing him the way. So, great was his surprise when one June day in 1084 he received a visit from the future Saint Bruno, professor in Cologne, along with six companions, who said they were looking for a "desert" where they could settle down to a contemplative life. The bishop took them into the "desert" of the Chartreuse, which nowadays appears pleasant and peaceful, but in those days was very remote from all civilization.

The monks went to work and built a primitive monastery and a chapel where the chapel of Saint Bruno is now located; they also established the rules of the Order of the Carthusians, which have remained unchanged. The monastery was destroyed several times over the centuries, sometimes by fire, sometimes by earthquakes, and its population was decimated by the Black Plague. The present house was built on plans established by the concerted efforts of one brother and one father after the great fire of 1676.

Like all religious orders, the Carthusians had to subsist by their own means. They started exploiting the forest, since cultivation at an altitude of 3000 feet can have its vagaries. They discovered iron ore, which they proceeded to extract and melt. For seven centuries they produced tools, knives, swords, and suits of armor, many of which are now displayed in museums. The Carthusian fathers became the first metallurgists in the French Dauphiné and started the industrial development of this mountainous area. If we believe the French Encyclopedia, the Savoie sovereigns looked upon that industry with, shall we say, "admiring eyes." The start of the Industrial Revolution put an end to these metal-working activities, and since King Louis XV had already reduced their activity in forestry, the fathers had to find another source of income.

In 1602, Marshal d'Estrées, companion of Henri IV of France, had donated to the Carthusians a strange manuscript that listed one hundred and thirty-some plants with which one should prepare an elixir of life, and gave the formula for its maceration and distillation. To this day, no one knows who the author was, most probably one of those alchemists of the sixteenth century who knew his plants perfectly.

In 1738, when the resources of the order were becoming meager, it was decided to start producing the elixir and Brother Jerome Maubec, at the time apothecary of the convent, was put in charge of the project. Brother Jerome worked without seeing the results and, just before his death, passed his secrets on to Brother Antoine. In 1755, the final formula having been established, the fathers started production.

Collected originally only in the mountains of the Chartreuse, the plants now come from all over the world. In 1792 the fathers were expelled from France during the Revolution and dispersed to the various Carthusian communities of Europe. The famous manuscript went through all kinds of regrettable adventures. Dom Sébastien Pallius, who had taken it away, gave it to Dom Basile Nantas before dying in exile. In 1800, not knowing how to use the manuscript, Dom Basile sold it to one Monsieur Leotard, a pharmacist in Grenoble. Napoleon, having ordered an inventory of all the remedies existing in France, received the papers from Leotard and with his lack of insight concerning anything but military matters, labeled them "without interest." Leotard received his papers back and quietly continued to produce his elixir under cover.

The fathers came back to their monastery in 1816. Leotard's heirs returned their manuscript, and they resumed distillation. It was in 1838 that the first commercial product, the yellow Chartreuse, was introduced by Brother Bruno Jacquet. For years, when no one knew of the liqueur, one Brother Charles sold bottles of elixir and yellow Chartreuse from the baskets attached to his donkey's back in the markets of Grenoble and Chambéry. The migrant Savoyard merchants who carried their little stores on their backs brought the Chartreuse with them, not only into their native country, but also to the four corners of France and Europe.

It was not until 1852 that the fathers had their trademark officially registered. To this day, it carries the name of their Father Procuror at the time: L. Garnier. The success of the liqueur extending more and more, it was necessary to build a new distillery in Fourvoirie. Then, in 1903, the French government voted for the separation of Church and State. The fathers were expelled again, and by the army at that!

All their acquired goods were sold at auction; their stock of liqueur was purchased by a wine and spirits merchant who proceeded to sell it, then produce an imitation, since he was not in possession of the original formula, which the fathers had taken with them to Spain. So, if you see an old Chartreuse bottle with a label dating between 1903 and 1929 that was made in France, you can be certain you have the copy, not the original. I have seen many of these bottles in the cellars of some of my elder friends.

The original, at the time, was called Tarragone, with the mention *liqueur fabriquée par les Pères Chartreux* clearly visible under that name. In 1929 friends of the fathers bought the distillery and its outbuildings back for them and they resumed production in France. They were in full production when, in 1935, the distillery collapsed under the weight of a landslide; everything but the inventory of liqueur was lost. The distillery was never rebuilt, and its walls are still standing, gray and sad, along the road of the Guiers Mort; the distillery was transferred to its present location in Voiron.

Still the French Carthusian Order did not have a home, and in spite of a petition of more than 200,000 names and a street demonstration in 1927 to try to force the French government to reinstate them in their former quarters, the fathers had to wait until 1940.

It happened in rather horrible circumstances. Since most of the fathers and brothers had taken refuge in their Italian community house at Farnetta, the Italian authorities, upon declaring war on France, gave them the choice of leaving or going to prison. So they left, and as they arrived in Saint Pierre de Chartreuse the mayor, Monsieur Villard, took it upon himself to let them into their house. No one ever objected and they have been there ever since, hopefully to stay forever.

Now there are always three brothers who know the famous formula. They travel each year to Tarragona, where they distill the liqueur for half the year. The distribution is handled by Chartreuse Diffusion all over the world. By all means, go to Voiron. You will see the incredible scenery of Les Abymes and the lovely village of Saint Pierre d'Entremont with its French church and its Savoyard church on either side of the Guiers, which until 1860 was the border between the two countries. After you see the distillery in Voiron, do not miss visiting the wonderful museum of Carthusian life that has been organized in the lay brothers monastery of La Correrie. I have taken this trip faithfully each year, enjoying the peace and total silence. I would recommend going as early in the morning as you can, to try to avoid the huge crowds that literally "invade" and are noisy in the afternoon. The off-season is especially wonderful and quiet. There is no admittance to the monastery, where thirty-seven fathers are now in residence, but you can walk quietly up to the entrance; it is most impressive.

Chartreuse comes in two colors: the original yellow, which I personally find a bit sweet; and green, which I prefer. The very best is sold in lovely old green bottles packaged in wooden boxes, and is called VEP Chartreuse, for *viellissement extra prolongé*, or a stay of seven years in a huge wooden vat, which you can see in the cellars of the distillery. Just so you know, the fathers are allowed to have some of their own liqueur only once a year, for Christmas. All three of these products are easily obtainable in the United States. Several other "monk" concoctions exist, an orange and a bilberry wine, a delicious walnut wine, and a wonderful liqueur called the Ninth Centenary. Try the beautiful chocolates sold at the Correrie and at Bonnat, the pastry shop in Voiron that has an exclusive to sell their products. If you like Gregorian chant, do not miss the two tapes that are on sale at the museum.

Daily Bread, Holiday Breads

Give us this day our daily bread was not an idle prayer in the old Savoie. All the sources to which I have referred for information have stressed that bread was no more no less than sacred to everyone. One look at the slopes on which the grains used to make it were grown gives away one of the reasons for this reverence. Cultivating and gathering this grain was exhausting work, and it was not unusual to gather barely enough to last the full year.

So whoever made the bread dough traced the sign of the cross on it; and so did whoever cut into a new loaf. The ritual was that the man of the house was in charge of preparing the dough, a charge that a husband would fulfill when he was present, but delegated to his wife or daughter when, out of necessity, he was away working in a foreign country (see emigration, page 73).

One baked more often during the good months of the year than during the winter. In winter the quality of the bread was poor; the loaves became so hard waiting to be used that they had to be rehydrated in wet towels before they could be sliced with the *copa* pan. The *copa* pan was a thick wooden board to which was permanently affixed a strong and heavy knife blade, always handmade by the head of the household or the village *magnin*. Often the edges of the board were beautifully carved with an Opinel knife, and the blade was always incised with the initials of its maker. The bread was, in many farms and houses, especially in the higher altitudes, stored in the *branlier*, a rack that could be brought up or down by a pulley and that was kept high under the roof of the attic to prevent small or large predators from reaching it. A *branlier* could contain up to two hundred loaves.

Bread was consumed with every component of a meal, often even with dessert. I remember seeing adults and children eating pears and apples with large slices of bread. Jean Nicolas, in his essay on food in the Savoie in the eighteenth century, made a complete study of bread consumption at that time: It was enormous. In the lower classes, two and a half pounds of bread a day was considered a strict minimum. As late into the twentieth century as the forties, I remember the village children eating the largest chunks of bread and cheese I had ever seen. I soon got used to it myself since we received at least one quarter pound of bread with a small tablet of Menier chocolate for *goûter*, the afternoon snack of French children. Consumption of bread among the bourgeoisie and the nobility was less impressive because there were many other good things available with which to satisfy their prodigious appetites.

The grains out of which the bread flours were prepared varied greatly. All white bread throughout the eighteenth and nineteenth centuries was definitely reserved to the very upper bourgeoisie and the nobility. To the lower bourgeoisie and house servants in cities went the *pain clair* or *pain clairet*, a shade or two darker since it contained whole coarsely milled wheat and/or rye. The common folks had to do with what was called the *gros pain*, a very dense, compact and dark composition of pure rye chaff, rye, oats (which are called in patois *bataille*), and barley (which was given the local name *cavallin*). I distinctly remember the expression *gros pain* still being used, even in Paris, while I was growing up. Most loaves contained a lot of barley until very late into the nineteenth century and even during the first decades of this century. In normal growing years one used what the soil in a given area could and would produce. It is well documented that during the years Louis XIV of France waged war against the Savoie, there were horrible famines, and flours made out of ground acorns, grape seeds, and walnut shells were used to make bread. History does not tell whether his egotistic French majesty ever tasted the bread thus made, which he was sent by the intendant of the Maurienne in 1690.

Late in the nineteenth century, it might happen that in one village some people would eat white bread because their fields were on the *adret* (see page 24), where wheat could grow, while others ate darker bread from lesser grains grown in fields located on the *envers*. Arsène Bourgeaux mentions that at the beginning of this century there was a lively interchange of lunch breads at school in Mont Saxonnex, since young children were always attracted to the color of the bread not baked in their own family.

If you travel in the Upper Maurienne during the summer, try to find your way to Bramans on the morning of August 15 to see the centuries-old ceremony of the benediction of the breads. Women dress in the local costumes of their grandmothers. The men dress in somber modern suits to carry the large arrangements of bread loaves decorated with flowers. The sight of the silk shawl, pink ribboned bonnets, and flower-decorated loaves of bread offers a true feast for the eyes.

The only time of year when everyone ate completely white bread was at *Chalande*, the Savoie name for Christmas. A wonderful custom lasted long enough into the twentieth century that I could witness it personally. Every Sunday the Communion bread was purchased by a different family; if the family was well off the bread was almost like brioche. I remember vividly how I loved to go to mass between 1937 and 1939 because of that delicious briochelike bread cut into large cubes that was passed down the pew in baskets lined with crisp linen. I regretted not daring to take more than one piece, and was secretly somewhat envious of some of my friends who apparently had not been warned as I had about the blackness of the sin of greediness. Marie Thérèse Hermann explains that a large piece of that Sunday bread was reserved for the priest and another for the family whose turn it would be to donate the Communion bread a week later. When I came back to the Savoie at the very end of the war, the custom had disappeared and never came back again. The Communion bread for High Holidays such as Christmas and the Assumption of the Virgin on the 15th of August was called *Riâme* in Northern Savoie and *Sarta* in Southern Savoie; sometimes it contained saffron and anise, sometimes it did not.

As they took Communion, older men and women murmured:

Pain bénit je te prends,
En mon cœur je t'attends
Si je meurs subitement,
Sers-moi de Saint Sacrement

which in English means approximately "Holy Bread, I receive thee with long-ing, should I die suddenly be my holy host." The French reader will appreciate the absolute faith expressed by the verse and its total simplicity.

Another bread made almost exclusively by bakeries was the *bescoin*, pre-pared with brioche dough containing saffron and anise, not too generously buttered. It was a longish oval loaf with a round ball at each end. Given as presents to godchildren by godparents, *bescoins* often showed the initial of the receiver's first name. *Bescoins* disappeared in 1939, but in Annecy, the residence of Marie Thérèse Hermann, where her book has met with quite a success, they are slowly making a comeback (see picture section). *Bescoins* seem to have been more popular in Northern than in Southern Savoie.

And then, there are *rioutes*. A true *rioutte* is a flexible piece of reed or wood with which a bundle of wood is tied; by extension, it is also a roll that looks suspiciously like a bagel, and is even made like one. Imagine a very crisp bagel, highly peppered and flavored with aniseeds. *Rioutes* are left to dry and are enjoyed as dry as rock dipped into a glass of wine. The Moors may have left this circular roll in the Savoie, just as they left those tiny peppered *échaudés* in exactly the same shape in Provence and the Languedoc; the only difference between the two is really the size. *Rioutes* are as large as bagels, but *échaudés* are no more than one and a half inches in diameter and barely one half inch thick. *Rioutes* are a bit difficult to locate nowadays; since I knew that they were more prevalent in Southern Savoie, I tried there and succeeded. On your way to visit the vineyards of the Combe de Savoie, you will have to pass through the village of Myans; stop at the only bakery; *rioutes* are sold there, as they always have been, by the dozen, tied together with a piece of regular string. I tried to convince the baker to let me take his picture but he was too shy, much to the regret of his wife, who would have liked this very much. But he is very proud of his *rioutes* and they are indeed excellent. By now, when

I pass through Myans, I arrive with my quarter pound of butter, get the Opinel out as soon as the rolls have been acquired, and spread merrily away while they are still fresh and crisp; it is not quite the traditional Savoie way, but it is certainly pure enjoyment of two excellent foods.

Everyday bread was kneaded into loaves at home, marked with the family wooden stamp in case one baked in cooperation with another family (those stamps are now quite difficult to find in antique stores and markets, and consequently are quite pricey; I have been chasing after an old damaged one to refinish myself for years), or in the *banal*, or communal oven. Keep your eyes open for these bread ovens when you travel. They are relatively plentiful in the vineyards around Apremont, but they are not the loveliest specimens. I can tell you of three excellent ones that are accessible in the good months of the year. One is in Alex, ten minutes from Annecy, just past the Col de Bluffy on the road to Thônes. The second is in La Frasse, close to the ski resort at Arâches (Haute Savoie) and can be reached from the expressway that goes to Mont Blanc by exiting at Cluses; a left turn unto the old National road will get you on your way. The last oven, the most moving of all, is way up in the Tarentaise, at one of the entrances of the National Park of the Vanoise, in a hamlet called Le Laisonnay. To reach it, you must first go to Champagny, then Champagny le Haut, then take the lesser road toward the entrance of the park. The view over the ski slopes of Courchevel is extensive and very beautiful from up there.

I found this little oven just like that—*par hasard*, as we say in French— and it went straight to my heart. On the edge of the oven floor there were still some of the ashes of a last baking that must have taken place years and years ago. I was alone, completely taken by the intense quietness of the Alps. On that September day, some leaves were starting to turn and the mineral world of La Grande Casse and its splendid glacier loomed so close and yet so far at the end of the narrow valley. Having one of my spurts of clairvoyance, I felt all of a sudden surrounded by the friendly warm crowd of all the souls who, for the last two centuries, had anxiously waited at the side of that oven for the loaves to come out. Whoever was around me knew that the oven had been a true find and meant a great deal to me. The truth of the matter is that

I cannot wait to go back up there. Maybe the new owners—obviously city folks from the type of renovations that have been made on the nearby old houses—will restore the old oven with as much style as they restored the houses.

Town and village ovens were not called *banal* without reason. The word comes from the medieval (and still modern but with another meaning) word *ban*, which in those days, and in the context of bread oven, meant "a fine." Throughout the Middle Ages most ovens belonged to feudal lords who could require the village folks to use their ovens and who would *ban*, or fine, people who did not. The privilege had disappeared by the sixteenth century. Later, many homes, as in Colonial America, had their own bread ovens; sometimes an old house still shows a telltale circular bulging outside wall. Georgette Reygrobellet's grandmother, who owned absolutely nothing when she was married, ended up being the owner of her own bread oven, which was her pride and joy. Later in this chapter you will find one of her bread recipes.

Baking a batch of bread was called *faire au four*. There was everywhere a well-organized system of taking turns at lighting the oven, which meant being responsible for producing the *fascines*, or large bundles of twigs and wood that were necessary to start the fire. The *fascines* were tied by true *riouttes*; if you visit the Upper Maurienne, look carefully at the many old houses still standing; one side of each house has a wooden balcony, often still filled with *fascines*.

Opinions differ as to whether the baking of such items as flat breads and pastries that were made with leftover dough after the regular loaves had been shaped, occurred before or after the baking of the loaves. From what I gathered after reading as much material as I could find, it seems that in the Lemanic areas, where the ovens were made of sandstonelike material, the smaller pastry items, which cooked fast, were put in the oven before the bread, while in ovens made of metamorphic stones in Southern Savoie, they were definitely baked after the loaves. These flat breads, practically identical to the *foccacie* of the Provence and Italy, were given the names of *Levèches* or *épognes*, and they could be sweet or savory.

Baking was not the only function of the bread oven; in its dying warmth one also dried fruit for the winter. Those ovens without a chimney but with a high ceiling space may also have been used to partially smoke hams and sausages. The saying went that the heat of the oven belonged to the baker; consequently, each family had a chance at drying fruit and vegetables on the day they provided the firewood.

The concept of the communal oven started slowly dying out in the 1870s as bakers began coming into some larger villages and renting the oven on a long-term basis. The higher the villages were located, the longer-lived was the old communal oven. They were, so to say, abandoned in the 1930s, but the Second World War saw them come back to life for a few years. I guess that nostalgia for them simply remained with the people after those difficult years, for many villages do use the oven at least once a year at the time of the Vogue; it is a pleasure to take part in such a celebration; our Swiss neighbors have restored a number of ovens in the Valais and the Pays de Vaud and follow the same custom, if not at the time of the Vogue, then at Christmas.

There is at least one old world–style bread oven in the United States. It is in Plainfield, Vermont, and was built by the capable hands of Jules and Helen Rabin, who, I can honestly say, bake the very best bread, probably in the whole country at this point; one of our food world colleagues, John Thorne, author/editor of *Simple Food*, is in the process of building one; I cannot wait to read about his experiences in future editions of his little magazine.

For a while the bread in Annecy was really not too good, but a number of modern bakers began, approximately ten years ago, to make all kinds of old-fashioned leavened breads; several have wood ovens and some really good loaves come out of them. In the recipes that follow I have included several modern recipes with the names of the bakeries who initiated them in Annecy. This bread renewal is not unique to Annecy; it has occurred in other larger cities of the Savoie, and I suspect that famous Monsieur Poilasne's enthusiasm in Paris has been contagious. What I know for sure is that our nostalgia for solid bread everywhere in the Western world is one of the expressions of our deep regret for the hard but so simple and spiritually rewarding life that we have lost to technology.

If you pass through Morzine, buy another quarter pound of butter and a local smoked *saucisson*, then stop at the center *Boulangerie* (bakery), just on the big hill going up to the top of the village, and buy yourself the beautiful bread they call a *roue*. It is a nice round loaf shaped like a very Celtic-looking wheel made by attaching together roll-size pieces of *baguette* dough. Each roll-size piece makes the best little sandwich of bread, butter, and *saucisson*; with a good bottle of Mondeuse, it is a perfect al fresco lunch.

In the recipes that follow, I have done my best to reproduce the old Savoie breads as closely as I could. But flours are always different, so if a dough is too soft, add flour and do not worry about following the recipes to the letter; recipes *will* vary enormously in every area of the United States; we do have nice strong flours that make up excellent breads. Another drawback is chlorinated water; may I recommend that you use spring water to prepare the doughs? I would not go so far as asking you to purchase Evian water, but in large cities, if expense is not an object, it would be perfect. Mountain people everywhere can use their own spring water. I do in New Hampshire.

One last word on what is called in French a *banneton*, which in the Savoie carries the name of *bennon* or *copon*. These are baskets in which breads rise before being baked. Crown-shaped *bannetons* can be purchased in the United States; I have seen them in many shops. The round *bannetons* you can make yourself by using a round Chinese basket and lining it with cotton cloth well stitched to the basket. You can unstitch it once in a while to wash it, then resew it into the basket.

BASIC TECHNIQUES FOR A TASTY BREAD

So much French-style bread made in America has absolutely no connection in taste, texture, or look to true French bread that I have had whole classes of students chasing after that "baked air" product rather than accept the fact that true French country—or city—bread is not light but chewy, substantial, yes, in some cases even rather heavy. The best French bread, made with strong European bread flour, shows big gas bubbles whose inner surface often looks fat and shiny with cooked gluten; often there is so much gluten that the dough is ever so slightly gray. I know that all over France there is nowadays some pretty bad bread, machine-made as quickly as possible, that has no taste at all and is comparable in its lack of quality to some American products. One of the distinctions of true French bread is that instead of being made with plain yeast, it is prepared with a leaven.

Leaven for Tasty Bread

When you prepare a leaven, you use a minimum amount of commercial yeast, introduce it into a flour and water paste to allow it to multiply, and thus grow your own fresh yeast. At the same time, you develop a lot of flavor in the leaven since the yeast produces alcohol, carbon dioxide, and a few other more complicated acids that give the leaven its very particular taste. Some of the yeast cells die every day and the potency of the leaven diminishes; this is why every day you feed the new yeast some fresh flour to permit it to multiply again. The leaven tastes rather acid; do not, however, expect your bread to have that wonderful sourdough taste unless you live in those areas of the United States on the northwest coast where the type of yeast called *Saccharomyces exiguus* is prevalent. This problem is also constant in France. Some areas can produce sourdough breads, some simply cannot. There are no real sourdough breads in the Savoie.

It will take three days to prepare a good leaven. Only on the fourth day will you be able to use it to bake bread. When you are ready to prepare your dough, use only two thirds of the leaven, and with the remainder of it, start another leaven, which will be usable on the fourth day after you start it. If you do not care for the taste of bread made with a full three-day-old starter, make a "short" leaven by using it the next day. I do not think the bread tastes as good, but that is my own taste. The cumin powder trick helps develop more sourness and was given to me by my baker in Annecy, Mr. Rotelli. *Note that positively no salt should ever go into a leaven.*

> *3 cups all-purpose flour*
> *¾ teaspoon cumin powder*
> *½ teaspoon active dry yeast*
> *Warm water (110°F) as needed*

Day one:

Mix 1 cup of the flour and the cumin powder with the dried yeast and enough warm water to make a batter as thick as a pancake mixture. Cover with cheesecloth and let stand at approximately 80°F.

Day two:

To the existing leaven, add another cup of flour and enough warm water to again obtain a pancake texture. Let stand another 24 hours, covered.

Day three:

Repeat the same operation using the last cup of flour and more warm water; let stand 24 hours, covered, again.

Now that you have a leaven, remove two thirds of it every time you want to make a batch of bread with approximately 4 cups (1 pound) of flour.

The making of the bread dough, a general description:

The basic technique is easy. You make a well in the 4 cups of flour, pour the leaven into the well, and start by gathering as much flour as the leaven will absorb; then add more warm water if needed, and sprinkle the salt over the yet unkneaded dough (see quantities, below).

Unfortunately, the exact amount of water cannot be indicated since different flours have various degrees of absorbency, and the degree of humidity in the atmosphere is very important. The wetter the surroundings (like Mississippi in the dead of summer), the less water the dough will take; conversely, the drier the atmosphere, the more water the dough will demand.

It is up to you to judge how much is needed in your surroundings, and *don't worry about exact amounts.* There is no problem anyhow; if the dough is too wet, add all-purpose or bread flour even in multi-grain breads. As soon as a ball forms, however unshapely, start kneading. Kneading should be done with each hand alternately, passing the dough from one hand to the other, rolling and flattening it on the countertop with one hand and crushing it with the fingers of the other hand; it is a rhythmical movement that will work your body all the way down to the waist and make you deserving of that nice crisp end, which in Savoie they call *l'quignon,* all nice and crunchy. *Never knead a bread dough more than a full 10 minutes.* And I hate to disappoint you, but no machine ever will knead as well and completely as your two hands; however, use any machine you like, if you prefer; it is your bread.

A well-kneaded dough should always keep the imprint of the thumb when one pushes it in; however, the surface of the bread should not be totally dry but slightly tacky; the gluten developed in the dough as you knead will absorb all the residual moisture while the dough rises, and you will be surprised to see that it does not stick to anything once it is fully risen.

Rising:

Let the dough rise until doubled in bulk in a lightly greased metal bowl, or without fat in a wooden bowl, lightly covered with a towel. This will take a good 2 hours in temperate climates, less in the summer or in warm climates. When the dough has doubled in bulk, pass your hands gently under it, deflate it, bring it back to the board, and reknead it 1 or 2 minutes to equalize the inner bubbles of carbon dioxide and even up the texture.

Shaping, proofing, docking:

Traditional Savoie breads are shaped into *couronnes*, or crowns, and *boules*, or round smaller loaves, or also *meules*, very large round loaves 15 inches in diameter. While the *couronnes* and *boules* are shaped in *bennons*, the *meules* are formed freehand.

Flour the *bennon(s)* well, shape the dough into round loaves or a crown, depending on the basket you are using, and put the dough to proof in the *bennon. Be careful:* Do not let the loaf completely double in bulk in its proofing container or it will deflate completely as you turn it over before baking. Let it rise only until 1½ times its original size. Sprinkle a black baking sheet with white bolted cornmeal. Gently turn the loaf of bread over onto the sheet so the bottom becomes the top, and immediately dock it ¼ inch deep with a razor blade. To dock, trace a large circle on crown-shaped breads, make a single diametrical slash on round loaves, or four perpendicular slashes for a double cross, if you prefer. Let the bread finish rising until almost doubled in bulk.

Baking:

To obtain a Savoie *pain fariné* (floured bread), do not brush the flour off the top of the loaves. Bake in a well-preheated 425°F oven. Brick tiles put on the bottom rack of your oven may help give you a crust that is closer to the crust obtained in a bread oven. Spray water onto the bricks and the bread 3 times during the first 10 minutes of baking, until a crust has built all around. Note that a black baking sheet absorbs more heat than a shiny light-colored one and bakes a better bread. If you own a pizza stone, do not hesitate to use it. You will know when the bread is ready: Your nose will tell you, so trust it;

also trust your eyes, you will see the dark golden crust. And finally, lift the bread loaf and trust your ears; they will recognize immediately the hollow sound of fully baked bread as you tap on the bottom of the loaf. There is no harm done, on the other hand, if a loaf overbakes; that is how the thick crust finally forms and stays crusty, because you have let most of the moisture evaporate in the oven. If you underbake the crust, all the steam contained in the bread moves toward the outside of the loaf and softens the crust as the bread cools.

Do resist the temptation to cut the loaf straight out of the oven. Give it an hour or so to cool gently on a rack, then cut *l'quignon,* spread it with butter, and tell me if it was not worth working for.

BREADS FROM THE PAST

The recipes that follow are old-fashioned and hope to be renditions of the traditional breads. The tests have been good. One Important point: *If in multigrain breads you must add more flour, make it bread flour to give them solidity since they tend to retain a lot of moisture.*

PAIN TOUT BLANC
All White Bread

This is the bread of the nobility and upper bourgeoisie in days gone by and that of daily consumption in the Savoie nowadays.

2 cups leaven (page 132)
2 cups each all-purpose and bread flours
1 tablespoon fine salt
Warm water as needed
1 tablespoon walnut or olive oil to grease the rising bowl

Follow the general directions given on pages 133–34 to prepare the bread dough, letting it rise, proof, then docking and baking it. This quantity will make 1 large crown 12 inches wide, or 2 large round loaves.

PAIN BIS DE LA TARENTAISE
Tarentaise Dark Bread

2 cups leaven (page 132)
1 teaspoon active dry yeast
½ teaspoon powdered cumin
½ teaspoon well-crushed
  caraway seeds
2 cups rye flour
2 cups whole wheat flour
1 tablespoon salt
Warm water as needed
1 tablespoon walnut or olive
  oil

Mix the dry yeast into the leaven and let stand 30 minutes; then add the cumin and caraway seeds and follow the general directions on pages 133–34 to prepare the dough, letting it rise in a bowl greased with the oil, shape and bake it. The teaspoon of yeast is added to help the heavy dough rise more easily by producing additional carbon dioxide, since the only gluten-containing flour is the whole wheat. The leaven cannot be considered a proper source of gluten since the gluten is weakened by the acids in the leaven. This bread is usually always shaped into 2 large or 3 smaller round loaves.

GROS PAIN
Coarse Bread

This has been a little more difficult to duplicate since I never tasted the original; it disappeared quite a few years ago. From what I have read, however, this could be a very legitimate version. There were many variations, depending on the availability of grains, and I suspect that this is still luxurious compared to what was really consumed. By our modern standards, it provides a healthy addition of good fibers to the diet; make a special leaven with whole wheat flour for this bread and notice the larger amount of yeast to start it, again because the minimum amount of gluten-producing proteins in the flours will result in a heavier dough, harder to leaven.

LEAVEN:
1 teaspoon ground cumin
2 cups whole wheat flour
2 teaspoons active dry yeast
Warm water as needed

Prepare a leaven with the cumin, whole wheat flour, yeast, and warm water, starting the leaven with 1 cup of flour and adding the second the next day, only 3 hours before making the bread. This leaven should "work" for a maximum of 24 to 36 hours.

Cook the pearl barley in salted water until almost tender; drain, pat dry, and cool it completely; break

DOUGH BULK:
¾ *cup pearl barley*
1 *cup white bread flour*
2 *cups rye flour*
1 *cup dry oat flakes*
1 *tablespoon fine salt*
Warm water as needed
1 *tablespoon walnut oil*

up the kernels in the food processor.

Mix the leaven, bread and rye flours, the oat flakes and barley; sprinkle with salt and add warm water if necessary. Knead into a smooth bread dough, drier than a regular white bread dough. Place in a bowl oiled with the walnut oil and let rise until doubled in bulk.

Deflate and shape into 2 large round loaves. Proof and dock according to the directions on page 134. As soon as risen to its maximum, bake in a preheated 425°F oven.

By our modern standards, this bread has no keeping capacities and will harden rapidly. Freeze one of the loaves after baking. If after cutting into a loaf you are left with some bread, rather than lose it, cut it into slices and freeze each portion in foil. Toast while still solidly frozen and the bread will taste as if it were fresh out of the oven.

BOGNONS AUX RAISINS ET CULS DE POULETS
Rye Rolls with Raisins and Prunes

These rolls are still sold in some country bakeries; they have a slightly acid taste since the prunes are home-dried and have no sweetness. I have limited the amount of prunes since ours are so sweet; soaking them in lemon juice does help.

1 *recipe* Pain Bis *(page 136)*
1 *teaspoon lemon juice*
4 *pitted prunes, diced in*
   ¼-*inch cubes*
⅓ *cup raisins*

Prepare the dough, and while it is rising marinate the diced prunes in the lemon juice. Do not use more lemon juice than the recommended teaspoon.

When you deflate the dough, knead the fruit into it and separate the dough into 18 equal balls out of which you can shape the rolls. Let them proof and bake them 15 to 20 minutes in a preheated 425°F oven on a dark baking sheet sprinkled with cornmeal.

RIOUTTES
Bagel-like Rolls

½ *recipe* Pain Tout Blanc
  (page 135)
1 *teaspoon coarsely cracked*
  pepper
1 *teaspoon crushed aniseeds*
1 *gallon boiling water*
3 *tablespoons salt*

Knead the black pepper and aniseeds into the dough before letting it rise.

Separate the finished dough into 12 equal-size small balls. Roll each ball of dough with the side of the hand to obtain a 10-inch-long piece of dough tapered at both ends. Meanwhile turn the water down to a simmer and add the salt.

Bend the two ends of each dough stick toward each other into a slightly oval circle. Bring the right end of the stick 1 inch above the other and fold the left tip back over the right one; pinch to seal well. Add the *rioultes* to the simmering water and poach until they have swollen and cooked; gently push them back twice into the water as they come floating to the surface to make sure that the center is done. Transfer them to a bath of salted cold water to cool them completely.

Lightly oil a black baking sheet and bake the *rioultes* 10 to 12 minutes in a preheated 425°F oven until evenly golden. Cool on a rack. To keep fresh, freeze. Otherwise let harden and dip in fortified wine.

ÉPOGNE, KOETA, OU LEVÈCHE
Flat Bread

These three names are given to flat breads similar to fougasse or foccacia.

¼ *recipe* Pain Tout Blanc
  (page 135)
1 *tablespoon walnut oil*

Oil a black baking sheet or prepare a pizza stone. Roll the dough out in a large circle ⅓ inch thick. Let rise until twice as high. Slash openings into the dough at 1½-inch intervals over the whole surface of the bread. Bake in a preheated 425°F oven approx. 20 minutes, or more if needed, until very crisp, and spray several times with water. Cool on a rack.

One of the best ways to enjoy this *épogne* is to slice it horizontally and fill it with butter and *saucisson*, or a nice reblochon (see next chapter). Then cut into portions with a large cheese knife.

ÉPOGNE À LA CRUTZE ET À LA TOMME
Flat Bread with Butter Skimmings and Cheese

This recipe comes from the kitchen of my stepgrandmother, Marie Becker, and dates back to approximately 1900; it was passed on to me by my mother.

¼ *recipe* Pain Tout Blanc
   (page 135)
⅔–1 *cup skimmings from*
   clarified butter (not the
   whey, only the solids)
Coarsely cracked pepper
1 *cup slivers of Tomme,*
   Reblochon, or even Raclette
   cheese

On a black baking sheet or a pizza stone, roll out the dough ¼ inch thick into a large circle. Spread the butter skimmings over the dough and let proof 20 minutes. Bake in a preheated 425°F oven until the skimmings turn light golden. Sprinkle then with the pepper and the slivers of cheese. Return to the oven until the cheese has just melted but not colored. Let cool a few minutes before eating.

CRÉPONS

Crépons are fried *grissini* to be sprinkled over a nice bitter salad dressed with walnut oil and a solid red wine vinegar.

½ *recipe* Pain Bis *(page 136)*
Frying bath of sunflower oil

Prepare the dough. Let it rise normally; after deflating and rekneading it, roll it into several sheets ⅙ inch thick, as wide as the cutter of the pasta machine and 3 inches long. Using the fettucine cutter, cut into strips. Let rise 10 minutes on a floured sheet. Heat the oil bath and fry the pieces of dough until golden. Drain on paper towels and use as a garnish on top of a salad.

PAINS GRISSINS
Breadsticks

These are breadstick cousins to the *grissini* of Piemonte. I remember crunching on these as a child. They have since disappeared from the bakeries but were mentioned by Mique Grandchamp in his 1883 edition.

½ recipe Pain Tout Blanc (page 135)

Follow exactly the preceding Crépon recipe. Bake the *grissini* in a preheated 450°F oven 5 minutes. Cool on a rack.

PAIN À LA CRASSE DEDANS DE MADAME MAILLET
Madame Maillet's Bread with Butter Skimmings Inside

This is Georgette's favorite memory of her grandmother's baking. It dates back to the 1930s.

½ recipe Pain Tout Blanc
    (page 135)
½ cup skimmings from
    clarified butter (not the
    whey, only the solids)
1 tablespoon walnut oil
Bolted cornmeal

Cut the dough into two equal pieces. Roll each piece into a ball.

Flatten the first ball to be approximately ¾ inch thick and as round as possible. Spread the top of this first layer with the skimmings, leaving ½ inch of dough free all around. Now roll the second piece of dough as you did the first, and put it over the first layer so the *crasse* is sandwiched between the two layers. Pinch the edges of the two layers together. Let the bread proof on a black baking sheet, rubbed with walnut oil and sprinkled with bolted cornmeal. When doubled in bulk, bake in a preheated 425°F oven, spraying as described on page 134. Cool on a rack.

RIÂME OU PAIN BÉNIT DU 15 AOÛT
Brioche Bread for High Mass on High Holidays

This is what we called *Le Pain du Saint Sacrement* (the bread of the Holy Sacrament).

2 cups unsifted flour
2 tablespoons cornstarch
1 envelope active dry yeast
2 eggs, beaten
¼ cup milk, or more if needed
2 tablespoons liquid honey
½ teaspoon salt
5 tablespoons unsalted butter
* at room temperature*
1 teaspoon orange flower water
* or*
⅛ teaspoon saffron threads
* and*
½ teaspoon crushed aniseeds

Mix the flour and cornstarch well. Add the yeast to one third of the flour mixture and just enough warm water to make a small softish ball of dough. Fill a bowl with warm water and immerse the "sponge" in it. Let stand 5 to 6 minutes, until the sponge comes popping up to the surface of the water.

Meanwhile make a well in the remainder of the flour; add 7 of the 8 tablespoons of the 2 beaten eggs. Add the milk, honey, and salt. Mix well and gather the flour into the liquid ingredients to make a dough.

By then the sponge will have risen to the top of the water bath. Open your hand and, using it as a ladle, gather the sponge in the hollow of your palm, allowing all the water to drip back into the bowl.

Add the sponge to the dough, and with your fingertips work them together; when homogenous, using 4 tablespoons of the butter, put 1 tablespoon at each corner of the dough; soften the butter with your thumb, and knead each piece into one quarter of the dough. Gather the dough and homogenize it well, add the chosen flavoring, and work the dough well by pulling it off the counter or board until it barely sticks anymore. Let it rise in a lightly buttered bowl 2 hours at room temperature. Deflate, rehomogenize well, and refrigerate overnight.

Butter a baking sheet with the remaining butter. Shape the dough into a 14-inch-long piece 1¾ inches thick. Twist into a full circle and set it on the baking sheet. Let rise until 1½ times larger than its original volume. With scissors, cut very regular pointed openings all around the top of the bread. Let rise again another 5 to 10 minutes and brush with the reserved egg.

Bake in a preheated 425°F oven 30 to 35 minutes. Cool on a rack and serve when completely cold.

BESCOIN

Using the very same dough as for the preceding *Riâme*, but flavored with saffron and aniseeds, shape a loaf 2½ inches thick and 12 inches long. Pinch a twist at each end of the loaf to make a ball approximately 1½ inches in diameter and cut small openings with scissors the whole length of the loaf, not including the two end balls. Let rise until 1½ times larger than the original size and bake in a preheated 425°F oven approximately 25 minutes. Cool on a rack, and serve when cold.

MODERN SAVOIE BREADS

This section is dedicated to the new breads that can be found all over the Savoie in modern bakeries. Most of the breads that follow are made by the famous Boulangerie Fontaine in Annecy, where the baker makes delicious bread as crusty as the personality of his wife, who sells it.

PAIN AUX NOIX, AUX NOISETTES, OU AU LARD
Walnut, Hazelnut, or Bacon Bread

Our whole wheat flour is not milled finely enough to obtain the same texture bread, so before you use it, put it into the food processor, then in the blender, and remill it yourself in both appliances so it is perfectly fine with no traces of the bran to be seen anymore.

2 cups leaven (page 132)

2 cups bread flour

2 cups whole wheat flour,
remilled as above

1 tablespoon salt

1 tablespoon walnut or other
oil of your choice (adapt to
the nuts)

1½ cups broken walnut meats
or unpeeled hazelnuts, or

1 cup smoked bacon, cut into
¼-inch cubes and cooked
but not brittle

Prepare the bread dough as indicated on page 133. Knead the nuts of your choice or the bacon into the dough. Let it rise at least 3 hours, covered. Deflate the dough. Shape into 2 round loaves. Proof until two thirds larger than the original size, dock, and let rise another 20 minutes. Bake in a preheated 425°F oven 30 to 35 minutes. Cool on rack. Let stand overnight before serving.

PAIN AUX SIX CÉRÉALES DE MYANS
Six-grain Bread from Myans

I found this great loaf at the same Myans Boulangerie as the *riouttes*. This is my version of their bread; they use a few linseeds.

1½ teaspoons active dry yeast

3 cups leaven (page 132)

2 cups bread flour

1 cup each *coarse whole
wheat flour, rye flour, fine
cornmeal,* and *dark
buckwheat flour*

1 cup dry oat flakes

4 teaspoons salt

Warm water as needed

Mix the yeast and leaven. Let stand 30 minutes. Mix all the flours and cereal together, add the leaven/yeast mixture, and prepare the dough as described on page 133. While you knead, dip your hands into bread flour if the dough is sticky, and if you have to add flour, use bread flour. Let rise in a large oiled bowl.

Expect the dough to rise until not quite completely doubled in bulk. Deflate the dough, knead again, and shape into 3 round loaves either freehand or using *copons* or *bennons*. Bake in a preheated 400°F oven 45 to 50 minutes. Cool and let stand 24 hours before cutting. Keep leftover portions or loaves frozen.

Vegetable *épognes* are identical to Mediterranean pizzas. In these modern versions, the vegetables are not blanched as they were in the old days. The taste remains fresher.

To make the dough easier to use in such small quantities, prepare regular batches, divide them in halves or quarters, and keep them frozen raw. They defrost and start fermenting again as soon as completely defrosted, working exactly like fresh dough.

ÉPOGNE AUX HERBES
Epogne with Greens

If nettles and strawberry leaves are not accessible to you, replace them with chopped escarole leaves.

TOPPING:
2 tablespoons butter
2 onions, slivered
2 cups spinach leaves, chopped
1 cup young nettle leaves,
*   chopped*
1 cup beet and Swiss chard
*   leaves, chopped*
5 strawberry leaves, chopped
6 carrot top greens, chopped
Salt
Pepper from the mill
1 cup coarsely grated Tomme
*   or Beaufort cheese*
Grated nutmeg

DOUGH:
¼ recipe Pain Tout Blanc
*   (page 135)*

To prepare the topping, heat the butter to the noisette stage in a large sauté pan, and in it cook the onions until translucent. Add all the greens, toss well, then add salt and pepper. Cover and let the vegetables lose all their water. Remove the lid, turn the heat down, and cook gently until all the water has evaporated. Cool completely.

Roll the dough out ⅛ inch thick into a circle 9 to 10 inches in diameter. Spread the vegetables into a thin and even layer on top of the dough. Bake in a preheated 425°F oven until the edges of the dough are golden. Sprinkle then with cheese and nutmeg, and return to the oven until the cheese has just melted. Serve very warm, but not piping hot, or you will not taste the cheese properly.

ÉPOGNE AUX POIRES, AU JAMBON, ET AU BLEU

Épogne with Pears, Ham, and Blue Cheese

Do not use any old blue cheese; it is essential that the cheese not be extremely sharp but just piquant enough to offset the sweet pears. The best is the Bleu de Bresse, of which some is now made in the United States. The Bresse is close enough to the Savoie that the substitution is acceptable.

TOPPING:

2 tablespoons butter

4 Bosc pears, not too ripe, washed, cored, and thinly sliced

Salt

Pepper from the mill

3 thin slices smoked, air-dried ham or prosciutto

1 cup slivered Bleu de Bresse (approximately ½ pound)

DOUGH:

¼ recipe Pain Tout Blanc (page 135)

Heat the butter in a 10-inch skillet and in it sauté the pear slices until brown. Turn the heat off, cover, and let stand until the juices run out of the pears. Salt and pepper, and cool completely.

Remove the fat from the ham and the rind from the cheese; cut each into slivers and keep on two separate plates.

Roll the dough out into a circle ⅛ inch thick and 9 to 10 inches in diameter. Top with the ham slivers, then the pear slices with their juices. Bake in a preheated 425°F oven until the edge of the bread is golden. Pull the *épogne* out of the oven. Top it with the cheese and return it to the oven for only 1 to 2 minutes, until the cheese melts. Serve warm.

ÉPOGNE AUX CHAMPIGNONS SAUVAGES

Épogne with Wild Mushrooms

During the fall the woods in the Semnoz forests, which are almost at my back door in Annecy, are full of great mushrooms. This *épogne* was made on an early October day, when my son Neil and I went up the Semnoz for a hike and came down with a booty of multicolored fall chanterelles plus 2 pounds of chestnuts for dessert.

Before you start cooking: Although Louis Krieger in *The Mushroom Handbook* identifies *Cantharellus lutescens* as edible, a few mushroom manuals in the United

States say nothing about their edibility. Please check first with your local mycology authorities, in case the soil in your area makes a difference. I have collected and consumed these mushrooms in New Hampshire. If you have no wild mushrooms, use those lovely brown cultivated mushrooms.

TOPPING:

2 tablespoons butter

⅓ pound chanterelles, well cleaned (Cantharellus cibarius)

⅓ pound craterelles, well cleaned (Cantharellus lutescens)

⅓ pound trumpets of death, well-cleaned (Cantharellus cornucopioides)

Salt

Pepper from the mill

2 cloves garlic, finely chopped

2 tablespoons chopped parsley

1¼ cups heavy cream

DOUGH:

¼ recipe Pain Tout Blanc (page 135)

Heat the butter in a large skillet. Add all the mushrooms, salt and pepper them, and toss well. Cover to draw the juices out and add half the garlic and half the parsley. Remove the lid to let the water evaporate. Add the cream and let it thicken and coat the mushrooms, salt and pepper. Do not let the cream reduce so much that the butter separates. Cool completely.

Roll the dough into a circle 9 to 10 inches in diameter and ⅛ inch thick. Spread the creamed mushrooms over it; let stand 10 minutes, then bake 10 minutes in a preheated 425°F oven; pull the épogne out of the oven and sprinkle the remainder of the garlic and parsley over the vegetables. Bake another 2 minutes. Cool slightly before eating to have the full flavor of the mushrooms.

Cheeses

That day of August 1980, Neil Kamman and I left to climb the Dent du Cruet, a 6000-foot mountain that dominates the village of La Balme de Thuy. Peppy Neil needed exercise, so we left early on a brilliant Sunday morning. I was actually quite excited; I had not been up there since I was in my teens and wanted to introduce my young fellow to the pleasures of *lait bourru*, the warm milk fresh out of the cow. I was also looking forward to seeing his face change on reaching the summit, when he discovered Mont Blanc in its glory. All the while I was wondering whether the friends I had made when I was young were still making reblochon in the fold of the mountain just below the summit. I huffed and puffed a bit, but eventually, before we climbed out of the forest, I had found that old mountain climbing rhythm again, acquired in childhood, which for me is the equivalent of meditation.

As we walked out of the trees, there was the first summer dwelling, the Châlet du Lindion, alive as usual in the summer heat weaving from the surrounding green pastures: a loud dog, the chime of cowbells, and half a dozen piglets lying flat and exhausted under the eaves of the roof—feasting on whey is a tough job for a piglet!

But I was heartened, hoping more and more that my friends at the upper "Châlet du Lindion dessus" would also be there. I was to be disappointed—the chalet was boarded up, not a soul was around, and the roof of what had been the cheese room had collapsed. I was saddened, for this was where I had helped make the reblochon when I was only a kid, and all I had left for Neil was just a great view, which seemed to satisfy him completely.

I am not the only one to mourn the disappearance of so many of the chalets of the Alpine pastures; books by Savoie historians are filled with the same nostalgia. So that you can understand why we are so sad, let me tell you the story of the great Alpine pastures, which have lasted for centuries.

As early as 500 B.C. the Salasses, Ceutrons, Medulles, and Graioceles settled in the intra-Alpine valleys may very well have initiated what is known to this day as *l'inalpage*. To make certain that the hay in the lower valley fields had time to grow a second time during the summer, the country folk would, between May 15 and June 15, depending on the area, put all their possessions—pots, pans, cheese-making tools—onto donkeys' and men's backs and migrate to the upper Alpine meadows they had cleared at the foot of the rocks and glaciers. Most of the life of a valley moved upward for a four-month stretch, during which one worked long hard hours to transform the huge amounts of milk from many cows into cheese and butter, which in turn would be used for winter survival. These movements of men and animals came to carry the name of *remues*, an expression still used nowadays. The Ligurian pre-Celtic populations understood well that where the forest had been cleared of the natural growth of low brush called in patois *arcosses* and *vernes*, it would soon start growing again unless preventive steps were taken, so they used their cattle each year for a full four months to naturally mow and fertilize the Alpine lawn.

As a witness to the role of the pre-Celtic populations, the very name of the whole chain of the Alps comes from their word *Alp* or *Aulp*, which in the Savoie dialects takes on many variations, such as *arpe*, *arpette*, *arpettaz*, or *alpettaz*, and means precisely "a high-altitude pasture." Another word with the same meaning is *Cha* or *Chau*, which can be found in the many *montagnes de la Cha* existing all over the Savoie.

This economic system, more or less formally organized, continued until the twelfth century, when the population explosion all over Europe reached the Savoie. Additional sources of food were needed, and private owners, along with a number of religious orders, in cooperation with the Savoie peasantry, found the way to produce it.

Among the religious orders were the Cistercians of the Abbey at Tamié, founded in 1132 on the spot where it can still be seen today, and which I cite here as a typical example. The fathers at Tamié put their lay brothers to work cleaning and clearing new Alpine pastures to produce more cheese. Much food was needed indeed for their congregation itself—for their poor, who were plentiful, for the travelers, who, on their way from Geneva to the Little Saint Bernard Pass, stopped at the abbey for food and lodging. For twenty-five years the brothers cleared new pastures, using the system known as *essartage* in which the natural brush is cut, uprooted, and burned, leaving the fields free for a dense growth of grass. Maps still show many places called to this day *Les Esserts* in all parts of the Savoie, particularly in the Tarentaise.

At that time a number of villages or hamlets received the names they still carry, which are very revealing of all the changes that took place in the countryside. Novalaise, for example, is now a small city and it means "freshly cleaned ground"; so do the names Nepvaux, Novalay, Novaux, and Nouvellets, which are frequent in all regions. Alex, the village close to Annecy, means "newly cleared forest," and Sagnes means "dried-out marsh."

The devoted monks went everywhere they felt needed, cleaning soggy terrain or digging ditches for irrigation, and, when they cleared the high-altitude meadows, they did so all the way up to 7500 feet. Exploiting these newly cleared grounds all through the thirteenth century, they created a whole organization to produce cheese on a large scale and to bring it down to the lower valleys for use. A complete system of halfway houses between alp and monastery was established, which made use of the nobility's skill at keeping the highways clear of troubles so the food could safely reach the *celliers* or *granges*, as these halfway houses were called. Nowadays, everywhere the name *Les Granges* appears on a road sign, there once was a transfer station, even if it is not in existence anymore. Two of them still stand and are quite accessible, in Gilly-sur-Isère (four miles from Albertville) and in Novalaise on the D916, three miles from Autoroute A41 out of Chambéry; both are handsome buildings and well worth a little detour in your itinerary. We have the fathers to thank not only for these granges but also for some of the wonderful little chapels that dot the length and breadth of the Savoie. There are two of them at least on the west side of the Annecy lake, at Sevrier and Saint Jorioz. Also the famous sanctuaries and pilgrimage churches of Notre Dame de Briancon and Notre Dame de la Vie date back to that time.

The Cistercians truly respected manual work and did so much of it themselves that the local populations were impressed and inspired by their efforts and their genuine charity. A great cooperation between monks and peasants resulted, as well as the widespread Christianization of the whole Savoie. This fact is worth mentioning, for it is in a way quite unique. In the neighboring kingdom of France, for example, conflicts between ecclesiastics and country folk many times ended in difficult confrontations.

The Black Death, which arrived in the first third of the "calamitous fourteenth century," as historian Barbara Tuchman called it, was instrumental in interrupting this great cooperation. After the plague reached Moûtiers, now capital of the Tarentaise, the good monks sold their refuge for travelers there to a good bourgeois, and slowly, all through the 1300s all the Alpine meadows became *albergés*, meaning that they were rented or even donated by the fathers to parishes and their elected administrators. By the fifteenth century, the cheese-making work on the alp had passed entirely into the hands of the peasantry, who organized it in different ways in each area. By the seventeenth century, the system, which on a reduced basis still exists today, was established.

In the Tarentaise, Haute Tarentaise, and Haut Faucigny, the high-altitude pastures were shared as community property. The parish owned the pastures and built on them all the buildings for summer housing: stables for the cattle in case of a storm and cheese-makers' chalets (the villagers worked four months on the mountain making cheese; the proceeds of their sale were called the *fruit commun*, and the whole system of high-altitude cheese production was called the *grande montagne*).

Each year after snowmelt the cattle from one or several parishes were brought up the mountain. The *inalpage* started officially on the first Sunday after arriving on the mountain by a benediction of the herd by the parish priest and a solemn mass held outdoors, facing the high Alpine summits, which were scintillating in their cloaks of glaciers and snow. A large meal often followed, and dancing on the grass as soon as the priest had departed; the next day everyone settled down to work. In some areas there was also a cow fight to find out which cow was the undisputed Queen of the Alp (see page 155).

There are, depending on the valley, many variations in the names given to the occupations of those hired for the making of the cheese. Those I give here are used in the Tarentaise, according to historian Marius Hudry. For the hiring of the personnel, each parish elected two *procureurs*, directors of sorts whose difficult task it was to select the *montagnards* who would spend the summer working in altitude.

The *fruitier* was in charge of making the cheese; in his hands rested its quality, which depended on how fast and efficiently he handled the milk to obtain maximum purity in the final products.

The *gouverneur* helped the *fruitier* and was in charge of brining the wheels of cheese and scrubbing them daily.

The *maître berger*, also called *gros berger*, was the head shepherd, responsible for alternating the grazing of the animals, one day in a patch of grassy plants, the next in a patch of leguminous plants. The thickness and richness of the milk depended entirely on his knowledge of the terrain and the plants growing in the meadows.

There was also a *séracier*, who, from the whey resulting from the making of the regular cheese called *La Gruyère*, made a skim cheese, *le sérac*, a white compact mass of proteins prepared for the consumption of the families who owned the cows. The large wheels of cheese were not for the farm families to feed themselves, but to turn into hard cash. An occasional farm was well off enough to buy one of these wheels and make it last for months, but this was a rarity rather than the rule.

Another important person on the alp was the *pachonnier*, who planted wooden pickets into the ground to delimit enclosures in which the cows were gathered for milking. He chose the place with great care, changing it every year so the soil would remain evenly fertilized.

Down the ladder of hierarchy there was the *kola*, who transported the milk from the *pachonnées*, or corrals, to the chalets and cleaned all milk cans and cheese-making equipment; his was certainly not an unimportant position, since in cheese-making sanitary conditions are so important.

Finally, the *bokatin* took care of the goats and made goat cheese. In the Tarentaise, before the school of cheese-making was instituted in Bourg Saint Maurice, one started as a *bokatin* at the age of twelve and ended up as *gouverneur* some twenty-five years later.

Some of the wonderful wood carvings I mentioned on page 52 were made during the *inalpage*, whenever one could catch a few hours of leisure and rest; I own a pencil box hand-whittled with an Opinel in the sixties by Salomon Devouassoud, who was one of the last shepherds on the alp of the Col de Balme.

An interesting custom existed in the Terra Santa (the Val d'Isère, Tignes area), where the shepherds slept in handmade *lits à parc*, closed wooden beds with a slanted roof brought outside on the alp so that they could listen for the baby lambs or any other problem. Woe to the poor shepherd who was a sound and deep sleeper and who did not become aware of a storm fast enough. It was not rare that the storm dismantled his small shelter in just a few seconds.

The *procureurs* came up the mountain regularly to check on all operations and were in charge, come the autumn fairs, of selling the Gruyère at the best possible prices. I saw this taking place in Saint Jean de Maurienne when I was a child, and these fellows did not seem to mind gigantic arguments for the sake of a penny to the pound. The benefits were split according to each cow's production of milk on the "weighing day," which always fell at the height of the season, toward the end of July.

In the Maurienne, the Upper Maurienne, the Beaufortain, and along the chain of the Aravis, things happened completely differently. The amount of communal property was not as large as in the Tarentaise and Faucigny, so private property dominated the system of the *Montagnette*, or *Petite Montagne*; there the mother of a family, accompanied by her numerous children, would pack her utensils for the summer and go spend the good months in a medium-altitude chalet making cheeses smaller than the Gruyère types. In the Beaufortain and some of the lower-altitude mountains, both types of land use existed at different altitudes. Around Arèches and Hauteluce, women made smaller cheeses at the lower altitudes while teams of men made the Beaufort at the Cormet de Roselend. Reblochons, tommes, persillés, and Chevrotins all come from the Petite Montagne (see cheese descriptions on pages 157–168).

All in all, this sounds pretty idyllic, doesn't it? In reality, it was anything but. Sure, the young people often had a nice time up there, much to the despair of the parish priests, but the archives of both the Savoie and Haute Savoie are full of minutes describing the dissensions between private owners, parishes, and often even bishops who were trying to infringe on some parochial right. This fascinating world still exists to some extent. An alp that in the 1930s could show a herd of 800 animals will have only 200 or so nowadays, if that many. And with the cows went the wonderful concert of the bells. When you ski up at Courchevel, Méribel, Val d'Isère, Val Thorens, Les Menuires, L'Avoriaz, or the top of the Chamonix valley, you are sliding on the long expanses of grass prepared for you by the pre-Celtic populations, the monks, and the medieval inhabitants of the Savoie. Since there are fewer and fewer cows to mow the grass, the low brush has a tendency to come back, and snow does not hold well on the long dry grass, which raises the danger of avalanches. It takes teams of men to dig out the bushes; in the process they often uproot the beautiful grass, as do the snow cats. The situation has changed radically because our world has. It would have been nice to preserve the *inalpage* on its original scale at the same time as one had skiing during the winter, but there is in France (as in all the EEC countries) an excess of milk resulting from the major producers of western France. The smaller *fruitières*, which still can be seen in Aime and Bourg Saint Maurice or Beaufort, will eventually be replaced by huge dairies handling hundreds of thousands of liters of milk per day, which is still small if one considers the gigantic scale of dairy production in Normandy. The danger is not only in the decline of the Alpine pastures, but also in the slow and insidious replacement of Savoie-born people in the dairy industry by people trained in the large milk centers of the western provinces. The firm of Entremont, for example, which is located exactly one hundred yards from my front door in Annecy, distributes exclusively Breton cheeses, which are imitations of the Savoie products. Their Breton Tommes are aged in the caves of Faubourg des Balmettes and, try as one will, the milk quality is just not the same. It is hard to say that Brittany cheese is not good, but it is just not true Savoie cheese, and all these western products are slowly but surely destroying the ancestral cheese-making vocation of the Savoie.

There is also another important angle: The people forming the teams on the alp fifty years ago were all local people involved in community affairs; nowadays, the social laws that govern labor in France are not made to further a cheese industry that requires as much concentrated work as *La Grande Montagne* did. The big dairy Emmental cheese (see page 165) is becoming more and more bland; only good old Beaufort holds the fort. I keep wondering why it is not receiving the same attention and commanding the same price on the market as the Swiss Gruyère, when it is definitely better tasting than its Swiss grandfather.

If you have not been to the Savoie, hurry up and come! In most areas of the Petite Montagne, many more herds go up for the summer than do now on the *Grand Montagne*. One of the nicest areas to see our Alpine pastures is around the Aravis and the chain of the Reposoir, where between June 8 and June 15 each year, the big *clarines* (cowbells) that hang in neat rows under the eaves of the houses during the winter are taken down and buckled around the cows' necks, and every woman and child walks up the mountain. If you cannot walk that high, you need not even go on foot: Drive to the Col de la Colombière on Route D6 between Saint Jean de Sixt and Cluses or on route D909 between La Clusaz and Flumet through the Col des Aravis early in the morning to avoid the crowds, and you will experience the pleasure of the *clarines* ringing, of the fresh air, and also, if you look at your feet, of the spring gentians peering from the bright green grass with the deep blue eyes of their corollas.

Let me tell you also that if you want your own *clarine*, nothing is easier. Antique stores sell them, complete with the leather collar; most of them come from Devouassoud Clarines in Chamonix, and they make a most nostalgic decoration and good luck charm. I have one in my New Hampshire kitchen as a reminder of the Chamonix valley I so dearly love.

You will notice on the Alpine meadows two very different breeds of cow. The first, living and "working" in Haute Savoie mostly, is the Abondance cow. Its robe is reddish, very well marbled with white, or as we say in French, *pie rouge tachetée de blanc*. It was brought into the Northern Alps by the Burgundians in the fifth century. The southernmost extension of the Abondance breed is to be found in the village of Hauteluce in the Beaufortain.

This cow is a descendant of the ancient *Bos Frondosus*. A good Abondance weighs around a thousand pounds and produces an average of six gallons of milk per day.

The other breed is the lovely little Tarine, which is descended from *Bos brachyceros*, the ancient Alpine breed out of which were issued both the Berner Oberland's Schwitz and our Tarentaise, shortened to Tarine. This little beauty weighs approximately nine hundred pounds and has a russet robe, darker in the male than in the female; a natural pigmentation all around the eyelids makes its eyes look as if they have been made up with mascara. These little Tarines are of sweet disposition, and the very best mountain climbers, with hooves adapted to the steep angle of the terrain. The Tarine sleeps outside on the alp without protection and is brought in only when a very nasty storm menaces. A Tarine produces just a little bit less milk than an Abondance, and both breeds have been registered in a Herdbook since 1888 and 1894, respectively.

The best place to see the Abondance is at the Aravis, and the Tarine reigns supreme up and down the slope of the Cormet de Roselend. Savoyards love their cows and have a personal relationship with them, giving each of them a name. If you read French, a lovely book entitled *La Vallée des Cyclamens*, by Madame Dubois, describes this lady's love for her animals and her very special relationship with them. The men used to train the larger cows to fight for the title Queen of the Herd. There was only one queen per year, except in the Chamonix valley, where there were always two: One was the queen because she fought out of territorial imperative, the other because she was the largest milk producer of the herd and was thus called *la Reine du lait*, leaving to her more combative sister the title of *Reine de l'Alpage*. I saw a real cow fight in the Chamonix valley, one of those spontaneous ones between two animals, not one organized for making money. It did not sit well with the young person I was then. The blunt shock of the foreheads hitting and the twisted intermingled horns were not to my liking, which caused me promptly to be labeled *fille de monchu* ("city man's daughter") by the kids my age who had been born in Les Praz de Chamonix and who had seen this as long as they had lived.

The quality of the milk made by the cooperation of Savoie grass and

Savoie cows is simply amazing. It is so rich that it looks like light cream, all ivory and opulent as it flows into the bins and cheese cauldrons. The cream skimmed off the milk is also quite amazing. You must see and taste it to believe it. Every week I take a bus to the mountains carrying a wide-mouthed jar and go to the most accessible farm to buy a liter or two of fresh cream to make my own butter. Make sure if you visit up there and decide to go on a cream expedition to take a jar with a wide opening because what will flow in there almost languorously is already semi-solid, and by the time you let it sit in a cool place overnight it will be completely solidified and could never ever come out of a regular bottle. In the old days, the ladies used to skim the cream off the milk with a wooden spoon called a *pochon; pochons* have never been great works of art in the Savoie, as opposed to the Swiss Valais *pochons*, which can be wonderful little masterpieces of whittling. To make my own butter is absolutely no problem: Out comes the good old food processor and in goes the cream; within two minutes I have a week's supply of both fresh butter and buttermilk, which is used to make pancakes, *matafans* (see page 201), or breads. I wash the butter under cold running water and wrap it in cheesecloth. One bonus comes out of the operation: soft, smooth hands, which for a cook is an occasion for celebration.

Up to twenty years ago, all the butter in the Savoie was made by women on the valley farms or at the "Montagnette" (see page 152). It came from raw cream churned by hand or from the cream gathered from the whey after the making of the tommes. Since one was not well off financially, one sold as much butter as possible for solid cash. Young girls or women often walked miles to reach a market for their butter, stood the four hours of the market's duration, and often did not sell one ounce of it because city ladies preferred fancy butter in colorful wrappers. By contrast, nowadays, many of us in the Annecy market are looking for the farm person—woman, couple, or man—who has brought raw butter made from unpasteurized cream. That little hazelnut and ever so slightly sour taste is simply incomparable.

Today a lot of small farms have cream separators and butter churners that work at the flick of an electric switch and do the work in a jiffy. To this day, any butter that is not sold, is melted and stored for the winter in pottery jars called *toupines*. There is so much butter that sometimes the *rezuls* (fried pastries, see page 376) are cooked in clarified butter, and always the butter solids, called the *crutze* or *crasse*, are kept to make a dessert.

What follows is a description of the most important cheeses produced in the Savoie; it is by necessity only a partial list. There are many more small cheeses than I can mention here, and I have tried to list only those that can be found easily nowadays on farms, in dairies, dairy stores, and restaurants.

CHEESE MADE WITH COW'S MILK

The VACHERIN is an ancient cheese that may go as far back as the pre-Celtic populations. It is known that cheeses were made in the first millennium B.C., for cheese molds, or *faisselles*, have been found in cave dwellings and dated back to that period. Van Gennep (see Selected Bibliography) insists that vacherins were exported to Rome, but no one has ever been able to prove whether his statement is accurate or not; it is a good possibility that they were. It is known with certainty that the cheese is most ancient and that for centuries Savoie ambassadors made it part of their state gifts. It is also said that the court of Louis XIV appreciated it.

The vacherin is unfortunately slowly disappearing, but it is still made in small quantities. Madame Gagneux believes that she is the only farm woman left making it in the Abondance valley. It is possible that a few are also produced in the Dranses valley, and in the Bauges mountains around the villages of Aillon and Le Châtelard. Many more are made in the Jura mountains. You may be able to find an occasional vacherin in New York; there is plenty of it sold all over France.

Vacherin is a winter cheese, prepared from the first to the last frost; it always contains the total percentage of cream to be found in the milk. The rennet is added to the milk still lukewarm from the cow, then heated just enough to allow the rennet to complete the clabbering. When the clabbering is finished, the curd is cut to allow the whey to escape fully; the cutting remains minimal and there is no stirring of the clabber at all. The curd is packed into wooden molds made of very thin spruce wood, which communicates to the cheese its pleasant aftertaste.

The best vacherins come just after Christmas. You will need at least four to six persons at your table to "finish" a good vacherin at one sitting. Here is the way to eat it, which is not that well known. Remove the lid of the wooden container, place the cheese in its box in a slow oven until the paste has mellowed or semi-melted. Lift the upper crust with a long, sharp knife blade; the semi-warm cheese is ready to be spooned over slices of plain, preferably not-too-white and not-too-fresh bread. If you can find a Savoie Crépy or even a Mondeuse, that would be splendid. As substitutes for these wines in the United States, use a Colombard or a light Zinfandel; the Swiss Dézaley is perfect.

As you enter the Thônes valley, just a few miles above the Col de Bluffy, you will see a large road sign on the right-hand side of Route D909 which reads:

YOU ARE ENTERING THE COUNTRY OF REBLOCHON

REBLOCHON comes to us from the recesses of the thirteenth century and from Alpine pastures cleared by the monks in the valleys of Thônes and Le Grand Bornand high on the slopes of the Reposoir and the Aravis mountains. These monks and a few private owners granted the local population the right to make cheese provided they pay a tax known as the *auciège*. The value of the *auciège* was measured in days of milk production. As early as the thirteenth century, so as to minimize the value of the *auciège*, tenant farmers would not draw all the milk from their cows and declare smaller quantities than what was really produced. Then they proceeded to a second milking and with it made a cheese that was not to be talked about or seen until all of a sudden its name, Reblochon, appeared in a notarized act of the sixteenth century. The name of the cheese contains its whole history. In patois, *rablassa* or *reblacha* means "stealing." Since the tenant farmers were stealing milk, in essence, the cheese made with that fraudulent milk was called reblochon. Another possibility is that the name came from another word, *blossi*, which in patois means "milking." If one adds the prefix *re* to that root to indicate repetition, one obtains *reblossi* or *reblochi*, hence *reblochon*. The two possibilities are equally plausible.

Originally the reblochon was made entirely during the *inalpage*, but during the seventeenth century the *auciège* was suppressed, the cheese started to be made year-round, and its popularity began. Like the vacherin, it made its way to Paris during the reign of Louis XIV through a woman named Angelloz, who was in the service of Madame de Conti. The original method of preparing reblochon, only with milk of the second milking, disappeared during the late 1880s, so that, as good as our reblochon may be nowadays, we can only dream of how deliciously rich it must have been then. The reason for the change was nothing more than cost. The demand for the cheese was growing, thanks to some pioneers who went on foot to markets peddling their *petites tommes grasses* (little fat cheeses), as they called them sometimes, as far as Lyon and Geneva. By 1889, reblochon was sold in all major French cities. In 1958 a law signed by General De Gaulle extended the *appellation contrôlée* to cheeses produced in the Chablais, the Arly valley, Albertville, and two villages of the Upper Maurienne. Having tried reblochons from all these areas, I can vouch for the fact that the best tasting come from its original area of creation.

Reblochon has always been made by women. The best way to purchase a reblochon is to stop at a farm. Many advertise on simple little wooden boards just at the entrance of the chalet. Do not hesitate to go knock on the door, and if you do not speak French you have only one word to say: reblochon; everyone will know why you came. I have my favorite farm in every township. My very favorite of all is that of Madame Bastard Rosset from Le Bouchet above Le Grand Bornand; she is the mother of seven children and to fifty cows; also the young peppy Madame Deloche, who makes her cheeses one mile from the center of Thônes, in the hamlet called Le Paradis. A paradise it is, indeed, if one does not mind the work. It is not unusual for these young women to get up as early as four in the morning to make the morning cheese, go to work in an office or factory during the day, and come home quickly to make the evening cheese.

I helped make the reblochon when I was very young. The rennet now comes from a manufacturer, but then it was homemade from a certain part of a calf's stomach—and how it smelled! The rennet is added to the milk just out of the cow and heated to bring on curdling; no cooking occurs, just plain reheating to body temperature. As soon as the curd is set, it is stirred to cut it as finely as possible. During stirring the molds are all lined up on a slanted wooden table; over them a large piece of linen is stretched and forced into every mold. The curd is hand-ladled into the molds, and as soon as most of the whey has dripped out, a heavy weight is put on each cheese for approximately twelve hours. The day-old cheese is then removed from the molds and immersed in brine. The length of salting varies with the taste of the cheese-maker, but it is never more than a few hours. The drying and aging starts as soon as the cheeses come out of the brine. They are washed and turned daily, and the wooden planks on which they sit are also turned each day. You will recognize farm-made reblochon by a little green label made of natural casein, not paper, that is still visible when you purchase it, partly dissolved into the crust (see picture section). If there is no green label, it is not a farm cheese but that of a small *fruitière* or even a large cooperative where reblochons are made with a mixture of milks of various qualities. It is better to eat farm cheese, but one can cook with the dairy cheeses; the *petit reblochon* that appears on the shelves of American supermarkets is always pasteurized. It is no competition for the real unpasteurized thing but in cooking it does well.

If you go to market in any of the towns or cities in the area of production, you may see a nice lady or two standing with a box of fresh white reblochons in their molds; they are unsalted and are known as *Tommes blanches*; they are enjoyed with boiled potatoes and butter. Believe it or not, I was fed tons of that when I was a kid; the *tomme blanche* is supposed to give women a wonderful complexion.

TOMME, TOMA, or TOME in patois, is the generic name given in the Savoie to all soft paste cheese not of the Gruyère type. The word is very ancient. In the first century A.D., when Lyon's Greek population was at its largest, the diet consisted of cheese called toma and tripe; they have both remained a specialty of the big city. Tomme is the ancestral protein food for the people of the Savoie for whom *un bocon d'pan et d'toma* represents a royal meal. Reblochon also carries the name of *tomme grasse*.

I often wondered how two cheeses made essentially with the same milk could be so different until I stayed at a farm for several days and followed closely the making of the cheeses. To make the tomme, both the morning and the evening milks are mixed and poured into containers called *seilles*. The cream, of course, comes to the top in one thick smooth beautiful layer and is lifted with a *pochon*. This allows the cheese-maker to prepare cheeses with more or less butterfat content. The best tomme is full cream with 45 percent butterfat; the least delicious, but one beating by all means the dietetic cheeses available in American markets, has only 10 percent butterfat. The texture of the more skimmed cheese is, of course, not as silky smooth, but the nutty taste is unsurpassable.

To make tomme one heats the milk to 95°F to allow the rennet to do its clabbering work. Once the curd is well set it is stirred, but not as thoroughly as for the reblochon, which accounts for the coarser texture of yet unripe tommes; as the tomme ripens the texture smoothes out, even in skimmed cheeses. Drained into a mold called a *faitire* that has been lined with fine linen, the whey is squeezed out and the linen removed two hours later. Each tomme is returned to its mold and put under weight until the evening milking, at which point it will be unmolded and hand-salted on its top and bottom but not on its sides. For ten days the cheese will be dried and turned daily, then ripening starts and lasts an average of two months, three for the very best cheeses, with turning every week.

Most tommes served in restaurants, even the best, are never as ripe as they should be; this is why I would recommend that you always purchase a tomme from a farm or a farmer at the market. A good tomme as it ripens develops a deep gray mold and stains of underlying orange mold; the more of those stains there are on the cheese, the riper it is and the better it will taste. There is nothing more disastrous than a semi-ripe tomme. Read the labels well when you purchase tomme, because tommes are made all over France, especially in Brittany, and neither their taste nor their texture is the same at all. Do not purchase tommes or reblochons in supermarkets; the farmers can use all the help they can get, and they make and sell the very best products.

There is a wide variety of weights and sizes and also a great variety of names in the tomme world. The term *Boudane*, in patois *Beudanna*, refers to large cheeses of six to nine pounds with a fat content of 30 percent that are made at the end of the summer season for family consumption during the winter months. Together with those, one still sometimes makes some *tome double pe cacon* (double tommes for special events) with a heavy butterfat content, which are kept for christenings and weddings. Fennel tomme, or *Tomme au fenouil*, is still made to order for the customers of some farmers in the Annecy market. The fennel is added to the warm milk before adding the rennet; this is called *tomme de chnu* in the Thônes valley. If you are not afraid of powerful good taste in cheeses with slight piquancy, ask any of the farm people who sell tomme at the entrance of the Pont Morens in the Annecy market to sell you some; they may very well have it, for they made it and aged it for me.

I must clear up something confusing. For a few years, we saw in the United States a type of creamy cheese surrounded by grape seeds; it was a major disaster in taste and was a cheap copy of the famous *tomme au raisin* made in vineyard areas. Already aged tommes are layered into barrels filled with grape rapes; the barrel is closed and the fermentation starts again so that the grape seeds adhere to the cheese crust and a powerful taste develops good enough to carry a strong and wonderfully aged red wine. Look for it in markets around the vineyards, such as Saint Pierre d'Albigny, Myans, and even Chambéry.

Finally, I would like to mention a very special cheese that can be found in the Giffre valley in the small town of Sixt. The farmers there age their tommes for two years, which results in a nice hard-grating cheese, very much in the vein of a great stravecchione Parmigiano-Reggiano. The last time I had some, I went begging for it on a farm, where I was given some as a special favor and treated to boot to a glass of wine, because the *tomme n'était point à vendre*, which means, "one did not sell it, one kept it for one's own use."

The only cheeses to be called *fromages* in the Savoie are the large wheels of the Gruyère type; all others fall into the Tomme category. All the large Gruyère types are made by the same method, definitely brought into the Savoie by immigrating Swiss families either from the Valais or from the Swiss Plateau, and by some shepherds from the Val d'Aosta in Italy. The method is as follows for all cheeses, with tiny variations, of course, for each one of them:

The milk is clabbered with rennet and heated, the temperature varying with the type of cheese. The paste obtained is known as *demi-cuite*, or half cooked. Beaufort and Emmental are heated more than Abondance. The curd is stirred steadily with a huge rake during the heating, and the stirring continues after the heat has been cut off. A huge piece of linen is stretched under the curd by two men, who lift, twist, and drop it into large wooden or metal molds; the technique takes on little variations with each type of cheese. The wheels are pressed, a stay in brine follows for several days, then drying and maturing begin.

The following cheeses are prepared according to this general method:

ABONDANCE is made in the valley of the same name, which does not mean what it seems to say. It comes from the two Celtic words *Habodan* and *Ty*, the first meaning "summer dwelling" and the second "house." Habodanty became Habundantia in Latin and Abondance in French, and its name is most fitting, since the Abondance valley was the summer cheese-making place for people of the lower Dranse valley around Thonon. The large wheels of Abondance cheese were made after the arrival at the Abbey of Abondance of busy Cistercian Fathers in 1607. Faithful to their tradition of well-kept Alpine meadows, quality animals, and quality milk, they spruced up the neglected domains of the abbey and employed throughout the seventeenth and eighteenth centuries a number of Swiss families well versed in the techniques of Gruyère-making.

The moderately heated curd of Abondance is divided into *meules*, or wheels, weighing an average of twenty-five pounds, which are pressed extremely heavily to obtain the smoothest melting cheese ever, with no holes in the paste at all, because of the lower temperature at which it is matured. It is the base for the *Berthoud* recipe that you will find on page 172. If you would like to see Abondance made, go to Vacheresse, a tiny village fourteen miles from Thonon and three or four miles from Abondance. There a small, very neat little *fruitière*, Laiterie Coopérative de Vacheresse, is open from nine to noon every day but makes the large Abondance only two days a week; the other days they prepare reblochon. Have a French-speaking person call for you ahead of time to know what is "brewing" on the day you would like to visit. The number is in the telephone book.

You must take a trip to peaceful Beaufort and to the two upper villages of Arèches and Hauteluce, but first and foremost you must drive above Beaufort to the Cormet de Roselend. A large artificial lake is now there; the road is open from late June through September, or until enough snow falls in the autumn to block it again for the remainder of the winter. It usually opens at the height of the Alpine flowering season. Several times I have had the great joy of leading groups of students through this enchanted world of flowers. By now you have discovered that the Alps send me into lyrical dithyrambs, but the Cormet is a sight of rare beauty on a late spring day when the sky is deep blue, the melting snow rushes down into quick white waters from high cliffs, and flowers of all colors blossom in the bright green background of the hardy grass. These flowers are what make the cheese, together with the knowledge of the cheese-makers.

Traveling through the Beaufortain, the intra-Alpine valleys of the Tarentaise, around the Col de la Madeleine in Lower Maurienne, around Mont Cenis and Praz sur Arly, you are in the area producing BEAUFORT cheese. Here, a loaf of bread and a wedge of the local cheese eaten sitting on the grass listening to the cowbells will change your notion of what makes a person happy for life.

Technically, the Beaufort is made like any of the Gruyère family members. It comes in two versions: the Beaufort d'Alpage, made during the summer months in altitude *fruitières* between 3000 and 8000 feet and containing a lot of good flower essences; and the Beaufort Laitier, made in small town *fruitières* during the winter months when the cows are down at lower altitude and fed on hay. The most interesting *fruitière* to visit is that at Beaufort, but those at Aime and Bourg Saint Maurice are also interesting. The advantage of the Beaufort *fruitière* is that it is set up to teach the visitor, with large explanatory boards and a balcony from which one can observe the making of the cheese; also, it sells the summer cheese year-round, since it keeps a supply from year to year to please its customers. The summer cheese is about 5 percent fatter than the winter one and carries the label *Beaufort Haute Montagne 50% de matières grasses* ("high-altitude Beaufort 50% butterfat"), by law; besides at the Beaufort *fruitière* and some exquisite cheese stores in larger cities, it is not available later than the May of each year following its summer of production. The high-altitude summer cheese is still packed in old wooden molds and pressed heavily. The wheels weigh from fifty to eighty-five pounds, and since aging takes place at cool temperature, there is not a single hole in the paste;

but the paste can show horizontal breaks called *lainures*, which are perfectly normal if they are not too wide. The Beaufort is immediately recognizable by its concave sides due to the way it is pressed.

It is obvious that the name EMMENTAL de Savoie is borrowed directly from the Swiss Emmenthal originally produced in the valley of the Emme in the canton of Bern. As much as I am ready to proclaim Beaufort the very best of all Gruyères in the world, I have to admit that I much prefer the Swiss Emmenthal to its Savoyard cousin. Still, the large wheels, which can weigh as much as two hundred pounds, yield a cheese that is pleasant to savor and makes a good fondue.

I have had the pleasure of spending a whole day at the cooperative dairy of Frangy where Emmental is made every day, brined, and aged, and it was a treat. Do not hesitate to visit any of the small *fruitières* that dot the Avant Pays of the Genevois. There are *fruitières* in Annecy-le-Vieux, Villaz, and Cusy where the cheese-making can be observed. Emmental is made of a mixture of collected milks, the quality of which changes every day, as do the quality of the rennet, the temperature, and the weather. Whereas in small *fruitières* the cheeses are still molded in wood forms, in the large modern ones you will see metal molds receive the curd and huge hydraulic presses squeeze the whey out of the *meules* in great big waterfalls. After being defatted, the whey is sent directly to the piggery usually attached to the *fruitière*—a fact of which you would want to be aware if you were to purchase a small dwelling in a Savoie village.

The maturing of the Emmental is done first in cool cellars, then finally in warmer ones where carbon dioxide develops in the paste and stretches those big holes you see in the finished cheese; ideally the holes should never be larger than a walnut. As you visit the maturing rooms a lovely warmth surrounds you, and you can almost hear and feel the cheese stretch. The huge wheels develop convex bellies on both sides; eventually a cheese wheel may burst open, and this will be used to prepare a delicious *crème de Gruyère* which is usually sold in foil-wrapped triangular portions.

SMALLER CHEESE MADE OF VARIOUS MILKS

The Trappist monks at the Abbey of TAMIÉ, still active to this day, produce a larger version of the reblochon. Some people say it tastes somewhat fruitier than the original. I say it depends on who made the reblochon. In their competition for the best possible taste, sometimes the monks beat the women, sometimes the women beat the monks. Tamié can replace reblochon, and vice versa, in any cooked dish. Should you be unable to find either reblochon or tamié in the United States, I know that you can find BEAUMONT. It is made in and around Saint Julien in the Genevois, right by the Swiss border. Some Beaumonts are still made on farms; those made by the Maison Girod since the last years of the nineteenth century are exported worldwide and are delicious.

Besides cows the Savoie sports quite a population of goats. Those of Thônes and Marthod seem to be the ancestral animals for the whole Savoie. These dear little Alpine goats are most impish. All through the summer they run the mountain to their heart's content, up and down incessantly, keeping people busy trying to get them back to the chalet by nighttime. If you walk up a mountain, do leave your cigarettes at home or the goats will follow you slavishly: They love the smell and taste of tobbaco. My first encounter with goats was in Thuy, on a country lane; it was, should I say, uneasy. I found on the ground what my city kid's eyes thought to be *des bonbons noirs*, those little round black licorice candies dear to all French seven-year-olds. Well, guess what? . . . Yes, you guessed; I am still laughing about it fifty years later.

Although some of the cheeses made with goat's milk have completely disappeared, quite a few survive. Ten families in Thônes still make the PER-SILLÉS; three or four of them still using the old-fashioned techniques. If made with 100 percent cow's milk, the cheese paste comes out a ripening yellow, whereas if made with goat's milk it comes out solidly white. Should one use half-and-half, the cheese paste will be marbled, since the two milks obstinately refuse to mix. Each day some of the curd of an older cheese, preserved in whey, is added in very fine crumbs to the newly clabbered milk. The mixture of the two curds gives the aged cheese a vaguely blue marbling. Originally around the Aravis, these little cheeses were rolled in a paper-thin sheet of spruce wood to prevent the formation of a hard crust called *casquette*. Any persillé should by law be made with 100 percent goat's milk, and the use of bread crumbs soaked in milk to bring on the bluish mold is fraudulent and considered heresy. At this writing, persillés sell for the small fortune of $10 a pound compared to the $6 asked for reblochon. Persillé is still made in the Aravis, in the Tarentaise at La Rozière de Valezan and Sainte Foy en Tarentaise, and around Mont Cenis in the Maurienne. There is in Termignon in the Upper Maurienne an elusive persillé known as the Bleu de Termignon as difficult to produce as it is to find. The cold damages the cheese intensely, which contributes to its rarity, and the Piemontese, who are extremely fond of it, razzia the whole new crop year after year come September in one little swoop over the mountains. I heard for years about the Orelle (Maurienne) cheese, which develops "yellow flowers" (read molds), without ever finding it, although I know it is still made. The same is true of the Grattairons, still made in the valley of the Bellevilles and the Giffre valley around Sixt.

CHEVROTINS are very modern little goat milk tommes made in the Aravis, looking every bit like a small reblochon, as opposed to the persillé, which looks like a small tomme in its thick coat of gray mold. In the vicinity of 200,000 chevrotins are made every year, although the poor little cheese is still fighting the vagaries of the successive French governments to obtain its *appellation d'origine contrôlée*. There are all kinds of new larger *tommes de chèvre* coming on the market nowadays, but they are not farm-made. Patricia Burgat of Serraval has introduced the little goat cheese Picodon, which originated in the Dauphiné, into the Savoie. Her experiment seems to be very successful; she makes the cheese from February through September and sells a great deal of it on the Annecy market; it is delicious and comes salt-free or salted, fresh or matured.

When I spent the winter in Savoie, I was fed more *caillé* and *sérac* than I ever wished to eat, though as I become older I like both better and better. The *sérac*, or *Céré* in patois, is made by recooking the whey of larger cheese production after the cream has been removed; it is a solid block of protein and extremely nutritious. It is not made very much nowadays and commands a remarkable price for that reason. Made on the farm, it can be delicious; once it is packed and pressed, it is much less attractive, which proves that I was not born in the Savoie; true Savoyards would never say anything so heretical.

I remember very well seeing Madame Déléan prepare it. She heated the whey rather high and the casein came floating to the surface of the liquid; with a slotted spoon she picked up the *fleurettes*, which were served to us with cream and sugar. Any leftovers were packed into a mold and dried. *Sérac* remains a favorite with the people of my generation; if you are curious, you can purchase some at the Fromagerie Gay, rue Carnot in Annecy. The *caillé*, or clabbered milk, you can prepare yourself if you have access to unpasteurized milk (see below).

All cheeses are prepared in the most beautiful cauldrons made of pure copper and kept shiny and pink by diligent hands. The size of a cauldron varies with the type of cheese made in it; the shape must be very ancient and probably Celtic in style, for I have seen in an Austrian museum an authentic Celtic cauldron resembling uncannily the cauldrons used to make cheese in the Savoie and Switzerland nowadays. In the *Petite Montagne* areas, a cauldron is passed from woman to woman in each family.

Here is a small list of very old-fashioned dishes coming straight from the farm or the bourgeois kitchens of the nineteenth century.

All Recipes in this section yield 6 servings.

LAIT CAILLÉ POUR FROMAGE BLANC FRAIS
Clabbered Milk for Fresh White Cheese

This is not the same as cottage cheese. If you prefer making the cheese with pasteurized milk, refer to the recipe given by Marion Cunningham in her delightful *Breakfast Book*. The recipe that follows is successful only if you use unpasteurized milk; no fresh cheese is ever made with pasteurized milk on a Savoie farm, so whatever cheese you would prepare with pasteurized milk would never correspond either in taste or texture to the real thing. If you have a source of unpasteurized milk, as a lot of people do, please observe carefully the following health notes:

Your milk must come from a certified source and be of first quality. Check the original packaging or, if you live in the country, *know* the farm and the farmers where you acquire it. Their cows should be healthy and tested. People with serious intestinal conditions must consult their doctor before eating cheese made with unpasteurized milk.

2 quarts raw, certified milk

Pour the milk into a large stainless steel bowl. Stretch a layer of fine cheesecloth over the milk to keep away insects. The cream will come to the top of the milk within 3 hours. Remove it with the side of a large spoon; refrigerate it to keep it sweet because in many areas of the United States raw cream turns bitter due to wild yeasts if left to stand unrefrigerated. The amount of cream gathered will depend on the richness of the milk; it will be larger in Wisconsin, Maine, Vermont, and Pennsylvania than in other states since their milk is so rich.

There will remain a thin layer of cream on the surface of the milk. Leave it there and let the milk clabber naturally, without adding any rennet. Obviously, it will work faster if the ambient temperature is high. The time for complete clabbering varies from 24 to 48 hours, depending on the climate. When the milk is solidly clabbered, remove all traces of the skin of dehydrated cream that has formed on its surface; you will lose a few tablespoons of the curd, but it does not matter. Cut through the curd with a large knife in a crisscross pattern to start releasing the whey. Ladled into bowls, at this stage the clabber is called *caillé* and eaten with sugar or honey.

If you prefer dripped cheese, rinse the cheesecloth in cold water, twist it dry, and stretch it into a strainer or a mold with holes (called *faisselles* in French; strawberry dishes work very well). If you care to keep the whey for making bread or pancakes, place the *faisselle* over a bowl to gather it. Fold the cheesecloth over the curd and let it drip as much as you like. You can retain a large percent of whey in the cheese or drip it completely dry to make a cake looking like farmer's cheese.

I prefer to drip approximately half the whey and beat the moist cheese with an electric beater to lighten and smooth it. I eat it completely skimmed to lose weight. To make cheesecake or serve to children (my children were given a lot of it while growing up), I drip the cheese completely and whip the reserved cream or any other fresh cream back into the cheese, thus obtaining the famous French *fromage à la crème*. In Savoie the dripped cheese is often served with a country-style compote (see page 377). Keep any leftovers refrigerated. The completely dripped cheese will keep a long time if it is refrigerated.

If eventually you leave the cheese a long time in the refrigerator, you will see it develop a fuzz and shrink as the bacteria that deposit on its surface soak up its moisture. After quite a long time you will obtain a matured cheese.

COMPOUTA OR TOMME FORTE
Strong Marinated Cheese

Be careful! This is only for people who love very strong cheese. This technique for refermentation is not unique to the Savoie; all other French provinces have a version of it.

3 cups grated Savoie Beaufort
   or Swiss Gruyère cheese
6 ounces dry, natural,
   unflavored goat cheese, finely
   grated
1 cup crème fraîche
¼ cup dry white wine
1 ounce brandy or marc
Salt
Coarsely cracked pepper from
   the mill

Mix well both types of grated cheese. Add the cream, white wine, and brandy or marc, salt and pepper to your taste. Put the cheese into a wide-mouthed jar with a lid. Punch several holes into the lid and let the jar stand in the refrigerator (or in cold climates in a very chilly cellar) until the whey comes floating to the top. It will take several weeks and there should be at least ¼ inch of whey covering the cheese; drain it completely. Mix the cheese again. Spread over garlic bread or spoon over plain polenta (see page 250). A powerful red wine is needed to stand up to the flavor of the cheese.

LA FONDUE DES BOURGEOIS
A Bourgeois-style Fondue

Every tourist restaurant in the Savoie will offer a fondue Savoyarde, an item that entered the Savoie culinary repertoire only very recently and is not Savoyard but Swiss. The fondue made in Savoie before the 1900s was more like this adaptation of a Mique Grandchamp recipe, which is very close to the Valdostana version. Mique Grandchamp even recommends a garnish of white truffles or mushrooms.

2 cups rich milk
1 pound Beaufort or Gruyère cheese, slivered
3 tablespoons butter
1 clove garlic, finely chopped
1 tablespoon flour
½ cup scalding light cream
3 egg yolks
1 pound button mushrooms cooked in butter and hot

Soak the cheese in the milk 1 hour.

Heat the butter in a *cocotte* or enameled cast-iron pan. Add the garlic and toss into the butter without browning. Add the flour and cook 3 to 4 minutes. Off the heat, whisk in the cream. Return to the heat, bring to a boil, and turn the heat off. Drain the cheese-soaking milk and whisk it into the already thickened cream. Add the cheese, and bring slowly to the melting point, stirring well with a wooden spoon. Avoid hard boiling. Add the egg yolks, mixing them first into some of the hot fondue, then whisking the mixture back into the pot.

Divide the mushrooms equally into 6 individual ovenproof dishes and spoon the melted cheese over the mushrooms. The best bread would be a loaf of *Gros Pain* (page 136). Serve with a Crépy, a Chignin, or a Dézaley. In the United States, a Colombard or a Sauvignon Blanc would be fine.

BERTHOUD

A Local Chablais Fondue

It has proved difficult to find the origin of the name. After years of searching, I opened the telephone book at the listing Abondance and found whole families of Berthouds in town. Since the original recipe is made with Abondance cheese, it must have come from one of these families; however, Dr. Ramain calls the dish a *berre-tout*, which would suggest that one should *berre* or *boire tout*, which means "polish off" the whole dish. The best version I ever had was at the Hôtel Albert ler in Chamonix; I was told that in the countryside this dish is prepared with old maderized white wine. You will need individual square oven-proof dishes such as Corning. This is an appetizer for a winter dinner.

2 large cloves garlic
1 pound finely sliced
   Abondance, Italian Fontina,
   or Swiss Appenzeller, or
   Vacherin cheese
1 cup Rainwater Madeira
Pepper from the mill
Sliced Pain Bis *(page 136)*

Crush the garlic cloves and with them rub 6 small oven proof dishes thoroughly. Discard the garlic pieces. Divide the cheese slices into the 6 dishes and sprinkle an equal amount of the Madeira over the cheese. Sprinkle lightly with coarsely cracked pepper. Melt without mixing in a preheated 375°F oven; when melted, serve promptly with the dark bread and a wine such as a Crépy or Dézaley, or in the United States, a Colombard or Sauvignon Blanc.

TARTE DE PACL'ONS AU BEAUFORT

Baked Dumplings with Beaufort Cream

Pacl'ons were dumplings very often so heavy that they were hard and chewy; they were rolled into a massive amount of melted butter. I have lightened the recipe considerably and used cream, which is a license, since cream would have been kept for butter-making on the farm. This dish is closer to a dish of bourgeois gnocchi than it is to true *pacl'ons*.

1 cup cold milk
5 tablespoons butter

Put the cold milk, 4 tablespoons of the butter diced, ½ teaspoon of salt, and the celery salt or Maggi

Salt as needed

⅓ teaspoon celery seed or Maggi seasoning

1 cup unsifted all-purpose flour

1 clove garlic, mashed

2 tablespoons chopped parsley

3 eggs, beaten

⅔ cup chopped walnuts

1½ cups scalding heavy cream

6 ounces diced Beaufort or Gruyère cheese

2 ounces grated Beaufort or Gruyère cheese

Coarsely cracked pepper from the mill

seasoning in a 2-quart saucepan. Bring to a boil and remove from the heat; add all the flour at once, return to the heat, and stir until a uniform ball forms. Add garlic, parsley, and the eggs, one at a time.

Bring a large pot of water to a boil, add salt to taste, then turn down the heat to a simmer; stuff the *pac'lons* dough into a pastry bag fitted with a plain nozzle with a ⅓-inch opening. Push ⅓-inch-long pieces of batter out of the bag, and with the back of a parer, cut them into the simmering water. They will fall to the bottom of the pot and then come floating to the top.

Butter a 9-inch porcelain pie plate with the remaining tablespoon of butter, add the chopped walnuts, and bake in a preheated 400°F over 5 minutes. Remove the dish from the oven, lift the *pacl'ons* out of the water with a slotted spoon, and toss them into the walnuts. Top with the scalding cream and the diced cheese and toss together. Bake 20 minutes, or until the *pacl'ons* have blown to twice their size. Top with the grated cheese and return to the oven until the cheese becomes golden. The *pacl'ons* can be cut into wedges like a tart. Season with coarsely cracked pepper. Serve as a winter main course with a salad.

You will need a sharpish little white wine to cut through the opulence of all that wonderful cheese; in Savoie it would be an Apremont, in the United States use a French Aligoté.

The dishes that follow have been popular since the beginning of this century, but especially so since the 1930s. You can see how the classic techniques of the French cuisine are completely assimilated into the recipes.

LA RACLETTE À LA MADELEINE
Raclette in a Baking Dish

The raclette is from the Valais, not from the Savoie, but has become extremely popular in modern Savoie, with many restaurants serving a more or less plentiful one. The best I know of in the two Savoie departments is at the interesting little Restaurant La Resse in Thônes; part of the dining room is built over a visible underground waterfall that, as late as the fifties, activated a little local woodcutting plant, or *resse*. Both the surroundings and the raclette are most enjoyable. This version is that of a modern cook, yours truly, who has no patience for little pans of cheese all over the place and uses market ingredients. To replace the tiny potatoes called *coeurs de pigeons* sold in Savoie markets, use any good diced potatoes; Patricia Burgat's goat cheese can easily be replaced by any one of our great goat cheeses made anywhere from Maine to California, passing through Texas and Vermont.

1½ pounds potatoes peeled, diced into ½-inch cubes or turned into olives
½ cup clarified butter
⅔ cup heavy cream
Salt
Coarsely cracked pepper from the mill
2 ounces fresh goat cheese, diced
2 tablespoons chopped chives
1 pound Raclette cheese, sliced
Strong mustard
A dish of French cornichons and pickled baby onions

Dry the potatoes in a tea towel and fry them in clarified butter until light golden and well done at the center. Drain off all the cooking butter (keep it, it can be reused). Put the potatoes in a 1½-quart baking dish.

Heat the cream, season it, and as you remove it from the heat, whisk in the goat cheese and chives; pour over the potatoes. Immediately top with the raclette slices and melt without browning in a preheated 325°F oven. Do not overcook. Serve for a winter lunch or dinner with a nice tart salad, mustard (I use the red-topped Moutarde de Pompiers), and both pickles. For wine, a nice and sharpish Entremont or Abymes or a French Aligoté or even small red Côtes du Rhone.

CHAUSSON OU TOURTE AU REBLOCHON
Reblochon Turnover or Pie

Presented as a turnover, this is a specialty of the Boulangerie Rotelli, Faubourg des Balmettes in Annecy. Many restaurants in the areas where reblochon is made present it as a tourte. The best replacement for reblochon is the Canadian OKA cheese.

1 pound puff pastry (see page 372)

1 full-size Reblochon (approximately 1 pound) or 1 pound OKA or Raclette cheese

One ¼-inch-thick slice smoked ham or baked Smithfield ham

Coarsely cracked pepper from the mill

1 egg, beaten to liquid

Be sure that the puff pastry is extremely cold. Remove the crust of the cheese, cut it into thick slices and keep it cold; dice the ham into ¼-inch cubes.

Cut the pastry into 2 equal parts. Roll out the first into a sheet ⅛ inch thick. Place the pastry on an unbendable black baking sheet. Cut a circle 9 inches in diameter. Put the slices of cheese at the center of the pastry, leaving 1 inch of pastry clear all around; return to the refrigerator.

Roll the second piece of pastry ⅛ inch thick and cut it into a circle roughly 9½ to 10 inches in diameter. Brush the edge of the bottom circle with the beaten egg. Wrap the second circle of pastry around the rolling pin, bring it over the first, and gently arrange the edges all around so they coincide as closely as possible; seal well, using the tines of a fork. With the tip of a knife, *chiqueter* the edge by cutting small indentations in it ⅙ inch deep at ½-inch intervals. Trace a crisscross pattern on the edge of the tourte with the fork and brush all over with the beaten egg. Refrigerate 30 to 45 minutes, then bake in a preheated 425°F oven approximately 20 to 25 minutes, or until deep golden. Let cool to lukewarm before serving.

To prepare turnovers, divide the cheese in half. Roll two circles, put one cheese in each, fold the pastry over the cheese, seal and crimp the edges, brush with egg, and bake as above.

TARTE AUX FROMAGES
Cheese Tart

This tart appears all over the Germanic countries from Alsace to the south-ernmost part of Switzerland, including some parts of Austria, under various names such as Quiche, Weihe or Waehe, or Salée in the Vaud countryside. It is sold all over in pastry shops, bakeries, and in the *traiteurs-charcutiers* (delicatessens) of the small Savoie towns and cities, where it definitely is an import. It is so delicious that it is addictive, and one wedge insidiously follows the other onto one's plate. The following is a personal version. You can use any cheese you like; I recommend here the three Savoie cheeses, but using any melting cheese from Wisconsin, Switzerland, or any other European country will do just as well for texture, with varied final tastes.

PASTRY:
1 cup sifted all-purpose flour
¼ cup coarsely chopped
  walnuts
5 tablespoons cold butter
½ teaspoon salt
1 egg

FILLING:
5 ounces each coarsely grated
  Beaufort, Emmental, and
  Abondance cheeses, or other
  cheeses of your choice
1 teaspoon potato starch
½ teaspoon Maggi seasoning
Cracked pepper from the mill
Grated nutmeg to taste
2 cups heavy cream
3 jumbo eggs
Salt

Put the flour, salt, and walnuts in the food processor and process until homogenous. Add very cold butter and process until the butter is in pea-size lumps; beat the egg and gradually add it to the processor until a lump forms. You may not need the whole egg. Flatten into a cake 1 inch thick and refrigerate wrapped in plastic 30 minutes.

Mix the grated cheeses in a bowl, and combine with the potato starch and all seasonings. Beat the cream and eggs together with salt and pepper. Set aside.

Roll the pastry out to a thickness of ⅛ inch and fit it into a 9-inch lightly buttered porcelain pie dish. Crimp the edge of the pastry. Add the cheeses to the pastry in an even layer; pour the cream and egg mixture evenly over the cheese. Bake on the bottom rack of a preheated 375°F oven 20 minutes, then raise the pie to the top rack and finish baking until the top of the tart is swollen and golden. Cool to lukewarm before serving. The best wine is a good Chignin de Bergeron or a Dézaley.

The hamlet of Le Manchet at the entrance of the Vanoise

Clarines hanging in the Thônes museum

The bread oven at Le Laisonnay

Tarine cows . . .

. . . and a shepherd

The perfect Tomme

Beaufort on the press

Madame Bastard-Rosset making the reblochon

The reblochon ripening

Faces of the Savoie

Savoie flowers

Gentian

Marsh marigold

Savoie arts

The modern pottery of Jean Christophe
Hermann

Baroque angels in the Termignon church

Foods of the Savoie

Bescoin

Riouttes

Farcement

House with columns at Le Miroir de Tarentaise

Fascines on the side of a Savoie house

The grenier at Sixt

The Cross of the Professions in Bessans

Madame Viallet in the native costume of Jarrier

GRILLAGE TOUS FROMAGES
Cheese Pastry

This is a good way to use all the small ends of cheeses that are forgotten in a refrigerator. The garnish of onions and shallots is one of the multiple versions of the *cerfuze*, or panful of sautéed onions described on page 209.

2 tablespoons butter
1 pound onions, thinly sliced
6 cloves garlic, finely chopped
½ pound shallots, thinly sliced
⅓ teaspoon crushed caraway seeds
Pepper from the mill
A sprinkling of Maggi seasoning
10 ounces of any melting cheese such as Reblochon, Tomme, Raclette, Beaufort, or Gruyère of any origin, mixed
1 pound puff pastry (page 372)
1 egg, beaten

In a large sauté pan, melt and cook the butter to the noisette stage. Add the onions and toss them in the butter until wilted. Add the garlic, shallots, caraway seeds, pepper, and Maggi seasoning. Cook until the vegetables have completely melted into a compote and are brownish and almost caramelized. Cool completely.

Cut the cheese into slivers and keep them cold. Roll the pastry out into two sheets each ⅙ inch thick. Place one on an unbendable black baking sheet. Using a paper pattern, cut a rectangle of dough 12 by 7 inches at the center of the sheet of pastry. Remove the excess dough. Place the onions and cheese on top of the rectangle, leaving ½ inch of pastry free; brush it with beaten egg. Cut a second rectangle 12½ by 8 inches out of the second sheet and, using the rolling pin, bring it over the first sheet. Seal the edges of both pastries with a fork and cut indentations ¼ inch deep into the edge, at ½-inch intervals. Using a razor blade, cut 7-inch-long diagonal openings into the top of the pastry, leaving 1 inch of uncut pastry all around to form a good edge. Brush the top of the pastry with beaten egg and refrigerate at least 30 minutes before baking.

Bake in a preheated 425°F oven 25 to 30 minutes, until deep golden. Cool slightly before serving either in small pieces as an appetizer or in larger portions as a lunch offering. A good salad should then round off the meal as well as a bottle of Chignin de Bergeron, Dézaley, or a good California Sauvignon Blanc.

And finally here are two modern dishes that I made up in Annecy using local ingredients.

POUDING AU PERSILLÉ
Goat Cheese Pudding

2 pounds baby onions
2½ tablespoons butter
Salt
Pepper from the mill
Pinch of sugar
⅓ cup chopped, unpeeled
   hazelnuts
8 ounces semi-dry goat cheese,
   crumbled
4 eggs
1 cup heavy cream
Grated nutmeg

Sauté the baby onions until brown in 2 tablespoons of the butter. Add salt, pepper, a pinch of sugar, and a bit of water; cover and cook until the onions are soft; remove the lid and continue to cook gently until the onions are brown and candied. Transfer them to a 9-inch porcelain pie plate buttered with the remaining ½ tablespoon of butter.

Put the crumbled cheese, eggs, and heavy cream in the blender. Add salt, pepper, and nutmeg and pour over the onions and hazelnuts. Bake in a preheated 375°F oven 30 to 35 minutes. The top of the pudding turns dark brown very rapidly, which is typical of goat cheese custards.

Serve with a nice salad and a bottle of Mondeuse or small Zinfandel.

RAMEQUINS AU FROMAGE BLANC SAUCE CHAMPIGNONS
White Cheese Ramekins with Mushroom Sauce

When one lives in a dairy-producing area and runs a cooking school, one often has all kinds of fresh cheese leftovers. I made these little ramekins with it. You will need six ramekins, three ounces in capacity. Use whichever mushrooms you like; I like brown chanterelles or oyster mushrooms.

8 ounces well-drained fresh
   white cheese or fine-curd
   cottage cheese
½ teaspoon fennel seeds
2 cups heavy cream
4 eggs
Salt
Pepper from the mill
2 tablespoons butter
⅓ cup finely chopped, very
   lightly toasted almonds
½ pound fresh mushrooms,
   preferably wild, cleaned
1 clove garlic, mashed
1 tablespoon chopped parsley

Put the cheese, fennel seeds, and 1 cup of the heavy cream into the blender container. Add the eggs, salt, and pepper and process until smooth. With 1 tablespoon of the butter, grease 6 individual ramekins and coat them with the chopped almonds. Fill with the cheese mixture and bake in a hot water bath in a preheated 325°F oven 20 to 25 minutes, or until a skewer inserted at the center of one of the puddings comes out clean.

Meanwhile sauté the mushrooms in the remaining butter. Salt and pepper them; cover them to extract their water. Uncover the pot and let the water evaporate completely and the mushrooms cook until they are nice and brown. Add the garlic, parsley, and the remainder of the heavy cream and reduce until the mixture lightly coats a spoon. Unmold the little ramekins onto warm plates and top each serving with a good spoonful of sauce.

Soups

In the summer of 1945, Simon and I took a liking to each other. His house was just across from ours, so we eyed each other for two and a half months without ever exchanging a word. We just looked—he from the doorstep of his house, I from the window of ours. We looked at each other at breakfast time: Simon was sitting on the windowsill peacefully eating his soup, while I was dipping my unbuttered bread into a huge bowl of milk barely cut with ersatz coffee. We looked at each other in church; as my teenagers would say later, that sneaking of mellow eloquent looks while the priest was raving on about the ills of the world was wicked great. And most of all, we looked at each other at night: While Simon was again eating his soup, this time on the doorstep, I was showing off like mad in the after-dinner volleyball game, which I otherwise hated passionately.

In essence, all Simon and I ever did during that summer of 1945 was to look at each other, talking being out of the question in those days. By 1946, Simon was gone; Mélanie the cook reported, "*Il est au service,*" meaning, of course, engaged in whatever the French government had by way of military duty in the yet unorganized France of the immediate postwar period.

As I arrived in Annecy to settle down in 1980, I rushed to market to buy some reblochon. I was at work on a pile of cheeses, gently pushing here and there with a testing finger, and as I raised my eyes toward the cheese man . . . Ah! there was Simon looking at me! We recognized each other, both laughing at once, "Oh, but I know you!" Nice as ever, those pink cheeks given by sun and air still there. Finally we talked of the old days, and of course I asked if he still ate soup for breakfast.

Since 1950 no one does that anymore, coffee is here to stay, but soup, that good old comforter of all people everywhere, is still loved, cherished, and fancied. It would have to be, since it was the survival food for centuries. In many families, soup, bread, cheese, and a piece of fruit is dinner to this day; in some rural communities where the budget is not enhanced by industry or tourism, the noontime meal for schoolchildren is soup and *pain d'épices* (honey cake).

For centuries, soup was made both for the main midday meal and for supper, the leftovers being carefully saved for the children's breakfast. The custom was smart: This was the best stick to the ribs food for young ones who had to stay in the cool mountain air to keep the cows en champ les vaches or who, before the advent of skis, had to walk to school through deep snow. Coffee in the morning was for the elders.

The soup was prepared with water in a *bronzin* or *bru* of black cast iron. Only in bourgeois households where one owned a farm kept by tenants or could afford to go to a butcher shop was there what the area called *bouillon*, the good old classic meat stock coming from the pot-au-peu. Using bouillon on the farm meant that one cooked for a wedding or Holy Communion, or later, toward the early 1900s, for Sunday dinner. The components of the soup varied with the season and the area. Obviously, during the summer all kinds of wild or homegrown greens were available, but toward the end of winter, when even root vegetables were becoming scarce, soup was plain salted water thickened with flour, grain, or a form of pasta. You will see in the recipes that follow some noodle-type garnishes called *galeots, calots,* or *danderiots,* which are equivalent to the Lorraine *totelots* or the Alsatian *spaetzle.* A lot of barley was used on the farm—the *gruau* or in patois *pekett* that one grew for bread flour. Flour- and grain-enriched soups were powerfully thick and substantial.

The soups were never creamed. What is called *be, bo,* or *betton* was used instead, especially in the Maurienne; *be* is the first very rich milk produced by a cow after calfing. But I have seen whey from white cheese–making also go into soups. Most people used rich milk and butter in abundance.

One *mitonnéed* the soup; that would correspond to the French term *tremper*, which means that the soup was a true soup: Bread slices plain or toasted, or sometimes even fried in butter, were used to thicken the liquid poured over them. I remember what we called, with the unending mockery of the young, "Mélanie's bouillabaisse." The dear lady piled layers of cheese and bread in tureens, poured the vegetable broth over that, and delivered to us a mass that may have looked like a mess but surely tasted delicious. And, of course, since the cheese made strings, our manners were put to the test every time the bouillabaisse appeared on the table. I had one of the greatest laughs of my life on the day that a not-too-well-liked counselor whom we called Tartuffe actually wrapped a string of Beaufort around the tip of her nose.

For the sake of authenticity of taste, I shall use a Mique Grandchamp recipe for the bouillon, which I would recommend you use for the bourgeois-style dishes. Farm women and city home cooks of modest households use a giblet broth that also follows.

TRADITIONAL SAVOIE SOUPS

The following soups come from the nineteenth century, but still exist nowadays in one form or another.

All recipes in this section yield 6 servings.

MIQUE GRANDCHAMP'S BOUILLON DÉMOCRATIQUE
Mique Grandchamp's Democratic Bouillon

Yes, you are reading correctly: democratic stock! The gentleman assures us that it does not cost more than 8 francs, and that one can make three meals for four persons out of the whole preparation. That was one hundred years ago. In our inflated world, 8 francs fluctuates between $1 and $2, depending on the spasms of Wall Street. The recipe is adapted for the American kitchen.

1 beef tongue
1 veal knuckle or large veal
    bone
4½ pounds boiling beef,
    preferably shank, bone in
4 large onions, peeled
4 medium carrots, peeled
6 leeks, white and light green
    parts only
4 cloves
Bouquet garni (1 celery sprig,
    1 thyme sprig, 1 bay leaf,
    and 10 parsley sprigs)
1 tablespoon salt
1 stewing hen

Blanch the tongue and veal knuckle, starting them in cold water. Rinse them and trim all fat from the underside of the tongue. Brown the beef shank, veal, and onions in a preheated 375°F oven until golden. Discard all fat and deglaze the pan with hot water. Carefully reserve the deglazing.

Put the tongue in a large stockpot and add 6 quarts of water. Bring to a boil, skim if needed. Add the beef and onions, reserved pan deglazing, carrots, leeks tied in a bundle, cloves stuck into the onions, and the *bouquet garni*, tied. Return to the boil and skim again; add salt. Simmer 2 hours.

Remove all visible fat from the fowl cavity. Truss the fowl, add it to the pot, and cook another 1½ hours. When all is cooked and the bouillon is tasty, you can serve the bouillon first and any of the meats you like. To use the bouillon for cooking, strain it carefully, cool it overnight, remove any trace of fat, and refrigerate or freeze as you would any stock.

BOUILLON AUX ABATTIS DE POULET
Farm-style Chicken Broth

Needless to say, in the countryside, chickens come whole to this day. Freezers are now common, although not necessarily loved or understood. Use your freezer: Freeze chicken giblets, wings, and carcasses of roasted chickens after the good parts have been eaten until you have five pounds and you will know what farm chicken broth tastes like. Of course, you can simplify matters by using only chicken wings and gizzards bought in the supermarket; the broth will be more expensive, but delicious, thanks to the gizzards.

5 pounds chicken giblets and carcasses
4 medium carrots
2 small purple-topped turnips
6 leeks, white and light green parts only
4 cloves
4 onions
1 celery sprig
1 thyme sprig
1 Turkish bay leaf or ½ California bay leaf
10 parsley sprigs
1 veal bone, blanched (optional)
1½ teaspoons salt

Put the giblets and carcasses into a stockpot. Cover with 4 quarts of water, bring to a boil, and skim well. Add all aromatics, bring to a second boil, skim again, add the veal bone, if using it, and salt. Cook 2 to 3 hours, or until tasty. Strain, and remove all fat if need be. Store in the refrigerator or freezer.

The traditional soups are cooked a very long time for maximum taste. The vegetables must all be wildly overcooked. When bread is used, any in the Bread chapter will work well. Or purchase any fine bread resembling the required bread in a good bakery.

MELANIE'S WINTER SOUP

4 tablespoons butter
3½ ounces slab bacon, cut into ⅓-inch lardons
6 onions, thinly sliced
6 leeks, thinly sliced
2 carrots, thinly sliced
2 quarts water
Salt
½ teaspoon Maggi seasoning
Pepper from the mill
6 slices Tomme de Savoie or Gruyère cheese, ¼ inch thick and 3½ inches long
6 slices, 3-by 2-inch, toasted Pain Bis (page 136) or equivalent bread

Heat the butter and in it sauté the bacon until golden; remove the lardons to a plate. Add the onions, leeks, and carrots to the pot and cook on slow heat until golden and compote-like. Add 2 quarts of water and the reserved bacon; add seasonings and simmer until reduced to 6 cups. *Do Not* strain or puree the vegetables.

Have the cheese at room temperature. Toast the bread slices. Put the bread at the bottom of an oven-proof soup tureen. Top with the cheese slices and ladle the soup slowly over the bread and cheese. Cover the pot. Put it in a low oven for a few minutes and serve in hot plates or bowls.

SOUPE À LA VIANDE FUMÉE
Smoked Pork Soup

This soup was still served in 1939 at a little hotel in La Clusaz that has now disappeared. The soup may be the same as what Marie Thérèse Hermann describes as *soupe à la viande des Aravis*. All I remember is that it was extremely smoky and that a nice and sticky dish of rice was served on the side with the overboiled vegetables.

1 smoked pork shoulder

1 pound slab bacon

4 pork hocks

1 head of Savoy cabbage, cut in quarters

6 leeks, tied in a bundle (white and light green parts only)

6 medium carrots, cut in quarters

6 purple-topped turnips cut in quarters

4 onions

4 cloves

Small bunch of celery leaves (not ribs)

10 parsley sprigs

1 Turkish bay leaf or ½ California bay leaf

1 thyme sprig

1 teaspoon Maggi seasoning

¼ recipe Fides (page 212) or ⅓ pound commercial angelhair pasta

Put all the meats into a pot, cover with cold water, bring to a boil, and blanch 5 minutes.

Drain completely, then cover the meats again with 5 quarts of water. Bring to a boil, add all the vegetables, aromatics, and the Maggi seasoning and cook approximately 3 hours, until the pork shoulder is done; you may remove the hocks as soon as you see them threaten to fall apart.

To serve, cook the *fides* in the bouillon and serve the meat on the side with the soup vegetables.

GRATINÉE MITONNÉE
Onion, Cheese, and Bread Soup

If brandy is not in your program, replace it with a pinch of saffron, as is done in the Maurienne.

5 pounds onions, thinly sliced
8 tablespoons butter
Salt
Pepper from the mill
1 cup dry white wine
2 quarts farm-style chicken broth (page 183) or water
Ten 3-by 2-inch slices of white bread, toasted
½ pound grated Beaufort or gruyère cheese
1 ounce marc or brandy or
⅛ teaspoon saffron threads

Sauté the onions in the butter; season and continue to cook them until mellow and brown. Add the white wine and reduce completely. Add the broth or water and cook very slowly until reduced to 6 cups. Put half the bread at the bottom of a large flameproof terrine or 6 smaller terrine. Top with half the cheese and top the cheese with the remainder of the bread.

Strain the soup through a food mill or put it in the food processor 30 seconds to coarsely break up the onions. Reheat the soup to the boiling point. Correct the seasoning, heat the marc or brandy, light and pour it, flaming, into the onion broth, or simply add the saffron. Pour the onion broth over the bread and top with the remaining cheese. Broil until the cheese is light golden and serve in hot soup plates or bowls.

LA SOUPE AUX HERBES ET À LA COURGE DE MADAME MAILLET
Madame Maillet's Herb and Pumpkin Soup

This is Georgette's grandmother's herb and pumpkin soup. If you have no strawberry leaves or nettles, use a bit of beet greens and spinach.

SOUP:
3 onions, finely chopped
3 leeks, finely chopped
⅓ cup butter

Sauté the onions and leeks in well-heated butter until translucent. Add 2½ quarts of water, bring to a boil, and add all the greens, root vegetables, and pumpkin; add salt, celery salt, and pepper. Return

2½–3 quarts water
¼ cup chopped strawberry
  leaves
1 cup chopped nettles
1 cup chopped Swiss chard
  leaves
3 large carrots, finely diced
3 large white turnips, finely
  diced
2 potatoes, peeled and finely
  diced
1 pound pumpkin meat, finely
  diced
Salt
½ teaspoon celery salt
Pepper from the mill

GARNISH:
⅓ cup Great Northern beans,
  soaked overnight
⅓ cup red beans, soaked
  overnight
½ cup chopped chervil
Light cream

to the boil and simmer down to 2 quarts. Pass the soup through a food mill or food processor.

Meanwhile cook both presoaked beans in just enough water to cover them. When they have cooked 30 minutes, add them to the soup with any remaining cooking water and continue simmering slowly until very well done. The beans should have split open. Add the chervil.

Add light cream to bring the soup back to a lighter texture and reheat well. Serve immediately.

LA SOUPE À LA BATAILLE DE MÉLANIE
Melanie's Vegetable and Oatmeal Soup

This soup was made in the summer with the vegetables donated by Madame Déléan next door and those that farmers brought in their old-fashioned trucks. Do not replace the fresh tomatoes with canned ones; the soup turns too tomatoey. The soup should not be strained.

4 tablespoons butter
2 cups sorrel leaves, packed
  and chopped

Heat the butter in a soup pot. Add the sorrel, carrot greens, leeks, onions, carrots, and turnips and toss into the hot butter. Add the water and bring to a

½ cup chopped carrot greens
6 leeks, chopped
4 onions, chopped
1 pound baby carrots, slivered
1 pound baby turnips, slivered
3 quarts water
Salt
Pepper from the mill
1 teaspoon Maggi seasoning
6 fresh tomatoes, sun-ripened,
  peeled, seeded, and chopped
⅓ cup oatmeal flakes
3 tablespoons fresh chives
Rich milk or light cream as
  desired

boil. Add salt, pepper, and Maggi seasoning and turn down to a simmer. Cook 45 minutes. Add the tomatoes and oatmeal and cook another 15 minutes, or until thickened. Add the chives. Serve with a pitcher of milk or light cream to add to the soup to personal taste.

SOUPE DE GALEOTS DU BAS FAUCIGNY
Flour Dumpling Soup from the lower Faucigny

This is true poverty cookery. It may seem awful to you, but you have no idea how good it tastes when one is ravenously hungry. It is a personal interpretation adapted from the many versions of the *galeots* soup of Mont Saxonnex as described by Arsène Bourgeaux in a lecture on the food of this village. The soup is made with water and flour with an occasional egg, nothing more. I have used the traditional Savoie spices of aniseeds, coriander, cumin, and dill to give it more taste, and farm-style chicken broth instead of water.

SOUP BASE:
3 onions, finely chopped
4 tablespoons butter
½ teaspoon crushed aniseeds
1 teaspoon crushed coriander
  seeds
½ teaspoon ground cumin
Salt
Pepper from the mill

Sauté the onions in the butter until translucent. Add the aniseeds, coriander, cumin, salt, and pepper. Cover with the water or broth and bring to a boil. Turn down to a simmer and cook 40 to 45 minutes.

Meanwhile prepare the *galeots*. Mix the flour and eggs, salt and pepper, and the aniseeds until smooth (do not overwork); gradually dilute with the milk. Put the paste into a pastry bag or funnel and, stir-

2 quarts water or farm-style
 chicken broth (page 183)

GALEOTS:
1 cup unsifted all-purpose flour
2 eggs, beaten
½ teaspoon salt
Pepper from the mill
½ teaspoon crushed aniseeds
½–⅔ cup milk

GARNISH:
½ cup chopped dill weed
1 cup buttermilk

ring, let it fall in irregular portions into the soup pot. Add the dill. Serve when the *galeots* come floating to the top of the soup. Correct the seasoning and serve with a pitcher of buttermilk for each person to add as he or she chooses.

SOUPE AUX FRIQUERONS
Cornmeal Soup

Friquerons are white when made with flour or yellow when made with polenta. The addition of fresh spinach and garlic is mine, to pep up the porridge, for it is definitely more a porridge than a soup. The chicken giblet broth also will do a lot for the taste.

6 cups water or farm-style
 chicken broth (page 183)
¾ cup fine cornmeal
Salt
Pepper from the mill
Grated nutmeg to taste
2 cups packed spinach leaves,
 chopped
3 cloves garlic, finely chopped
Hot milk or light cream to
 taste
Grated Beaufort, Tomme, or
 Gruyère cheese

Bring the water or broth to a boil; stirring constantly, add the cornmeal in a steady rain. Lumps may form, but please do not destroy them. The more lumps, the better the soup is considered. Cook until the soup thickens, then add salt, pepper, and nutmeg. Cook down until quite thick, to approximately 4 cups. Add the raw chopped spinach and garlic, stirring well. Thin the soup with milk or cream to taste, and serve with a bowl of grated cheese for personal use.

SOUPE À LA FARINE DE BLÉ DE TURQUIE
Polenta Soup

For more details on the importance of cornmeal in Savoie food see the chapter on Exotic Grains, page 248. This was a great favorite in both my restaurants. If yellow tomatoes are not available in your area, use twice as many red ones.

½ cup butter

3 onions, very finely chopped

4 cloves garlic, mashed

1 large zucchini, diced into ¼-inch cubes

2 large, red sun-ripened tomatoes, peeled and cubed

2 large, yellow sun-ripened tomatoes, peeled and cubed

½ cup medium cornmeal

1 cup cold farm-style chicken broth (page 183)

5 cups milk

Salt

Pepper from the mill

Freshly grated nutmeg, to your taste

1 cup light cream

3 tablespoons chopped chervil leaves

Grated Beaufort or Gruyère cheese

In a large saucepan, heat half the butter to the noisette stage. Add the onions and half the garlic. Cook slowly until very mellow and compote-like.

Meanwhile sauté the zucchini and the other half of the garlic in the remaining butter on high heat so both take on a brown color; add the red and yellow tomatoes, toss well, cook another 15 minutes, then remove from the heat.

Mix the cornmeal with the cold chicken broth. Bring the milk to a boil, stirring the cornmeal slurry into the milk to thicken it. Turn down to a simmer and cook 5 minutes, then add the onions and garlic with all their butter. Add salt, pepper, and nutmeg and cook 15 minutes, stirring occasionally.

Add the zucchini and tomato mixture, stirring well again. Just before serving, add the cream and chervil. If you allow the soup to stand too long before serving, it may thicken again; add broth or more cream to dilute it again.

SOUPE À LA LIVÈCHE
Lovage Soup

In the mountain villages this soup was made with wild mountain celery, which is a type of lovage. The replacement ingredients in this recipe are close enough to the original, which I enjoyed a long time ago in a Valaisan village inn in Trient, while waiting for a rainstorm to pass.

Since there is a lot of sodium in celery and the Maggi seasoning is quite salty, watch the salt seasoning.

½ cup butter

6 onions, finely slivered

3 cups celery ribs, cut into ⅛-inch-thick slices

1 very large potato, diced small

1 teaspoon Maggi seasoning

Salt if needed

Pepper from the mill

½ teaspoon celery seeds

1 teaspoon crushed coriander seeds

2 quarts water or farm-style chicken broth (page 183)

Six 3- by 2-inch slices of bread

Six 3- by 2½-inch slices Beaufort or Gruyère cheese, ¼ inch thick

¼ cup chopped lovage leaves or pale green celery leaves

In a large pot, heat half the butter; add the onions and sauté until lightly browned. Add the celery and potato and toss into the onions. Add the Maggi seasoning, salt, pepper, celery seeds, and ground coriander and toss well. Add the water or broth, bring to a boil, turn down to a simmer, and let cook gently until the water is reduced to 5 to 6 cups.

Brown the bread on both sides in the remaining butter. Put the bread slices into a flameproof soup tureen; top it with the cheese slices. Ladle the soup over the mixture, sprinkle with the lovage or celery leaves, and cover the tureen. Let stand a few minutes on the lower rack of a preheated 275°F oven before serving in hot plates or bowls.

SOUPE DE L'ALPAGE DE COUTERAY

Soup from the Couteray Alp

When I was young I kept climbing mountains with a bunch of friends. We met whenever business for everyone would let us, to climb whatever we were in shape to climb. On a nice day in July 1959, four of us arrived at Le Couteray in the upper Chamonix valley to try to make our way to a beautiful summit called Le Buet, which sits some 11,000 feet above the village of Vallorcine.

The weather quickly became extremely bad, with lightning in all directions. Whoever was protecting us put us in view of a chalet, where we were gladly welcomed and spent the night. I was so frightened that, crawling under a rock overhang, I pulped the two pounds of fresh tomatoes I was carrying in my backpack; the tomato pulp became my contribution to that night's soup made by our hostess, Madame Bossonaz, and Le Buet was never climbed. The best cheese for this soup is Swiss raclette.

½ cup butter
3 medium onions, sliced
6 leeks, thinly sliced
2 pounds sun-ripened
   tomatoes, peeled, seeded,
   and coarsely chopped
½ cup all-purpose flour
6 cups scalding water
Salt
Pepper from the mill
1 teaspoon Maggi seasoning
1 cup heavy cream
Six 3- by 3-inch Pain Bis
   (page 136) or other dark
   bread, diced and air dried
½ pound Swiss Raclette, diced

Heat half the butter in a large saucepan. Add onions and leeks and brown well. Add the tomatoes and toss into the pot. Sprinkle the flour over the vegetables, mix well, and, off the heat, gradually add the hot water. Bring to a boil, stirring constantly. Add salt, pepper, and Maggi seasoning and turn the heat down to a simmer. Cook 45 minutes to 1 hour, until nice and tasty. When ready, add the cream and correct the seasoning.

Toss the bread cubes into a skillet containing the last 4 tablespoons of butter and heat gradually until the croutons turn golden. Place a handful of croutons and diced cheese into each soup plate or bowl, and ladle the soup over the garnish.

SOUPE À LA FARINE BRÛLÉE
Burned Flour Soup

This soup is probably of Germanic origin since it is also a specialty of the southern Alsace and the area of Basel and several other cantons of Switzerland. The Savoie bacon makes it especially delicious. Please use a very well smoked bacon; the Vermont cob-smoked product would be the best. Mélanie used to prepare it for us, and we rejoiced every time it came to the table. You can reduce the amount of butter if you want, but with it goes the great taste; it is better to prepare the soup only once in a while but to make it the right way.

5 ounces slab bacon, cut into ¼-inch cubes
1½ pounds onions, finely chopped
¾ cup butter
¾ cup all-purpose flour
2 quarts hot water or farm-style chicken broth (page 183)
1 teaspoon Maggi seasoning
Salt
Pepper from the mill
1 cup light cream
½ pound slivered Tomme, Beaufort, or Gruyère cheese

In a large sauté pan, render the bacon cubes slowly; let them color to a nice golden without crisping. When the bacon is ready, remove it to a plate. In the bacon fat, slowly sauté the chopped onions until mellow and brown. Mix the bacon into the onions.

In another saucepan, heat the butter well. Add the flour and cook slowly—at least 20 minutes—until nice and dark brown (two shades deeper than a hazelnut shell). Whisk in the hot water or broth, bring to a boil, and pour over the onions and bacon. Add Maggi seasoning, salt, and pepper. Simmer approximately 45 minutes, or until tasty and reduced to 5 cups.

Add the cream and mix well. Serve in hot plates or bowls with a dish of cheese slices for your guests to help themselves. The tomme is to be slivered into the soup.

SOUPE DE BOLETS
Wild Boleti Soup

I do not remember exactly which species of mushrooms were used for this soup, but there were many kinds, all coming in August/September, after a solid rain and several days of high sunshine, under the evergreens. I distinctly remember *Boletus edulis*, of course, for we had to race the *artisons* (worms) if we wanted to eat the stems. There was also *Boletus castaneus* with its yellow-green tubes, *Boletus badius* in generous quantity, *Boletus aureus*, and the less attractive *Boletus luteus*. We were taught to recognize them by the mysterious Mademoiselle Riondet, a dynamo who at nearly eighty was going up and down those slopes as if she were still twenty. The recipe is Mélanie's; the soup was served once a year, in coffee cups because it was so precious and there was not enough to fill our gigantic pottery bowls.

10 tablespoons butter
2 cloves garlic, chopped
3 tablespoons chopped parsley
2 carrots, finely chopped
1 onion, finely chopped
1 leek, finely chopped
5 tablespoons all-purpose flour
*4–6 large fresh boleti, or 2
    ounces dried**
*6 cups farm-style chicken stock
    (page 183), scalding*
Salt
Pepper from the mill
¼ cup sour cream
¾ cup heavy cream

Heat 8 tablespoons of the butter in a large sauté pan. In it brown the garlic and parsley; add the carrots, onion, and leek and cook until the onion is translucent. Add the flour and cook no more than 5 minutes. Set aside.

Meanwhile clean the boleti carefully: Cut out the dirty stem ends, removing any trace of *artisons* in them, and gently pull out the tubes from under the caps. Quickly rinse the mushrooms under running water, pat dry, and sliver the stems and caps. Set aside.

Bind the *roux* with the broth, bring to a boil, and turn down to a simmer. In the remaining 2 tablespoons of butter, toss the boleti; salt and pepper them, then cover the skillet to extract all their water. Add the mushrooms and their liquid to the soup pot. Simmer 45 minutes. Finish the soup by adding both creams mixed together; correct the seasoning.

*If you use the dried boleti, soak them in water and use the soaking water, well filtered, to make the soup exactly as instructed, skipping the sautéing of the mushrooms in butter.

SOUPE DE GRUAU
Pearl Barley Vegetable Soup

This barley soup is a composite of three soups described by Marie Thérèse Hermann, all coming from the Maurienne; it is sometimes called *soupe de pekett*. Notice that I use a salted and cured pork since one seems to prefer it to smoked pork in Maurienne soups, another indication of the different tastes that result from the different ethnic backgrounds of the cook; Provence, which is also Ligurian, uses salt pork rather than smoked bacon.

1 cup dried beans
½ cup pearl barley
*3 ounces pancetta, diced into
    ⅓-inch cubes*

Soak the beans and barley overnight. In a large pot, cook the pancetta in half the butter until golden but not crisp or brown. Add the onions, carrots, and leeks; cook slowly without coloring. Cool completely.

½ cup butter

1½ pounds onions, finely slivered

½ pound carrots, finely slivered

3 leeks, finely slivered

Thyme

1 Turkish bay leaf or ½ California bay leaf

Salt

Pepper from the mill

2 potatoes, peeled and diced in to ¼-inch cubes

Milk as needed

3 cloves garlic, chopped

3 tablespoons chopped parsley

Add to the pot 3 quarts of cold water, the beans and barley, the thyme, bay leaf, salt and pepper. Bring to a boil and simmer approximately 1 hour, or until the beans and barley are barely tender. Add the potatoes and continue cooking until the whole pot is a mass of vegetables, compact and almost without any liquid. At this point, add enough salted water or milk to bring the soup back to the texture you prefer. Fry the garlic and parsley in the remaining butter and add it to the soup just before serving with good crusty bread.

LA BREGYE DE MAGLAND
Cherry Soup from the Village of Magland

Called *bregye* by one author and *breglie* by another, this cherry soup is most definitely German (it can be found in Scandinavia, the Black Forest, and northern Germany). How did it arrive in the Faucigny? Through Alamanni or with an immigrant returning from Germany? It is found only in this small area of the Faucigny, so the immigrant theory is the more probable.

I serve it as breakfast fare on pilaf of polenta (see page 255).

2 cups water

Pinch of salt

2½ pounds dark sweet cherries, stemmed

1 tablespoon brown sugar, or more to taste

⅔ cup butter

½ cup all-purpose flour

Bring the water to a boil and add salt. Add the cherries. Lift them out of the water as soon as they rise to the surface, put them into a bowl and add the sugar. Reserve the poaching water. Let the cherries stand until cool, then pit them, working over a bowl to collect the juices as they drip down.

Melt the butter and add the flour, stirring, to make a *roux*; bind it with the cherry poaching water and cook until well-thickened. Add the cherries and their juices. Serve lukewarm, in ramekins or on fried polenta croutons.

NOTE: The traditional recipe has no other flavoring, but I add a little more sugar, lemon juice, lemon rind, and cinnamon, plus a touch of Kirsch as befits the cherries with which I am working. Do experiment with the quantities of these ingredients to obtain a taste you will enjoy.

SOUPE DE FIDES
Large Vermicelli Soup

Every source I have found states that this soup was reserved for sick people. You can, if you want, add some peeled, sliced, blanched asparagus, which does wonders for the broth, but I doubt that it would have been done on the farm, only in those bourgeois households of Chambéry and Annecy.

2 quarts bouillon (page 182) or farm-style chicken broth (page 183)

1 cup asparagus, peeled and cut diagonally (optional)

⅓ recipe Fides (page 212) or ½ pound vermicelli

Chopped dill

Bring the bouillon or broth to a boil. Add the asparagus and cook them *al dente*. Remove to a bowl with a slotted spoon. Add the *fides* or vermicelli and also cook *al dente*. Return the asparagus to the soup, add the chopped dill, and correct the final seasoning.

MODERN SOUPS

To distinguish them from the country soups made with bread or flour, I shall, in French, call these soups *potages*, which immediately intimates a bourgeois preparation, less substantial and more adapted to entertaining than family fare. These soups were all prepared in Annecy with the glorious ingredients of the farmer's market; the seasonings remain completely Savoyard by tradition.

POTAGE CRÈME DE RAVES AU CARVI
Cream of Turnips with Caraway

½ cup butter

2 onions, finely chopped

2 pounds small purple-topped
  turnips, peeled and sliced

Salt

Pepper from the mill

Pinch of sugar

½ teaspoon crushed caraway
  seeds

2 quarts farm-style chicken
  broth (page 183)

¼ cup sour cream

¾ cup heavy cream

GARNISH:

3 tablespoons butter

3 tablespoons semi-dry goat
  cheese

1 clove garlic, finely chopped

2 tablespoons chopped dill

Salt

Coarsely cracked pepper from
  the mill

Heat the butter in a large sauté pan and in it sauté the onions until translucent. Add the turnips and toss well. Season with salt and pepper. Cook, covered, until all the juices have come out of the vegetables. Add a pinch of sugar and continue to cook, uncovered, until the juices evaporate and the turnips have caramelized. Toss every 5 minutes or so.

When the turnips are browned and candied, add the caraway seeds and the stock; salt and pepper again and bring to a boil. Turn down the heat to a simmer and cook until the turnips fall apart. Puree in the blender. Add the creams mixed together and reheat just below the boiling point.

To prepare the garnish, cream the butter, then add the goat cheese, garlic, and dill. Season with salt and coarsely cracked pepper.

Serve the *potage* in hot plates, dropping a dollop of the garnish butter at the center of each plate.

POTAGE AUX POIS GOURMANDS ET AUX CHANTERELLES
Snow Pea and Chanterelle Potage

Snow peas from the Annecy market and brown chanterelles from the Semnoz woods entered the first version of this soup. Use whichever chanterelles you prefer. The brown and yellow ones do, of course, make the best color combination, and the taste also happens to be the best.

½ cup butter
2 onions, finely chopped
1½ pounds snow peas, cut in half
Pinch of sugar
Salt
Pepper from the mill
1½ quarts farm-style chicken broth (page 183)
2 cloves garlic, finely chopped
¼ cup chopped parsley
½ pound chanterelles, cleaned
1 cup heavy cream

In 6 tablespoons of the butter, sauté the onions until translucent. Add the snow peas and stir-fry 2 to 3 minutes. Add the sugar, salt and pepper, and the stock. Bring to a boil and simmer 10 minutes. Puree in the blender and strain through a fine strainer to discard all skins.

In the remaining butter, brown the garlic and half the parsley, add the chanterelles, salt and pepper, and sauté until brown. Add the cream to the soup, then the mushrooms, and correct the final seasoning. Serve sprinkled with the remaining chopped parsley.

POTAGE DE COURGES JAUNES ET VERTES
Pumpkin and Zucchini Potage

2 pounds fresh pumpkin in one large piece
2 very large zucchini
2 tablespoons chopped parsley
4 cloves garlic, chopped
1½ quarts farm-style chicken broth (page 183)
Salt
Pepper from the mill
¼ cup clarified butter
1 cup ⅓-inch French bread cubes, air-dried
⅓ cup sour cream
⅔ cup heavy cream

Bake the pumpkin until it releases its water. Scrape it from its skin with a spoon and mash it coarsely. Put it into a large sauté pan.

Box the zucchini—that is, remove the skin with no more than ⅛ inch of pulp attached to it on all four sides of each vegetable. Reserve the skins, chop the inner pulp of the zucchini and add it to the pumpkin. Add the parsley and half the chopped garlic. Cover with the stock and bring to a boil. Season to taste and cook until reduced to 4 to 5 cups of liquid. Puree in the blender.

While the soup is cooking, heat the clarified butter. All at once add the remaining garlic and the bread cubes. Toss until the cubes are golden; drain on paper towels. Cut the zucchini skins diagonally into ⅛-inch julienne and add them to the pan in which the bread cubes browned and toss 1 minute; season well.

To finish the soup, add the two creams mixed together and the zucchini julienne. Correct the salt and pepper. Serve the soup in heated plates, with a sprinkling of croutons on the top of each portion.

CRÈME DE CORNICHONS AU CERFEUIL
Cream of Pickling Cucumbers

Use pickling cucumbers, as small as you can possibly find, for the garnish.

½ cup butter
2 onions, chopped
3 shallots, chopped
1 English cucumber, thinly sliced
8 large pickling cucumbers
Salt
Pepper from the mill
1½ quarts farm-style chicken broth (page 183)

GARNISH:
8 pickling cucumbers, as small as possible, or 4 larger ones
1 tablespoon butter
1 tablespoon cider vinegar
2 tablespoons chervil
2 tablespoons chopped tarragon
¼ cup sour cream
2 tablespoons Dijon-style mustard
½ cup heavy cream
Salt and pepper
Garlic bread

Heat the butter in a large sauté pan, add the onions and shallots, and cook only a few minutes; add all the cucumbers, season to taste, cover, and cook 15 minutes. Add the chicken broth and cook, uncovered, approximately 40 minutes, until tasty. Puree in the blender until perfectly smooth.

Meanwhile sauté the sliced pickling cucumbers in butter. Add the cider vinegar and remove from the heat; add the chervil and tarragon. Add to the soup. Mix the sour cream, mustard, heavy cream, light salt and pepper. Add some of the soup to the mixture, then reversing the process, add the cream liaison to the bulk of the soup. Correct the seasoning and serve with garlic bread.

POTAGE AUX NOISETTES SAUVAGES
Wild Hazelnut Potage

Until quite recently I searched the woods to find wild hazelnuts; now I go peacefully down to market and purchase them from the farmers. The little hazelnuts that grow wild in the forests of the Pre-Alps are milkier than our filberts. Were you to have access to wild hazelnuts, double the amount indicated here.

¾ cup butter
¾ cup hazelnuts, peeled and
   chopped
½ cup all-purpose flour
1½ quarts excellent chicken
   stock, scalding
⅛ teaspoon dried orange peel
½ cup chopped chervil
1 cup heavy cream
1 tablespoon lemon juice
1 tablespoon green Chartreuse
   (optional)
Salt
Coarsely cracked pepper from
   the mill
2 tablespoons chervil,
   separated into single whole
   leaves

Heat ½ cup of the butter to the noisette stage and in it cook the hazelnuts to deep beige. Remove only the hazelnuts from the pan and set them aside.

Add the remaining butter to the pan, melt it, and add the flour; cook to a lovely beige. Bind with the stock, bring to a boil, and add the orange peel and the chopped chervil. Simmer until reduced to 5 cups, skimming the impurities as you go along.

Strain the obtained *velouté* into a saucepan, add the hazelnuts, then, all at once, the heavy cream soured with the lemon juice and the green Chartreuse, if you use it; correct the seasoning with salt and pepper. Stir in the whole chervil leaves and serve.

Matafans

Jean Nicolas has called the world of the common folks of the Savoie in former centuries *ce monde de crève la faim* ("this world of forever famished people"). As we have seen, difficulties in finding food were many, and the one type of dish more evocative than any other of that dire state of necessity is the *matafan*, or *matefaim*, the rustic semi-pancake, semi-crêpe prepared to *mater la faim*, or kill hunger.

Descended directly from the Stone Age gruel spread thin on hot stones to obtain thin flat breads, *matafans* as we know them now have captured the fancy of small restaurants and bistros, which serve them to the tourist trade with a salad. It was serious food for the people working in the fields, since it often came in the lunch baskets brought by children or grandmothers. I remember stopping for lunch during a climb and finding in my backpack *matafans*, nice, cold and hard, left over from the previous dinner, together with large precut portions of reblochon and tomme and a big bagful of Lombardes, the purple plums of the area. I felt heartened at the sight of farm people lunching on the very same fare while haying a nearby field. I am pretty sure that a bit of investigation in areas where one still cuts and stores the hay would probably show a lot of *matafans* still on the lunch menu, brought up nowadays in a rickety four-wheel-drive Jeep.

We had high stacks of *matafans* at dinner in many diverse colors, as Mélanie, forever gifted at recycling food, enclosed a lot of leftovers in her batter. Building on her ideas, I have presented my own children with *matafans* filled with all kinds of vegetables or fruits. I have not found in all my reference books any *matafan* made with fillings and fillers, but since Mélanie made them they must have existed; she came from the countryside and and obviously did things the way she had learned them there. A long time ago I had some *matafans* made with pumpkin puree in a small bistro on the left side of the Isère, way up there where the road twists and turns up and down in the area of Notre Dame des Prés, but since at the time I was not yet totally food-oriented, I do not remember the village or the restaurant.

The modern recipes use mostly white flour. But again there is no reason to believe that some did not contain buckwheat, corn, rye, or even potato puree, since numerous potato pancakes are sold in modest local restaurants year-round. The liquid used to mix the flour and eggs is well documented: lukewarm water, which is supposed to make the *matafans* "fluffier." But I have seen them done in private homes with *be*, that rich after-calving milk, or even buttermilk or whey. Some were prepared with hemp oil and turned green as a consequence (the Villards Valley), while in the Arvan valley one used pig's blood to prepare *matafans* rather than blood pudding. *Matafans* are such a daily article on the Savoie table that Mique Grandchamp called them a "national dish." Well, Savoie was a nation when he was a child, and I have had more than one *crispelle* in the valleys around Suza and Aosta, now in Italy, which is most definitely a relation to the *matafan*. As a matter of fact, the higher up into the mountains one climbs on that southern slope of the Alps, the heavier the *crispelle* become.

Here is a basic recipe followed by many variations. Because our American flours are heavy in proteins, I have modified the mixing method to lighten the final texture and produce a *matafan* that is pliable even when cold. I have often precooked *matafans* for my children, who refried them crisp before eating them. If you choose this method, do not crisp them too hard on your first cooking.

All recipes in this section yield 6 servings.

BASIC MATAFANS

For 12 *matafans* cooked in a 22- or 24-inch crêpe pan:

1 cup unsifted all-purpose flour
6 eggs, separated
¾–1 cup lukewarm water or
buttermilk or whey
½ teaspoon salt
Melted butter as needed

Put the flour in a bowl. Make a well in the center and add the egg yolks. Break them and gradually incorporate them and the lukewarm water into the flour with a metal whisk. Add the salt and 4 tablespoons of melted butter.

Whip the egg whites only to the soft peak stage and fold them into the batter base.

To cook the *matafans*, heat a good piece of butter in the pan, pour a ladleful of batter at its center and spread it toward the edge of the pan to a thickness of ¼ inch. Flip over as soon as the first surface is crisp.

VARIATIONS:

BUCKWHEAT MATAFANS
½ cup dark buckwheat flour
⅔ cup unsifted all-purpose flour

POTATO MATAFANS
⅔ cup cold mashed potatoes
½ cup all-purpose flour

PUMPKIN MATAFANS
⅔ cup mashed pumpkin
⅔ cup all-purpose flour
Always use buttermilk

CORNMEAL MATAFANS
½ cup each fine cornmeal and
flour

MATAFANS AUX HERBES FRAÎCHES
Fresh Herb Matafans

1 recipe Basic Matafan *batter (page 203)*
2 tablespoons mixed chopped parsley, chives, chervil, and tarragon
6 eggs, panfried
6 rashers bacon, crisped and crumbled
Chopped parsley

Add the herbs to the *matafan* batter; cook the cakes as usual. Top each *matafan* with a panfried egg, and sprinkle with chopped bacon and parsley.

MATAFANS DE COURGE AU JAMBON
Pumpkin Matafans *with Ham*

1 recipe Pumpkin Matafan *batter (page 203)*
6 thin slices baked ham, preferably Smithfield
½ cup heavy cream
½ cup grated Gruyère cheese
Pepper from the mill
Grated nutmeg

Prepare the batter. Cook 6 *matafans*; roll one piece of ham into each cake. Meanwhile heat and lightly reduce the cream, add the cheese, pepper, and nutmeg and stir over medium heat until melted. Spoon an equal amount of the fondue over each cake. Serve hot.

MATAFANS DE POMMES DE TERRE AUX POIRES
Potato Matafans *with Pears*

3 unripe Bartlett or Bosc pears, cored and sliced
Salt
Pepper from the mill

Slice the pears, put them in a baking dish, sprinkle them with salt and pepper. Render the bacon and sauté it until golden, then remove it to a plate. Remove most of the bacon fat from the pan, and

3 ounces slab bacon, cut into
⅓-inch cubes
1 recipe Potato Matafan batter
(page 203)

in the bit left, sauté the pears until brown, return the bacon to the pan, and mix with the pears.

Cook one or two *matafans* per person. Put a small portion of pears and bacon on each cake and roll.

MATAFANS DE POMMES DE TERRE AUX FROMAGES
Potato Matafans *with Cheeses*

1 recipe Potato Matafan batter
(page 203)
6 onions, slivered
2 tablespoons butter
⅓ cup each grated Emmental
and Beaufort or Gruyère
and Emmenthal cheeses

Cook the *matafans*. Sauté the onions in the butter until very soft, and top each *matafan* with an equal amount of the onion compote. Sprinkle with the mixed cheeses and put in a preheated 300°F oven until the cheese has melted. Serve promptly.

MATAFANS AU VERT
Green Matafans

½ pound raw spinach, very
finely chopped
1 tablespoon butter
1 recipe Basic Matafan batter
(page 203)
6 eggs, fried
½ cup heavy cream
½ cup sour cream
6 rashers bacon, cooked and
crumbled
Salt (optional)
Pepper from the mill
Grated nutmeg

Sauté the spinach in the butter until dry and completely free of moisture. Cool completely. Add the spinach to the egg yolks in the basic *matafan* batter before preparing the batter, which may require slightly less liquid. Fry 6 *matafans*, top each with a fried egg and with both creams mixed together, heated, and seasoned with the crumbled bacon, salt if needed, pepper, and nutmeg.

MATAFANS DE MAÏS AUX BOLETS
Corn Matafans *with Creamed Boleti*

1 recipe Cornmeal Matafan
   batter (page 203)
1 pound fresh boleti
   mushrooms, cleaned and
   sliced
1 small zucchini, cut in
   ⅛-inch-thick slices
2 tablespoons butter
Chopped parsley and basil
Salt
Pepper from the mill

Prepare the *matafans* and keep them warm. Sauté the boleti and zucchini together in the butter; add the parsley and basil. Correct the seasoning with salt and pepper. Top the *matafans* with some of the mixture, roll, and enjoy.

This mixture can also be creamed: Add the vegetable mixture to 1 cup of cream reduced by almost half and well seasoned.

VARIATION: Include the sautéed boleti in the *matafan* batter and cream the zucchini; spoon the creamed mixture over the mushroom *matafans*.

SWEET MATAFANS

This is probably a modern modification and variation, since I do not remember having been served dessert *matafans* anywhere, even in a private home; there are too many imported Brittany crêpes floating about Savoie cities nowadays to think of making the old *matafans* a dessert, but they are delicious with honey mixed with soft butter. Pumpkin, cornmeal, and potato *matafans* especially marry very well with the taste of evergreen honey.

MATAFANS AUX FRUITS
Fruit Matafans

Add to the basic *matafan* batter modified with any spice marrying well with the berries and a dab of honey or sugar, any berries you like. If you use cherries leave them unpitted and warn your guests; the cherry juice makes them too soggy. If you use apples, pears, or bananas, sauté the slices in butter before adding them to the batter. Very juicy fruits such as plums and ripe peaches or apricots are better cooked into compotes and served on the side as here.

MATAFANS DE POMMES DE TERRE AUX COMPOTES
Potato Matafans *with Fruit Compotes*

Prepare potato *matafans*, adding 1 tablespoon of sugar and a sprinkle of cinnamon to the batter. Serve with any fruit compote: apricot, rhubarb, plums, and strawberries are the best. See page 377.

Mix, match, and enjoy substitutions of batter and fruit to your heart's content.

Pasta

The self-sustaining family in many a Savoie valley reserved a small field for Manitoba Spring Wheat, which was grown with more or less difficulty, depending on the exposure of the field and the particular weather of the year. The flour made from this wheat was reserved for the making of pasta during the winter months while snow curtailed all outside activities.

One category of pasta, the *fides*, was purchased at the grocery store and mostly used to thicken broth or light soups for people who were ill; the other types were called *grosses pâtes* and were homemade. The thickness was never so perfected that one could read the newspaper through the sheet and depended very much on the manual dexterity of the individual pasta-maker. I experienced some pretty thick and hard products during the winter of 1940, when Mélanie made pasta. It was thick all right, and most of the time she overcooked it in what can only be called an uncivilized manner. But many women were able to make *taillerins* as supple and silky as any professional pasta-maker.

You must have noticed the similarity of the word *taillerin* to the Italian *taglierini*, but it would be wrong to believe that the Savoie learned its pasta-making from Italy. Pasta was there historically among the Ceutron, Graiocele, and Medulle populations that, centuries before the opening of the Alpine passes, made tiny squares of dough, which they called *crozets*, using a mixture of wheat, rye, and buckwheat flours.

While *taillerins* have, so to say, disappeared, or rather still exist under the

French name *nouilles*, *crozets* have retained their name and are still made both at home and commercially. They now can be purchased in pretty square boxes all over the Tarentaise; they thicken soups and make excellent pilafs. In those regions of Italy also of Ligurian descent, *crozets* appear under the name *corzetti* or *scorzetti*.

There existed, and perhaps still exists, in the Upper Maurienne an elbow-shaped type of pasta called *dialinces* with which one prepared a stick-to-the-ribs dish called *frequesses*, which was a mixture of *dialinces*, *crozets*, rice, and potatoes. If it sounds like a *Bourre-Chrétien* (Christian-stuffer!) type of preparation, well it was, but it was also a smart nutritional item loaded with long-lasting energy for people who did hard physical work.

All one did to season the pasta was to sprinkle cheese over it and toss it with a wonderful concoction of onions sautéed in butter, most of the time precooked to the dark noisette stage. This concoction was and still is called a *cerfuse, cerfuze, serfuse,* or *starfuze*. The difference between *serfuze* and *starfuze,* if there is really any, is minor. It seems that in the first the butter is simply heated while in the second it is cooked to the deep noisette stage. The *cerfuze* is not made exclusively with onions; sometimes it is made with regular shallots or with those wonderful large red shallots known as *Cuisses de Dame*, or even with garlic slivers, as Georgette's grandmother was in the habit of doing.

There is also mention of cream and bacon bits added to the pasta after cooking. To replace the Savoie cream, I slightly undercook the pasta and use plain American cream well preheated; the pasta absorbs all the excess water in the cream, then I add sour cream at the last minute. You will notice that I use enough butter to compensate for the extreme difference in the quality of American supermarket cream and the Savoie product. Those cooks who live in dairy areas such as Vermont, Wisconsin, and Pennsylvania, with thick green grass and cream that is far superior to the average, can use their cream as is, just heating it to the scalding point.

Tomato sauce is relatively modern and became more important at the end of the nineteenth century. The tomato did not play a major role among the traditional Savoie vegetables because of the climatic conditions, but nowadays farmers of the Avant Pays and the Combe de Savoie grow tomatoes locally and very successfully. The crop arrives from September to almost the beginning of November in three colors: red, yellow, and green. The yellow tomatoes make a most delicious *coulis*.

The use of saffron was reserved for special occasions, and was used especially in food for funerals. Since other areas of France with a deep Celtic background also use saffron for funeral foods (*Mourtayro*, the Soup of the Dead, in Périgord and Rouergue), I have often wondered whether this was a custom brought by the Saracens.

Nowadays, pasta is as often boiled—a bit overboiled even—as it is prepared as a pilaf, by browning it, then cooking it in its own approximate volume of broth or salted water. When it has absorbed all the liquid, garnishes go in, mostly cream, cheese and bacon, herbs, but more rarely vegetables.

In the recipes that follow, the *fides*, the *taillerins traditionnels*, both the *crozets* of the Tarentaise and Thônes, and the *agneletti* belong to the nineteenth century or earlier. The other recipes are modern concoctions that I prepared in Annecy with local market ingredients. I have not hesitated to prepare *taillerins* containing greens because all Savoyards love *les herbes* (see Soup and Vegetable chapters). I have mixed flours since traditional *crozets* were always made with mixed flours. I see very little reason some women would not have mixed flours, dependent as they were on the constant changes in the crops from year to year.

I still vividly remember the strikingly beautiful mother of my friend Mimi, always immaculate in a white, rough-textured hemp apron as she sat in front of her house slivering cheese to season whatever smelled so good inside. She used to make some mighty spirited fennel-flavored tomme, which ripened with grace, that she used to season her *crozets*. Since you will have problems finding fennel-flavored tomme, you will see me use fennel seeds in the cream to replace its flavor.

Remember, when you want to prepare a Savoie dish, to use as ripe a cheese as you can find. Tomme is available in big cities, as is reblochon, which is always overripe; but there is also some great Fontina from Aosta that you should not hesitate to use in place of any missing Savoie cheese. Cooks from the Terra Santa around Val d'Isère probably used Fontina themselves, since a type of Fontina was and still is made, if in very small quantities, up there. OKA cheese from Canada can be a very good replacement for reblochon.

ABOUT PASTA-MAKING TECHNIQUES

Although I vastly prefer pasta totally handmade and hand-cut, I have reached that stage of my life where the whole operation becomes life threatening by the time I have finished hand-rolling the dough out as thin as I possibly can, so I now use a hybrid method. I give approximately 10 minutes of hand-kneading and finish the smoothing work with the machine. Then I roll the sheets of dough into flat cigars and cut the noodles in ¼- or ⅓-inch-wide bands, which I shake to unroll. I then put the ribbon pasta to dry. In the recipes that follow, you can do what you please; the more you do by hand the better the pasta will be.

When you have finished kneading the pasta by hand, make sure that you work it long enough with the machine to force the gluten to absorb 95 percent of the moisture, so that you will have just enough water left to make the dough workable. Your sheets should show no traces of tackiness or they will stretch and stick when you attempt to cut them. Let each sheet air-dry approximately 5 minutes before passing it through the cutter, or rolling and cutting it by hand.

For the *fides*, cut them with the small cutter of the machine to achieve regularity of size. *Fides* were store-bought only because no one had the time or manual dexterity to cut pasta as small as *fides* were.

All pasta recipes yield 8 servings.

FIDES

Sorry, no translation exists, but they will look familiar to you since, indeed, they are cousins to spaghettini. Try them as soup pasta in an excellent chicken broth garnished with baby peas and a bit of saffron. The recipe is no different from plain noodle dough, although I often add more egg yolks for better texture; the proportions here are those of the Savoie countryside.

BASIC FIDES

2 cups unsifted all-purpose flour
3 eggs, beaten
½ teaspoon salt

Make a well in the flour, add all but 3 tablespoons of the eggs and slowly draw the flour into the liquid. Add the salt. Knead into a smooth dough 10 minutes, flouring your hands lightly if the dough is too wet or, on the contrary, rubbing them with the reserved egg if the dough is too dry.

Divide the semi-finished dough into 6 equal pieces; let it stand under a bowl turned upside down 15 minutes. Pass each piece of dough through the machine until smooth and dry; roll out to number 3 so the thickness is 1/16 inch. Cut through the small cutter of the machine. Roll into nests and let dry 1 hour. Turn the nests over and let dry another hour on the other side. If you would like to keep some *fides*, simply put them into a metal tin.

PILAF DE FIDES AU SAFRAN
Saffron Pilaf of Fides

½ cup butter
1 onion, finely chopped
2 shallots, finely chopped
2 cloves garlic, coarsely
    chopped
1 recipe Fides (above),
    completely dried
1½–2 cups excellent chicken
    broth
Salt
Pepper from the mill
1 cup fresh, blanched baby
    peas

Heat the butter to the noisette stage and in it mellow the onion, shallots, and garlic. Using a slotted spoon, remove the vegetables to a plate. In the same butter, brown the nests of *fides* on both sides, proceeding in several batches if need be. Return the vegetables to the pot, arrange the *fides* nests on top of them, and add the broth just to cover. Bring to a boil, then turn down to a simmer. Season with salt and pepper, cover the top of the pot with several layers of paper towels and the pot lid, and cook from 4 to 8 minutes, the length of the cooking depending on the strength of your flour and the richness of your broth. Stir the peas into the pasta. Mellow the saf-

¼ teaspoon saffron threads
Grated Beaufort, Gruyère, or
  Fontina cheese (optional)

fron threads in a tablespoon or so of broth or water and fluff through the pasta with a fork. Serve quickly, with or without the cheese.

TAILLERINS

The recipe for *taillerins traditionnels* is a key or master recipe. In all those that follow, I shall use the same basic ingredients. Watch for variations in the pasta dough; if you see additional egg yolks, it is to give a better texture to pastas made with softer flours. When greens enter the composition of the dough, I shall reduce the amount of whole egg but add egg yolks to compensate for the water in the greens.

TAILLERINS TRADITIONNELS
Basic Recipe for Traditional Taillerins

TAILLERINS:
2 cups unsifted all-purpose flour
3 eggs, beaten
½ teaspoon salt
*1–1½ cups diced Tomme de
  Savoie or other similar
  cheese*

CERFUZE:
1 cup butter
*4 large yellow onions or 2
  Texas onions*
Salt

Make a well in the flour. Set 3 tablespoons of egg aside and pour the remainder into the well. Add the salt. Draw the flour into the liquid. Knead into a smooth dough approximately 10 minutes; flour your hands lightly if the flour is too wet or moisten them with egg if the flour is too dry. Cut the dough into 6 pieces. Pass each through the machine until smooth and dry; roll out into sheets ⅟₃₂ inch thick and cut either by hand or by machine. Gather the pasta into nests and let dry on a baking sheet.

To prepare the *cerfuze*, heat ¾ cup of the butter in a large sauté pan until the foam starts receding. Add the onions and cook until all the water has evaporated; let the onions cook until limp and light golden.

To put the dish together; boil the *taillerins* in abundant salted water. Butter a baking dish with 2 tablespoons of the remaining butter. As soon as the pasta is cooked, put half of it into the dish and top with the diced cheese; cover the cheese with the remainder of the pasta. Sprinkle the *cerfuze* evenly over the *taillerins*. To the pan in which the onions cooked, add 2 to 3 tablespoons of the pasta-cooking water; add the remaining 2 tablespoons of butter and heat well, scraping to dislodge the browned onion glaze. Spoon over the pasta.

GROS TAILLERINS À LA FARINE COMPLÈTE
Whole Wheat Flour Taillerins

TAILLERINS:

1½ cups unsifted all-purpose
    flour
1 cup unsifted whole wheat
    flour
3 eggs
2 egg yolks
½ teaspoon salt

FENNEL CREAM:

4 tablespoons butter
4 cloves garlic, coarsely
    chopped
2 cups heavy cream
Pinch of salt
Pepper from the mill
½ teaspoon crushed fennel
    seeds
⅓ cup sour cream
1–1½ cups finely slivered
    Tomme or Fontina cheese

Prepare the *taillerins* exactly as described in the master recipe on page 213. To prepare the fennel cream, sauté the garlic in the butter until it starts coloring. Add the heavy cream, salt, and several grindings of pepper and bring to a boil. Add the well-crushed fennel seeds. Keep warm and steep 15 minutes. Fluff in the sour cream.

Cook the *taillerins* in boiling salted water and layer them with the Fontina; pour the fennel cream over the pasta and serve promptly on hot plates.

GROS TAILLERINS AUX TROIS FARINES ET AUX CUISSES DE DAME
Three-flour Taillerins *with Red Shallot Cerfuze*

TAILLERINS:
1¼ cups unsifted all-purpose
  flour
½ cup unsifted rye flour
½ cup unsifted buckwheat flour
2 eggs
3 egg yolks
½ teaspoon salt

CERFUZE:
1 cup butter
1½ pounds shallots, preferably
  the large Cuisses de Dame,
  sliced ⅓ inch thick
Salt and pepper
½ pound slivered Beaufort,
  Gruyère, or Fontina cheese

Prepare the *taillerins* as indicated on page 213. Meanwhile heat the butter to the dark noisette stage, and in it sauté the shallots until very mellow. Season well.

Cook the pasta in boiling salted water; as soon as it is ready, drain and add it to the *cerfuze*. Transfer to a hot serving dish and sprinkle with the Beaufort or other cheese. Serve on hot plates.

TAILLERINS À LA LIVÈCHE
Lovage-flavored Taillerins

Wild celery is among the most important herbs of Savoie country food. The Swiss put lovage in Maggi seasoning, which every one of my Swiss friends sprinkles generously on whatever is served at any meal. I use Maggi seasoning, reinforcing its taste with a bit of celery seeds. If you have no lovage, you can use a mixture of parsley and celery leaves finely chopped. This is a modern use of old ideas. Maggi seasoning is available in most supermarkets or, if not, in gourmet food stores.

TAILLERINS:

2 cups unsifted all-purpose flour

2 eggs

2 egg yolks

1 teaspoon Maggi seasoning

¼ teaspoon powdered celery
  seed

GARNISH:

4 tablespoons butter

4 cloves garlic, coarsely
  chopped

½ cup coarsely chopped
  walnuts

2 cups heavy cream

¼ cup finely chopped lovage
  leaves or celery leaves

⅓ cup sour cream

Maggi seasoning

1½ cups grated Beaufort,
  Gruyère, or Fontina cheese

Pepper from the mill

Prepare the *taillerins* as indicated on page 213.

To prepare the garnish, heat the butter in a large sauté pan; add the garlic and walnuts. Toss until golden; pour in the heavy cream, bring to a boil, and add the lovage or celery leaves. Whisk in the sour cream and season with Maggi seasoning instead of salt.

Toss the pasta into the hot cream and serve piping hot, topped with the Beaufort and pepper from the mill.

TAILLERINS À LA FARINE DE MAÏS
Corn Flour Taillerins

Please use corn flour, not cornstarch or cornmeal or polenta; if you cannot find corn flour, put cornmeal in the blender and process until flour is obtained. The food processor is not useful for this operation.

TAILLERINS:

3 eggs

2 egg yolks

1 large clove garlic, chopped

1 large shallot, chopped

To make the *taillerins*, mix together in the blender the eggs, egg yolks, garlic, shallot, and pepper. Prepare the *taillerins* as indicated on page 213.

To prepare the garnish, peel and slice the garlic cloves. Cut them into paper-thin slices. Heat the

½ teaspoon ground black
  pepper
1¾ cups unsifted all-purpose
  flour
⅔ cup corn flour
½ teaspoon salt

GARNISH AND TOMATO
FONDUE:
1 whole large head of garlic or
  2 smaller ones
¼ cup clarified butter
½ cup butter
2 large zucchini, cut into
  ¼-inch julienne sticks
8 large yellow tomatoes, peeled,
  seeded, and coarsely diced
Salt
Pepper from the mill
3 large red tomatoes, peeled,
  seeded, and coarsely diced
½ pound Beaumont cheese,
  slivered
¼ cup chopped dill

clarified butter in a skillet and fry the garlic slivers until golden. With a slotted spoon, remove the garlic to paper towels and set aside. Add the butter, the zucchini julienne and sauté 1 to 2 minutes. Remove to a plate.

To the same skillet add the yellow tomatoes, salt and pepper them, and cook to a very liquid fondue; then add the red tomatoes and cook only a few minutes so the red tomatoes do not fall apart. Season carefully.

To put the dish together, boil the *taillerins*; in a baking dish or large sautée pan, blend the zucchini and *taillerins*. Correct the seasoning. Spoon the tomato fondue over the noodles. Sprinkle the slivered cheese, the dill, and the garlic cloves over the noodles. Toss first before serving on hot plates. Pass the pepper mill.

TAILLERINS AUX HERBES
Soup Greens Taillerins

If Patricia Wells reads this text she may remember the fresh *Persillé de la Rosière* that she brought me back from the Tarentaise in August 1980. After a very nice long stay in my cellar in Annecy, it turned all moldy and gray. I crumbled it into the green *taillerins* here, made with the soup greens sold by the farm ladies at the market. Even not-too-dry goat cheese does very well in this dish, which may also be creamed if you like, although I prefer it plain.

TAILLERINS:

1 tablespoon butter

2 cloves garlic, chopped

1 whole large leek, chopped

1 cup each spinach leaves,
    Swiss chard, and nettles,
    very finely chopped

Salt

Pepper from the mill

2 eggs

3 egg yolks

2½ cups unsifted all-purpose
    flour

½ teaspoon salt

GARNISH:

3 red onions, slivered

Salt

¾ cup butter, or more if
    needed

1½ tablespoons vinegar of
    your choice

1½ cups cooked Silverqueen
    corn kernels

1 cup grated or crumbled, aged
    or semi-dry goat cheese

Chopped parsley

Coarsely cracked black pepper
    from the mill

To prepare the *taillerins*, heat the butter in a large sauté pan, add the garlic and leek, and toss in the hot butter 3 to 4 minutes. Add all the greens, salt and pepper. Cover the pot to draw the water out of the vegetables. Remove the pot lid and cook, stirring occasionally until all the water has evaporated. Cool completely. Beat the eggs, egg yolks, and cooked greens together. Make a *taillerin* dough using the green mixture as described on page 213.

For the garnish, sprinkle the red onions with salt. Let stand 15 minutes. Pat dry with paper towels. Heat the butter in a large sauté pan, add the onions and the vinegar, toss well together, then add the corn.

Cook the pasta in boiling salted water. Drain, and add it to the mixture of corn and onions; sprinkle with the goat cheese, parsley, and coarsely cracked pepper.

TAILLERINS AUX RADIS ET AU CARVI
Red Radish and Caraway Taillerins

Caraway, or *carvi*, is usually used in the making of sausage and sometimes in tommes. Why not use it in a pasta dish? The idea is probably not new, but I never saw it in any of the texts I studied.

TAILLERINS:

2 cloves garlic, coarsely
   chopped
2 eggs
3 egg yolks
1 cup packed radish leaves
   (from 3 bundles of fresh
   radishes)
2¼ cups unsifted all-purpose
   flour
½ teaspoon Maggi seasoning

GARNISH:

3 tablespoons butter
Radishes from 3 bundles, sliced
   ⅙ inch thick
1½–2 tablespoons red wine
   vinegar
Salt
Pepper from the mill
1½ teaspoons caraway seeds
⅓ cup sour cream
Dijon mustard to taste
2 cups heavy cream
Chopped parsley

Put the chopped garlic, eggs, egg yolks, and radish greens in the blender container and puree until smooth. Set ¼ cup of the mixture aside. Prepare the pasta as indicated on page 213, using the radish green mixture and the flour mixture with the Maggi seasoning.

To make the garnish, heat the butter in a sauté pan, add the radish slices, vinegar, salt and pepper. Stir-fry until bright red. Add the caraway seeds and set aside. Mix sour cream and mustard. Set aside.

In another sauté pan, heat the heavy cream to the scalding point; season well. Cook the pasta, add it to the cream, keep on low heat while you toss in the sour cream and mustard mixture. Serve topped with the caraway, radishes, and chopped parsley.

CROZETS

Crozets are very small pieces of dough, no larger than ¼ inch square. Feel free to make them larger if you please; the larger they are, the more water they will need to cook. The smaller ones are best cooked in broth using the pilaf method; the larger ones must be boiled.

CROZETS DE THÔNES

Thônes Crozets

Thônes *Crozets* are first cousins to the Italian potato gnocchi.

One of Mélanie's colleagues in the kitchen used to make these by the ton; she was from Thônes. Sometimes they came in plain butter with cheap old endives or cabbage cooked to death; other times they were coated with *béchamel*. Here is one of those dishes.

FOR THE CROZETS:
3 cups unsifted all-purpose flour
2 very large, hot baked
    potatoes
1 tablespoon oil of your choice
    (not olive)
Warm water as needed
1 teaspoon salt

GARNISH AND SAUCE:
1 large Savoy cabbage
¾ cup butter
1 large onion, chopped
Salt
Pepper from the mill
3 tablespoons flour
1½ cups scalding milk
Grated nutmeg
⅔ cup slivered Tomme or
    Beaufort cheese

To prepare the *crozets*, put the flour on the countertop. Scoop out the hot potato pulp and rice it over the flour; sprinkle the oil over the mixture and gather it into a ball as much as you can without adding water. If the mixture crumbles, dip your hands into warm water, sprinkle a few drops at a time over the dough, and knead until it is smooth and homogenous. Cut into 8 pieces. Roll these pieces into strips ⅓ inch wide and cut them into triangular pieces. Let stand on a floured baking sheet, covered with a towel until ready to cook . . .

Clean the cabbage leaf by leaf. Pat dry in a towel and squeeze it to remove all water. Roll the leaves and chop them finely. Heat ½ cup butter in a sauté pan. Add the onion and the cabbage, salt and pepper, and cook covered until the cabbage forms a thick compote. Transfer the cabbage to a 9″ round porcelain dish.

Bring a pot of water to a boil. Add salt and the *crozets*. Let them come back to the surface of the water, then turn the heat down. Cover the pot and let them blow up in the warm water. Once they have done so nicely, transfer them on the bed of cabbage.

With the remaining butter, the flour, the scalding milk, and the nutmeg, prepare a light white sauce. Pour it over the *crozets*. Top with the slivered cheese and bake a few minutes until the cheese turns golden. Serve on hot plates.

CROZETS DE LA TARENTAISE EN PILAF
Tarentaise Crozet Pilaf

It would be nice if you could find Beaufort for this dish, since so much of it is made in the Tarentaise.

1¼ cups unsifted all-purpose
    flour
½ cup rye flour
½ cup buckwheat flour
2 eggs, beaten
½ teaspoon freshly grated
    nutmeg
½ teaspoon salt
Broth or other meat stock as
    available
¾ cup butter
2 large yellow onions, slivered
6 shallots, slivered
3 ounces slab bacon, cut into
    ¼-inch cubes
Salt
Pepper from the mill
1–1½ cups grated Beaufort
    cheese

Mix the three flours. Prepare the *crozet* dough exactly as the *taillerin* or *fides* dough. When you pass the dough through the machine, make certain it becomes as dry as possible, almost on the verge of being too dry. Pass the dough immediately through the fettucine blade. Lay the bands of pasta flat on the floured table and recut them into squares. Dry completely before using. Before storing in a tin, put the *crozets* in a colander and shake off the excess flour.

Measure 1 cup of scalding broth for each cup of dry *crozets*; set aside. Heat the butter in a sauté pan, add the onions and shallots, and cook until mellow and candied. Remove to a plate, leaving the majority of the butter in the pan. Blanch the slab bacon if it is very salty and sauté the tiny cubes in the same butter as the onions. Add the *crozets* and toss them into the hot butter. Add the measured broth, salt, and pepper and bring to a boil. Cover with paper towels and the pot lid, and cook until all the broth has been absorbed. Toss in the Beaufort and serve immediately.

NOTE: Any soup pasta, such as *orzo* and *tubbettini*, for example, can be used if you do not care to make the *crozets*. The nice taste of the rye and buckwheat will be missing, though.

AGNELETTI

The name, of course, is almost the same as the rounded Piemontese *agnolotti*, and like their cousins they are destined to receive all kinds of leftover meats after a Sunday or holiday dinner. The recipe given by Mique Grandchamp as "à l'Italienne" is a triumph of bourgeoise cuisine. Not so the country *agneletti*, square and small like the raviolis used to thicken clear soups or prepared as a gratin in a sauce made of meat juices and cheese.

Here are two recipes for *agneletti*, cousins to ravioli: one with duck stuffing, the other with pumpkin and hazelnut stuffing, since pumpkin is so popular in the Savoie. To imitate the local pumpkin, use half buttercup squash and half American pumpkin. For entertaining, make the *agneletti* ahead of time and freeze them. They go directly from the freezer to the boiling water.

AGNELETTI AUX RESTES DE CANARD
Agneletti *of Leftover Duck*

I always make these when I have served roast duck at dinner; carefully reserve the cooking juices from ducks roasted at 325°F and preferably use meat from the legs. If you have access to duck legs only and want to avoid the "powerful mess" of duck-roasting, prepare a dinner of slowly baked duck legs covered with mustard and bread crumbs and keep all the gravy for the *agneletti* dish. Shape the *agneletti* into ravioli freehand or using a simple ravioli tray, whichever is easier for you.

PASTA SHEETS:
3 cups unsifted all-purpose flour
4–5 eggs
¾ teaspoon salt

FILLING:
4 cooked duck legs, bones and
  skin removed
2 tablespoons chopped parsley

To prepare the pasta, mix the flour, eggs, and salt, knead 10 minutes. Divide the dough into four balls and allow them to rest 30 minutes under an upside-down bowl. Work each ball into two sheets large enough to cover *raviolini* trays and stretched as thin as possible on the pasta machine (Number 1 or 7, depending on the brand). Keep between towels.

To prepare the filling, put the duck meat, parsley, and garlic in the food processor and process as fine

1 large clove garlic
Cream as needed
1–2 tablespoons bread crumbs
   (optional)
1–2 gratings of nutmeg
Salt
Pepper from the mill

SAUCE:
½ cup duck gravy or
   homemade meat glaze
1 cup veal stock
2 cups heavy cream
1 cup slivered Beaufort or
   Gruyère cheese

as possible. Add a bit of cream to obtain a soft forcemeat. Add the bread crumbs only if, having made a mistake, your filling has become too thin. Add the nutmeg, salt and pepper.

To prepare the *agneletti* freehand, place the sheet of pasta on the counter. At 1- to 1¼-inch intervals, place half teaspoonfuls of forcemeat. Dip a pastry brush lightly in water and paint the dough between the dabs of forcemeat in both directions: top to bottom and left to right. Cover with a second sheet of pasta and with the fingertips seal the top sheet to the bottom one. Cut with a pizza wheel. Repeat with the other two sheets.

To prepare the *agneletti* with ravioli trays, stretch one sheet of dough over two or three trays. Add the forcemeat into the small depressions. Top with a second sheet of pasta and pass the rolling pin firmly over the trays to cut the ravioli.

In both cases you may cook the ravioli immediately or freeze them, and when you are ready to cook them put them solidly frozen into boiling salted water. Cook them until the skins are nice and soft, which will happen fast.

To prepare the sauce, mix the duck gravy and stock and reduce to ½ cup; at the same time, reduce the cream a bit and blend the cream and reduced juices. Put the *agneletti* in a baking dish. Pour the sauce over them and top with the Beaufort. Bake in a preheated 350°F oven until the Beaufort has just melted. Cool slightly before serving to enjoy the full flavor.

AGNELETTI À LA COURGE ET AUX NOISETTES

Agneletti *Stuffed with Pumpkin and Hazelnuts*

Use the same pasta dough as in the preceding recipe and fill with the following:

⅔ cup cooked buttercup
    squash
1 cup cooked pumpkin meat
Salt
Pepper from the mill
1 tablespoon marc or brandy
½ cup mashed, semi-dry goat
    cheese
½ cup chopped, toasted
    hazelnuts
½ cup butter
1 tablespoon lemon juice
Chopped parsley

Mix both squash meats, add salt and pepper, and cook until the puree turns brown and caramelizes on the bottom of the pan. Stir occasionally to prevent burning. Cool completely. Add the marc or brandy.

When cooked, add the goat cheese, well mashed, and the hazelnuts. Stuff the *agneletti* with the mixture (see page 223). Cook them in a bath of boiling salted water a few minutes.

To serve, bring the butter to the noisette stage, add the lemon juice, and toss the well-drained *agneletti* into the mixture. Serve on hot plates sprinkled with parsley.

Farcements, Farcis,
and Farçons

The Thônes valley is beautiful, airy, full of wild fragrant cyclamens in the summer and crystal-clear during the sunny days of winter. Historically it is quite interesting since it offers ancient Stone Age dwellings, small castles, and fortified farms, or *maisons fortes*, dating back to the 900s, if not earlier. The little town is dominated by the bulbous steeple of its baroque church, and as one leaves town toward the east, slowly the majestic cliffs of the Colombière appear to the left while the sierralike Aravis peek through the smaller ranges to the right. The road passing through La Clusaz climbs up to the Aravis Pass.

It was in La Clusaz, during the Christmas week of 1939, that I discovered skiing and that gem of Savoie food, *le farcement*. My parents had come from Paris to visit me and had taken me skiing; in those days skiing was done literally on wooden boards; a snapshot commemorates the event. There I stand, with my mother in a smart 1939-style felt crusher, looking at me half in motherly appreciation, half in doubt that I am going anywhere on those long wooden contraptions. I knew enough to reach the dining room at the bottom of the hill where midday dinner (not lunch) was waiting.

I was only nine years old, but the symphony of smells that reached my child nose as soon as we sat down at the table has remained with me ever since and literally haunted my gurgling stomach during the war years that followed.

The hotel has disappeared in the almost violent modernization that took place in the early eighties, but I can still see the sharp, forward-slanting handwriting in black ink on one of those old-fashioned menus advertising Pastis 51, of all things. Some of the offerings were:

Jambon de Montagne

air-dried mountain ham, which came on a huge platter, in large translucent red slices, surrounded by tiny cornichons and vinegar-preserved baby onions. The smoky smell was unbelievably pleasant. If you ever go up there, do not miss that ham; it is still there to enjoy, as sweet as Parma, with the smoke but none of the high salt of our best Smithfield. Then came:

Quenelles de Veau à la Savoyarde

rich veal *boudins*, hand-shaped, completely smothered with creamy mushroom sauce and some of those melting puff pastry *fleurons* that can be made only with soft French flour. And then, the star dish:

Le Farcement

When Maman saw this high pudding, all pinkly clad in bacon slices, she let out an enthusiastic "Oh, what is it?" much to the dismay of the waitress, who was a young girl, probably from the village, and whose holiday feasts had probably so far consisted of nothing but *farcements*. I could see her thinking, "Where is this woman coming from who doesn't even know what a *farcement* is?"

She thought better of us when, after hefty portions of tomme and reblochon, we all complimented her on the dessert of

Oeufs à la Neige and Gâteau de Savoie

the usual custard with poached egg whites floating in it, for which the French all over the territory seem to have a primeval craving; the dish appears on three-star tables as well as in smoky bistros every Sunday noon. There was also the famous biscuit, nice, dry, and ideal to soak up the custard, called *Gâteau de Savoie* by the frugal Savoyards.

It was that young waitress, whose name I never knew, whom I never saw again, although she is probably still somewhere around La Clusaz now busy grandmothering some red-cheeked urchins, who explained to us that *farcement, farcis*, and *farçons* are simply the great foods of the Savoie, served at least twice a week, on Sundays, and always for weddings, Holy Communions, at Christmas, and for funerals.

As a dish it is now in serious decline because of the introduction of meats into everyone's daily diet, but it remains a beloved preparation that many people are trying to preserve for posterity. Before I start on descriptions and bits of history, let me tell you where, at this late stage of the twentieth century, you can sit at a friendly table to enjoy this masterful piece of food preparation as it has passed to us slowly and surely from the Stone Age. At the Nouvel Hôtel du Commerce, rue des Clefs in Thônes, Monsieur and Madame Bastard Rosset serve a Savoyard dinner at the most moderate price together with a wonderful *carte* of other very tempting specialties.

The second exceptional *farcement* was made in Chamonix by Madame Dufour who, up to a few months ago, operated a neat little traditional restaurant, La Tartifle, rue des Moulins. Madame Dufour has just retired and I only hope that she has passed on the recipe to the new owners; hopefully, they will have the same culinary touch, since recipes, alas, are not enough to make a superior dish.

In Les Praz de Chamonix, at the Hôtel de l'Arveyron, Alain Schmidt, the patron, also makes a good one among all his very good dinners. I met Alain when he was a kid in 1959, before I left for America; his parents are old friends.

More and more local dishes are being revived nowadays, thanks to the wonderful work of Marie Thérèse Hermann; so look, because more and more country restaurants are sure to reintroduce *farcements* and *farçons* in the years to come, and I would not be surprised if a few in the Albertville-Moûtiers axis were to activate regional menus during the 1992 Olympics.

So, after all these tourist details, what is a *farcement*? It can be many different preparations. Those I just mentioned are made as follows:

A high tube pan called a *rabolire* is lined entirely with slices of smoky bacon; layers of raw, yellow hand-grated potatoes mixed with very little egg and milk fill the mold, separated by dried prunes and raisins and occasionally *per se* or *cruchons*, known to us as dried pears. The layers are baked in a hot water bath, tightly covered like a steamed English pudding, and unmolded onto a platter. It is quite a sight, the smell is heavenly, and the taste a revelation. Well at least it is, as far as I am concerned; I have had some contrary souls wriggle their noses daintily and tell me what heavy food it was! Why sure, when one walks up and down mountains, draws the milk out of a hundred cows, makes cheese, skis more than a few miles a day to get to "civilization," and has to contend with snow up to one's face, one does not have to worry as much about excess pounds and one eats a sturdy dish with gusto instead of being on the sempiternal diet because one cannot take off from one's chair. This is all a matter of philosophy; I have to admit that some country dishes are anything but light, but they are historical features that do not have to be consumed more than once in a while or can simply be tasted just so one knows what it is. These dishes are a reflection of a way of life that, of course, is far from our own, but is still most interesting.

Farcement is the name given to this potato pudding in the Arve valley, all the way up to the upper Chamonix valley; the same name is also used in the upper Arly valley on the eastern slopes of the Aravis.

Farcements can be made the ancient or the new way. In Mont Saxonnex, it was made in a terrine lined with a piece of linen called *la patta du farcement*; inside the linen went a pastry into which were put cooked potatoes mixed with milk, eggs, raisins, prunes, and quite a bit of sugar; one closed the pastry, linen, and terrine, and the whole was steamed exactly like a pudding. The *farcement* just described, made in the metal *rabolire*, is the most recent recipe of the collection; the *rabolire* did not arrive until the beginning of our century.

Historian Jean Nicolas places the arrival of the potato at 1733–44, so all *farcements, farcis*, or *farçons* made with potatoes must date after that time. There are much more ancient *farsman* made only of cabbage and bacon and cooked in a net called a *gwefa*, which was immersed in the soup pot. Can anything more Celtic exist? These are found in the Chablais, around Abondance, as well as near Lake Leman, in Habère Poche.

In the valley of the upper and lower Arc, and the Upper and Lower Maurienne, these puddings are given another name, which denotes yet another cooking method; the *farci*, as it is called there, can be steamed in a towel or bag as described, or simply baked in a terrine as is done for meat terrines and meat loaves nowadays. According to Marie Thérèse Hermann in *La Cuisine Paysanne de Savoie*, the people of Termignon used to stuff the *farci* mixture into a lamb stomach when an animal happened to be killed or had to be slaughtered. This practice was common to all ancient people of the Stone Age, and the bags or vegetable leaves used as containers are more modern replacements for the animal stomachs used in prehistoric times when no vessels of either clay or metal existed. Other countries or provinces have identical preparations: the clay-baked birds of the Longobards, the *Haggis* of the Scottish people, the *Gefuellte Soymage* of the Alsatians, the *Far'sach* of the Bretons, and the *Sou Fassum*, or stuffed cabbage, of Provence.

The Combe de Savoie and the Tarentaise offer *farçon*, which is evocative of the more modern gratins, but is of different origin and made mostly with cooked potatoes.

In each of the three names you can see the common root *fars*, a word still used currently in the Breton-speaking part of Brittany to name their numerous flour and grain puddings. Basically, the less potato and the more bread and vegetables a *farçon* contains, the more ancient it is. Those recipes containing cabbage, turnips, and carrots are probably the most ancient.

May I recommend to those who read French fluently and who are interested in French Provincial cuisines the chapter "*Le Farçon*" in Ms. Hermann's book cited earlier. The diversity of preparations is unbelievable. One anecdote struck me as more typically Savoyard than all the others:

According to Ms. Hermann, *farçons* and their cousins were long-cooking preparations that could be baked slowly, buried into the cinders of the hearth or in the bread oven while one walked to mass on Sunday, far away from home. Those women who did not have a bake oven at home deposited the *farcement* or *farçon* at the baker's shop, which in Thônes has "always" faced the church. Ms. Hermann colorfully describes how the women of the Thônes valley carried the *farcement* for the family on their heads, well tucked into a roll of material called the *torche*, and walked three to four miles from their homes to the Thônes church, knitting. I happen to know all the paths leading to that church very well, and they are not exactly smooth for walking, so it was quite a feat.

Each *farcement* was duly marked with the family name to prevent confusion. Alas, in the maze of all those identical pans or molds, the mark would sometimes be lost and disaster would strike as one would have to consume the *farcement* or *farçon* of strangers. My friend Georgette, next door in Annecy, confirmed this as being the utmost source of distress.

Farcements keep hot for such a long time that some have been said to arrive in Geneva warm, after being taken there on foot from Mont Saxonnex, a distance of some twenty miles.

In the recipes that follow, you will find various combinations of ingredients, most savory, some sweet, and a lot of different cooking and baking techniques. These very ancient dishes have been staples in my family's after-ski fare in the Alps or the White Mountains for the last fifteen years. My favorite are the *Farcement du Faucigny* and that marvel of *Farçon de Saint Ferréol*, all fragrant with chervil. With the exception of the Faucigny *farcement* on page 233, which is a combination of different versions I enjoyed in many homes and/or public places, the other recipes are taken from ideas cited by Marie Thérèse Hermann and adapted for the most authentic possible taste one can achieve with American ingredients.

Choice of Potatoes

The choice of potatoes is extremely important. Idaho potatoes will not work because they contain too much moisture and starch and fall apart too easily; keep them for baking. The best potatoes to use for the *farcement/farci/farçon* family of dishes are:

> Yellow Finnish potatoes
> White Rose potatoes
> Maine Round flat potatoes
> Long Island potatoes
> Prince Edward Island potatoes
> California September new potatoes

They all keep well through February in a cold cellar covered with a blanket.

All recipes in this section yield 8 to 10 servings.

FARÇON DE SAINT FERRÉOL

Farçon *from Saint Ferreol*

The *farçon* that follows comes from Saint Ferréol in the Genevois part of the Haute Savoie, perched high up halfway between Thônes and Faverges on Route D12. It is accessible only by the most amazing road turning and twisting over a gorge. This is taken from the recipe of Madame Blampey cited by Ms. Hermann and adapted to American ingredients. The original recipe calls only for chervil, but the strength of this herb as grown in the United States requires the addition of parsley and tarragon to be approximately equivalent to the original taste.

½ pound butter

Cloves from 1 large head of garlic, peeled and slivered

2 pounds baked Maine or California potatoes, hot from the oven

½ cup chopped fresh chervil

¼ cup chopped Italian parsley leaves

3 tablespoons chopped tarragon leaves

½ cup scalding light cream, as needed

Salt

Coarsely cracked white pepper from the mill

Heat the butter in a large skillet. Add the garlic slivers and cook them to golden, no deeper. Remove them from the butter and keep them to garnish a salad. Set aside a third of the garlic butter in a small bowl.

Scoop the insides out of the potatoes directly into the skillet containing the garlic butter and mash coarsely with a fork. Heat the pan to cook the puree so it crusts on the bottom of the pan. Mix well and repeat the crusting and mixing another time. Add the herbs, and only if too dry add the cream. Correct the seasoning with salt and cracked white pepper.

Butter a 1-quart baking dish with half the reserved garlic butter. Pour and smooth the puree of potatoes into the dish. Sprinkle the top with the remaining garlic butter and bake in a preheated 300°F oven approximately 1½ to 2 hours, until golden. Serve with a salad of lamb's lettuce containing the browned garlic slivers.

VARIATION: Spread one layer of potatoes on the bottom of the dish, add ½ pound of crumbled fresh goat cheese, top with another layer of potatoes, and finish baking as just described.

FARCI DE BESSANS
Farci *from Bessans*

This comes from Bessans, the second-to-last village before the Iseran in the Upper Maurienne and a mecca of interesting cultural and artistic life. Bessans women used to prepare small linen bags to receive this pudding, which was then steamed in water. The American ingredients did not poach well, so I transferred the whole mixture to an enameled cast-iron *cocotte*, the mixture now resembling many of the old Celto-Ligurian *tians* of Provence. The mustard gravy is a personal addition; the true seasoning was chopped garlic infused in water, which is a little thin. A bitter green salad is the best companion to this sturdy preparation.

FOR THE FARCI:
½ cup butter
2 leeks, finely chopped
2 yellow onions, chopped
1 large Savoy cabbage, shredded
Salt
Pepper from the mill
½ pound thick-sliced bacon, finely diced
½ pound smoked pork shoulder, finely diced
½ pound ground lamb
½ pound lean Italian sweet sausage
4 cloves garlic, mashed
1 teaspoon caraway seeds
½ teaspoon grated nutmeg
1½ cups cooked short-grain rice, warm
½ cup fine cornmeal
½ cup flour

In a large sauté pan, heat 6 tablespoons of the butter and sauté the leeks and onions in it until the onions are translucent. Add the cabbage, salt and pepper, and toss well; cover, and cook on low heat until the moisture has completely evaporated and the cabbage is overcooked and falling apart. Set aside in a large bowl.

In the same pan, render the bacon until golden but not crisp, and remove to the bowl containing the cabbage; add the pork shoulder and sauté it a few minutes in the bacon fat. Remove the shoulder to the bowl. To the bacon fat, add the ground lamb, flattening the meat well on the bottom of the pot to extract the fat. As the meat browns, bring it to the handle side of the pot and with your spatula push on it at the same time as you tilt the pot to let the fat drain out. Spoon the fat out and discard it. Add the lamb to the bowl. Finally render the sausage, browning it lightly and discarding as much fat as possible. Add the sausage to the bowl, as well as the 4 garlic cloves, the caraway seeds, grated nutmeg, rice, cornmeal, and flour. Beat the eggs

10 eggs
1 cup whole milk

FOR THE GRAVY:
3 tablespoons butter
2 tablespoons flour
1½ cups farm-style chicken
   broth (page 183)
⅓ cup sour cream
½ tablespoon Dijon mustard
2 cloves garlic, finely chopped
2 tablespoons chopped parsley
Salt
Pepper from the mill

and milk together, and blend the dry and moist ingredients until the mixture is homogenous.

Butter a 3-quart *cocotte* with the remaining 2 tablespoons of butter and turn the *farci* evenly into the pot. Cover and bake in a preheated 300°F oven until a skewer inserted at the center comes out clean and hot. Cool 10 minutes before serving with a salad and the mustard sauce.

To prepare the mustard sauce, cook half the remaining garlic in butter until golden. Add flour and butter and cook to a hazelnut color. Bind with the broth and cook 10 minutes. Mix the sour cream and mustard together and blend into the sauce. Add the remaining raw garlic and parsley and correct the seasoning.

NOTE: If there are leftovers, a cold slice of *farci* on a piece of country bread with mustard makes a great sandwich. For breakfast, I cook cold slices as I would scrapple.

FARCEMENT DU FAUCIGNY
Farcement *from the Faucigny*

This is the king of them all! It is strikingly attractive, cooked in its tall tube pan, the *rabolire*, which if you are in Haute Savoie can be purchased in all *quincailleries*, or hardware stores, and household equipment stores in Cluses, Sallanches, and Saint Gervais. But a great *farcement* can be made in any American tube pan, tightly covered with heavy foil.

This version is made with raw grated potatoes, a composite of the best I have had in restaurants and private homes. Watch the potatoes—they are extremely important—and never ever put flour in the pudding. If you can find Yellow Finnish potatoes, use them; they will give you exactly what is called in Megève a *farchment rosset* ("yellow *farcement*"). If you cannot find any of the potatoes listed here, do not hesitate to go to the recipe I published in *When French Women Cook* using cooked mashed potatoes, which has worked like a charm. The taste will be the same; only the texture will vary.

And yes, you are reading correctly. It takes *seven* full hours to steam the *farcement*, and make sure that you have the full seven hours or the taste simply will not be there and you will think I am crazy in my enthusiasm. Customarily, ham, rolled pork shoulder, and the *pormonaises*, for which a recipe is given on page 320, are served with it. You will need a good crisp salad after that, and no dessert—there is enough dried fruit in the pudding—but let the wine flow freely. Your wine should be a Chignin de Bergeron, a Dézaley, or a Sauvignon Blanc. It is the most perfect food I know after a day of great skiing.

ESSENTIAL IMPLEMENTS:
one 9⅝- by 3¼-inch tube pan
Heavy-duty aluminum foil

12 potatoes, Yellow Finnish, Maine, Long Island, or California new, peeled and washed (The potatoes are listed in order of preference.)
4 rashers thick-sliced bacon, preferably Virginia- or Vermont-smoked
3 eggs
⅔–1 cup milk, or more if needed
½ cup cornmeal
¼ cup currants
2 dried pear halves, without sulfur dioxide, diced into ¼-inch cubes
Salt
Pepper from the mill

Hand-grate the potatoes on the coarse blade of a grater (positively no food processor). Let the potatoes stand in a bowl so the water oozes out. Cover with plastic wrap and do not worry about browning. After 1 hour, rinse the potatoes under cold running water until the water runs perfectly clear. Dry the potatoes completely in tea towels.

Meanwhile render the thick-sliced bacon and cook it until golden, not crisp. Cut into ⅓-inch square pieces. Do not remove the fat remaining in the bacon; it is needed. In a large bowl, beat the eggs and ⅔ to 1 cup of milk; add the cornmeal, cooked bacon, currants, and diced pears and blend well. Add the potatoes; salt and pepper well. Keep covered while you line the mold entirely with the thin-sliced bacon, letting the ends of the rashers hang over the edges of the tube pan on the outer and inner rims. Spoon half the potato mixture into the mold; pack down by tapping the bottom of the mold on the counter. Top with the soft prunes and add the remainder of the potatoes. Tap again to pack down.

Flip the bacon hanging out of the mold over the

2 pounds thin-sliced, any old-
   fashioned bacon (but not
   cured with replacement
   sugar)
12 soft pitted prunes

top of the filling. Cover the mold tightly with heavy-duty aluminum foil, dull side out. Put the mold in a 1½- to 2-gallon soup pot and slowly pour enough water into the pot to reach 1 inch below the rim of the mold. Bring to a boil on top of the stove and immediately bake in a preheated 325°F oven 7 hours. Cool slightly before unmolding onto a platter and serving on hot plates.

FARCI AU FROMAGE BLANC
Farci *with Fresh White Cheese*

Another specialty of the Maurienne where, instead of our cottage cheese, they use a tomme, nice and fresh, just as soon as it has been dripped of all its whey. Lining the baking dish with cabbage leaves is also common in the Auvergne. The cabbage leaves caramelize as the *farci* bakes, giving the potatoes a wonderful taste.

2 pounds Maine potatoes or
   other choices (page 230)
1 cup heavy cream
¼ teaspoon grated nutmeg
1 pound creamed cottage
   cheese
¼ pound rich cream cheese,
   whipped
6 eggs, well beaten
⅔ cup fresh rye bread crumbs
Salt
Pepper from the mill
½ cup melted butter
2 tablespoons cold butter
12 large outer leaves of Savoy
   cabbage, blanched

Boil the potatoes in their jackets. Scald the cream in a large saucepan and add the nutmeg. As soon as the potatoes are cooked, skin them and rice them quickly into the cream. Add the two cheeses, the eggs, the bread crumbs, salt and pepper, and 4 tablespoons of the melted butter. Mix very well.

Butter a 2-quart *cocotte* with the cold butter. Remove the ribs of the blanched cabbage leaves; line the bottom and sides of the *cocotte* with the cabbage leaves. Empty the potato-cheese mixture onto the leaves. Pour the remaining melted butter on top of the pudding and cover. Bake in a preheated 300°F oven at least 2 hours. Cool slightly before serving with a salad.

FARÇON DE LA COMBE DE SAVOIE
Farçon *from the Combe de Savoie*

This is a light preparation that can also be used as a companion to a stew or civet, as on page 334, rather than only as a vegetarian main course. The end product is a creamy rather than a stiff and cuttable mixture.

2 pounds Maine potatoes,
  boiled in their jackets
½ pound slab bacon, cut into
  ⅓-inch cubes
2 onions, finely chopped
Pinch of sugar
2 tablespoons flour
1 cup scalding heavy cream
Salt
Pepper from the mill
4 tablespoons butter
Outside leaves of a Savoy
  cabbage, blanched

While the potatoes cook, slowly render the bacon in a sauté pan, cooking it until golden but not crisp. Remove the bacon to a plate.

In the bacon fat, cook the onions slowly until they are candied; add the sugar and let it caramelize. Add the flour and cook a few minutes; off the heat, stir in the scalding cream; return to the heat and thicken on medium-high.

Peel the cooked potatoes, and while they are hot, rice them into the onion-cream sauce. Add the bacon, mix well, and season to taste. Add 2 tablespoons of the butter.

Butter a 2-quart *cocotte* with the remainder of the butter. Line it with the cabbage leaves. Pour the potato mixture over the leaves and cover the edge of the potato mixture with the tips of the cabbage leaves. Bake, uncovered, in a preheated 300°F oven 1 to 1½ hours. Serve with a salad.

FARÇON DE TARENTAISE ET DU BEAUFORTAIN
Farçon *from Tarentaise and Beaufortain*

This *farçon* seems to be on the sweet side, so sweet that I would almost consider it a dessert. It is a composite of several recipe descriptions given by Marie Thérèse Hermann.

2 pounds potatoes, boiled in
   their jackets, then peeled
3 cups milk
6 slices of white bread, crust
   removed, crumbled
Seeds of 1 vanilla bean or 1½
   teaspoons pure vanilla
   extract
½ teaspoon grated nutmeg
⅛ teaspoon Quatre Epices
¼ teaspoon saffron powder
2 tablespoons currants
1 teaspoon aniseeds
2 tablespoons chopped dried
   figs
6 dried prunes, chopped
2 eggs
1½ tablespoons sugar
Salt
Pepper from the mill
½ cup butter

Rice the potatoes into a large bowl. Keep them warm over the water in which they cooked.

Scald half the milk, add the crumbled bread, bring to a boil, and stir gently into the potatoes. Scald the remaining milk, add the vanilla seeds or extract, the nutmeg, Quatre Epices, saffron, currants, aniseeds, chopped figs, and prunes. Blend into the potatoes. Beat the eggs and the sugar well, and blend into the potato mixture. Add salt, pepper, and 4 tablespoons of the butter.

Butter a 2-quart *cocotte* with 2 tablespoons of butter. Add the *farçon* mixture and bake, covered in a preheated 300°F oven 1½ to 2 hours. Serve lukewarm with a fruit compote of your choice (see page 377).

FARCEMENT DU GRAND BORNAND
Farcement *from Le Grand Bornand*

Le Grand Bornand made news in the United States during the summer of 1987 when flash flooding brought disastrous results. A beautiful village overlooking the Aravis, it is a great little place for not-too-expensive skiing. No baking for this *farcement*, only a nice slow—forever—cooking in a *cocotte* until all the ingredients are reduced to a compote. Enjoy it with a salad. It is an adaptation of the recipe idea of Sister Cecile Blanchet, as cited by Marie Thérèse Hermann.

1 large Savoy cabbage,
   blanched
3 Bosc pears, almost but not
   quite ripe, cut into ¼-inch
   cubes
5 rashers thick-sliced bacon
4 large yellow onions, sliced
1 tablespoon flour
¼ cup raisins
8 potatoes, baked and hot
   (any kind)
1–1½ cups scalding light
   cream, as needed
Salt
Pepper from the mill

Mix the cabbage and pears. Set aside. In a 2-quart *cocotte*, render the bacon until golden. Cool and chop them, then set aside. In the bacon fat, sauté the onions until golden. When they are cooked, press out the bacon fat and discard it.

To the *cocotte* add the cabbage and pear mixture, the reserved bacon and onions, the flour, and the raisins; stir well together. Peel the potatoes and rice them into the mixture. Dilute with hot cream as needed. Season lightly and cook slowly on very low heat, stirring occasionally. Cook at least 1½ hours. The longer it cooks the better it tastes. If the mixture seems too dry, add small amounts of cream. The texture should be that of a compote. Serve with a salad.

Gratins

The word *gratin* was explained on Channel 2 of French National Television in 1981 by a professor at the University of Grenoble as deriving from the Latin name for Grenoble: Gratianapolis. It is probable that it was applied to dishes of vegetables or of meats and vegetables, which were baked in the various metal dishes illustrated in the Apicius cookbook. The brown earthenware dishes in which gratins are baked now resemble those dishes, sometimes in shape and always in depth.

If gratins really originated in the Dauphiné, they then inched their way north, for they are also found in the mountains of the Savoie and the Jura. Both in the Savoie and the Jura the faïence and ceramic dishes in which gratins have been made since the eighteenth century can be identified as to their origin by their shape and workmanship. They are mostly oval, although a few are round or rectangular, very shallow, with rims no higher than 1½ to 2 inches; some have straight sides and a flat bottom, while others show a scalloped design inside.

In the Savoie there is a relationship between the gratins and some of the *farçons*: the basic difference between the two preparations is that in the Savoie *farçons* the potatoes are always precooked and pureed, however coarsely, while in the gratins they are generally in slices, mostly raw but sometimes precooked, so that the *gratin de courge* on page 243 should really be called a *farçon de courge*.

Everyone in the United States is familiar with gratins; they are prepared all over the country since scalloped potatoes are potato gratins, even if made with a technique other than the French ones. I can vouch that Maine potatoes and American heavy cream make as good a *Gratin Dauphinois* as any made in France; the taste and texture are a bit different, but perfectly delicious. In my other cookbooks I have included many types of potato gratins, made plain or in combination with other vegetables such as leeks, celeriac, fennel bulb, and mushrooms. Here you will find three other potato gratins different from the Dauphinois.

The Savoie likes, more so in its modern kitchen than in its traditional one, to prepare gratins with all kinds of vegetables. So classic have the gratins of cardoons and of Swiss chard become that by now they have found their way into all French cookbooks and are already well known in the United States, so you will not find them in the following pages. Instead, I have included gratins that I have enjoyed more or less well executed in small restaurants all over the Savoie, and a few I have made up myself.

One thing should be well understood. It is absolutely essential that gratins be made with bouillon or broth or heavy cream, not ever with *crème fraîche*, which coagulates like baked white cheese when submitted to the steady heat of an oven. The baking heat must be very slow and steady, never higher than 300°F to 325°F, to imitate the heat of the dying bread oven. Gratins know neither exact science nor exact timing; they bake as they please, in the time they feel like, and can be contrary if one is in a hurry. This is because no two ingredients entering a gratin are ever identical: Every cream and stock texture and heaviness will be different, and each vegetable will have its own speed of softening and of absorbing the cream. No recipe followed to the ¼ teaspoon will ever give you a civilized gratin. Some mountain people say that the gratin makes the cook. That may be true, but the cook need understand only one thing: that cream or stock, when it bakes at length, reduces letting its water content be partly absorbed by the vegetables and partly evaporate while its proteins concentrate and eventually coat the outside layers of the vegetables. This is more visible with stock or broth than it is with cream; with cream the gratin is ready when the cream breaks butter all around the edge of the dish.

No two vegetables once sliced give the very same volume when measured in cups; so if a dish is too large, use a smaller one, and if it is too small, obviously, use a larger one. The same applies to the amount of stock or cream needed; if there is not enough cream or stock to cover the vegetables, by all means add more without worrying whether you are doing the right thing or not. Worrying about amounts of ingredients takes all the fun out of cooking. Make sure that you always have enough cream or broth, or both, when you make a gratin, and proceed from there, cooking the gratin with your eyes and your nose; both will tell you when it is done. One thing is certain, it should look tight and well reduced, not soggy with unreduced liquid. Now good luck, you will make it, I am certain; generations of peasant women have done it very successfully before you.

Patience is of the essence because this is old food that we have had to adapt from the old way of cooking in brick or stone ovens; just remember that easy does it for gratins and that slow, ever so slow, is the rule. When you plan your dinner, just organize your time so you always have at least 1½ hours at your disposal to bake a gratin, and remember that your oven will be in use for that amount of time. Oh yes, the microwave cooks a gratin, but not a Savoyard one; a modern microwave gratin bears no resemblance at all to a true gratin.

All gratins yield 6 servings.

TRADITIONAL GRATIN DE POMMES DE TERRE À LA SAVOYARDE
Potato Gratin the Savoie Way

The best will be made with Yellow Finnish, White Rose, or Maine potatoes.

6 medium potatoes, peeled and
   cut into ⅛-inch-thick slices
Salt
Pepper from the mill
4 tablespoons butter
1½ cups grated Beaufort or
   Gruyère cheese
1–1½ cups bouillon or broth

Toss the slices of potato with salt and pepper. Butter a shallow baking dish with a full 2 tablespoons of the butter. Arrange one layer of potatoes on the bottom of the dish, top it with half the grated cheese, arrange the second layer of potatoes on top of the cheese, and pour enough bouillon or broth over the potatoes to barely cover them. Dot with the remaining butter. Bake in a preheated 325°F oven until the stock has been completely absorbed and the potatoes are tender when tested with a knife. Sprinkle the remainder of the cheese over the potatoes and bake again until the cheese has turned golden. Cool a few minutes before serving.

GRATIN DE CHOUX
Cabbage Gratin

This is the exquisite recipe of Madame Maillet. If none of the French cheeses are to be found, substitute Gruyère or Emmenthal.

2 large heads of Savoy cabbage
5 ounces slab bacon
4 tablespoons butter
Salt
Pepper from the mill
1½ cups heavy cream, or
*   more as needed*
1½ cups grated Beaufort or
*   Emmental cheese*

Core and quarter each head of cabbage. Blanch the pieces of cabbage twice, starting both times in boiling water. Cut the cabbages into ¼-inch slivers; discard the cores.

Cut the bacon into ⅓-inch cubes and render them in a large sauté pan until golden. Discard most of the bacon fat, add the butter to the pan and heat it well, toss the cabbage into the bacon cubes; salt and pepper and cover. Cook the vegetables until their volume has reduced by half.

Pour ½ cup of the heavy cream into a 1-quart baking dish. Add the cabbage in one layer of even thickness, pour another ½ cup of cream through the cabbage, punching holes in its mass to let the cream flow through. Bake slowly in a preheated 300 to 325°F oven until the cream has completely reduced; add another ½ cup of cream, salt and pepper the top of the gratin, and top with the cheese sprinkled evenly over the surface of the vegetables. Bake until bright golden; let cool a few minutes before serving.
VARIATION: I have made a personal variation of this gratin using well-blanched caulifower and Brussels sprouts, which are not traditional vegetables in the Savoie but taste very good.

GRATIN DE POIREAUX
Savoie Leek Gratin

The Madeira is not typical of country food, but can be acceptable in *cuisine bourgeoise.*

2 tablespoons butter
12 large but not huge leeks, blanched
Salt
Pepper from the mill
1–1½ cups bouillon or broth
¼ cup Sercial or Rainwater Madeira
½ cup heavy cream

Butter a 2-quart baking dish with the butter. Line the blanched leeks in the dish. Salt and pepper them. Pour on enough bouillon or broth to barely cover and add the Madeira. Bake in a preheated 325°F oven until the leeks are caramelized in the stock; should they color too much, cover them with parchment paper. When the stock has evaporated completely, add the cream and let it reduce until it coats the leeks completely.

GRATIN DE COURGE
Gratin of Pumpkin or Winter Squash

As mentioned in the title, this can be made in the United States with butternut or buttercup squash.

One 4- to 5-pound piece of dark orange pumpkin
1 tablespoon evergreen or other honey
Salt
Pepper from the mill
2 tablespoons butter
1 cup heavy cream
Freshly grated nutmeg
1 cup very coarse fresh bread crumbs from French bread

Put the piece of pumpkin or the whole squash in a large baking dish. Bake in a preheated 350°F oven until the outside caramelizes and the juices have flooded the dish.

Remove the pumpkin meat with a large spoon and mash it well with a fork or masher; add the honey, salt, and pepper.

Butter a 1½-quart dish with the 2 tablespoons of butter. Add the pumpkin and smooth the top well. Bake in a 300°F oven at least 2½ hours, or until the top starts caramelizing once more.

Mix the heavy cream and nutmeg with a dash of salt and pepper. Pour evenly over the gratin. Sprinkle evenly with the bread crumbs. Raise the heat to 325°F and continue baking until the crumbs are golden and crusty. Let cool a bit before serving.

GRATIN DE RAVES CARAMÉLISÉES
Gratin of Caramelized Turnips

Mélanie used to prepare this dish, and I never quite liked it until, one day, I decided to sauté the turnips. I let them color well and the whole dish turned around; so here is the fruit of our cooperation over a span of forty years. I used the fresh chestnuts of La Grande Jeanne above Annecy.

3 pounds purple-topped
    turnips, peeled and sliced
4 tablespoons butter
Salt
Pepper from the mill
1 cup cooked, crumbled
    chestnuts
2 cups bouillon (page 182) or
    farm-style chicken broth
    (page 183)
½ cup heavy cream
⅔ cup fine dry bread crumbs
1 clove garlic, finely chopped
2 tablespoons chopped parsley

Blanch the turnip slices in plenty of salted boiling water; drain and pat dry in a tea towel.

Heat 2 tablespoons of the butter in a sauté pan; add the turnips and, on medium-high heat, brown them as evenly as you can. Salt and pepper the vegetables, cover the pan, turn the heat down, and cook, covered, until the vegetables are evenly brown all around.

Butter a 1½-quart baking dish with the remainder of the butter; arrange half the turnips on the bottom of the dish, top with the crumbled chestnuts, and add the remainder of the turnips. Add just enough stock to barely cover and bake in a preheated 325°F oven until three quarters of the stock has evaporated. Add the heavy cream seasoned with a bit of salt and pepper. Mix the bread crumbs, garlic, and parsley and sprinkle the mixture over the gratin. Bake until golden.

GRATIN DE POMMES DE TERRE, POMMES, ET POIRES VERTES
Gratin of Potatoes, Apples, and Green Pears

A Mélanie version of a very Alemannic dish, which in the Alsatian part of my family was called *Schnitten* (in Germany it is called *Himmel und Erde*, meaning "Heaven and Earth"). Marie Thérèse Hermann has another version of it cooked in a *cocotte*, which she calls *Lou Cartis* ("the quarters") because the fruit is cut into quarters.

4 large potatoes

3 onions

3 Red Delicious apples, washed and unpeeled

3 not-so-ripe Bosc pears, washed and unpeeled

¾ cup butter

Salt

Pepper from the mill

2 cups bouillon (page 182) or farm-style chicken broth (page 183)

1 cup coarse fresh bread crumbs from French bread

Peel and slice the potatoes and onions; core and slice the apples and pears, all into ¼-inch slices.

Heat ½ cup of the butter in a large sauté pan, toss the onion slices in it until lightly colored, then remove to a plate. In the same butter, sauté successively the potato, apple, and pear slices. Salt and pepper all fruits and vegetables.

Grease a 1½-quart baking dish with 2 tablespoons of the remaining butter. Build three layers as follows: one with half the potatoes and onions mixed, one with all the apples and pears, and the last one with the remainder of the potatoes and onions. Add just enough stock to cover. Sprinkle with the bread crumbs and dot with the remaining butter. Bake in a preheated 325°F oven until all fruits and vegetables are tender, the stock has been absorbed, and the crumbs are golden. Add more stock during the cooking if needed.

GRATIN DE MANIGOD
Gratin from the Village of Manigod

In this dish, if you leave out the bacon you will not be too far from a Central European potato kugel. It is adapted from a recipe description given by Marie Thérèse Hermann.

3 ounces slab bacon, diced
    into 1/3-inch cubes
6 medium potatoes, peeled and
    grated
Salt
Pepper from the mill
2 eggs
1½ cups milk
2 cloves garlic, finely chopped
2 tablespoons chopped parsley
4 tablespoons butter

Render the bacon until golden but not crisp; drain and set aside.

Put the grated potatoes in a colander, rinse them thoroughly under cold running water until the water runs clear, and pat dry in a tea towel. Season the potatoes with salt and pepper.

Beat the eggs and milk together with salt and pepper; add to the potatoes. Add the garlic, parsley, and the reserved bacon.

Butter a 1½-quart baking dish with 2 full tablespoons of the butter. Pour in the gratin mixture and dot with the remaining butter. Bake in a preheated 325°F oven until golden.

GRATIN DE RACINES MÉLANGÉES
Gratin of Mixed Roots

An idea from the very nice small restaurant Le Grand Alexandre in Annecy revised my way of making this dish.

2 leeks, white part only
4 tablespoons butter
2 potatoes, peeled and sliced
Salt
Pepper from the mill
2 very large carrots, sliced and
    blanched
3 large purple-topped turnips,
    sliced and blanched
2 cloves garlic, finely chopped
2 cups broth or stock
1½ cups grated Beaufort or
    Gruyère cheese

Slice the leeks very thin and sauté them in 2 tablespoons of the butter until translucent; mix the leeks into the potato slices.

Butter a 1½-quart baking dish with the remaining butter, add half the potatoes and leeks, and season well. Add the carrots and turnips mixed and season well again; top with the remaining potatoes and leeks and season with garlic, salt, and pepper. Add just enough broth or stock to cover and bake in a preheated 325°F oven until most of the liquid has been absorbed. Top with the grated cheese and continue baking until golden.

GRATIN DE CHÂTAIGNE ET CHOUX DE BRUXELLES

Gratin of Chestnuts and Brussels Sprouts

This is a modern preparation; Brussels sprouts are not a traditional Savoie vegetable. If you use peeled chestnuts sold in a jar, do not precook them in water.

1 pound Brussels sprouts
1 pound peeled chestnuts
Salt
Pepper from the mill
2 tablespoons butter
1½–2 cups bouillon (page 182) or farm-style chicken broth (page 183)
½ cup heavy cream
½ pound Tomme de Savoie or Fontina cheese, sliced

Blanch the Brussels sprouts, drain them well, and set them aside. Cover the peeled chestnuts with water and cook them until half tender. Mix the sprouts and chestnuts; season with salt and pepper.

Butter a 1½-quart baking dish. Add the vegetables and stock to cover them; salt and pepper. Bake in a preheated 325°F oven until most of the stock has evaporated. Add the cream and finish baking until a light golden crust builds over the vegetables. Top with the cheese and let it just melt without browning at all.

NOTE: The cabbage gratin on page 242 can also be made the same way if one adds chestnuts before baking.

Exotic Grains

POLENTA

The tendency would be to pronounce the word *polenta* as in Italian, but in Savoie one says "Polinte," with that for-the-Anglo-Saxon-tongue quasi-unpronounceable nasal central syllable noticeably accentuated, and no trace of the *a* at the end.

The word *polenta*, as is well known, comes from the Latin *pulmentum*, the good old cereal gruel that old civilizations of the Mediterranean prepared for their common folks and their armies. Depending on the climate, the grain used varied from one area to the next; one did not use the same grain in Sparta as one used in Rome.

The seventeenth century saw a general popularization of corn all over Europe, and it was inevitable that the semolina made with the milled corn and called in Italy *polenta* would reach the Savoie. It happened through an enterprising landowner who brought some planting seeds from Piemonte around 1730. Xavier de Maistre assures us that only after 1780 did people start to consume polenta. Before that, corn had been reserved for animals. One fact is certain, and it is reported to us by Joel Barlow in his famous Hasty Pudding poem so popular that it is cited in all encyclopedias. Barlow was served polenta daily in Savoie inns while he was traveling through its countryside in 1793. Since this was the height of the French Revolution, shortages of all foods probably hastened the use of cornmeal on a general basis. Polenta *galettes* (maybe *matafans* made with cornmeal instead of flour where flour happened to be in short supply), topped with delicious fried onions, appeared first in all the little towns of the Tarentaise close to the Little Saint Bernard, and obviously the golden mush made its way slowly toward regions lying to the west.

Polenta slowly became a staple farm food, especially when a large group of people got together to celebrate or work, as during the summer *remues*, for example, or even during the *Vogue* in some villages. The sight is not common in Savoie anymore, but if you want to know what it was like, one little jump over the border to the communities of Northern Piemonte, Lombardia, Veneto, or Friuli, where the huge pots are still active, will give you the exact idea. In Savoie, another type of glorification of polenta has taken place. Since with tourism plain people foods have become attractive, polenta has been for the last twenty-five years very popular in small restaurants during the tourist season.

While in part of Northern Italy, polenta and polentina are often made with part cornmeal and part corn flour, such is never the case in Savoie, where one uses the meal exclusively. There are three calibers to the meal: The small caliber is used generally for mush, the medium caliber for both mush and pilaf, and the very coarse caliber of $\frac{1}{12}$ inch is used only for pilaf.

The mush is prepared exactly as it is in Italy and is called *Polenta au Bâton*, because it is always stirred with a large stick in a large cauldron for a very long time. It should not be surprising that the second technique used to cook polenta was adapted from the Classic French cuisine after the annexation: The pilaf method of cooking rice was applied to polenta, and the very coarse polenta meal was probably created originally for this method of cooking.

The polenta mush is enjoyed hot out of the pot with stews and rabbit civets, or it is poured onto a slab as in Italy and cut into slices to be floured and refried in butter. The ladled mush is interchangeable with the croutons, depending on the personal taste or flair of the cook, to receive a garnish of lightly sauced meat, fish, or melted cheese.

As in the Val d'Aosta and all other northern regions of Italy, polenta is often baked with garnishes of cheese and wonderful sauces based on tomato and/or meat. For a startling polenta, try spooning the pungent *Compouta* of aged cheese (page 170) over steaming polenta.

POLENTA AU BÂTON
Stirred Polenta

This is a master recipe to allow you to prepare the five recipes that follow. Use a large flat-bottomed sauté pan so that evaporation will take place a bit faster. While in the old days, when one worked on the hearth or a small inefficient stove, the pot was large and rounded at the bottom to catch all the heat from the flames, we need flat-bottomed pans to catch all the heat from our flat gas and electric burners.

When you check the polenta for doneness, tilt the pan and bunch the polenta toward the side opposite the handle, so there is a good thickness of it. Then and only then stick your wooden spoon into the mass of mush: If the spoon stands the polenta is ready.

6 cups boiling water or broth,
    or half water half milk
2 cups cold water or broth, or
    half water half milk
2 cups cornmeal
Salt
Pepper from the mill
Nutmeg to taste

Keep the boiling liquid simmering. Mix the cold liquid and cornmeal and pour, stirring, into the simmering liquid. Add salt, pepper, and nutmeg and stir until the spoon stands in the polenta to obtain a mush. If you want to prepare croutons, pour the mush onto a buttered board or sheet and let it cool; cut only when cold.

LA POLENTA DU VENDREDI SAINT DE 1940
Polenta for the Good Friday Dinner of 1940

I truly believed that Mélanie could outcook anyone, including my extremely gifted mother, because she found a way to make us love polenta and dried cod all at once. For Paris kids mostly raised on thin *bifteck* and *pommes frites*, that was an achievement.

FOR THE COD:
1 side of a medium salt cod
    soaked in water 24 to 48
    hours

To prepare the cod, soak it until fully rehydrated. Bring the water to a boil, add the onions, garlic, thyme, bay leaf, and parsley and simmer 15 minutes;

3 quarts water

2 onions, finely chopped

3 cloves garlic, finely chopped

1 thyme sprig

1 Turkish bay leaf or ½
California bay leaf

10 parsley sprigs

10 peppercorns

6 tablespoons butter

4 tablespoons flour

2 cups cod cooking water

1 tablespoon lemon juice

½ cup heavy cream

2 tablespoons chopped parsley

FOR THE POLENTA:

1 recipe Polenta au Bâton
(page 250), cooled into a
cake

All-purpose flour

4 tablespoons clarified butter

3 cloves garlic, finely chopped

3 tablespoons chopped parsley

3 tablespoons butter

add the peppercorns, turn the heat off, and cool to barely lukewarm.

Add the cod and very slowly bring the water back to a bare simmer; as soon as the water simmers, turn the heat off, cover the pot, and let stand 5 minutes. Remove the cod with a slotted spoon. Cool the cod and clean it of all skin and bones; keep the obtained cod flakes warm on a plate placed over the cod cooking liquid and covered.

To prepare the sauce, make a *roux* with butter and flour, cook 3 to 4 minutes and bind with 2 cups of the cod cooking liquid. Bring to a boil and cook 10 minutes. Add the lemon juice and cream, add the cod, and reheat well. Keep warm, correct the seasoning, and add parsley.

Cut the cake of polenta into slices ½ inch thick, flour them, and brown them in the hot clarified butter. Put them into a large baking dish or on a platter and keep warm. To the pan in which you just cooked the polenta, add the garlic, parsley, and butter and cook until golden. Spoon half of these aromatics over the polenta croutons. Top each crouton with an equal amount of sauced cod and sprinkle the remainder of the garlic, parsley, and butter over the dish. Serve quickly.

POLENTA AUX ARTICHAUTS
Polenta with Artichokes

The summer of 1947 was so very hot that one of the citizens of La Balme was able to grow a whole field of artichokes; those not consumed were allowed to grow to the most gorgeous purple flowers I have ever seen, even in Provence; this is how those that did not reach the flower stage were served to us. You can substitute frozen artichokes; trim the tips of the leaves a bit, as they can be tough.

FOR THE ARTICHOKES:

24 artichokes, 2 inches in
    diameter
Lemon or vinegar water
2 onions, finely chopped
4 tablespoons butter
3 cups tomato puree (use
    Tomi as sold in Parmalat-
    brand boxes)
1 cup farm-style chicken broth
    (page 183)
2 cloves garlic, finely chopped
2 tablespoons chopped parsley
⅔ cup sour cream
4 ounces Bleu de Bresse or
    Gorgonzola cheese,
    crumbled
Salt
Pepper from the mill

FOR THE POLENTA:
3 tablespoons butter
3 onions, finely chopped
1 recipe Polenta au Bâton
    (page 250)

Clean the artichokes, remove the stems and tips, and gently remove the leaves until the white inner leaves appear. You will have tiny artichoke hearts no bigger than ¾ inch in diameter, and they are delicious; boil them in acidulated water until *al dente*. Meanwhile prepare the tomato sauce.

Sauté the onions in the butter until brown, add the tomato puree, the broth, garlic, and chopped parsley. Add the artichokes and one ladleful of the acidulated water in which they precooked and simmer until the artichokes are very tender. Add the sour cream and crumbled cheese. Mix well and correct the seasoning with salt and pepper.

When you prepare the polenta, sauté the onions first in the butter, then add the large amount of water, bring to a simmer, and continue as in the master recipe on page 250.

Serve the artichoke sauce over portions of polenta.

MADAME MAILLET'S FRESSURE DE VEAU À LA POLENTA
Madame Maillet's Tripe and Polenta Dish

Fressure is a type of organ meat not used in the United States. I am replacing it here with tripe, since the taste is almost identical. Do not be surprised by polenta and potatoes together; this is traditional in Savoie cookery—the potato here is a meat extender. Please make sure to overcook the tripe; one of the reasons people do not like tripe so much is because in this country, even in

Italian-American neighborhoods, it is always terribly undercooked and thus never given enough time to develop its very characteristic robust flavor. This is another "patience" dish.

FRESSURE:

1½ pounds tripe, slivered

½ cup butter or lard

3 onions, slivered

3 cloves garlic, slivered

1 quart farm-style chicken broth (page 183) or water

1 beef bouillon cube

Bouquet garni

2 tablespoons tomato paste

1 cup dry white wine

Salt

Pepper from the mill

2 tablespoons flour

3 potatoes, peeled and slivered into 1½- by ⅓-inch sticks

POLENTA:

1 recipe Polenta au Bâton *(page 250) made with onions if desired*

Blanch the tripe even if it was sold as blanched in the store. Pat dry in a tea towel.

Heat 3 tablespoons of the butter in a sauté pan and sauté the onions until brown; remove the onions to a plate and sauté the tripe to make sure that all the blanching water has evaporated. Return the onions to the pan, add the garlic, enough broth to cover, and the bouillon cube, the *bouquet garni*, tomato paste, and white wine. Add salt and pepper. Cook until very tender, adding a bit more stock or water if needed.

When the tripe is done, remove it from the gravy. With flour and 2½ tablespoons of butter, prepare a kneaded butter and whisk it into the gravy to thicken it; simmer 10 minutes. Keep hot.

In the remaining 2½ tablespoons of butter, sauté the potatoes until golden, then turn the heat down to mellow them. Raise the heat again to brown them. As soon as you raise the heat, add the well-drained tripe and correct the final seasoning.

Serve portions of the tripe over the polenta and spoon the sauce over all.

LA POLENTA POUR LES AMÉRICAINS

An Annecy Polenta for American Boys

What do you do when a crowd of American boys arrives in Annecy on a surprise visit? Open the icebox, find bacon, fresh plums and cornmeal, and start cooking. As it turned out, we all loved it. Use Italian prune plums for the true taste. A lamb's lettuce with walnut oil dressing rounded out the meal.

3 large onions, finely chopped
½ cup butter
5 ounces slab bacon, cut into
  ⅓-inch cubes
6 cups boiling water
2 cups cold water
2 cups cornmeal
4 pounds Italian prune plums
¼ cup brown sugar
Grated rind of 1 lemon
½ teaspoon cinnamon
4 tablespoons butter
Pinch of salt

Before cooking the polenta as indicated in the master recipe on page 250, sauté the onions in the butter and remove them to a plate; in the same pan, cook the bacon and discard its fat; return the onions and bacon to the pan, add water, and proceed to prepare the polenta. It will be nicely flavored and contain protein for hungry boys.

Cook the plums in a large pot with the brown sugar, lemon rind, and cinnamon. Reduce to the texture of thickish applesauce. Do not strain; add butter to the hot compote and a pinch of salt.

Serve the polenta in one bowl and the plum compote in another, but enjoy both together.

MADAME BERTHOD'S POLENTA
Mrs. Berthod's Polenta

Madame Berthod has been my hostess for the last ten years at Le Vieux Pommier in Courmayeur on the Italian side of Mont Blanc. She is the last in her family to speak French as a home language; the younger members all speak Italian. From that, I deducted that exactly as much time was needed for French to be almost lost in favor of Italian in the Val d'Aosta as it took for the Savoie patois to be almost lost to academic French—approximately one hundred and twenty-five years. The term *boleti* can be considered synonymous with the Italian *porcini*.

3 cups tomato puree (use
  Tomi as sold in Parmalat-
  brand boxes)
1 cup dry white wine
1 cup water
3 tablespoons scissored basil
  leaves

Mix the tomato puree, white wine, and water, bring to a boil, and add basil. Simmer while you prepare the boleti.

Remove the tubes under the caps. Cut the mushrooms in ¼-inch-thick slices. Sauté them in 2 tablespoons of the butter; add the garlic, anchovy paste, salt and pepper from the mill; as soon as the

1½ pounds fresh boleti or
    brown cultivated mushrooms
4 tablespoons butter
2 cloves garlic, finely chopped
1 teaspoon anchovy paste
Salt
Pepper from the mill
1 recipe Polenta au Bâton
    (page 250) made with plain
    water
1 pound Fontina cheese,
    slivered

water comes out of the mushrooms, add the tomato sauce and cook together until reduced to 4 cups altogether. Correct the seasoning.

Cook the polenta. Then butter a 1½-quart baking dish with the remaining butter. Add half the polenta, top with half the Fontina. Add the remainder of the polenta, spoon the sauce over the whole dish, and top with the remainder of the cheese. Bake in a preheated 350°F oven 20 minutes to melt the cheese. Do not brown the cheese too much.

POLENTA EN PILAF
Pilaf of Polenta

A typical example of what politics can do to cooking. Made the Italian way all through the nineteenth century, all of a sudden the polenta found itself transformed into a pilaf. This method is so recent that Mique Grandchamp in the 1880s still made the polenta only *au bâton*. Use as coarse a meal as you can find.

This is the basic recipe to be used for the three dishes that follow:

2 onions, finely chopped
4 tablespoons butter
1½ cups coarse cornmeal
5 cups boiling water, farm-
    style chicken broth (page
    183), or bouillon (page
    182)
Salt
Pepper from the mill

In a 2-quart *cocotte*, sauté the onions in 2 tablespoons of the butter until translucent. Add the cornmeal and toss well together. Add the boiling liquid, salt and pepper, and stir well. Cover and cook in a preheated 300°F oven 30 to 45 minutes, or until all the liquid has been absorbed. Add the remaining butter and fluff with a fork. Serve as plain starch or garnish as in the next dishes.

POLENTA AU LARD, AUX POIRES SÈCHES, ET AUX PRUNEAUX
Pilaf of Polenta with Dried Pears and Prunes

An excellent winter vegetable for grilled meats or stews of wild meats.

1 recipe cooked Polenta en Pilaf *(page 255)* made with farm-style chicken broth *(page 183)*

4 dried pear halves, cored and diced

6 soft pitted prunes, diced

3 ounces smoky bacon, diced into ⅓-inch cubes

1 tablespoon butter

To the cooked pilaf of polenta add the diced pears and prunes. Cook the bacon cubes in a skillet until golden; discard the fat and add the bacon to the pilaf. Deglaze the pan in which the bacon cooked with a dash of water or broth and add to the pilaf. Fluff the pilaf with a fork, adding the butter.

POLENTA À LA FRICASSÉE D'ESCARGOTS
Polenta with Snail Fricassee

The snail fricassee would have been a Lent or meatless day dish at mid-nineteenth century in any household; of course the snails would have come in their shells and had to be cleaned instead of easing gently out of a can. Please, please do not rinse the snails under water as is so often done; the poor things already have trouble tasting like themselves. Use the French imported snails which are cooked in a good court bouillon that can be used in a sauce.

72 French snails

Canning juices of the snails

Same amount of dry white wine

Same amount of water

1 onion, chopped

2 shallots, chopped

Bouquet garni

Drain the snails of all their juices. Set them aside. Measure the juices and put them in a saucepan, add the same volume each of dry white wine and water. Add the onion, shallots, and *bouquet garni* and reduce by one third.

Strain the reduction into the heavy cream and reduce again by one third to one half; add the sour cream, mustard, and hazelnuts.

1 cup heavy cream

2 tablespoons sour cream

1 tablespoon Dijon mustard,
  or more to taste

3 tablespoons coarsely chopped
  hazelnuts

2 tablespoons butter

2 cloves garlic, finely chopped

2 tablespoons chopped parsley

Salt

Pepper from the mill

1 recipe cooked Polenta en
  Pilaf (page 255)

In the 2 tablespoons of butter, brown the garlic and parsley; add the snails to reheat well, and, finally, blend in the hazelnut sauce, correct the salt and pepper and serve over the polenta.

POLENTA AUX SAUCISSES
Polenta and Sausage

8 Diots (page 317) or Italian
  sweet sausage links

1 recipe cooked Polenta en
  Pilaf (page 255)

Put 1½ cups of water in a large skillet and add the sausages. Bring to a simmer. Prick the sausage skins as the cooking goes on to release the fat; continue browning slowly until a good gravy caramelizes on the bottom of the skillet and the links are completely browned. Discard the excess fat.

Slice the sausage links and arrange them on the dish of polenta. Dissolve the juices in the skillet with water and boil hard for a minute or so. Pour the gravy over the sausage slices and polenta.

POLENTA À LA BREGYE
Polenta with Cherry Ragout

Serve a large dish of Bregye (see page 195) on a pilaf of polenta. Excellent for Alpine climbers and even regular folks.

RICE

I still remember the days when rice was a luxury item all over France; a dish of Patna rice brought a relatively high price in any good restaurant. In Savoie it was a luxury item until at least 1930. The rice used in bourgeois households came from the Piemonte and after the annexation in 1860 it became an imported item, hence a more expensive one, until less expensive rices started to arrive from all the overseas possessions of the then French "empire."

In the country, rice was used only for holidays: in the Maurienne *farcis*, which were special dishes, as a great favorite for dessert, as a garnish for meats such as tarragon chicken or stew at weddings. Here, for fun, is one risotto we used to prepare in Annecy using 100 percent Northern Savoie ingredients.

RIZ CHAMBÉRY
Chambéry Risotto

½ cup butter
3 onions, chopped superfine
1½ cups uncooked rice, either
    Arborio or Vialone
1 cup dry Savoie Vermout or
    French Vermouth (page
    119)
3 ounces smoky bacon, diced
    into ¼-inch cubes and
    rendered
4 cups broth of your choice
1 whole Reblochon cheese,
    peeled and slivered, or ¾
    pound Fontina, slivered
Salt
Pepper from the mill

Heat the butter well; add the onions and cook 5 minutes. Add the rice and mix well, stirring until the grains turn deep white. Add the dry vermouth and let the rice absorb it. Add the bacon.

Add the broth until it has been absorbed 1 cup at a time. When the rice is done, fluff it with a fork and add the cheese, mixing well with a fork. Correct the final seasoning. Serve immediately on hot plates.

If the rice gets heavy because it is cooling fast, just add a bit of broth.

Not So Green Greens and
A Few Words on Potatoes

Greens have been of major importance on the Savoie table. Before the arrival of polenta and potatoes, for centuries bread, cheese, and greens, and sometimes a bit of preserved pork, were all one had or could afford, at least on the farm. You will see the preserved pork give to many of the vegetable preparations their wonderful dusky flavor.

To this day the favorite *herbes* are still popular and sold in the markets already cut up for soup or gratins; they will invariably end up overcooked, but strong in taste and flavor. As late as the 1940s some upper valleys consumed no salads or greens in the raw state; salads were known early, but later mostly by the upper classes in the cities. In the remote countryside, every vegetable, before ending up on the table, passed through a long period of cooking in the *bru* or *bronzin*, or in a baking dish. Gratins were numerous and baked after bread, or in the oven of the simple wood stoves of the beginning of this century.

Each house or farm has to this day a lovingly tended vegetable patch; vegetable patches even appear in city neighborhoods with predominantly private homes. Modern concrete-building dwellers are in the market as early as seven-thirty in the morning to purchase their farm vegetables, and it is not unusual to reach one's favorite stall by eight-thirty and find several of its baskets empty. Farm vegetables are literally swept up by those small restaurants that prepare relatively good food, and I have seen one local luxury greengrocer or two picking up fresh herbs at farmstand prices and reselling them at city prices thirty minutes later; city life in tourist towns has its demands . . .

In the old days Savoie herbs came not only from the garden patch but also from the wild meadows of the valleys and the alp. Although the wild artichoke, *Regina acaulis*, does not seem to have been praised as much as in the Savoie as it was in the Auvergne, other greens such as the wild caraway, were picked directly from fields of wildflowers. Some wild greens were also used to prepare clabbering mixtures to replace rennet, as was the case with wild thyme, *Thymus serpyllum*, in the Beaufortain.

At the break of spring, when the snow has barely left the ground, the first dandelion sprouts come out and are picked enthusiastically; nowadays they are offered by the farmers in market stalls.

Common knowledge of wild greens and flowers was extensive all the way up to the beginning of this century. I remember our Mademoiselle Riondet bringing back baskets of blue bonnet sprouts that she had picked along the roads while they were no higher than an inch, just after the April thaw. Mélanie made them into a great salad. During the great famines of the seventeenth through the beginning of the nineteenth centuries, people survived on wild greens, picking and consuming whatever they could find to survive: martagon lilies, wild tulip bulbs, and irises, which, of course, are extinct or almost extinct nowadays.

I was extremely surprised when I studied Marie Thérèse Hermann's book not to find more mushroom dishes. Morels seemed to be in good favor, but not the local boleti or chanterelles that find their way to the market throughout the summer and fall. Tiny, old Mlle Riondet, who took us chasing after low-altitude mushroom crops, knew her boleti and was one of my mushroom mentors; whenever we went with her, boleti would surface, brown with beige or greenish tubes, tan with white tubes. But come to think of it, she never kept any for herself; we always took the basketful home for Mélanie to prepare. It is possible that some famous historical error would have caused death and put a damper on the general consumption of mushrooms, but I think I can explain this in a much more rational manner. In August/September everyone was busy with the second haying or on the alp making cheese, and there was no time to explore the forest for mushrooms.

My last and most vivid memory of Savoie boleti is recent and comes from the Plateau de Beauregard, just above La Clusaz. My class and I climbed up there the day before our final exams of June 20, 1981, and looking under one of the spruce, I saw the largest *Boletus edulis* I had found in my whole life, totally out of season, as if it knew the right person was due to come along. It weighed almost one and a half pounds and found its way into the after-exam feast gratin. The modern cuisine has caught up with mushrooms, as many wild and cultivated varieties now reach the table in the form of garnishes for meat or fish.

I have often wondered how difficult it must have been to survive in the Savoie before the eighteenth century, which heralded the advent of polenta and potatoes, since both of these ingredients took such an important place in the kitchen of the nineteenth century. Potatoes arrived in 1733 and were in regular markets by 1742, which shows how fast they were adopted. Like bread, they became a staple food, mixed with many other vegetables; the dishes of mixed potatoes, rice, and pasta of the Maurienne epitomize the life-sustaining foods of an area not too rich in fresh vegetables for long months. The Savoie is a great potato producer, and a look at the market stalls will tell you the story: Sizes, shapes, and dimensions vary from barely a half inch to the size of an Idaho Russet. But it is not always the size or shape that is important; it is the taste, texture, and flavor, ranging from hazelnut in the large ones to chestnut and a bare reminder of chocolate in the famous quenelles grown locally. The growing soil for a potato is critical, for I have grown quenelles in New England without ever obtaining the pronounced Savoie characteristics. In other parts of France they are called *Hollande*, but nowhere do they acquire that wonderful candylike flavor that one finds in the mountains. In the United States, you can obtain something identical by baking Finnish Yellow potatoes slowly in their jackets until the skin is almost caramelized inside; at this point, there is only one way to go—add as much butter as there is skin, and if you close your eyes while enjoying this delectable food, you can smell the Savoie forests.

From May through almost July, behold the lovely white asparagus; they appear in all market stalls, and if you buy them you must be very choosy: Select asparagus as fat as possible. Two hundred years ago these stalks were such a luxury in mountain areas that among the bourgeoisie and the nobility they were given as presents. Large asparagus always allow the making of two dishes, one using the tips, of course, and with the peeled stems a lovely soup or a salad.

The recipes that follow will appeal immediately to all Southerners who are familiar with that very overcooked texture and discolored look. For all other Americans, unless they are first generation, still with vivid memories of Europe, these dishes will not look very attractive; but as everyone says in Savoie, "*Goûtez seulement*" ("just have a taste").

The recipes will present mostly vegetables that would grow in the mountains: cabbages, leeks, Swiss chard, turnips, celeriac, pumpkin, twisted and turned in many ways. When the vegetable is new and modern and not necessarily popular, I shall mention it. Many of these dishes can be vegetarian main courses since bacon, if an ingredient, can easily be left out. I am including some salads made entirely with vegetables found in the Annecy market. Some are modern, some from the late nineteenth century and the beginning of the twentieth.

All recipes in this section yield 6 to 8 servings.

ASPERGES AU JAMBON
Asparagus and Ham

This is the last Sunday dish we had in La Balme in May 1940, the day before we all left to go back to Paris because of Mussolini's threats. Use fat white asparagus if you can; white asparagus must be almost overcooked, or *moelleuse*, as the term goes. If you have green asparagus, use the California jumbos and bring them to the edge of losing their *al dente* texture. This was a luxury dish in bourgeois households, eaten as a first course.

12 jumbo asparagus, peeled
6 slices boiled ham

Boil the asparagus as just described. Remove from the water and immediately wrap 2 stalks into each

2 tablespoons butter, cooked to
    the noisette stage
6 tablespoons cold butter
3 tablespoons flour
1½ cups cooking water from
    the asparagus
2 egg yolks
Juice of 1 lemon
1 teaspoon grated lemon rind
2 tablespoons chopped parsley
Salt
Pepper from the mill

slice of ham. Put the rolls into a baking dish and spoon the noisette butter over them. Cover with parchment paper and keep warm.

Prepare a *roux* with the cold butter and the flour; cook it only a few minutes. Whisk the hot asparagus cooking water into the *roux*, bring to a boil, stirring to thicken, and cook 5 minutes. Mix the egg yolks and lemon juice. Add some of the asparagus sauce to the mixture, stirring well, then whisk this liaison back into the bulk of the sauce, again whisking well. *Please* bring slowly back to the boil or the sauce will not stay thick and become soupy. Turn the heat off as soon as you see a few bubbles through the sauce. Add the lemon rind and parsley, correct the salt and pepper, and pour over the asparagus and ham rolls and serve promptly.

CAROTTES AU LARD ET PETITS RAISINS
Carrots with Bacon and Raisins

For the true taste and texture, please overcook the carrots slightly; this dish is wonderful with all kinds of roasted or sautéed birds.

3 ounces slab bacon, cut into
    lardons ⅙ inch thick
12 baby onions, peeled
1 pound baby carrots, peeled
    and blanched
2 tablespoons currants
1 tablespoon all-purpose flour
1 cup farm-style chicken broth
    (page 183)
Salt
Pepper from the mill
1 tablespoon butter

Render the bacon until the lardons are golden but not brittle. Remove them to a plate. Add the baby onions to the bacon fat and sauté them until golden. Add the blanched carrots and the currants and mix well. Sprinkle with the flour, toss 1 to 2 minutes, add the broth, salt and pepper to taste, and cook, uncovered, until very tender. When the carrots are done, toss the butter into the pot.

CÉLERI RAVE, CHÂTAIGNES, PETITS OIGNONS, ET CHOUX DE BRUXELLES
Fricassee of Celeriac, Chestnuts, Baby Onions, and Brussels Sprouts

This is a fricassee we were often served during the winter months and which I have served with great success in my restaurants. The use of Brussels sprouts was a luxury until very recently. Serve with rabbit and wild meats.

½ pound celeriac, peeled, cut into ½-inch cubes, and blanched until tender

1 cup cooked chestnuts

½ pound Brussels sprouts, blanched

½ pound baby onions, peeled and blanched

2–3 tablespoons butter

Salt and pepper

⅓ cup reduced bouillon (page 182)

Sauté each ingredient separately in butter; add salt and pepper, then mix, and, just before serving, roll into the reduced bouillon.

BEIGNETS DE CÉLERI RAVE
Celeriac Fritters

These delicious *beignets* appearing on the table once in a while on Sunday were always the object of lively food exchanges; I sacrificed my portion of fruit compote for two of these *beignets*. They are delicious with roast or sautéed chicken.

1 large celeriac, cut into regular ¼-inch slices, fully cooked

⅔ cup flour plus ¼ cup

3 eggs, separated

1 cup milk

Make sure that the celeriac is cooked very tender. Cut the slices in regular shapes: triangles, rectangles, or circles; keep the trimmings to use in a soup.

Put the ⅔ cup of flour into a bowl. Mix the egg yolks and milk and add, stirring, to the flour until the batter is smooth; salt and pepper well. Beat the

Salt
Pepper from the mill
Frying oil of your choice

egg whites until they can carry the weight of a raw egg; mix one third of the whites into the batter and fold in the remainder.

Heat the oil almost to the smoking point. With the remaining ¼ cup of flour, coat the slices of celeriac and dip them into the batter; drop them immediately into the hot oil and fry them to a rich golden color. Remove to crumpled paper towels to absorb the excess oil and serve piping hot. Do not salt before serving; let your guests salt the fritters themselves to better preserve their crispness.

GROS CHOU FARCI AUX CHÂTAIGNES
Cabbage Stuffed with Chestnuts

This is very popular in the Savoie and in the Lyon area. It makes a great vegetarian meal if cooked with vegetable broth instead of bouillon. Also good with any meat, especially veal and all wild game.

1 large Savoy cabbage
2 tablespoons butter
1 pound peeled chestnuts,
  cooked half tender
1–1½ cups bouillon (page 182)
Salt
Pepper from the mill

Carefully remove the outer leaves of the cabbage until you reach the inner core; blanch the outer leaves. Drain and refresh under cold running water; remove the rib of each leaf. Set the leaves aside. Keep the white inner core to add to a soup or for a cabbage salad.

Rub the inside of a 1½-quart cast-iron enameled pot (*Creuset*) with the 2 tablespoons of butter; use all the butter.

Stretch two pieces of cooking string at right angles and let them hang over the edges of the pot. Line the pot over the string with as many layers of cabbage as you can. Add the chestnuts at the center and tightly fold the cabbage leaves back over the chestnuts. Tie the strings over the cabbage leaves to keep the package tight.

Add half the bouillon, bring to a boil on top of the stove, add salt and pepper, and bake in a preheated 325°F oven 45 minutes. Using a small bowl, turn the cabbage over, and return it to the pot, adding the remainder of the bouillon. Finish baking, still covered, for another hour, or until the cabbage is candied in the stock.

For full flavor, cool slightly before serving.

VARIATION: Madame Maillet made this preparation using a forcemeat of leftover meats chopped and mixed with sausage meat and bread crumbs to replace the chestnuts.

RAVES AU SUR
Soured Turnips

Again, who brought this completely Germanic preparation, exactly identical to the Alsatian *Suri Ruwi*, to the Savoie? Alamanni, immigrant or emigrant, or commercial traveler? My great-aunts in Alsace made exactly the same recipe with rutabaga. Use it with winter meats. The original description for this Savoie version of the dish is in Marie Thérèse Hermann; the caraway addition is mine.

3 pounds purple-topped
    turnips, peeled and cut into
    ¼-inch sticks
1½ ounces kosher salt (please
    weigh carefully)
1 teaspoon caraway seeds
5 juniper berries, crushed
4 tablespoons butter or lard
2 onions, finely chopped
Pepper from the mill
Salt if needed
12 Diots, sautéed in butter
    (page 317)

Place the julienned turnips in a glass container, alternating layers of turnips with layers of salt. Place a plate over the top of the turnips. Top the plate with a heavy weight and let the bowl sit on the bottom shelf of the refrigerator or in a chilly country cellar 2 to 3 weeks. Discard the water that comes to the surface of the cabbage at regular intervals.

When ready to prepare the dish, wash the turnips thoroughly under plenty of cold running water; letting the turnips soak in water overnight will give a mellower taste. Pat dry the turnips and toss them with the caraway seeds and juniper berries.

Heat the butter to the noisette stage, toss in the

onions until translucent, add the turnips and toss well. Add pepper, salt only if needed, cover, and cook on low heat until very mellow. The length of the cooking varies with the size of the turnips. This dish must be deeply cooked for reasons of taste and digestion.

When the *diots* are cooked, discard their fat completely from the pan, remove the *diots* to a platter, and dissolve the cooking juices of the sausages with a bit of water; pour into the turnips and serve the turnips with the sausage.

EPINARDS AU REBLOCHON
Spinach and Reblochon

Since spinach does not grow well at high altitudes, people of the mountain used *Chenopodium bonus Henricus*, a large leaf that grows wild around the base of chalets and, unfortunately, close to manure piles, according to both Marie Thérèse Hermann and Robert Fritsch (see Selected Bibliography). I probably ate plenty of it without knowing, thinking it was spinach. "Bon Henri" was also believed to cure tuberculosis.

3 pounds spring spinach, stemmed and washed
1 cup heavy cream
⅓ cup sour cream
Salt
Pepper from the mill
2 tablespoons butter
2 onions, finely chopped
Dash of nutmeg
1 whole Reblochon cheese, or ½ pound Beaumont or Gruyère, crust removed and thinly sliced

Do not blanch the spinach. Pass it quickly through the food processor to coarsely chop the leaves.

Reduce the heavy cream by half, add the sour cream, salt, and pepper. In a large sauté pan, heat the butter, add the onions, and sauté until translucent. Gradually toss in the spinach and raise the heat, stirring constantly until all the spinach water is gone; add the cream and nutmeg. Correct the seasoning. Empty into a 1-quart baking dish. Top with the slices of cheese and put in a preheated 350°F oven to allow the cheese to heat and mellow. Do not brown the cheese. Serve with a dish of plain buttered pasta or any of the grilled meats in the meat section.

FARCETTES OU GOURRES
Stuffed Vegetable Leaves

Marie Thérèse Hermann calls them *farcettes* and Monsieur Bastard Rosset calls them *gourres* or *gourdes*. They are vegetable leaves filled with either more vegetables or a combination of vegetables and meat. The concept is ancient and probably dates back to the cave-dwelling age when containers in which to cook were scarce or nonexistent; it is common to women cooks all over the world but especially in the Périgord, Normandy, and Central Europe. For more details, read the *Farcement* chapter beginning on page 225. The Savoie *farcettes* that follow are from Mélanie's repertoire.

FARCETTES DE POIRÉE
Stuffed Swiss Chard Leaves

Swiss chard is also called *bettes* or *blettes*; it is a favorite Alpine food both in the north and south of the chain. The lemon and flour in the water keep the chard pieces from browning.

1 large heart of Swiss chard or
   3 small ones
Juice of 1 lemon
6 tablespoons all-purpose flour
2 onions, finely chopped
Butter as needed
4 large baked potatoes, hot out
   of the oven
Salt
Pepper from the mill
1 clove garlic, finely chopped
Grated nutmeg
4 ounces fresh or semi-fresh
   goat cheese
Fruit compote of your choice
   (page 377)

Remove the leaves of the Swiss chard carefully so they remain large enough to be stuffed. Bring a large pot of water to a boil and blanch the leaves quickly. Refresh the leaves under cold water and keep cool rolled in tea or paper towels.

Into the same water, whisk the lemon juice and 4 tablespoons flour. Chop the chard ribs into 1/3-inch cubes. Add them to the lemon water and cook 35 to 40 minutes, or until very tender. Drain the cubes well and pat dry. Put in a bowl.

Sauté the onions in 2 tablespoons of butter. Add the Swiss chard cubes. Remove the pulp from the baked potatoes and rice it over the onions and Swiss chard cubes; add at least 2 more tablespoons of butter, salt, pepper, the garlic, nutmeg, and goat cheese. Mix until homogenous.

Using this mixture as stuffing, prepare as many *farcettes* as you can, wrapping an egg-size lump of stuffing into one or two chard leaves combined. Flour the *farcettes* with the remaining flour and fry in butter until crisp on both sides. Serve with a fruit compote of your choice.

FARCETTES DE CHOUX
Cabbage-stuffed Cabbage Leaves

2 large Savoy cabbages
3 ounces slab bacon, diced
  into ⅓-inch cubes
4 tablespoons butter
Salt
Pepper from the mill
2 tablespoons blue cheese
2 tablespoons chopped walnuts
2 tablespoons all-purpose flour

Remove 6 large outer leaves from each cabbage. Blanch them, remove the ribs, and set aside. Cut the cabbage hearts into 4 pieces each and blanch them; chop them into ¼-inch slivers. In a large sauté pan, render the bacon and sauté it until golden but not crisp; discard the bacon fat, replace it with half the butter.

Add the chopped cabbage to the pan, salt and pepper; toss well and cook, covered, until the cabbage is totally overcooked and candied. Add the blue cheese and walnuts. Divide into 12 equal parts.

Put one part of the stuffing over each of the reserved cabbage leaves and wrap the leaf tightly around the stuffing. Flour the leaves. Heat the remainder of the butter in a large sauté pan or skillet and fry the *farcettes* until crisp on both sides. These are excellent with pork.

GOURRES DE COURGE
Cabbage Leaves Stuffed with Pumpkin or Squash

Pumpkin is more Savoyard than our buttercup or butternut squashes, but the American squashes produce a tastier final product than the pumpkin ever does in the Savoie.

3 pounds cooked pumpkin,
  buttercup or butternut
  squash
10 tablespoons butter
½ cup chopped, toasted
  hazelnuts
Salt
Pepper from the mill
12 large Savoy cabbage leaves,
  cooked al dente
2 tablespoons all-purpose flour

Reduce the cooked pumpkin or squash until thick and brownish; let it attach to the bottom of the pan, then stir again and repeat the operation several times. Add ½ cup of butter and the hazelnuts and season to taste.

Wrap an equal amount of puree into each cabbage leaf. Flour the *gourres* and brown them in the remaining butter until crisp on both sides.

VARIATION: You can replace the squash with well-crumbled chestnuts, plain or mixed with cooked sausage.

FÈVES À LA VERVEINE
Verbena Mint–flavored Fava Beans

The Savoie does not use as many fava beans as other Romanized areas of France. Quite a bit of fava beans do come to market in the late spring, though, and the two very modern dishes that follow created a stir with my Annecy friends, as did all my other crunchy vegetables. This is work shelling and peeling, but absolutely delicious. Favas are found in Italian neighborhoods; an excellent vegetable for veal or poultry. *Do peel off the skins of the beans. Some people are highly allergic to some of their contents.*

5 pounds fava beans in their
  shells
3 tablespoons butter
Salt
Pepper from the mill
1 tablespoon chopped mint
2 tablespoons very finely
  chopped fresh verbena, or
1 teaspoon water-revived dried
  verbena

Shell and peel the favas; boil them in salted water until still a bit crunchy; toss them in the butter heated to the noisette stage and, off the heat, season with salt and pepper and add the fresh herbs. Excellent for veal and lamb.

FÈVES ET POIS GOURMANDS
Fava Beans and Snow Peas

3 pounds fava beans in their
    shells
2 tablespoons butter
½ pound snow peas
1 clove garlic, finely chopped
Salt
Pepper from the mill
2 tablespoons fresh chopped
    peppermint leaves

Shell and peel the fava beans. Boil them in salted water until still a bit crunchy.

Heat the butter in a large sauté pan and stir-fry the snow peas with the garlic until crunchy but hot to the core; add the fava beans. Season with salt and pepper and add the mint. Serve with fish or white meat of poultry.

FRICASSÉE DE CHOUX RAVES
Kohlrabi Fricassee

Kohlrabi is plentiful in the Savoie; according to Marie Thérèse Hermann, its skin was cleaned and removed carefully to form long ribbons that were hung to dry and used in stews as we use dried mushrooms.

2 pounds kohlrabi, peeled and
    cut into ⅙-inch slices
2 tablespoons butter
½ teaspoon ground caraway
    seeds
Salt
Pepper from the mill

Blanch the kohlrabi slices until quite tender. Drain well; sauté in very hot butter until the slices brown lightly. Season with caraway, salt and pepper.

The recipe below can also be made with kohlrabi.

BÉBÉ NAVETS GLACÉS
Glazed Baby Turnips

An almost classic preparation made with those small purple-topped turnips that arrive in Savoie markets at the very beginning of summer; try to choose them no more than an inch in diameter; they exist in the United States, but if only large turnips are available, quarter them and turn their angles to round them off.

1½ pounds baby purple-topped turnips
2 tablespoons butter
Pinch of sugar
Salt
Pepper from the mill
⅔ cup chicken broth or bouillon (page 182)
1 tablespoon chopped parsley

Peel and blanch the turnips until par-cooked. Heat the butter in a sauté pan and brown the vegetables well. Add the pinch of sugar to help bring on good color. Season with salt and pepper. Cover the pan and let the turnips finish cooking on low heat.

When they are tender, raise the heat and add the broth or bouillon while you shake the pan back and forth to coat them well. Add the chopped parsley. Perfect for lamb.

LES HERBES
Greens

This should not necessarily be prepared with "bought" greens; do as Savoyard cooks do—look around and use the outer leaves of any lettuce or bitter greens, beet greens, Swiss chard greens, put on your rubber gloves and go pick young nettles that grow abundantly in all our mountains and plains, add the green tops of leeks, and finally, only if there is not enough, go buy some spinach. It does not look great, but it tastes grand and is an excellent source of fiber. The method is Madame Maillet's, the lemon flavoring and currant additions mine.

5 pounds greens of all types as above washed
4 tablespoons butter
Salt
Pepper from the mill
2 tablespoons all-purpose flour
1½ cups scalding farm-style chicken broth (page 183)
2 tablespoons currants, soaked

Blanch the beet greens, Swiss chard leaves, nettles, and bitters; do not blanch spinach, strawberry leaves, or carrot tops—the taste of the dish will be brighter.

First sauté the unblanched greens in 2 tablespoons of butter, then add the blanched greens. Toss well and cook until most of the moisture has evaporated. Salt and pepper.

With 2 tablespoons of butter and of flour, make a golden *roux*; bind with the chicken broth and

in 2 tablespoons lemon juice
1 teaspoon grated lemon rind
1 cup dry bread crumbs

thicken on medium heat to obtain a *velouté*. Blend the sauce into the greens, add the currants and their soaking lemon juice, as well as the lemon rind. Empty into a baking dish and top with the bread crumbs. Bake in a preheated 350°F oven 30 minutes. Excellent for all pork and veal dishes.

CHÂTAIGNES AU VIN D'ITALIE
Chestnuts in Italian Wine

Chestnuts in Italian wine were a sweet delicacy throughout the seventeenth century; which wine was never mentioned, however, so I made up this recipe, which proved quite good. Use chestnuts that do not fall apart; those sold canned dry in glass jars are extremely expensive but work well for this recipe.

1 pound cleaned, cooked
* chestnuts*
½ cup dry Marsala wine
⅔ cup bouillon (page 182)
2 tablespoons butter
Salt
Pepper from the mill

Macerate the chestnuts in half the wine 1 hour. Mix the remainder of the wine with the bouillon; reduce to ⅓ cup. Add the chestnuts and the butter and shake the pan back and forth on the stove until the nuts are glazed. Correct the seasoning.

MÉLANIE'S PÉLA

There is no possible translation to the title of the dish, *péla* being "pig's food." It is prepared in a large part of the Genevois, especially around Thônes and the Aravis. Mélanie used to prepare it for us in what are now known as large hotel pans. One large pan came per table and the counselor had to be firm in her distribution of portions, especially of the crust at the bottom. Serve with a salad as a main course. There are very many variations of this dish. Red Bliss are the most common red potatoes that do not fall apart when boiled.

4 tablespoons butter
1½ pounds Red Bliss potatoes, peeled and sliced ¼ inch thick
Salt
Pepper from the mill
1 whole Reblochon or 1 pound Italian Fontina cheese, crust removed and thinly sliced

Spread a square 1½-quart Corning Ware baking dish with all the butter. Put the slices of potato in the dish to form a 1½-inch-thick layer, no thicker. Salt and pepper well. Barely cover the potatoes with water. Cook, covered, on medium heat approximately 20 minutes.

When the water has been totally absorbed, the butter is left at the bottom of the pan; continue cooking until the bottom of the potatoes is nice and crisp, remove the pot from the heat. Drain and store any excess butter. Top the potatoes with the slivers of cheese, cover again, and cook 5 more minutes; the cheese will melt into the potatoes. Enjoy as a main course with a salad.

POMMES DE TERRE DE MARIE BECKER
Marie Becker's Potatoes

See Marie's story on page 99. This dish probably came into her life through her husband Paul Guimard, a native of Saint Pierre d'Albigny in the Combe de Savoie.

4 tablespoons butter
1½ pounds Red Bliss potatoes, peeled, quartered, and turned
Salt
Pepper from the mill
2 shallots, finely chopped
1 clove garlic, finely chopped
1 tablespoon finely chopped parsley

Heat the butter to the noisette stage in a 2-quart *cocotte*. Toss the potatoes in the butter until they start browning; add just enough warm water to cover them; salt and pepper them. Cover the pot and cook on medium heat 20 to 25 minutes, until all the water has been absorbed; let the potatoes stick to the bottom of the *cocotte* and brown. Turn the heat off.

Squeeze the shallots in the corner of a towel to remove the harsh juices; mix the shallots, garlic, and parsley and sprinkle over the potatoes. Cover the pot a few minutes to let the flavors blend and serve with a salad.

FRICASSÉE DE COEURS DE PIGEONS ET PETITS OIGNONS

Baby Potatoes and Baby Onions

If you have no baby potatoes in their skins, wash some Yellow Finnish, White Rose, or California new potatoes; cut them unpeeled into ½-inch cubes, then turn the angles of the cubes to make them as large as the onions and to prevent the angles from falling off and burning while cooking.

1 pound baby potatoes,
    unpeeled
1 pound baby onions, peeled
Butter as needed
Salt
Pepper from the mill
Chopped parsley

In two separate skillets, brown the potatoes and onions in butter until golden; when almost cooked, pour the potatoes into the onions, or vice versa, and finish cooking, covered, 5 minutes. Season with salt, pepper, and chopped parsley. This is an excellent vegetable for all meat dishes.

FRICASSÉE D'OIGNONS, POMMES DE TERRE, ET POIRES VERTES

Fricassee of Onions, Potatoes, and Green Pears

This was another one of Mélanie's specials; the pears came from the *verger*, or orchard, in back of the house. Our hard American Bosc pears should be very good in this dish. For white as well as wild meats.

Butter as needed
4 large onions, peeled and
    sliced ¼ inch thick
4 large, unripe, unpeeled Bosc
    pears, halved then cut
    crosswise into ¼-inch slices
6 cooked Red Bliss potatoes,
    peeled and cut into ¼-inch
    slices
Salt
Pepper from the mill

Heat 2 tablespoons of butter in a skillet; in it sauté the onions on medium heat until translucent. Then raise the heat and brown them lightly. Remove the onions to a plate.

In the same butter, and adding a tablespoon or so more if needed, brown the pear slices until they mellow a bit but still stay crunchy. Remove to the same plate as the onions.

Still in the same skillet and the same butter, but adding more if necessary, brown the potatoes until crispy all around the edges. Drain any excess butter to reuse later. Return the onions and pears to the skillet and mix well with the potatoes. Season with salt and pepper and serve as a vegetarian main course with a salad, a piece of cheese, a loaf of bread, and a good bottle of Savoie or other wine.

RAGOÛT DE POMMES DE TERRE
Potato Ragout

From Saint Pierre d'Albigny again via Marie Becker. Use Yellow Finnish potatoes if you can, otherwise Red Bliss will be fine.

1½ pounds potatoes, peeled and cut into 2½- by 1-inch pieces
3 ounces smoky slab bacon, cut into lardons ¼ inch thick
2 tablespoons butter
3 cloves garlic, peeled
3 shallots, peeled
2 tablespoons flour
2 cups water or, better, farm-style chicken broth (page 183)
1 Turkish bay leaf or ½ California bay leaf
½ teaspoon dried thyme
Salt
Pepper from the mill

It is essential for proper cooking that the potatoes be uniform in size. In a *cocotte*, render the bacon until golden but not crisp; remove the lardons to a plate. Discard the bacon fat, replace it with the butter, and in it lightly sauté the garlic cloves and shallots.

Add the flour to the *cocotte* and cook it 2 to 3 minutes. Bind with the water or broth and bring to a boil. Add the bay leaf, thyme, salt and pepper, the bacon, raw potatoes, garlic, and shallots; bring to a boil, turn down to a simmer, and cook, covered, on low heat with the pot lid askew approximately 20 to 25 minutes, or until the potatoes are tender. Serve as dinner with a nice salad.

LA MATOUILLE DE MADAME MAILLET

Another untranslatable title. The recipe is Georgette's grandmother's. There are several *matouilles*, all mixtures of vegetables that become shapeless and taste grand. In the Maurienne there is another *matouille* in which the vegetables are pureed by stirring with a wooden spatula with an addition of butter that even I, with all my love for butter, would consider unreasonable. This is messy food; for home fare only.

Butter as needed
3 large yellow onions, sliced ¼
* inch thick*
8 medium California or Maine
* potatoes, cooked, peeled,*
* and sliced*
1 pound baby carrots,
* blanched and thickly sliced*
Salt
Pepper from the mill
1 clove garlic, finely chopped
2 tablespoons chopped parsley

Put 4 tablespoons of butter in a skillet, add the onions and toss them in the butter over low heat until they have mellowed. Remove the onions to a plate; add 2 more tablespoons of butter and sauté the potatoes so they brown at the edges; add the carrots and continue tossing together until the potatoes start breaking. Mix in the onions, salt and pepper. Cover and cook on medium-low heat until the vegetables brown at the bottom; serve sprinkled with garlic and parsley. Good with ham or sausage, or alone with a good salad.

RAVIULES DE POMMES DE TERRE
Potato Gnocchi

Make absolutely certain that you use either eggs or flour, but not both, or the *raviules* will not be solid enough to poach. Use California new potatoes.

6 large California new
* potatoes, baked and hot*
1 egg or
⅓–½ cup all-purpose flour
4 cloves garlic, finely chopped
Salt
Pepper from the mill
Butter as needed
2 tablespoons chopped chervil
1 tablespoon chopped parsley

Rice the potatoes, and, while they are still hot, add the beaten egg or the flour, 1 garlic clove, salt and pepper. Knead into a smooth and elastic dough. Shape into little quenelles 1½ by ½ inch and poach in simmering salted water.

Cook no less than 4 tablespoons of butter to the noisette stage in a skillet, roll the *raviules* in it, and just before serving, add the remaining garlic, the chervil, and the parsley. Serve with sausages and a salad.

LES POMMES DE TERRE FARCIES DE MIQUE GRANDCHAMP

Mique Grandchamp's Stuffed Potatoes

This is an adaptation of one of Mique Grandchamp's recipes combined with an idea given by Marie Thérèse Hermann as coming from a lady in Grand Bornand; it consists of putting a nugget of cheese at the center of the stuffing. Stuffed potatoes are also a specialty in Lyon; if you have any leftover cooked meat, do not hesitate to use it in the stuffing.

2 tablespoons butter
2 onions, finely chopped
2 shallots, finely chopped
½ cup chopped boiled ham
1 pound Italian sweet sausage
2 eggs, beaten
Salt
Pepper from the mill
Grated nutmeg
6 peeled Idaho Russet
   potatoes, baked and hot
Hot milk or light cream, as
   needed
12 sticks of Reblochon,
   Fontina, or Gruyère cheese,
   2 by ½ inch
½ cup bread crumbs of your
   choice
2 cups chicken broth or
   bouillon (page 182)

Heat the butter in a sauté pan, add the onions and shallots and cook until translucent. Add the chopped ham and broken-up Italian sausage meat. Toss together until the fat runs out of the sausages. Discard the fat, turn the heat off, and cool. Add the eggs and all the seasonings.

Halve the baked potatoes, scoop out and rice their centers, leaving ¼ inch of potato meat to form the boats. Mix the potato pulp into the sausage stuffing and add as much milk or cream as needed to prepare a wet but not too loose stuffing. Fill each potato half with some stuffing, enclosing the piece of cheese in the center. Sprinkle with bread crumbs.

Put the potatoes into a 2-quart baking dish. Add 1 cup of the broth to the dish and bake in a preheated 350°F oven until the stuffed potatoes turn golden; during the baking, baste with the remaining chicken broth. Serve as a main course with a crisp salad. Dissolve the caramelized broth at the bottom of the dish with a bit of hot water and spoon around the potatoes when serving.

MODERN SALADS

Salads, as I shall write them up in the pages that follow, contain ingredients found in the markets of Savoie cities throughout the seasons.

If in the countryside greens were mostly cooked, such was not the case among the sophisticated upper classes; it is obvious from Jean Nicolas's work on the seventeenth and eighteenth centuries that the well-to-do consumed food as merrily in the Savoie as they did everywhere else in Europe at the time; salads were part of these feasts, seasoned with olive oil at that. Down the Rhône valley, Provence is not so far, and merchants called *citronniers* brought to city markets lemons, oranges, and pomegranates, which were in demand among the aristocracy. The use of olive oil is the only reference I could find to the components of salad dressings; although Marie Thérèse Hermann mentions seasoning a dressing with shallots, nothing appears on oils, vinegars, or mustard. As a matter of fact, mustard is nowhere to be found.

So, in the salads that follow, I am going to assume that walnut oil was used. There are still too many walnut trees around for this not to be so. If walnuts were used in desserts, and oil was pressed by the millers, there is no reason it would not have been used for salad dressing. I am also going to use mustard because it was affordable to the upper classes who prepared the salads.

That leaves hazelnut oil. Hazelnuts in the Savoie are the wild type, not the very rich avellina type, so if you see hazelnut oil somewhere it is a thoroughly modern idea of this writer.

Vinegars must have been of both the wine and cider varieties since the Savoie has wonderful wines and a cider called *La Maude*, made with 50 percent each of pears and apples, that could certainly deliver a great vinegar.

Here are a few ideas for flavorful vinegars to be made at home:

Flavored Vinegars

If, again, I give the Latin names of berries or plants in this section, it is not to seem learned in any way but to make certain that the user of this book can check the names of similar vegetables or fruits available in the United States. Unless otherwise indicated, the maceration of the berries or herbs in the vinegar should last six months. I indicate cider vinegar, but if you prefer white or white wine vinegar, that is also fine.

All areas of the United States that at one point were covered by the ice cap have the wild berries mentioned here, or, if not, some that are very similar; I have seen them in Maine, New Hampshire, and Vermont in the East, and in Alaska, Washington, Montana, and Wyoming in the West, but all the northern states bordering Canada could also possibly have them.

Bilberry Vinegar *Vacillium Myrtillus (A Small Wild Blueberry)*

Macerate ⅔ cup of wild blueberries in 1 quart of cider vinegar.

White Raspberry or Cloudberry Vinegar *(Rubus chamaemorus)*

Macerate 1 cup of either berry in 1 quart of cider vinegar.

Fennel Vinegar

Macerate 3 tablespoons of crushed fennel seeds in 1 quart of cider or white wine vinegar.

Pear Vinegar

Macerate 2 ripe sliced pears, cored but not peeled, in 1 quart of white vinegar.

Fraises des Bois Vinegar *Fragaria vesca*

Crush 1½ cups of wild strawberries (from white-flowering strawberry plants, not yellow-flowering ones) and macerate in 1 quart of white vinegar.

Wild Cherry Vinegar *Prunus avium*

Crush the flesh *but not the pits* of ½ cup of wild cherries in 1 quart of cider or white vinegar.

Sorbus Fruit Vinegar *Sorbus aria*

Macerate 12 well-crushed serviceberries in 1 quart of white wine vinegar. Before using, please check the edibility of serviceberries in the United States.

Alpine Cranberry Vinegar *Vaccinium vitia idaea*

Macerate ½ cup of Alpine or regular cranberries in 1 quart of cider vinegar.

Be careful not to confuse the berries with *Daphne mezereum*, which looks almost identical but is very poisonous and swells the mouth tissues dangerously.

Wild Cumin or Caraway Vinegar *Carum carvi*

Macerate 2 teaspoons of the crushed seeds of wild or cultivated caraway in 1 quart of white vinegar for a year.

About Dressings

I have become more and more weary of giving proportions for dressings, since I have not yet found two human beings with the same perception of acid levels. As a result, I shall indicate the components of a dressing, but not the exact amounts, since everyone likes a different taste. However, since young cooks often do not know how to cope with acids, here are the most important guidelines:

- For a salad made for 6 people, 3 to 4 tablespoons of dressing should be sufficient. Start with this amount; if it is insufficient, add another tablespoon.
- Do not use more than one quarter acids for the total volume of dressing. Mustard counts as an acid, so if you use mustard, use less vinegar
- Dissolve the salt into the acid, then whisk in the oil.
- Shallots should be chopped, then squeezed in the corner of a towel before being added to the dressing, to discard strong juices that are hard to digest.
- Add fresh herbs just before making the salad, but add dried herbs as soon as the dressing is finished and let them steep in it.
- There are two philosophies on dressings:
  —either one uses the blender and makes the dressing an hour before using it, *or*
  —one whisks the elements of the dressing together at the last minute.
- Serve salads on ice cold plates with Evian or other spring water.
- A large head of lettuce or 1 pound of baby lettuce, 3 large tomatoes or 4 medium ones, are enough to make a salad for 6 people.

All salad recipes yield 6 servings.

SALADINE DU MARCHÉ
Seedling Salad of the Annecy Market

This type of lettuce, made of all the young plants gathered after the sown seeds are "cleared" to make space for only a few heads to come to maturity, can now be found in fancy grocery stores in all large American cities. Use walnut or olive oil and lemon juice dressing. Do not dress as an ordinary salad or the fragile greens will wilt.

Wash your hands carefully. Pour a small amount of well-homogenized dressing into your left hand, rub the dressing into your right hand, and let the greens roll into your hand as you toss them over a bowl. Serve without delay to prevent wilting of the fragile greens.

SALADE DE PETITS PISSENLITS DE PRINTEMPS
Baby Spring Dandelion Salad

These dandelions are found bunched inside the smallest heart leaves, no longer than 1 to 1½ inches. You can dig them yourself out of the fields come the first sunny days of spring wherever you are in the United States.

You will need 1 pound of dandelions for 6. To dress the salad, render 3 rashers of bacon very crisp; completely discard the fat by soaking it up with bunched paper towels. Dissolve the bacon glaze with cider vinegar, add pepper and oil, and mix well with a whisk. Check the salt; none should be needed because of the bacon. Pepper well.

Toss with the dandelions and sprinkle with chopped walnuts.

SALADE DE POUSSES DE CHICORÉE
Baby Blue Bonnet Salad

This is made with the tiny shoots of blue bonnet that appear in the spring. When they are this young they have absolutely no trace of bitterness. You can substitute the very tender yellow centers of the hearts of curly chicory (use the outside large green leaves to make *Herbes* on page 272 or soup). Place the chicory on a bed of deep green lamb's lettuce. Prepare a dressing made of mustard, wine vinegar of your choice, salt, pepper, and walnut oil. Sprinkle with ¼ to ⅓ cup of diced Beaufort or Gruyère cheese.

SALADE DE MÂCHE
Salad of Lamb's Lettuce

Also called *rampon*, lamb's lettuce is extremely easy to grow almost anywhere, and, of course, it is for sale in fancy greengroceries. I serve it with garlic croutons, 2 chopped boiled eggs, and 2 rashers of rendered bacon, crumbled. For dressing, I use 6 garlic cloves cooked in water and pureed in the blender with a mixture of blueberry vinegar and walnut oil. If you care to, you can fry a few chips of garlic in the oil used to prepare the dressing and sprinkle them over the salad.

SALADE DE POMMES DE TERRE ET RAVES AU CARVI
Salad of Potatoes and Purple-topped Turnips

Made of 4 medium Red Bliss potatoes cooked in their jackets and sliced and 4 small, cooked purple-topped turnips also sliced, the salad is dressed with caraway seeds, scallions, mustard, cider vinegar, and walnut oil dressing. Serve on a bed of red radicchio leaves.

SALADE DE TOMATES ET ROQUETTE AU CHÈVRE FRAIS
Tomato, Arugula, and Fresh Goat Cheese Salad

Put 6 peeled, sliced, and seeded tomatoes on a bed of arugula leaves and season with a dressing of raspberry vinegar, 1 chopped shallot, 1 mashed garlic clove, and chopped parsley. Sprinkle the dressing over the salad top with 2 ounces of diced semi-fresh goat cheese.

SALADE AUX FLEURS
Nasturtium and Borage Salad

This is a salad of mixed green- and purple-tipped salad bowl lettuces with 12 nasturtium flowers or nasturtium leaves and 12 blue borage flowers (no borage leaves, they are irritating to the mouth). For the dressing, use cranberry-flavored vinegar (see page 280) and walnut oil. Use chives as the fresh herb and not too much pepper, since nasturtium is peppery.

SALADE DE CHOU RAVE À L'ANETH
Kohlrabi and Dill Salad

For the salad, use 1 pound of peeled, cooked, and sliced kohlrabi with a lot of chopped dill. Prepare a dressing of caraway vinegar, sour cream, mustard, walnut oil, and more chopped dill. Serve on a bed of mixed red and green salad bowl lettuce leaves.

SALADE AUX DEUX TOMATES
Two-tomato Salad

On a platter, alternate slices of peeled, seeded yellow tomatoes with slices of salted red onion and peeled, seeded green tomatoes. Serve with a dressing made of orange and lemon juices, grated orange and lemon rinds, chives, olive oil, salt, and pepper.

Be careful: Use pale green tomatoes, just before they turn, with just a few blush spots. The deep green ones are too hard and must be kept for pickling.

SALADE AU DEUX AUTRES TOMATES
Another Tomato Salad

On a bed of Italian parsley leaves and pale green celery leaves, alternate slices of peeled and seeded red and yellow tomatoes with slices of Tomme, Reblochon, or Fontina cheese. Serve with a dressing made of a pinch of saffron threads, basil, tomatoes, fennel vinegar (page 280), and olive oil.

SALADE DE TOUS HARICOTS
All Bean Salad

Mix cooked green beans, wax beans, cooked Northern beans and red beans, cooked chick peas, and coarsely chopped salted red onion. Add cubes of cold hard cooked polenta (page 250) and serve with a dressing of plain wine vinegar, mustard, chopped shallot, a lot of chopped Italian parsley, and walnut oil.

SALADE DE ROMAINE AUX POIRES DE CURÉ
Romaine and Seckel Pear Salad

Marinate 10 cored and sliced Seckel pears in 1 tablespoon of Marc de Savoie or brandy. Serve on a bed of romaine lettuce, not forgetting the soft inner heart that everyone in America seems to throw away. Serve with a dressing made of a bit of walnut wine or Madeira, pear vinegar, the white part of 3 scallions, and hazelnut oil.

Fish and Fish Cookery

The 15th of August, Feast of the Assumption of the Holy Virgin, is a big celebration everywhere in the very Catholic Savoie; our children's home participated in the festivities. In the morning there was a long mass, as long and solemn as these deeply religious people could make it, with a procession in the cemetery afterwards. Some older women wore long black and blue dresses and, instead of hats, white or black lacy *fanchonettes*, the little bonnets that took the place of the traditional coifs before the final invasion of city hats.

In the afternoon, as soon as our religious duties were over, we were packed into a bus and went off to Veyrier-du-Lac, where some generous industrialist opened his lakeside lawn to our bunch of ragamuffins. I fondly remember this lawn, which is still in existence and lined with the most beautifully rounded linden trees. It was such fun looking at the boat traffic: small canoes, sailboats, and those large red and white steamboats that to this day crisscross the lake with their loads of loud tourists. There was a private landing on the property where one of the big boats would pick us up later for a ride around the lake; in those days *le tour du Lac*, as it is still called, was something very special for all of us, however poor or well-to-do our families may have been, something almost as important as crossing the Channel to go to England. In that European world of the late thirties, when bathing publicly in a maillot was not yet quite part of a good Christian girl's life, we all sat in rows in our blue skirts, white Lacoste shirts, and berets, looking longingly at those few young girls and women who seemed to dare the undarable: to put on a true, hugging, if one-piece bathing suit and go into the lake!

And, of course, there was a picnic lunch with a small pastry called a *réduction* to close the feast. These *réductions* are half-size tartlets, or *petits gâteaux*, of which, even at my present semi-venerable age, I can polish off almost a dozen without difficulty. I grabbed my loot and looked for a convenient lunch place for the *gobe-la-lune* that I was then (a *gobe-la-lune* in colloquial French is the name given to naïve and distracted persons). I left so fast that I did not hear the most important information, which was not to sit anywhere close to the edge of the water. Worse than the edge of the water, I found for myself an old boat sitting peacefully in the water under an old wooden shed; the boat was long and narrow, with a very flat bottom and two tall, skinny masts lying flat across the bridge, but still leaving space enough for me to sit and enjoy my repast, lulled by the small swells that passing canoes and sailboats were sending my way. One has to get up at 4 a.m. in our days of loud motorboats to enjoy the peace I felt on that day.

Disaster struck at just about the time I was getting ready to enjoy my dessert: It appeared that everyone had been anxiously looking for me. The verdict was severe when it fell: No big boat ride for such a disobedient girl, "you stay right here, my dear, and wait for us with Mademoiselle." Ah! that I could have done without, but as it turned out, Mademoiselle, looking about ready to crumble and not too attractive at that, gave me the best time, for she knew a lot about the fateful boat that had brought about my disgrace. I ended up having a wonderful time listening to her explain how the Savoie lakes had been used in the old days as a means of communication, with three different kinds of boats: the *barques*, the *bricks* or *brigantins*, and the *cochères* crisscrossing them incessantly. All three types of boats were used to transport merchandise or passengers from town to town around the lake, as well as building stones, coal, and often food for the villages that were still not very well connected to cities by road. Fifty years later, as I started reading about all the boats on the Savoie lakes, I realized that Mademoiselle had been a scholar.

Barques and *bricks* had a bridge, the flat-bottomed *cochères* did not. What had gotten me into trouble was an old *cochère*, totally unsafe, that was slowly falling apart; by 1947, it had sunk into the water, completely disintegrated, and of course, in 1980, when I looked for it, it was gone: not a trace of what had been a true museum piece.

The dukes of Savoie had instituted a true flotilla of these boats on Lake Leman for merchandise and, if necessary, transportation of troops, but their main goal remained fishing, not fun or sport fishing, but commercial fishing practiced as a trade to deliver supplies to the big cities. All one had in those days were those fish that lived in the lakes; ocean fish did not appear on any regular basis before the rapid overnight trains arrived in the mountains at the beginning of the twentieth century.

There are still a number of fishermen who catch considerable amounts of various fish in the Savoie lake; Lake Leman, of course, has the lion's share with fifty totally active and thirty semi-retired professional fishermen. In Annecy and Le Bourget/Aix les Bains there are fewer. Still, these people form an *Association Interdépartementale des pêcheurs professionnels des lacs alpins*, with headquarters in Thonon-les-Bains. They bring up quantities of fish that end up on restaurant plates throughout the Alps.

The lake areas were always good fish consumers, since the well-to-do classes observed a strict fasting on Fridays and during some of the High Holidays. In the countryside, fish was less prevalent, since no one had time to go fishing; all one could have was dried cod, bought at the *épicier* or from a peddler, and snails and frogs most of the time gathered by children. After cleaning the frog meat, one gave it a nice long rest on a bed of snow to firm up the meat. And once in a while, a field accidentally filled by a flash flood would yield stranded trout as the water receded.

The quantity of fish taken out of the lakes is still considerable, but with the problems of the modern world ecologists have been put to the test. The Swiss have had to control their Valais industries, but pollution of the lakes continues to come not only from industrial wastes but also from gasoline leaks from cars, asbestos from brakes, salt from the wintering of the roads, herbicides, and—I could not believe this one—DDT, still. There have been merciless reddish-blue "tides" on Lake Leman, which have been fought successfully, but all lakes are slowly losing their natural reed beds, and no reed beds mean no place for minnows to grow up in peace; maintaining the ecological balance presents Europeans with the same problems it does Americans and Canadians. As a result, the fish population has become unbalanced, with whitefish out-numbering the more fragile trout and salmon. As we take a tour of the fish still to be found, I shall mention all the known steps that French and Swiss ecologists have taken to maintain the balance of nature. The work on Lake Leman, which is like an ocean, is continuous; in Annecy the *lac pur* project has been completed, and in the Le Bourget/Aix les Bains lake it is in the process of completion.

Approximately twenty-four different species of edible fish developed in the Alpine lakes precisely because of the local geology. Before the Rhône River built its cluse through the Valais, the waters of Lake Leman ran northward toward the Rhine River system. As soon as enough erosion had taken place to allow the waters of the lake to flow south toward what is now the Rhône valley and the Mediterranean, the species of fish existing in the northern Swiss lakes disappeared from Lake Leman. Nor did it receive any Mediterranean fish, such as shad and lampreys, because until the recent building of the Genissiat dam, the Rhône went underground at Bellegarde for several miles; the passage to the headwaters of the lake was so narrow that only eels could squeeze through. Shad and lampreys went instead to the Le Bourget/Aix les Bains lake. Even the fatty little sweet water lotte could not be found in Lake Leman until an artificial waterway was opened in the twelfth century between it and Lake Neuchâtel, which sits some thirty miles north, at the foot of the Jura mountains.

Following is a list of the fish to be found in the Savoie lakes. I use the Latin name not to be complicated, but because some identical species of fish exist in our northern lakes of glacial origin and can be recognized more easily this way. If the American fish is not quite the same, it will be close enough that one can use it; my own three fishermen have done it successfully.

Salmonidae

OMBLE CHEVALIER, found in the Leman, Annecy, and Le Bourget/Aix les Bains lakes, and called in Latin *Salvelinus alpinus* (Alpine salmon), has been undergoing a dramatic decline since 1850. Publications in the late 1800s already deplored the situation. The egg-laying grounds, or *omblières*, are located on the lake bottom, on what used to be large natural gravel beds, which are now being invaded by oxygen-deprived mud. The small fish die of asphyxiation. Annecy has remedied the problem by pouring tons of natural gravel on the sites of the *omblières* that were established by stocking in 1890 since there was no omble in the original natural fish population of the lake.

In an effort to raise again the omble population the La Puya pisciculture station in Annecy monitors those bottom grounds by video camera in order to maintain the correct conditions for the minnows to mature. All the lakes of the area are now being well stocked with ombles. In Annecy alone up to 400,000 eggs are hatched to minnows 2 to 3½ inches long and released yearly into the lake. Everywhere hatcheries are being built to grow the minnows to a size of 6½ inches to prevent them from being feasted upon by pikes.

An omble is a gorgeous fish; normally gray with deep orange spots, it turns reddish-orange at the time of reproduction, which takes place between October and the end of February. When selling omble, fish merchants will often tell you it is *omble grise*, as if gray omble were inferior, but if it is fresh and shiny-looking, you have the correct fish, since it is not legal to sell the orange omble. The true omble is extremely expensive and not to be found in many restaurants; one is almost certain to find small wild, local omble during the summer at l'Auberge du Père Bise, coming directly from the *omblières* located right along the Roc de Chère in the Talloires bay. It is simply prepared with plain noisette butter, as good small omble should always be, to avoid overpowering its delicate flavor. I have purchased an eight-pounder from Lake Leman, which was successfully baked with light garnishes.

In the summer, all Savoie fish stores offer *omble* from Finland to supply the huge demand of the tourist restaurants. It probably is very good in Finland, but when served in the Savoie it definitely shows traces of having traveled. The omble is identical to our arctic char and first cousin to the French-Canadian ouananiche, both of which also carry the name *Salvelinus*.

LAKE TROUT, in Latin *Salmo trutta lacustris*, can be found in Lakes Leman and Annecy; also called *fario*, it is absolutely delicious and not in such danger of destruction as the omble because it reproduces in the small streams that drain into the lakes, not on the lake bottoms themselves. To control the reproduction, fish filled with eggs are caught and the eggs are gently squeezed out and raised in hatcheries to be released as large minnows. This lake trout looks exactly like the omble without the orange spots. Lake trout (*Salmo trutta namaycush*) from the glacial lakes of North America is an exact equivalent, although larger.

Coregoni

What a complicated family! Coregoni are related to our Great Lakes whitefish, which, therefore, can be used as a substitute when cooking. Coregoni are to be found in all three Savoie lakes; those in Lakes Leman and Annecy are known as *Coregonus fera*. Again the Annecy lake did not include the coregonus in its original fish population; it was implanted with minnows from the Bodensee (Lake Konstanz) in 1888. Overexploitation has been a problem since tourism became a major industry, so that when the population dropped too low in the Leman and Annecy lakes, one used the Le Bourget fish called *Coregonus lavaretus*, or LAVARET, to prop it up.

The demand for this fish is absolutely extraordinary during the summer months, and often the fish supplied is not true lavaret but the small pan-size fish known as GRAVENCHE. You will recognize gravenche; it is approximately the size of a trout, and, unfortunately, the tendency is to overcook it, which, of course, destroys it completely. When you see lavaret offered on the menu, ask whether it is filleted or not. If it is the whole fish, it is better to avoid it. You are almost certain to be served gravenche in all medium- to low-priced restaurants. If you are a good fisherman, you can catch your own lavaret, féra, or gravenche and avoid the problem by either grilling or panfrying it until just done right; then it is good. Fishing equipment stores sell a special legal artificial lure called a green Scoubidou, which resembles the mudworms that lavarets, féras, and gravenches relish.

Omble, trout, and féra or lavarets are considered the "noble" fish of the Alpine lakes, but they are given quite a competition for survival by all the other types of whitefish that cope better with not-so-clean waters. Choice morsels are the PERCH (*Perca fluviatilis*), which comes large enough to provide delicious little fillets that crumble under the tooth. You may have had them served with mayonnaise in Switzerland, where they abound in all northern Alpine lakes. In the United States, we have *Perca flavescens* to replace the European *fluviatilis*.

Another choice morsel is the PIKE, identical to our *Esox lucius*, the northern pike. In dishes it can be replaced by yellow pike and even walleye pike. The minimum legal size for pike in the French Alpine lakes is 14 inches. They make delicious eating and are extremely popular. Carp, tench, and bream are also relatively easy to catch, but are not as well-liked by the local population.

The European catfish (*Aurerus nebulosus*), much smaller than our channel catfish or even the brown bullhead of the eastern United States, is considered a nuisance since it was accidentally released in Lake Leman; so are redfish, whose population tends to explode ever since a child lost his pets in the lake, and the awful sunburst perch that breeds profusely and is nothing but bones.

The famous *Friture de Lac* (page 294), crisp mountains of deep-fried small fish served in all lakeside *petits restaurants*, should normally be made of vairons (*Cyprinus foxinus*), small bream (*Abramis brama*), and roach (*Leusceicus rutilus* or *Rutilus rutilus*), as well as baby perch and goujon (*Gabio fluviatilis*). Since most of these fish are no longer easy to find and are relatively expensive, moderately expensive restaurants do not hesitate to replace them with small frozen smelts.

There is only one fish that cannot be replaced at all in the United States or Canada, it is the freshwater LOTTE (*Lota vulgaris*), not to be confused with the *Lotte de Mer*, which we call monkfish. Lake lotte grows to no more than 6 or 7 inches long. It is yellow with lovely brown markings coming down from the dorsal area, and its head is somewhat like that of a very small catfish. In years when lottes are plentiful one can see them swimming in schools in the canals of Annecy-le-Vieux, much to the pleasure of all the little boys who unsuccessfully try to catch them with bait that is ten times too large for this small variety. Lottes are coated with a layer of thick algae, which makes them slippery. Make a point of trying a *friture* of lottes; it is wonderful when golden, crisp, and straight from the oil bath. Some lottes grow large enough for their livers to be accumulated, then floured and sautéed in plain butter. Some people love them, others do not; I myself am indifferent.

A multitude of small Alpine lakes exist in the mountains; some have no fish population at all, but some are stocked, and out of these some fine morsels can be fished since reproduction goes on peacefully up there. Most of the mountain lakes lie at the end of a nice vertical hike, which keeps the city folks away. Those interested in finding out about these lakes should consult the excellent book *Lacs de Savoie* by S. Coup and J. P. Martinot (Glénat, 1982); this is the best manual I know for serious fishermen with good hiking legs.

For those who cannot or do not care to hike, there are several hatcheries in the Savoie, one of them accessible by car or the loveliest walk on a small country road through well-preserved ancient villages and hamlets. From Thônes (Haute Savoie), look for the Tronchine road and drive or walk to its end at Montremont; a hatchery there serves a luncheon of trout straight out of the clearest-ever mountain brook, which has been diverted into basins to give the trout its wild taste. It works, and this is a most charming place; no telephone, it is just there . . . well known, popular, and open only from June through the end of September.

Shellfish in all Alpine lakes and streams mean crawfish or crawdads. The Alpine stream-dwelling species with the white legs has not yet quite disappeared, but Europeans have made such a tremendous habit of consuming "crayfish bushes" that one must now import the poor critters from Turkey! Since we have some 250 different species of crawfish in the continental United States, there will be no problem preparing the few recipes that follow. The most commercially available American crawfish are the Bayou and Sacramento delta crayfish, but we have plenty of Alpine-type crayfish as well. Use whatever you can find. The Bayou type has large red legs, the Alpine type translucent grayish ones. The gray critters are so prevalent in glacial lake areas that my children used to catch them for me in Massachusetts when they were young boys; so send your boys on a merry chase anywhere in the northern states—they will be successful. I shall gladly communicate privately to anyone the way to catch crawfish in large quantities, but I refuse to describe it in such a happy book.

FRITURE DE LAC
Lake Fish Fry

Use North American smelts that are as small as you can find, and the small lake perch (*Perca flavescens*) that, when it crowds our northern lakes in such quantity in April and May, remains tiny; the smaller the perch the softer the bones will be. If you can obtain roach in unpolluted waters, do not hesitate to use it, as well as any small fish you may be able to obtain in local water that you know are perfectly edible.

3 pounds small frying fish (see above)
Flour as needed
Salt
Pepper from the mill
At least 2 quarts oil for frying
2 cloves garlic, finely chopped (optional)
2 tablespoons chopped parsley (optional)
Lemon wedges

Clean the small fish very carefully, wash under cold running water, and pat very dry with paper towels, then again in tea towels (soak these immediately in soapy water after use and rinse them well; no fish smell will be detectable afterwards in your general load of laundry).

Put ¼ cup of flour per ½ pound of fish into a large paper bag. Add ½ teaspoon each of salt and pepper; add the fish and shake the bag well. Empty into a colander and shake again to remove any excess flour.

Heat the oil almost to the smoking point. Add ¼ pound of fish at a time and fry until deep golden and very crisp. Serve topped with a mixture of garlic and parsley, if you wish. Salt again just before serving and serve with the pepper mill and wedges of lemon.

To remove the smell of frying fish from the house, grill the skin of an apple on the electric or gas burner of your stove.

OMELETTE AUX GRENOUILLES
Frogs' Leg Omelette

This omelette is delicious, but it is essential to have small frogs' legs; those large bull frogs imported from the Far East will not do, they are too tough.

24 small fresh frogs' legs
2 tablespoons chopped parsley
24 cloves garlic, peeled
24 small shallots, peeled and thickly sliced
Butter as needed
Salt
Pepper from the mill
Flour as needed
8 eggs, beaten

Soak the frogs' legs in cold water, or let them sit 2 to 3 hours on crushed ice. Meanwhile sauté the parsley, garlic, and shallots slowly in 2 tablespoons of butter. Salt and pepper well, cover, and cook slowly until tender. If necessary, add a tablespoon or so of water every now and then to prevent burning. When the garlic cloves are tender, remove the aromatics to a plate.

Pat dry the frogs' legs. Flour them and cook in 2 tablespoons of hot butter until the meat starts separating from the bones. Bone the legs and add the meat to the aromatics.

Heat 3 tablespoons of butter in a large omelette pan. Beat the eggs 40 to 50 strokes; salt and pepper them well. To the skillet add the aromatics and frog meat. Raise the heat very high and add the eggs. Continue beating until the eggs are well scrambled but mellow. Roll the omelette and invert it unto a platter. Serve piping hot, with a nice salad and a bottle of Crépy or Chignin, or, in the United States, Colombard or Sauvignon Blanc.

OMBLE AUX CÈPES
Traditional Alpine Salmon with Boleti

For this dish use arctic char, large brook, brown, cutthroat or steelhead trout, or even, if you have to, the hatchery rainbow trout. Use plain brown mushrooms if you cannot find fresh boleti. In this dish, dried boleti would be too overbearing for the delicate taste of the fish.

*1 pound fresh boleti or brown
    mushrooms*
Butter as needed
Salt
Pepper from the mill
1 clove garlic, finely chopped
2 tablespoons chopped parsley
1 cup dry white wine
*4 pounds whole fish, as
    available (see above)*
½ cup heavy cream

Remove the tubes from the undersides of the boleti, wash them well and rapidly, pat them dry, and slice them. Sauté them in 1½ tablespoons of butter, then salt and pepper them; reduce the heat, cover, and steam to extract the mushroom juices.

Butter a baking dish large enough to contain the fish. Add the boleti with their juices, the garlic, parsley, and wine. If the fish is large, cut three ¼-inch-deep slashes on its top side. Brush a tablespoon of butter on the fish and bake in a preheated 400°F oven until done. The length of the baking will depend on the size of the fish. A medium fish will take 15 to 20 minutes, a very large one 30 minutes at the most. Remove the top skin of the fish and, using two long spatulas, transfer it to a large fish serving platter. Keep warm.

Empty the mushrooms and their juices into a skillet, bring to a high boil, add the cream, and reduce to a lightly coating texture. Correct the seasoning and spoon over the fish. Serve with Crépy, Chignin, or Ripaille, or in the United States, with a French Colombard or a Sauvignon Blanc.

MORUE AUX TAVAILLONS EN FRICASSÉE
Cod and Sautéed Potatoes

Another one of Mélanie's Friday specials; it was good and I always prepare it on Good Friday. Purchase the cod in Italian markets. Fill a tub with water, soak the cod in it and let a thin stream of water run through it overnight.

*1 pound boiling potatoes,
    cooked in their jackets, cold*
*½ pound dried cod, soaked
    overnight under running
    water*

Peel and slice the potatoes. Set aside. Remove the cod from its water bath, put it into a pot, cover with fresh cold water, and bring slowly to a boil; turn off the heat as soon as the first boil occurs and let stand 5 minutes off the heat.

3 onions, peeled and thinly
    sliced
Butter as needed
Pepper from the mill
Salt
⅔ cup heavy cream
⅓ cup sour cream
2 tablespoons chopped chives

Meanwhile sauté the sliced onions in butter until golden, set aside and keep warm; in the same butter, sauté the potato slices until golden, mix the potatoes and onions. Keep warm.

Clean and flake the cod, pat dry in paper towels. Add the cod flakes to the pan containing the vegetables. Mix gently, reheat well, and keep very hot; pepper well, and add salt if needed.

In a small saucepan, bring the heavy cream to a boil, add sour cream, salt, pepper, and chives. Pour over the hot cod and potatoes. Serve with a good Chignin or even with a Mondeuse; in the United States use a Colombard or a very light Zinfandel.

SEMI-CLASSIC AND MODERN FISH DISHES

The following dishes were all prepared in Annecy using either classic or modern cooking techniques and typical Savoie ingredients from the market and the lake.

TRUITE NOIRE DE COURMAYEUR
Blackened Courmayeur Trout

Friends of mine rented a summer home in Courmayeur that had a huge vine running on a pergola and a trout pond next door. A quick fire of dried vine twigs in the chimney would yield these lovely fish, all black outside and dripping with juices inside. The same technique is used in vineyard areas of the Savoie. *Keep your face away from the fire.*

6 trout, any species
Butter as needed
Salt
Pepper from the mill
Lemon wedges

Clean the trout; set the fish in one or two metal broiling baskets. Pack your chimney or barbecue pit with paper topped with small, very dry vine cuttings. Set the basket containing the fish directly on the wood. Light a match and throw it into the mixture of wood and paper. *Be careful, the fire will flash,* sending up high flames and singeing the trout so that it looks black and sooty. As soon as the high flames have died out, using a large kitchen mitten, remove the basket and transfer the fish to a platter. No service. Each guest removes the skin, and salts, peppers, lemons, and butters the fish to his or her taste. This dish is the essence of goodness and simplicity.

Serve with a Chambave, which can be located in many wine stores. Chill it well. In the Savoie a Mondeuse is usually served or any dry white wine.

NOTE ON SAFETY: You are responsible for yourself when you try this recipe; your chimney must draw properly and should have been cleaned regularly to avoid chimney fires. A chimney fire can be put out by throwing several onions into the hearth. Your barbecue pit, if you use it, must be placed in the center of an empty area so the fire has no possibility of catching on to anything. This is not for balcony barbecuing, in any case, or even for preparing in the tiny yards of apartment buildings or condominiums.

TRUITE BRAISÉE AU VIN DE NOIX
Braised Trout in Walnut Wine Sauce

See page 409 for a walnut wine that can be used to prepare this recipe, or use Italian Nocino in lesser quantity; since Nocino is sweet, rebalance the sauce with lemon juice.

6 trout of your choice
½ cup butter
2 leeks, coarsely chopped, white part only
1 pound baby mushrooms or large mushrooms, quartered
Salt
Pepper from the mill

Clean the trout carefully. In a skillet, heat 2 tablespoons of the butter, add the leeks and mushrooms, salt and pepper, and toss well together; cook and let the juices of the mushrooms come out over low heat.

Butter a 2-quart baking dish with another tablespoon of butter; add the prepared vegetables and top them with the fish. Butter a piece of parchment

½ cup walnut wine, or
⅓ cup dry white wine plus 3
   tablespoons Nocino
⅓ cup chopped parsley
2 tablespoons sour cream
½ cup heavy cream
Lemon juice as needed

paper with another tablespoon of butter. To the baking dish add the walnut wine or a combination of white wine and Nocino mixed; add generous amounts of salt, pepper, and parsley, to the trout, cover with the prepared parchment paper and bake in a preheated 375°F oven 14 to 20 minutes. When the trout is done, remove it to a platter and keep hot.

Empty the cooking juices and vegetable garnish into a skillet and add both creams mixed; reduce to a slightly coating consistency, correct the seasoning carefully with salt, pepper, and lemon juice if needed, and pour into a sauceboat without straining. Serve with the trout.

The best wine in the Savoie would be a Chignin de Bergeron and in the United States a great little Sauvignon Blanc.

TRUITE FARCIE AUX NOISETTES
Hazelnut-stuffed Trout

This recipe was made with small trout, with larger féra and lavaret, with a great eight-pound omble in France, and with the corresponding fish in the United States: It was particularly successful with lake trout and one splendid arctic char that had lost its life at the end of a friendly line in Maine.

6 trout cleaned or even boned,
   or
1 larger fish, to serve 6 people
2 tablespoons butter
1 shallot, finely chopped
½ pound mushrooms, finely
   chopped
2 tablespoons fresh bread
   crumbs

Clean the trout or larger fish carefully. In a skillet, heat the butter and in it sauté the shallot and mushrooms until the juices start coming out of the mushrooms. Add the bread crumbs, garlic, parsley, hazelnuts, heavy cream, salt and pepper; cool completely. Add an equal amount of this stuffing into the cavity of each trout or, if using a large fish, stuff the cavity with all of it. If you have boned the fish, spread the mixture between the two fillets and press

2 cloves garlic, finely chopped
2 tablespoons chopped parsley
⅓ cup peeled, toasted
   hazelnuts, finely chopped
2–3 tablespoons heavy cream
Salt
Pepper from the mill
4 tablespoons all-purpose flour
½ cup clarified butter

well together, but do not squeeze the stuffing out.

Flour the trout and panfry it in clarified butter a few minutes on each side so the skin turns very brown, crisp, and very delicious. If you prepare a larger fish, it is better to broil it approximately 6 minutes on each side, using a broiling basket. Serve plain, without any other sauce.

FILETS DE LAVARET OU FÉRA MARINÉS AUX NOISETTES ET AU CERFEUIL
Fillets of Whitefish Marinated in Chervil and Hazelnuts

Besides whitefish, you can use that wonderful catfish that is raised nowadays, and pike, either northern, yellow, or walleye.

2 shallots, very finely chopped
¼ cup hazelnuts, peeled,
   toasted, and very finely
   chopped
Salt
Pepper from the mill
3 tablespoons cider vinegar
⅓ cup plus 2 tablespoons each
   hazelnut and corn oil
⅓ cup chopped fresh chervil
6 large fish fillets (see above)

Prepare the dressing by mixing the shallots, hazelnuts, salt, pepper, cider vinegar, the larger amount of both oils, and the chervil. Emulsify well and pour half this dressing into the bottom of a large baking dish.

Rub a tablespoon each of the smaller amount of oil on the bottom of two skillets. Add the fish fillets, seasoned well with salt and pepper on both sides. Over very low heat, steam the fillets, covered, for just a few minutes, or until the fish turns translucent. Transfer the fillets to the prepared baking dish, and spoon the remaining dressing over them. Cover with plastic wrap and deep chill 24 hours before serving.

Serve with a Ripaille or a French Colombard from California.

FILETS DE FÉRA OU LAVARET AUX CUISSES DE DAMES
Fillets of Whitefish with Large Red Shallots

This preparation is good for whitefish, catfish, or pike, but a bit too rustic for refined arctic char or lake trout. The *cuisses de dames* or *cuisses de dindes*, as they are sometimes called, are large red shallots found in all Savoie markets and are also available from farms in California.

1 pound large purple red shallots known as cuisses de dames
Oil of your choice, preferably sunflower or grape-seed oil
Red wine vinegar or flavored vinegar of your choice (page 280)
Salt
Pepper from the mill
Dijon mustard to taste
3 tablespoons chopped parsley
6 large fillets of whitefish, catfish, or pike

Peel the shallots and cut them into ⅙-inch-thick slices. Heat ½ tablespoon of oil in a skillet and in it gently sauté the shallots; add a tablespoon of vinegar, season with salt and pepper, and cook on low heat until tender. Set aside when done.

With Dijon mustard, vinegar, salt and pepper to taste, and oil, prepare a dressing using your preferred proportions for more or less acidity. Add 2 tablespoons of the chopped parsley.

In two large skillets, pan-steam the fish fillets, well seasoned with salt and pepper. Remove the fillets to a platter; serve them topped with the cooked shallots and the remaining chopped parsley, and pass the bowl of dressing for your guests to help themselves.

Any crisp white wine will be fine, especially a Crépy or a California Sauvignon Blanc.

FILETS DE POISSONS DE LAC AU BEURRE D'OSEILLE CRUE
Fillets of Lake Fish with Raw Sorrel Butter

If you enjoy the crisp skin, do not skin the fillets; if you would rather avoid their fat content, do skin them. Use pike, whitefish, catfish, or trout of any species.

12 fillets of lake fish (see above)

3 tablespoons all-purpose flour

Salt

Pepper from the mill

Clarified butter as needed, approximately ½ cup

½ cup butter at room temperature

¼ pound fresh sorrel leaves, finely chopped

Coat the fillets in flour seasoned with salt and pepper. Fry them golden on both sides in clarified butter.

Using a fork or the tip of a chef's knife, mix the room temperature butter with the raw sorrel. Add salt and pepper. Spread half the sorrel butter on the bottom of a warm platter; add the fillets and decorate the top of the fillets with the remainder of the sorrel butter.

This should be served with an Apremont or an Abymes or, in the United States, with an imported, slightly fresh and sharpish Aligoté. The sorrel, excellent at accentuating the sweetness of the fish, would destroy any great California or French white wine.

FILETS D'OMBLE CHEVALIER AUX CERISES AIGRES
Fillets of Arctic Char with Sour Cherries

You can also use any other Salmonidae or whitefish. This dish was conceived on a day when fresh ombles arrived from Thonon at the same time the first sour cherries of 1984 graced the Annecy market. I also presented it in my New Hampshire restaurant prepared with fillets of landlocked hatchery salmon parrs and canned sour cherries. Canned cherries must be fortified with a droplet of Kirsch.

6 fillets of arctic char, small coho salmon, or other Salmonidae of your choice

Salt

Pepper from the mill

3 tablespoons all-purpose flour

1 cup sour cherries, stemmed and pitted

Salt and pepper the fillets, flour them, and set them on a rack. Puree the cup of cherries in a blender and pour the puree into a saucepan. Add the white wine, the chopped aromatics, and the wine vinegar; bring to a boil, turn down to a simmer, and reduce to approximately ⅓ cup. Add salt and pepper. Bring to a high boil and fluff in the butter and reduced cream, reduce a few minutes, and strain into a clean

½ cup dry white wine

4 shallots, finely chopped

1 small onion, finely chopped

1 small carrot, peeled and
  finely chopped

1½ tablespoons strong red
  wine vinegar

½ cup butter

3 tablespoons reduced heavy
  cream

2 tablespoons chopped parsley

1–2 tablespoons Kirschwasser,
  if needed

Clarified butter, approximately
  ½ cup

12 fresh sour cherries on their
  stems, with leaves if possible

saucepan. Add the parsley and keep warm. Add Kirschwasser only if you use canned cherries.

Heat ½ cup of clarified butter in a large skillet and quickly panfry the fillets. Serve them with the cherry sauce, on plates decorated with the raw cherries on their stems. Serve a Chignin de Bergeron with this dish or a French Colombard.

SAUMON AUX PASSE-PIERRES ET GROSEILLES À MAQUEREAU
Salmon with Sea Green Beans and Gooseberry Sauce

This dish has been prepared successfully with salmon, arctic char, and lake trout. Gooseberries complement the flavor of coho salmon best. Sea green beans, called in French *passe-pierres*, are the tender shoots of seaweed. They are slowly appearing in better supermarkets. *Darnes* are pieces of large salmon fillets cut across the fillet.

1 cup gooseberries, preferably
  fresh, crushed

2 shallots, finely chopped

1 small onion, finely chopped

1 cup dry white wine

½ cup fish fumet *or* water

Put the crushed gooseberries, shallots, onion, white wine, and fish *fumet* or water in a saucepan; bring to a boil, add a dash each of salt and pepper, and simmer until reduced to ½ cup. The sauce will be thickish and pink. Strain it into a clean saucepan and blend with the heavy cream. Correct the salt

Salt
Pepper from the mill
½ cup heavy cream
½ pound sea green beans
2 tablespoons butter
6 fillets of coho salmon, skin
    left on, or 6 darnes *or*
    steaks of salmon ½ inch
    thick
3 tablespoons oil of your
    choice
Chopped parsley

and pepper and set aside.

Blanch the sea green beans in three successive boiling waters to remove their salt. Toss them into 2 tablespoons of hot butter; pepper them rather strongly and set them aside.

Preheat your broiler; brush the fish on both sides with oil and cook it very close to the source of heat until crisp outside and very moist inside. It will take 2 to 3 minutes for the small fillets and approximately 5 minutes for the thicker salmon darnes. Serve the fish with a garnish of sea green beans on the side and top it with a few spoonfuls of the sauce and chopped parsley.

As wine, a Chignin de Bergeron will be the best or a full-bodied California Chardonnay.

SALADE D'ECREVISSES ET D'ARTICHAUTS AUX NOISETTES
Salad of Crawfish Tails, Artichokes, and Hazelnuts

Use crawfish as large as you possibly can purchase or gather. Also, preparing your own artichoke bottoms makes a great deal of difference in the final taste of the dish. To prepare artichoke bottoms, see any manual of Classic French cuisine or my own book *In Madeleine's Kitchen*, page 389. You can also simply boil artichokes, remove the leaves and chokes, and use the bottoms for this recipe; the texture, however, is not as attractive as when the bottoms are cooked separately. Of course, you can always use canned artichoke bottoms if you can find a brand that does not contain too much citric acid. Watch that live crawfish; it pinches fingers gladly. To devein it, hold each critter between the index finger and thumb of your left hand, with the head under your palm. With your right hand twist the center tailfin and pull gently; the blue vein will come out at once.

60 large crawfish from the
  Bayou, Delta, or a glacial
  lake
20 hazelnuts, peeled, toasted,
  and cut in half
3 tablespoons red wine vinegar
  or other vinegar of your
  choice
1 teaspoon or more Dijon
  mustard, to taste
2 tablespoons heavy cream
¼ cup each hazelnut and
  sunflower seed oils
Salt
Pepper from the mill
6 artichoke bottoms cooked
¼ cup coarsely chopped chervil
12 large ruby red lettuce leaves

Wash the crawfish well and devein them (see above). Boil them in well-seasoned, rapidly boiling water 8 to 10 minutes; drain and refresh under cold running water. Shell the tails and keep the heads to prepare a good bisque. Put the tails into a bowl and mix them with the hazelnuts.

Prepare a good salad dressing with the vinegar, mustard, cream, and both oils; season well with salt and pepper and brush some of this dressing into the artichoke bottoms. Toss the shellfish and hazelnut mixture in the remainder of the dressing. Add half the chervil and arrange 10 shellfish tails on each artichoke bottom. Serve on lettuce leaves sprinkled with the remainder of the chervil. A Good Chignin de Bergeron will be pleasant or, in the United States, a Riesling, even if it has a pinch of sweetness.

QUENELLES AND FISH MOUSSES IN SAVOIE COOKERY

Obviously, such elaborate fish preparations would not have appeared on farm dinner tables, the general lack of fresh fish and of the expertise to prepare them being the two main reasons. The upper bourgeoisie, however, was always very much in the know, and quenelles were served at celebrations in many middle-class households and at receptions in upper-class ones, especially after 1860, when the Classic French cuisine, then at the height of its development, spread to all the better hotels and restaurants. The preference in the Savoie was for the quenelles of veal that you will find on page 339, but many tourist restaurants also served fish quenelles in many forms and variations. One great favorite is a *mousseline* of trout with a wild mushroom sauce, which, created at l'Auberge du Père Bise, seems to have made its own tour of the Savoie over the last twenty years.

The two preparations that follow are based on the same quenelle/*mousseline* paste that I have always used; it is made of fish puree, eggs, and cream properly seasoned, no bread, no frangipane, no flour.

The amount of cream will depend on how the mixture is to be used and on the texture of the fish. The amounts I indicate here are for the freshest fish, bought whole and filleted just before being used either by the fish merchant or at home.

For the trout, use if you can the beautiful northern lake trout (*namaycush*), and for the pike, northern or yellow pike. The walleye, being a bit soft, is less desirable. Regular trout meat is perfectly usable if less tasty than that of lake trout.

Using a fish *fumet* made with sea fish for a sweet-water fish preparation is not desirable. Prepare a simple *fumet* with the head and backbone of the fish you are using. From a large trout or pike you will obtain approximately 1 cup of light but excellent fish *fumet*, which is enough to prepare a sauce for 6 people. Simply mix the well-cleaned bones, 1 large chopped onion, and a small *bouquet garni* with half water and half white wine to cover the fish bones and simmer no more than 30 minutes.

One important point: If you have access to the freshest lake fish caught by a friend or family member, wait until the stiffness present in the freshly caught fish has receded before preparing the *mousseline*; the stiffness disappears in approximately 1 hour in small fish and 2 in larger ones. The meat prepared while the fish is stiff tends to turn the cream.

TERRINE FROIDE DE BROCHET AUX DEUX SAUCES SALASSES
Cold Pike Terrine With Two Valdostani Sauces

Yield: 8 portions

This recipe was prepared with a huge pike fresh out of the lake and green asparagus, which in the Savoie are a rarity. The terrine is served cold, so there is relatively a large amount of salt in the *mousseline* paste.

FOR THE TERRINE:

1 pound pike meat, no skin,
   no bones
2 eggs
1/3 cup light cream
2 teaspoons salt
35 turns of the peppermill
1/4 teaspoon freshly grated
   nutmeg
1/8 teaspoon cayenne pepper
1/2 cup butter at room
   temperature
3 cups heavy cream
1 pound small asparagus,
   peeled, blanched, and cut
   into 1 1/2-inch pieces

FOR THE DRESSINGS AND
GARNISH:

3 tablespoons balsamic vinegar
   (''Modena'' style, not
   ''tradizionale'')
6 tablespoons red wine vinegar
1 1/2 cups light olive oil
Salt as needed
Pepper from the mill, to taste
1/2 cup packed basil leaves,
   finely scissored
Fresh basil bouquets
3–4 tablespoons tomato puree
   (use Tomi as sold in
   Parmalat-brand boxes)
1 pound jumbo asparagus,
   peeled and blanched
3 tomatoes, peeled, seeded,
   and sliced

Prepare the mousse exactly as described in the preceding recipe, adding all the heavy cream in the food processor.

Line a 1 1/2-quart rectangular terrine mold with parchment paper. Alternate three layers of mousse with two layers of small asparagus stems, starting and ending with a layer of mousse.

Bake in a hot water bath in a preheated 350°F oven, approximately 2 hours, uncovered. Cool completely in the water bath and deep chill overnight.

Prepare the dressing in the blender using only the vinegars, olive oil, salt and pepper. Separate the dressing into two equal parts. Blend one part with as many basil leaves as you like to make a pungent, thickish basil dressing, correct the seasoning, and pour into a bowl. Repeat the same operation, adding as much Tomi as you like; correct the seasoning and pour into a bowl.

To serve, slice the terrine and arrange the slices on a platter. Surround the terrine with alternating jumbo asparagus and tomato slices, and spoon a bit of alternating green and red dressings over the center of the slices. A few basil leaves at each side of the platter will finish the look nicely.

The best wine would be an Apremont or, in the United States, an imported Aligoté or Macon Villages.

MOUSSES DE TRUITE CHAUDES À LA CRÈME DE LAITUES ET DE CÉBETTES

Warm Mousse of Trout with Lettuce and Scallion Sauce

This was made with a 35-inch trout straight from the Annecy lake, and with vegetables from a nearby farm. Use as bright green a lettuce as you can find and do not overblanch either the lettuce or the scallions to preserve their fresh coloring.

FOR THE MOUSSE:

1 pound clean trout meat, no skin, no bones (see above)

2 egg whites

1 egg yolk

1/3 cup light cream

1½ teaspoons salt

35 turns of the peppermill

½ cup butter at room temperature

¼ teaspoon freshly grated nutmeg

2 cups deeply chilled heavy cream

FOR THE SAUCE:

1 head of Boston lettuce, well cleaned

2 bunches of scallions, chopped

1 cup fish fumet (page 306)

1 cup dry white wine

6 shallots, finely chopped

1 small onion, finely chopped

1 small leek, finely chopped, white part only

Small bouquet garni

To prepare the mousse, process the fish meat, egg whites, and egg yolk in a food processor with the light cream until perfectly pureed. Strain if you care to. Put the puree into a stainless steel bowl embedded in a larger bowl containing crushed ice. Refrigerate at least 2 hours. This operation can be done 24 hours ahead of time.

Put the salt, pepper, nutmeg, and butter in the food processor; process 15 seconds, then gradually add the fish meat. When homogenous, open the lid of the processor and add 1½ cups of cream. Stop the processor as soon as all the cream has been absorbed. Remove the mousse to a bowl and place it again on ice. With a large rubber spatula, fluff the remaining cream into the mousse. Refrigerate until ready to use. The shelf life of this *mousseline* is 24 hours uncooked.

To prepare the sauce, blanch the ribbed lettuce leaves and scallions in boiling salted water 1 minute. Drain well and puree in the blender. Strain through a fine strainer and set aside.

Mix the fish *fumet*, white wine, shallots, onion, and leek with the *bouquet garni* in a large saucepan. Add a dash of salt and pepper and reduce to ½ cup of solids and liquids. Bring back to the boil and

Salt
Pepper from the mill
Heavy and sour creams as
needed, approximately ½
cup each
10 tablespoons butter

FOR THE GARNISH:
2 tablespoons butter
8 currant bunches, preferably
with a tiny leaf attached
Green tips of scallions, cut
diagonally to obtain ¼ cup
slivers

whisk in the heavy and sour creams. Reduce for a
few minutes and whisk in the butter. Strain well.
Blend in as much puree of lettuce and scallion as
you like for taste and color. Correct the final seasoning and keep warm.

Butter 8 glass or ceramic ramekins with the 2
tablespoons of butter listed in the garnish. Pack the
forcemeat into the containers, place them in a large
baking dish, and cover them with a sheet of parchment paper. Bake in a hot water bath in a preheated
325°F oven 15 to 17 minutes, until a skewer inserted
in the center of one of the ramekins comes out clean
and feeling burning hot to the top of the hand.

Invert the *mousselines* onto hot plates and surround them with the sauce. Decorate one side of
each *mousseline* with a small bunch of red currants
and top with a few slivers of scallion. The best wine
is a Chignin de Bergeron or a good California Sauvignon Blanc.

Meats in Traditional Savoie Cookery and in the Modern Savoie Kitchen

The quantity of meat consumed and prepared in a traditional Savoie kitchen depended, of course, on the level of society in which one lived. I know from reading Jean Nicolas's texts on the bourgeoisie and the nobility that meat was not lacking on the tables of the well-to-do. Expense lists from the eighteenth century prove that one ate well in cities and towns, in all private hotels, *maisons fortes*, and castles where the upper classes resided. The categories of meats were varied, but those most used were the barnyard animals or, during the winter season, the small game animals that were, most of the time, delivered by tenant farmers.

Among the common people, meat consumption was and remained a problem until the late 1890s. One can include farmers among the poor people, for only in a few areas were farmers able to produce enough funds from the sale of their cheeses to afford a bit of fresh meat for family consumption. It was not until late into the nineteenth century that *le petit boucher* ("the small butcher") would deliver small cuts to villages and small towns in his horse-drawn wagon. The wagon was replaced in the late 1920s to 30s by a truck, and the custom continues in very remote villages even today. As I arrived in Le Miroir of Sainte Foy, all the way up the Upper Tarentaise, such a truck was behind me with its horn tooting mightly, not because my driving was especially bad but because the driver was simply warning everyone up there of his arrival.

The Sunday pot-au-feu of boiled beef was a true luxury. It spread more and more after the arrival of industrialization, which provided steady salaries, but even after the onset of industrial development many people used fresh, always quite fat, boiling beef only for special occasions such as High Holidays or ceremonies. Georgette talked to me extensively of her grandmother's and mother's Sunday pot-au-feu as she was growing up during the same decades I did, the thirties to the fifties. A few villages retained longer than others the custom of the Easter steer, in patois *le bè de poques*, which was decorated and paraded through the village before being slaughtered and bought in cooperation by the whole community. Sometimes a large meat supply became available accidentally when a cow that had lost itself was irreparably injured and had to be slaughtered. Each home in the village able to afford it would, out of community feeling, purchase a piece of meat to help the family regain some of its enormous financial loss. The wealthier families purchased the choice roasts, while the less well-off were content to buy the less costly cuts, which were boiled and served with whatever condiments one could afford to purchase or prepare for the occasion. In the recipe that follows you will see two condiments recommended by Mique Grandchamp to accompany pot-au-feu. To this day, many families whose ancestry is 100 percent Savoyard consume meat only at what we consider lunchtime and make supper consist of a large plate of vegetable soup and a comfortable slice of tomme on a no less comfortable slice of country bread, dessert being the fruit of the season or often, nothing. Meat nowadays is plentiful; local restaurants and fancy home cooks prepare lovely dishes when they entertain, but even among the present-day upper classes, meat consumption is, by American standards, limited.

Antoine Bourgeaux, in his excellent report on food and cooking in Mont Saxonnex (Faucigny) during the 1920s and 30s, gives more information on meat consumption than any other author. He cites this wonderful story: To the priest who asked during catechism class which was the most important feast of the year, one innocent little soul enthusiastically replied, "*La Fête de Cochon*," the feast of the pig. The story does not tell what the priest's reaction to that perfectly lovely answer was, but the child certainly knew what he was talking about. The slaughtering of the porker, called in patois *Le Cochon*, was as important in the Savoie as it was all over France and rural Europe during the last two centuries. It is still important nowadays. I remember witnessing, in the late fifties, the dispatching of a venerable 500-pound pig, an event I could never forget.

One or two porkers per family were the object of total attention for several months and of frantic activity for both men and women for several days. Depending on the mood of each individual family, the slaughtering of the pig was either an outright joyous feast or a totally serious business in which men and women involved all their energies, for from *Cochon* came almost all the meat protein one would consume for almost a year.

Cochon's odyssey started in June, when it went up the alp with the family to be fed on whey. This happened mostly in the *Petite Montagne* (see page 152), since pigs do not seem to tolerate the greater variations in temperature that occur above 6500 feet. After coming back down to the valley, the family fed it the biggest possible potfuls of potatoes mixed with all the still edible waste from the household and often some wild greens called in patois "monk's rhubarb," which resembles elephant grass. The Feast of the Pig took place during the latter part of December or in January, when the weather had turned very cold and the meat would not ferment too fast.

One retained, well in advance, the services of the *grand boucher*, who specialized in the slaughtering of larger animals. As everywhere else in Europe, many superstitions surrounded the proceedings. Some zodiac signs had to be avoided to prevent parasites from growing in the hams; the position of the moon was most important for, depending on whether it was waxing or waning, the meat, it was feared, would shrink or not while cooking. Rituals were many and orchestrated all the operations involved in the carving of the carcass; some areas removed the silks by singeing the animal's skin, others by immersing it in boiling water. The animal was carved with great care, every bit of its carcass being used, generally as follows:

On the first day, soon after carving, all the innards were cleaned, blanched, and prepared for tripe dishes and sausage skins. All tripes, sausages, and the famous *Fricacha*, or fricassee, for which a recipe follows, were prepared almost immediately to prevent the loss of any piece of meat tainted with traces of blood. Part of the *fricacha* was donated to a poor family. The preparation of the sausage meat, which nowadays is made with electric grinders, was done entirely by hand with a fast-moving cleaver on a wooden block. The filling of the sausage skins was also done by hand, with a funnel and a wooden pestle. With the blood one prepared the black pudding, which was always flavored with onions and which often contained a significant amount of cream. You will see here the types of sausages prepared and often smoked for longer conservation.

The quarters of meat were left to stiffen in the cold air before being carved into hams, shoulders, and sides of bacon. One had the choice between salting and/or smoking. The ham skin was removed very carefully without making a hole or tear, the femur bone was removed, only a short part of it being left on to hang the ham. A mixture of juniper berries, pepper, salt, and saltpeter nicely pounded to a powder was sprinkled and massaged all around the ham; finally, the skin was put back over the meat, tightly pulled, and sewed to pack the muscles well together, and the ham was salted either by being immersed in brine or set to rest in deep salt. The length of the salting period would vary with the local climate and, of course, the taste of the individual. The best hams came, and still come, from higher altitudes where the climate is dry. Most hams were hung above the hearth in the large chimneys designed especially for this particular work. If you travel in the northern Pre-Alps you will notice the large, squarish, squat chimneys that are visible on all old roofs. In some villages, as I have mentioned in the Bread chapter, the high-ceilinged bread ovens were also used for this purpose. Juniper boughs were put on the burning wood to add their incomparable flavor to the smoking meat. When the smoking was finished, each ham was wrapped in a fine linen bag to prevent insect contamination and hung in a safe place, its smell hauntingly appetizing to everyone in the household. There is a standing joke in every family that Mother is never ready to release full slices of ham.

A lot of excellent smoked ham is still prepared in all Savoie valleys and the treat should not be missed; the flavor, savor, and texture show off best on coarse, sliced country bread slathered with a respectable layer of butter. The Savoie ham slice presents the same characteristic translucency as prosciutto or Lachsschinken, plus a wonderful juniper flavor. Notice as you pass through towns and villages, which to this day operate a cheese *fruitière*, that, very often, there is behind the cheese-making room full of beautiful copper cauldrons another long, dark room housing a large colony of porkers, which are fed on whey and its derivatives.

Besides pork, other animals would also be salted and air-dried at higher altitudes. Such was the case for some cuts of beef; some of these are still produced in the Tarentaise, around the Trois Vallées, where specialty stores sell an air-dried beef in every way as delicious as the air-dried meat from the Grisons in Switzerland. Much more common than beef in the upper valleys of the Tarentaise bordering the Italian Val d'Aosta was salted and air-dried chamois, or goat meat. Although this type of meat is still prepared on some farms, it is not as often served in restaurants, and one has to cross the border into Italy to find the traditional product sold under the name of Motzettaz. In Courmayeur, it comes accompanied by coarse whole wheat bread spread with butter and a thin layer of mountain honey. I have not been able to verify whether the same custom once existed in the Terra Santa since the latest documentation published on its food is mute on this subject.

Wild animals, of course, were a source of fresh meats. In upper altitudes chamois and ibex were much beloved and, as we have seen in the section on natural resources, very much abused until the creation of the National Park of the Vanoise. Ibex is now rare and extremely protected, as are chamois, but around the Iseran and in the Bauges, one can still shoot a good and delicious specimen. In areas where pork and other smaller barnyard animals were readily available, small game was sold to local inns and restaurants; but in higher altitudes too cold for small domestic animals one did consume whatever wild game one could catch. Marmots were as popular as squirrels were in Colonial America, and it was the children who often flushed the little animals out of their winter quarters.

Since the availability of wild meats varies greatly across the United States,

I shall indicate in the recipes that follow how to treat husbanded animals so that they may pass on the plate for the original wild species.

COCHONNERIES

Cochon being *Cochon*, *cochonneries* is the name given in Northern Savoie especially, but also in other areas, to all the sausages and salted or smoked products resulting from the slaughtering of a pig. All the recipes that follow are very traditional, still executed nowadays, and relished by the Savoie people, many people from other parts of France, and a few Americans I know well.

Le Boudin Noir

Le boudin in French and in the Savoie always means "black pudding"; when one wants to speak about the now-famous *boudin blanc* made with quenelle paste, it is essential to specify the color, or one is certain to receive a plateful of black pudding with sautéed apples.

It is impossible for the great majority of American cooks to prepare *boudin* since we have absolutely no source of pig's blood that would be fresh enough to render a flawless product, but for anyone interested in a good *boudin*, let me mention that in northern New Hampshire, especially around Berlin, northern Maine, French-speaking Canada, and many Italian and Portuguese neighborhoods, some great blood pudding, is produced.

If you like blood pudding, buy it, heat a bit of butter, and fry the pudding in it until the skin is very, very crisp. Meanwhile, per pound of *boudin*, reduce ½ cup of heavy cream by half, add to it a a couple of tablespoons of sour cream, salt, and a generous amount of pepper, and as you remove the pudding from its crisp skin, mash it on your plate with as much of the cream as you like.

The best garnish for *boudin* is a panful of mixed sliced onions, apples, and none-too-ripe pears, sautéed in butter and spiked with a swig of excellent vinegar, salt, and a lot of pepper. I have seen on a plate of *boudin* in one of the villages around Le Grand Bornand, a nice compote of Lombardes, those Savoie Italian prune plums that you will see me, on several occasions, call by the truculent name *culs de poulets*. For those of you who are fluent in French, I am certain that it sounds awfully inelegant, but this is the term used around Annecy at least.

A Collection of Savoie Sausages

This section is especially dedicated to my students Roy Palmeri and Bruce Tillinghast and to my younger son Neil, in view of their exceptional understanding and appreciation of Savoie sausages!

The sausages featured in the following pages are still prepared in the Savoie, and there is not a *petit boucher* in Annecy, Chambéry, or any other Savoie city or small town that does not present a delicious array of each category of sausage. There is often from shop to shop a great variation in types of sausages, so I have relied heavily on the descriptions given by Marie Thérèse Hermann, using my complete familiarity with the taste of each product to establish recipes.

To prepare a good sausage forcemeat, not only is the choice of meat important, but also the choice of pork fat and the quantity of fat used. You must use brown meat from the Boston butt or from the short ribs after they have been boned carefully; in the traditional Savoie, meats were not selected especially for sausages; one used what was available—scrapings of bones, any little trimming, etc. But I watched at least two women prepare sausage and noticed that they carefully selected brown meat rather than lighter-colored tissues. I tried it both ways and noticed the absolute superiority of the lightly marbled darker meat. For the fat, be certain to use exclusively unsalted fatback, not sowbelly, which is too granular and does not blend well into the forcemeat. Salt pork is absolutely inadequate, since the salt has absorbed all the available moisture in the fat and through its crystals has sent it back into the atmosphere. What is important in the fat is not the grease, which will be rendered anyway during cooking, but the large amount of water locked into that fat.

Positively do not use the food processor to prepare Savoie sausages or the texture will be all wrong. To obtain a homogenous forcemeat, grind it once, then work the mixture well with your working hand, protected if possible by a surgical plastic glove. You can also use a sterilized spatula, but it does not do as well as the warmth of your hand.

One word about saltpeter, which you can purchase in any drugstore. Using it will give the sausage forcemeat the characteristic pink coloring, but it is by no means essential and you can skip it if you wish; the sausage will be browner in appearance and must be consumed within three days of being prepared.

Do let the sausage links "ripen" a bit before cooking them; they will taste considerably better. Do the ripening in a very cold refrigerator, and be careful of old wet and drippy refrigerators, which will make your sausage links "sweat" and spoil. A good sausage must always be overcooked to be safe and must have lost over three quarters of its fat content to be as the French so elegantly say "digestible."

Smoking all the sausages mentioned below is very feasible; remember only that home smoking implements are far from being as efficient as the commercial apparatus and that even after smoking the sausage must be cooked. To smoke, I use a small Smoke n' Pit, then I cook the sausages but never preserve them in oil, cinders, or loose wheat berries as the Savoie folks do. Where some of us in the cold climates of the northern United States could preserve at length this way, no one living in hot and humid climates could ever do it safely. Follow the directions given with your personal smoking apparatus to the letter when you smoke sausages.

LES DIOTS
Sausage Links

Diots are sausage links 3½ inches long and barely 1 inch in diameter, which are prevalent in all vineyard areas such as the Chautagne and the Combe de Savoie but can easily be found all over and are even sold in supermarkets and in all city *charcuteries* and *boucheries*; in the small vineyard cottages called *sartos* (see page 116) they are cooked over vine cuttings and wine, red or white. *Diots* can also be smoked; here is a recipe for approximately 12 links:

3½ teaspoons fine salt
1½ teaspoons coarsely cracked
   black pepper
Tiny pinch of saltpeter
   (optional)
1/16 teaspoon ground cloves
½ teaspoon freshly grated
   nutmeg

Mix all the seasonings together.

Grind the meat through the coarse blade of a grinder. Grind the fatback separately through the fine blade of a grinder. Spread half the lean meat into a baking dish. Sprinkle one third of the seasoning over it. Spread the ground fatback over the first layer of meat. Sprinkle it with another third of the seasoning. Finally spread the remainder of the

3 cloves garlic, mashed
2 pounds Boston butt or
   boneless short ribs, at room
   temperature
1 pound fatback
Sausage skins to open ¾ inch
   wide when rinsed

lean meat over the fatback and sprinkle the remainder of the seasoning over it. Mix well until smooth and homogenized.

Rinse the sausage skins well inside and out. Fill them with the forcemeat. Twist the obtained long sausage every 3½ inches to obtain links and tie well over each twisted part. Let dry 3 days before using.

LES DIOTS COMME À FRANGY
Frangy-style Diots

This is the typical vineyard way of cooking diots and the way they are served at La Cave de la Ferme in Frangy, Haute Savoie, where the *roussette* is made. If you have no vine cuttings, steam the sausages over white wine.

1 bottle dry white wine
Vine cuttings to fit the bottom
   of a 13-quart creuset pot to
   a depth of approximately 2
   inches
12 Diots (page 317)

Put the wine at the bottom of the pot; add the vine cuttings, and place the sausage links, pricked with a very fine needle, on the cuttings. Slowly steam the sausages approximately 10 minutes. Remove the sausages to a ribbed-top stove grill and continue grilling them slowly to allow the fat to drip thoroughly. To prevent smoking, drain the fat or collect it with a wad of paper towels as it melts. Serve with boiled potatoes and a salad or a dish of polenta.

LES DIOTS DE MADAME ARNAUD GODDET
Diots as Prepared by Mrs. Arnaud Goddet

Monsieur and Madame Arnaud Goddet were the butchers who, during all my years of work in Annecy, served me with excellent meats. We used to chat quite a bit, and in the course of one of those conversations came this recipe:

2 tablespoons butter
2 large yellow onions, slivered

Melt the butter in a large skillet. Add the onions and toss them in the butter, add the shallots, toss

6 shallots, slivered
Salt
Pepper from the mill
½ cup dry white wine
1½ cups heavy cream
1 cup water
12 Diots *(page 317)*

them among the onions, salt and pepper well. Cover and cook until the vegetables are soft. Remove the pot lid and raise the heat slightly to color the vegetables lightly. Add the white wine, raise the heat again, and allow the wine to evaporate completely. Finally add the cream and reduce until the sauce barely coats a spoon. Remove to a bowl and set aside.

To the skillet add the water and the *diots*. Cook on low heat until the water has evaporated and the fat completely melted out of the sausages. As the sausages brown in their own fat, prick them lightly with a needle to release more fat. When the sausages are done, discard all the fat in the pan. Return the cream sauce to the skillet and, using the blunt end of a spatula, scrape well to loosen the deglazing of the sausages. Serve with a dish of plain polenta, if you wish, and/or a nice salad with a sharp dressing to refresh the palate.

VARIATION: You may, if you like, add 1 tablespoon of tomato paste to the cream sauce for a pleasant pink color.

LES LONGEOLES
Savoie Large Sausages

Longeoles are slender *sausages* shaped in skins approximately 1½ inches in diameter and definitely cousins to the *cotecchino* of the Emilia-Romagna of Italy. If you are in the Haute Savoie and stop at any supermarket, you will find *longeoles* prominently displayed; they are made by a small and very good factory in Bons en Chablais, to which they are indigenous. These proportions will yield one large sausage to serve 6 people, which tastes best as served on pages 321–322. Any leftovers are usually sliced to make a mean sandwich with dark bread. *Longeoles* can be smoked.

1 large sausage skin, 1½ inches in diameter

1 pound fresh pork rind, fat-free, cut into 1-inch squares

Salt as needed

Pepper from the mill

1½ pounds boneless Boston butt, cubed

12 ounces fatback, cubed

1½ teaspoons black pepper, ground medium coarse

2 cloves garlic, mashed

1 teaspoon powdered caraway seeds

½ teaspoon cumin powder

Pinch of saltpeter (optional)

Rinse the sausage skin well inside and out. Dry carefully with paper towels.

Put the pork rind in a pot; cover it with cold water. Slowly bring to a boil, add salt and pepper so the water tastes almost oversalted, and simmer until the rind is swollen, soft, and can be cut easily with a fingernail.

While the rind is cooking, grind the meat coarse and the fatback fine, mix with 2½ teaspoons of salt, the pepper, garlic, caraway, cumin, and, if you wish, saltpeter.

When the rind is soft, drain and pat dry; grind while still very warm or it will turn stiff and unmanageable.

As soon as the rind has been ground, add it to the forcemeat and mix well. While still lukewarm, stuff the forcemeat into the skin; tie the *saucisson* well but not too tight and let it cool completely at room temperature. Refrigerate 3 to 4 days before using, and serve as described on page 321.

LES PORMONAISES
Savoie Smoked Sausages with Herbs

Also called *Pormoniers*, *Pormonières*, or in patois *Pornejhes*, these large sausages take their name from the meat they are made of, namely the lungs, or *poumons* in French. They are made with parts of the pig that are not always found in supermarkets, and you will have to go to an Italian butcher to locate them. I know . . . you will look at the ingredients list and say whatever one says when one does not want to think about what one eats, but this is wholesome poor people's food. It tastes absolutely delicious and is no worse in composition than Pennsylvania scrapple. Fresh pork brisket is the French *lard de poitrine*, which we smoke to prepare our bacon. The lungs are not totally essential, so do not worry if you cannot find them. The kidneys are easy to locate. Some *pormonaises* also contain a bit of pork rind and always a healthy addition of blanched greens, which can be beet greens, Swiss chard greens, or leek greens. As far as I am concerned, leek greens are best. No spices other than salt and pepper are used. *Pormonaises* are always smoked. Their texture is not solid when cut, but is identical to corn beef hash.

This recipe yields 2 sausages to serve 8.

2 large sausage skins, 1½
 inches in diameter
¾ pound fresh pork rind, fat-
 free, cut into 1-inch squares
Salt as needed
2 teaspoons coarsely ground
 black pepper
1½ pounds fresh pork brisket
3 pork kidneys (5 if lungs are
 omitted)
2 pork lungs (optional)
1½ cups packed chopped beet
 or Swiss chard greens
 blanched 5 minutes
1 cup packed chopped leek
 greens blanched 5 minutes
Smoking wood of your choice
24 juniper berries, if needed

Rinse the sausage skins inside and out and pat dry with a tea towel. Cover the rind with cold water, bring slowly to a boil, add salt so that the water is almost too salty, ½ teaspoon of pepper, and simmer until the rind can be cut with a fingernail.

Meanwhile grind all the meat with the fine blade of the grinder. Drain the blanched greens, squeezing them well in a tea towel to extract all the moisture. Rechop them so they are no larger than ¼ inches.

Grind the pork rind while still very warm. Mix the rinds, meats, greens, approximately 2½ to 3 teaspoons of salt, and 1½ teaspoons of pepper and stuff into the sausage skins. Cool and refrigerate overnight. The next day, soak the smoking wood in a bit of water 5 minutes, smoke the sausages 3 hours over a mixture of wet wood of your choice and a bit of juniper bough if you can find them. If you cannot locate juniper wood, add 24 crushed juniper berries to the wet wood while you are smoking.

THE SAVOIE WAY TO ENJOY *LONGEOLES* AND *PORMONAISES*

In Annecy we used to make a Saturday lunch out of sausage and potatoes followed by a salad of bitter greens garnished with walnuts. For this dish, use

White Rose potatoes peeled and cut in half; Yellow Finnish or Red Bliss potatoes will also do well. The dish will serve 6 to 8 people.

1 Longeole *or* 2 Pormonaises
1½ pounds potatoes as mentioned above, halved or quartered
1 head of escarole
Vinegar of your choice
Walnut oil
1 shallot, very finely chopped
⅓ cup walnut halves
Salt
Pepper from the mill

Do not prick the skin of either sausage. Put the chosen sausage in a large pot containing enough water to cover well. Bring slowly to a boil and simmer 20 minutes for the *longeole* and 10 minutes for the *pormonaises*.

Add the potatoes and bring back to the boil; turn down again to a simmer and continue cooking until the potatoes are done. Serve with the sliced *longeoles* or with the *pormonaises* cut into chunks.

With the remaining ingredients, prepare a salad to serve with the sausage and potatoes.

NOTE: A jar of strong mustard is enjoyable and a vigorous walk in the afternoon is highly recommended. Keep the cooking juices of the sausage and potatoes refrigerated; remove all traces of fat, and use the liquid to make a good vegetable soup.

ATTRIAUX
Sausage Patties

These sausage patties are made exactly like *Pormonaises* (page 320) but contain ½ pound liver and half as much greens. Like the French *crépinettes*, they are wrapped in small pieces of pig's cawl before being cooked in butter or lard. If you go skiing at La Clusaz, do not miss the *attriaux* at a small restaurant called Le Foly at the Lac des Confins; they are absolutely delicious.

There are many other pork products: In Magland, one still preserves small pork sausages in oil; In Bourg Saint Maurice, you will still be able to locate *saucisses au sang*, made with pork forcemeat, potato pulp, and some pig's blood. *Landelets* are large sausages made exactly like *Longeoles* (page 319) but only with beef marinated in a garlic condiment and pork rinds, the important cumin and caraway being omitted.

At the many Alpine passes where one goes nowadays for a nice excursion, one can find many gift shops that sell great little *saucissons*. Enjoy them on the spot, as part of the Alpine experience.

They are all made of salted and air-dried meat, and we in the United States are missing just the right amount of that balsamic air, so well balanced in dryness and oxygen, to be able to make them ourselves. Some are plain pork sausages, others are made with donkey's meat; some are heavily smoked with juniper, others are plain.

Of course, you should try the ham I discussed earlier (page 313), as well as the "heart of the ham," which is treated the very same way. There is a very modern *saucisson* called *Les Miches de la cousine*, which looks so obvious that you will have no problem figuring on the spot which part of the anatomy of the cousin is meant. It is all well worth going off your diet. So get yourself an Opinel knife in the Savoie—it costs about one quarter of what it resells for in the United States—a loaf of bread, half a pound of butter, and a bottle of Mondeuse, and head for the market. All these wonderful, usually forbidden things are to be found at at least two stands per market. And usually, the cheese stand is just next to the sausage stand, so you cannot win even if you intend to . . . Come now, do not fight it, sit ye down folks at the edge of a swift torrent, slice away, and enjoy. It may be peasant food, but as far as I am concerned it is food for the gods.

Just clear the palate with a tomato or two, run the woods in search of mushrooms and the alp for flowers the whole afternoon; the scale will not even dare to tip.

SAVOIE BACON

It is difficult with our American low-sugar, lightly smoked bacon to duplicate the true smoky taste of Savoie bacon. So here is how to prepare yourself something that will be more or less identical. What we are truly lacking is the long smoking that occurs in the chimney.

But I have been successful in preparing a bacon that tasted at least more European, if not 100 percent Savoisien, than what we find in supermarkets.

Pennsylvania, Vermont, and Virginia residents have products closer to that taste than anyone else in the United States, but still there is a bit of difference.

Procedure:

Use a 5-pound slab of fresh brisket of pork, which in cities can be bought from any butcher upon request, or at farmers' markets in many rural areas. With a thin trussing needle, punch holes in the meat at 1½-inch intervals, to allow the salt to penetrate to the center of the cut.

Weigh exactly the following ingredients:

1/12 ounce saltpeter (do not omit it)
3½ ounces coarse salting or kosher salt

NOW MEASURE:
1 teaspoon thyme leaves, dried
3 bay leaves, Mediterranean type
15 juniper berries, powdered

Mix all these ingredients together and rub them well into all sides of the meat. Leave any excess salt equally distributed between the bottom and the top of the cut. Place the meat in a glass baking dish and place a board over it, as well as a weight equal to the weight of the meat. Let the meat stay under full salt 8 days. *Do not do this type of operation in the summer;* should you have to, however, the salting time should be reduced to 6 days. During the war we had such emergencies and the summer bacon never came out as tasty as the winter one.

If you prefer, you can use the brine recipe given with all commercial smokers, but add all the aromatics to it. As for the smoking, follow the directions of your personal smoker. I had to repeat the operation several times to obtain the taste I like; during one of the tries, I even had the impression I was eating smoke, and I had to blanch my bacon twice. The combination of woods for smoking is:

Apple woods *plus* juniper boughs, or, if no juniper boughs are available, a handful of coarsely crushed juniper berries. Juniper will be available in all northern mountains.

Curing the brisket in full salt means that there will be none of the usual mildness that you are used to in bacon; if you use this bacon in cooked dishes, please blanch it first or you will salt your dish desperately.

Try, and if it does not work out for your taste, go back to a good Pennsylvania, Vermont, or Virginia product. All the dishes I prepared with those bacons were always very successful.

La Fricacha

La Fricacha is a stew that in the old days was prepared with the neck of the pig and sometimes the heart, kidneys, and also the lungs. Prepared on killing day, it was a celebration dish for the whole family and for those who had helped with the slaughtering. Nowadays it is made with the same ingredients if one still kills a pig—which happens and not rarely—or with pork shoulder meat from the butcher.

There has been a great diversity of cooking methods and garnishes: The sauce may be prepared with water, red or white wine, or as in Mélanie's version with *maude*, the Savoie cider made of 50 percent apple juice and 50 percent pear juice. The garnishes were mostly onions, carrots, and potatoes, alone or in combination, or if one had them left over from the winter, some wrinkled old apples.

From the study of Marie Thérèse Hermann's book I gathered that the name *Fricacha Manette* was used in Northern Savoie while *Fricacha à la Sauce Coffe* appeared in the Combe de Savoie and in the Tarentaise; both terms mean "dirty" in patois, an indication that the sauce is darkened by traces of cooked blood, or even a deliberate addition of pig's blood as a binder. The more southern Maurienne gives the name *Sauça* to the same culinary preparation.

FRICASSÉE DE MÉLANIE
Fricassee Melanie Style

This fricassee was served by Mélanie at least once a week, without ever showing the slightest variation in taste or texture. Toward the end of fall the carrots were replaced by chestnuts, while in the late winter they were replaced by sautéed, cubed old apples.

Yield: 6 servings

3 tablespoons butter

3 pounds Boston butt, cut into
   1-inch cubes

Salt and pepper

2 medium onions, sliced

4 cloves garlic, thickly sliced

3 shallots, peeled and sliced

1 medium carrot, peeled and
   sliced

1½ cups dry white wine

2½ cups natural unsweetened
   cider

1 semi-ripe Bosc pear, finely
   chopped

Bouquet garni

GARNISH:

½ pound Red Bliss potatoes,
   peeled and cut into 1½-inch
   cubes

2 tablespoons butter

½ pound peeled baby carrots

½ pound silverskin onions,
   peeled

⅔ cup heavy cream

Chopped parsley

Heat 3 tablespoons of butter in a 2-quart *cocotte*. Brown the cubes of pork, salt and pepper them well, and remove them to a plate. Add the onions, garlic, shallots, and carrot to the pot and toss in the butter until golden. Return the pieces of meat to the pot. Add the white wine, cider and chopped pear. Bring to a boil, and add the *bouquet garni*. Cover with a piece of foil placed flush over the meat and forming an upside-down lid. Top with the pot lid. Bake in a preheated 325°F oven until a skewer inserted in one of the largest pieces of meat comes out without resistance.

While the meat bakes, brown the potato cubes in 2 tablespoons of butter; set aside. In the same butter, successively brown the carrots and the silverskin onions; set aside with the potatoes. Deglaze the browned juices of the garnish vegetables with the heavy cream. Set aside.

Remove the cooked meat from its cooking juices. Strain the aromatic vegetables out of it. Put the potatoes, carrots, onions, and meat back into the pot and finish cooking on top of the stove until the vegetables are tender. Add the reserved heavy cream, correct the seasoning, and serve sprinkled with parsley.

The obvious vegetable is a sturdy dish of plain polenta and the wine a bottle of Gamay de Savoie or Mondeuse.

FRICASSÉE À LA SAUCE COFFE
Black Sauce Fricassee

In this recipe I imitate the look and taste of blood by using cocoa and liver. Use chicken liver, which is milder than pork liver, and be sure to let stand

15 minutes after binding, since the liver poaches then and becomes totally undetectable to the palate.

Yield: 6 servings

3 cups dry red wine

1 cup dry white wine

2 medium onions, peeled and sliced

3 large shallots, peeled and sliced

6 cloves garlic, sliced

4 cloves, crushed (heads only)

1 teaspoon dried thyme

1 crushed bay leaf

3 tablespoons chopped parsley stems

6 crushed juniper berries

3 pounds Boston butt, cubed

Butter as needed

1 tablespoon natural unsweetened cocoa

2 tablespoons all-purpose flour

4 large red potatoes, peeled and cubed

1 large celery root, peeled and cubed

½ small chicken liver

⅓ cup heavy cream

Chopped parsley

Mix the red and white wines in a large saucepan. Add all the aromatics. Bring to a boil, turn down to a simmer, and cook 20 minutes; cool completely.

Put the pork in a large baking dish and cover it with the marinade. Marinate 6 hours, no more. Drain and reserve the marinade. Pat both meat and vegetables very dry. In a *cocotte*, heat 3 tablespoons of butter and brown the meat on all sides. Remove the meat to a plate and, in the same pot, brown the marinade vegetables until light golden. Sprinkle the vegetables with the cocoa and flour mixed. Cook, stirring together for a few minutes, and bind with the reserved marinade. Bring to a boil and thicken. Add the meat and cook, covered, until tender.

Meanwhile cook the potatoes and celery root in boiling salted water to almost well done for authenticity of taste and texture.

When the meat is done, turn the heat off under the pot and add the potatoes and celery root. Place the chicken liver and the heavy cream in the blender; start the blender on medium-high speed, add a large ladleful of liquid gravy and switch the blender to puree to homogenize the liver. Strain the liver binding and stir it into the stew with a spatula. Let stand 15 minutes, covered and off the heat.

When ready to serve, reheat well without boiling; turn into a country serving dish and sprinkle with chopped parsley.

The best vegetable is again a polenta, and the red wine should be the same as the wine used to prepare the fricassee.

Cochonnailles à la Bourgeoise

In traditional cookery, the Savoie does not offer many terrines or pâtés. Cooks in upper-class households prepared them as party fare, but in the kitchens of common folks they were almost nonexistent and replaced by the *Gelée* on page 338. They have always been served at inns and restaurants to the tourist trade and at weddings and other ceremonies.

The following terrine is the specialty of Monsieur and Madame Mahaut, owners and wonderful hosts of the delightful tiny Hôtel du Col du Cucheron in Saint Pierre de Chartreuse. Saint Pierre is in the Dauphiné, not in the Savoie, but so close to the border that some of the mushrooms in the terrine are bound to be picked in the nearby Savoie forest. The terrine is always the first course of a lunch that continues with trout from the outside pond, a gratin of potatoes, a nice walnut salad, and the best fresh white cheese with cream from the Saint Pierre Laiterie and the walnut tart on page 369.

TERRINE DU COL DU CUCHERON
An Alpine Terrine

Yield: 12 servings

½ pound Boston butt
½ pound boneless veal shank (osso bucco)
1 pound pork liver
¾ lb fresh fatback
3 ounces dried trumpets of death (Cantharellus cornucopioides)
½ teaspoon Quatre Epices
2 cloves garlic, mashed
2 shallots, finely chopped
1 onion, finely chopped
2 teaspoons salt

Grind all the meats and the large piece of fatback with the fine blade of your grinder; regrind half the mixture once more. Mix well.

Add the crumbled, unrevived mushrooms, all the seasonings and aromatics and the small cubes of fatback. Transfer to a mixer bowl and beat, adding the eggs one at a time and, gradually, the vermouth. Fry a small patty of the mixture on both sides until well done. Cool and test for seasoning; add whichever seasoning is needed.

Line a 2-quart terrine mold with parchment paper. Turn the forcemeat into the mold and refrigerate 6 hours before baking.

Bring back to room temperature 1 hour. Bake in a hot water bath in a preheated 325°F oven 1½ to

1 teaspoon coarsely cracked
   black pepper
Large pinch of cayenne pepper
¼ pound fatback, cut into
   ¼-inch cubes
4 eggs
⅔ cup vermouth, preferably
   Boissière

2 hours, until a skewer inserted at the center of the terrine comes out dry and burns the top of the hand, and the fat runs clear. Cool in the water bath until lukewarm, then remove from the water and place under weight until cold. Refrigerate 3 days before serving to develop the full flavor.

NOTE: The same forcemeat can be enclosed in the pastry of your choice to make a pâté; consider the pastry on page 376–377 and use a 10-inch porcelain pie plate.

WILD MEATS

Chamois and Its Replacement

In the Rocky Mountain area, chamois can be replaced by any mountain goat–type animal that is not protected and can be hunted legally. In other areas, it is best and more than adequately replaced by young lamb, the best being those tiny baby lambs sold around Easter in all Italian neighborhoods. Capretto, the baby goat, can also be substituted and is absolutely delicious. Older goat legs are not recommended, but heavy legs of lamb can be used once the fell has been removed.

To obtain a wild taste from farm-raised animals, one must marinate. The younger and smaller the joint of meat is, the shorter the marination should be. Generally, the century-old marination called *en chamois* is done with red wine. Serve the same red wine with dinner as you use for the marinade.

PETITS GIGOTS EN CHAMOIS
Baby Leg of Lamb Chamois Style

Use two little legs and cook them in one of those huge brown earthenware baking dishes. For the spirit, use marc or any good American whiskey, since Savoie marc varies widely. Jack Daniels would be a bit too dominant, though.

Yield: 8 servings

1 bottle light red wine
    (Mondeuse or young Côtes
    du Rhône)
12 juniper berries, crushed
1 yellow onion, peeled and
    sliced
1 small carrot, peeled and
    sliced
1 large Mediterranean bay leaf
1 teaspoon dried thyme
3 cloves garlic, mashed
5 cloves
10 black peppercorns
¼ cup tawny port
1 ounce marc or spirit of your
    choice (see above)
2 legs of baby lamb
Butter as needed
Salt
Pepper from the mill
6 White Rose potatoes, peeled
    and quartered
½ pound silverskin onions,
    peeled

Mix the wine and all the aromatics and reduce to 2 cups. Add the port and spirit to the hot marinade. Cool completely.

Marinate the lamb in this mixture no more than 2 hours. Reduce the marinade again to obtain only ½ cup of thick and syrupy liquid; strain it. Pat each leg very dry, brush well with butter, and bake in a preheated 450°F oven 10 minutes. Turn the oven down to 375°F, salt and pepper the lamb well, and roast to an internal temperature of 135°F, brushing at regular intervals with the reduced marinade. The roasting time will vary with the size of the roast from 30 to 45 minutes.

Meanwhile brown the potatoes and onions in butter in a skillet; 10 minutes before the meat is done, add them to the baking dish. Let the little legs rest 5 minutes after taking them out of the oven. Salt and pepper well, and slice. Serve with the vegetable garnish on very hot plates.

GIGUE DE CHEVREUIL OR GIGOT DE MOUTON EN CHEVREUIL
Leg of Deer or Leg of Lamb Deer Fashion

If you have a leg of deer, do not marinate it; it would spoil its wonderful natural flavor. Simply roast it on a rack and deglaze the pan with half white wine and half stock, reducing well. If you can only use a leg of lamb, choose the classic method of marination (page 330), this time in white wine to obtain a *sauce chevreuil*; do not omit the Madeira, and use marc or whiskey as spirit. As vegetable, serve whatever you like, a gratin, a polenta, a dish of pasta. This is sturdy late-fall and winter fare. Note that the longer the meat marinates, the faster it will roast.

Yield: 8 servings

1 bottle dry white wine
  (Crépy, Sauvignon)
12 crushed juniper berries
1 teaspoon dried thyme
1 large Mediterranean bay leaf
5 cloves
10 black peppercorns
2 onions, peeled and sliced
1 small carrot, peeled and
  sliced
½ cup Madeira (Sercial or
  Rainwater)
¼ cup marc or other spirit of
  your choice
1 very large leg of lamb
Oil of your choice
Salt
Pepper from the mill
1 cup stock (page 182)

Mix the white wine and all the herbs, spices and aromatics in a saucepan and reduce by one third; remove from the heat and immediately add the Madeira and chosen spirit. Cool completely.

Completely trim the leg of lamb, removing all the fell and fat. A few traces of fat will not hurt, but do not leave large blocks. Carefully excise and remove all traces of the femoral artery and of blood left on the underside of the leg; you will locate it easily—it is bright red.

Marinate the meat 2 to 4 days in a glass dish; the wild flavor will become stronger with the number of days. Remove the leg from the marinade, dry it well, and let it air-dry 2 hours. Brush well with oil and roast on a rack in a preheated 500°F oven 10 minutes; reduce the temperature to 400°F and continue roasting to an internal temperature of 135°F, adding the marinade liquid into the pan at regular intervals. The roasting time will vary from 40 minutes to 1 hour, depending on the size and length of marination.

When the meat is done, remove it to a board, salt and pepper it, and let it rest 5 to 10 minutes. Meanwhile add the stock to the pan and deglaze well; strain the gravy into a boat, correct its seasoning, and serve on the sliced meat.

You will need a good full-bodied red wine such as a strong Côtes du Rhône.

COMPOTE DE PETITS OISEAUX
À LA CRÈME DE GENIÈVRE
Compote of Small Birds with Juniper Cream

I observed Madame Folliguet, wife of the then-postmaster of Les Praz de Chamonix, prepare this dish while I was chatting with her one late fall day of 1959; since she had a large family, she was cooking on the side the most enormous tub of polenta I ever have seen.

Yield: 6 servings

6 *partridges or pigeons*, or
12 *large quail*
2 *tablespoons butter*
Salt
Pepper from the mill
1 *ounce marc or cognac*
2 *large onions, sliced*
6 *shallots, sliced*
12 *juniper berries, crushed*
1 *cup heavy cream*
3 *tablespoons sour cream*
Lemon juice to taste

If you use partridges or pigeons, quarter them. If you use quail, leave the birds whole. In a large sauté pan, brown the birds or bird parts in the hot butter. Salt and pepper, add the chosen spirit and let it evaporate. Remove the birds to a plate.

To the pot add the onions, shallots, and juniper berries. Toss in the hot butter so the wet vegetables deglaze the pan well. Continue cooking the vegetables until mellow; return the birds to the bed of vegetables, cover with the lid kept slightly askew for the steam to escape, and cook 30 to 40 minutes, until the birds are well done.

Remove the birds to a country-style serving dish. To the pot add the heavy cream; raise the heat and reduce to coating consistency. Off the heat add the sour cream and lemon juice to your taste. Correct the seasoning with salt and pepper; do not strain the sauce; spoon it over the birds.

Serve a sturdy red wine.

WILD BOAR OR ITS REPLACEMENT

Since it is unlikely that anyone will be able to obtain wild boar, here is a recipe for a nice shoulder of pork prepared in the same manner as a leg of wild boar. I enjoyed it at the table of a friend of mine while vacationing in Les

Bois, three miles up the Chamonix valley. It was prepared by her Savoie-born cook. I hardly spoke with the cook, since she was one of those house "servants" who, in those days, slid silently in and out of bourgeois French dining rooms.

Yield: 6 servings

1 cup dry white wine
2 cups dry red wine
⅛ teaspoon ground cloves
½ teaspoon each ground cinnamon, allspice, and nutmeg
1 teaspoon dried thyme leaves
1 large onion, chopped
1 Mediterranean bay leaf, crushed
½ cup dry Madeira (Sercial or Rainwater)
1 boned, rolled, and tied Boston butt, approximately 3½ pounds
Salt
1½ pounds whole peeled shallots
2 tablespoons butter
Pepper from the mill
Chopped parsley

Mix the wines, half of all the dried spices well mixed, half the thyme, the whole chopped onion, and the crushed bay leaf in a large saucepan. Reduce by one third, remove from the heat, and, while hot, add the Madeira. Cool completely.

Marinate the roast in this mixture 2 days. When ready to roast, remove from the marinade, pat dry and air-dry 2 hours. Mix the remaining spices and aromatics and rub them all over the meat. Roast in a preheated 325°F oven 2 to 2½ hours; salt generously during the last 30 minutes of baking.

Meanwhile strain the marinade and discard its vegetables. Sauté the shallots in the butter until golden; add half the marinade to the shallots in successive additions until they are cooked and very mellow; set aside and keep warm.

Remove the cooked meat to a board; deglaze the baking dish with the remaining marinade and a ¼ cup of water, add salt if needed, and pepper, and strain into a gravy boat. Add the chopped parsley.

Serve with a light red wine and a dish of *Herbes* (see page 272).

SMALL GAME

I remember well the hunters coming back home during the fall of 1940 with strings of birds, everything from grouse to ptarmigan, pheasant, woodcock, and quail. Since we still have plenty of these birds in the United States we can use them. They need absolutely no marination; even the farm-raised quail have a wonderful flavor. We also have plenty of hare and rabbit. Farm rabbit can be used but will need a bit of marination.

CIVET

A peasant dish *par excellence*, this preparation mostly applies to rabbit but can also be used for smaller animals such as squirrels and marmots, and to a cubed shoulder of deer or any other mountain goat. Marination should be 48 hours if you use farm rabbit. The following recipe is a composite of three different ones coming from Mélanie, Les Praz de Chamonix, and Courmayeur. The anchovy is obviously from the Italian side of the Alps and smoothes over the sharpness of the country vinegar. Do not use the *loin* of hare or rabbit in a stew; it turns stringy. Go instead to page 347 for another recipe. Rabbit, when cooked to the European taste, almost—but only almost—falls off the bones! Amazingly enough frozen California rabbit tastes better for this dish than any freshly killed rabbit!

Yield: 6 servings

3 pounds shoulder of deer,
  cubed, or
Legs, shoulders, and ribs of 2
  rabbits
1 bottle red wine (Mondeuse,
  Chambave, or light Côtes
  du Rhône)
2 tablespoons red wine vinegar
  (6 percent acetic acid)
2 onions, peeled and sliced
2 chopped sage leaves, or ⅓
  teaspoon dried sage
2 tablespoons chopped parsley
  stems
1 crushed Mediterranean bay
  leaf
4 cloves
Butter as needed
Salt

Put the meat in a large glass baking dish. Pour the bottle of wine over it. Sprinkle all the aromatics over the meat and push the meat down so the liquid covers it well; marinate 48 hours.

Remove the meat from the marinade, pat it very dry, and brown it well in 2 tablespoons of butter in a *cocotte*. Salt and pepper and remove to a plate. Add the vegetables and aromatics from the marinade to the *cocotte* and sauté them on high heat to evaporate all moisture. Sprinkle the flour over the vegetables and cook 5 minutes, stirring occasionally; bind with the marinade and bring to a boil. Simmer a few minutes until well bound and return the meat to the pot. Add 1 mashed anchovy and cover, leaving the lid slightly askew; cook approximately 1 hour.

When the meat is done, remove it to a country-type serving dish. If more anchovy is needed, add 1 more, mashing it with some butter; if no more is needed, simply whisk 2 to 4 tablespoons of butter

Pepper from the mill
2 tablespoons all-purpose flour
1–3 anchovy fillets, to taste
Chopped parsley

into the sauce. Strain the sauce over the rabbit pieces, sprinkle with chopped parsley, and serve with nothing more than polenta and the same wine as used to marinate.

LATE NINETEENTH-CENTURY TO LATE-1940s DISHES

Among the Sunday and holiday dishes that were most popular in all parts of society was the pot-au-feu, the famous boiled beef that to this day is prepared throughout the winter by a large percentage of French families.

Mique Grandchamp, in his concern for good food in the bourgeois household, gives a recipe for Tenderloin of Beef à la Savoyarde, which he lards with salt pork, garlic, and truffles, and garnishes with artichoke bottoms stewed with tomato essence and green olives. This may sound very Provençal but it is not. Mique was using expensive imported ingredients, which he knew a certain part of the bourgeoisie was very well able to afford; the hostess received from him this eminent piece of advice: "The tenderloin à la Savoyarde served cold surrounded by aspic is marvelous for formal dinners, formal lunches, and formal evenings and can replace a galantine."

On the farm, the ceremonial dinner fare was more likely to be *La Zalia* or *La Gelée*, a supreme luxury all wrapped in good meat jelly, which could be prepared with pork on *cochon*'s demise day or with veal or a large bird. *La Zalia* could be served hot, but as a showpiece it was preferred cold.

LE POT-AU-FEU ET SES CONDIMENTS
Boiled Beef and Its Condiments

The recipe for pot-au-feu is in the Soup section on page 182. Since boiled beef tastes better when added to boiling water, you may want to add the tongue to the cold water to obtain a good bouillon, then add the beef to the already boiling bouillon to obtain a good piece of moist beef.

In the Savoie, and mostly all over France, the boiled beef is always well done. But I have seen several instances, in well-to-do private homes in Annecy, where the pot-au-feu was kept to make a shepherd's pie and a piece of tenderloin was poached in the bouillon only to medium rare. This is a modern variation. Usually the vegetables from the pot are served around the meat. Here is my Annecy way of serving the potatoes, without which boiled beef is nothing; compare it with Marie Becker's potatoes on page 274.

Yield: 6 to 8 servings

6 *Red Bliss potatoes, peeled*
  and quartered
Salt
Pepper from the mill
Enough beef stock from the pot
  to cover the potatoes
2 *tablespoons butter*
1 *clove garlic, chopped*
½ *teaspoon caraway seeds*
1 *tablespoon chopped parsley*

Put the potatoes in a 2-quart *cocotte*. Add the salt, pepper, bouillon, and butter. Cover and cook until all the bouillon has been absorbed and the potatoes start to fry in the butter. Delicately remove the potatoes to a serving dish.

Toss the garlic, caraway, and parsley into the butter at the bottom of the *cocotte* and sprinkle over the top of the potatoes.

Condiments for the Pot-au-feu

Mélanie used to serve a bowl of vinegar chock-full of chopped garlic and shallots as a condiment for her boiled beef. Here are two of Mique Grandchamp's favorite condiments for the same dish:

ESSENCE D'AIL DE MIQUE GRANDCHAMP
Mique Grandchamp's Garlic Essence

This is a direct translation from Mique's text; I have tried this garlic essence and found it a great asset to flavor a number of stews, grilled fish, and white meat of chicken (low cal!).

In parentheses I have added important information: "Choose six (large) garlic cloves, stick a clove into each of them; take two bay leaves and enough salt (1 teaspoon); (add) the mixture to one bottle of dry ordinary white wine and reduce by one half; strain your essence, pour it into a bottle, seal it well and place it in a dry cool place (your refrigerator). This essence keeps several months; it is wonderful to perk up fish sauces and even those of cooked and roasted meats."

RAGOÛT NATIONAL
National Ragout

Another direct translation from Mique, with parentheses still mine; the ragout tastes best when prepared with goose fat, which is not in the Savoie tradition:

"Put in a pot either some butter, lard, goose or duck fat, or oil (2–3 tablespoons, depending on the fat); (in it) sauté some (3 tablespoons) raw ham (prosciutto) diced small; add two tablespoons flour; let it brown moderately, add water or bouillon (3 cups); also add a chopped shallot, pepper, little salt since the ham is already salty, two tablespoons tomato sauce, a drop of (meat or vegetable extract) if necessary (when you use water), two dozen silverskin onions and as many button mushrooms. Let cook at least one half hour (until the sauce is reduced to 2 cups and coats the vegetables well). Thus prepared the *Ragoût National* can be served with all kinds of meats boiled and roasted."

POITRINE DE VEAU FARCIE EN GELÉE
Stuffed Veal Breast in Jelly

This came faithfully to the lunch table for the celebration of the 14th of July with a great tomato salad and small pastries. It must have exhausted the staff seriously, since all we had for dinner on that day was bread, butter, and café au lait. Typical country fare, it can be served either hot (the sauce is then very rich in proteins and thick) or cold, but shows off better cold since the jelly is so delicious. Do not clarify it; straining it through a tea strainer is sufficient. Pig's feet are available in many supermarkets and, in any case, in Italian neighborhoods.

2 pig's feet
4 ounces ground veal
4 ounces ground pork meat
½ pound Italian sweet
    sausage, skinned and broken
    up
1 slice boiled ham ¼ inch
    thick, cut into ¼-inch cubes
2 shallots, grated
3 cloves garlic, mashed
1 egg
Salt
Pepper from the mill
¼ teaspoon grated nutmeg
1 teaspoon celery seeds
1 side of veal breast, boned
2 tablespoons chopped lovage
    leaves, or celery leaves
3 tablespoons fat of your
    choice
1 large onion, peeled and
    sliced
1 large carrot, peeled and
    sliced
1½ quarts bouillon (page 182)
1 cup dry white wine
Bouquet garni

Blanch the pig's feet starting in cold water. Change the water and boil the feet in 2 quarts of fresh water until they fall apart. Drain but do not discard the cooking water. While still warm, bone and completely chop one of the feet. Keep the second foot as is.

Mix the ground veal, pork, sausage, boiled ham, chopped pig's foot, shallots, garlic, egg, approximately 1 teaspoon of salt, pepper, nutmeg, and celery seeds, and mix until very homogenous. Spread the veal breast on a board, sprinkle it with the lovage or celery leaves; and spread the forcemeat over all the meat leaving 2 inches free at one of its edges. Roll the meat and tie it with kitchen string at ½-inch intervals.

In a large oval *cocotte*, brown the rolled veal breast in 3 tablespoons of fat or oil; remove it to a plate; brown the onion and carrot in the same fat. Return the meat to the pot. Add the second pig's foot, enough bouillon to cover the meat, the white wine, and the *bouquet garni* and bring to a boil. Cover with foil formed to create an inverted lid and the pot lid; bake in a preheated 325°F oven approximately 2 to 2½ hours, until a skewer inserted at the center of the shoulder comes out freely.

Strain the cooking juices into a measuring cup and, using a baster, separate the lean gravy from the fat.

If you serve the meat cold, pour the gravy into a jelly roll pan and refrigerate it until solid. Using a knife, cut it into ⅓-inch cubes. Put the cubes of jelly around the sliced meat and garnish with cornichons. Pass a jar of mustard separately.

If serving hot, add the gratin of leeks on page 243 to your menu and pass the gravy in a preheated gravy boat.

A FAVORITE SAVOIE COMBINATION
Meat Garnished with Crawfish

Most Alpine lakes and streams, like our own Appalachian mountain streams, are full of small crawfish known as *écrevisses à pattes blanches*. Nowadays it seems less expensive to have crawfish flown in from Turkey than it is to run around the countryside gathering the local critters in remote streams. But occasionally, during the summer, when the airlifted supply is stretched to the limit by the tourist trade, a Talloires "mystery person" traps crawfish descended from a batch escaped from the Auberge du Père Bise supply into the Talloires bay; their taste and texture, as they come out of the cold lake, is superior to any crawdads I have ever enjoyed.

To devein a crawfish is easy, but watch your hands, they pinch! Hold the head between the index finger and thumb of your left hand, and with your right hand, twist the center tail fin; pull, and the vein full of bluish material will come out easily. Once a crawfish is deveined, it must be cooked immediately.

QUENELLES DE VEAU À LA SAVOYARDE
Veal Quenelles Savoie Style

I tasted them for the first time at Christmas in 1939 with the famous *Sauce Savoisienne*; they were delicious but far from smooth. Monsieur Arnaud Goddet, my butcher, also made them somewhat coarse. Quenelles have been typical hotel fare since the turn of the century and are still very popular; it is not rare to find them on the Sunday dinner menu even in smaller towns.

Yield: 6 to 8 servings

QUENELLES:
7 tablespoons unsalted butter
6 tablespoons flour plus ¼ cup
1½ cups scalding milk
2 eggs

To prepare the quenelles, make a *roux* with 6 tablespoons each of butter and flour. Cook to golden, bind with the scalding milk, and cook into a *béchamel* sauce. Cool completely.

Beat the eggs and egg yolks together. Process the *béchamel*, veal meat, veal kidney suet, and beaten

4 egg yolks
1¼ pounds veal top round, slivered and free of connective tissues
½ pound veal kidney suet, finely crumbled
2 small cloves garlic, finely chopped
⅓ teaspoon freshly grated nutmeg
Salt
Pepper from the mill
2 tablespoons chipped ice
2 quarts farm-style chicken broth (page 183), lukewarm

SAUCE:
½ pound mushrooms, sliced
Butter as needed
Salt
Pepper from the mill
18 deveined crawfish (see above)
3 tablespoons all-purpose flour
Reserved quenelles poaching broth
⅓ cup heavy cream
2 tablespoons sour cream
1 truffle, finely julienned (optional)
Puff pastry fleurons (optional)

eggs until very coarse; add the garlic, nutmeg, salt, pepper, chipped ice, and process until homogenous but still slightly coarse. Empty into a glass baking dish, smooth the top of the mixture, cover with plastic wrap, and refrigerate overnight. (Process in two batches if your food processor is too small.)

The next day, flour your hands with the remaining flour and shape the paste into twelve to eighteen 2½- by ¾-inch quenelles. Grease a sauté pan with the remaining tablespoon of butter and deposit the quenelles on its bottom. Gently pour the broth over the quenelles, slowly bring to a simmer (without ever allowing the broth to boil), and cook until the quenelles come floating to the surface of the broth. Remove them from the heat; cover, and let them puff a bit; remove them to a gratin dish (their shelf life is 2 days well covered and refrigerated). Reserve the broth.

To prepare the sauce, sauté the mushrooms in 1 tablespoon of butter; salt, pepper, and cover them to extract their juices. Add the crawfish and steam 8 minutes or so.

With 3 tablespoons each of butter and flour, prepare a blond *roux*. Bind with 3 cups of the poaching broth. Bring to a boil, turn down to a simmer, and skim a bit. Meanwhile shell the crawfish, crush 6 heads completely, and add them to the simmering sauce; also add the mushroom juices and reduce to approximately 2 cups. Strain. Finish the sauce by adding both creams, the mushrooms, and, if used, the truffle. Correct the final seasoning. Reheat the quenelles in the remaining broth. Serve 2 quenelles per person and spoon the sauce over them. Decorate with *fleurons*. A good Chignin or Roussette will go very well.

POULET SAUTÉ AUX ECREVISSES
Chicken and Crawfish Fricassee

This is Georgette's specialty when she entertains; in the absence of crawfish, she does not hesitate to use Norwegian lobsters, which we call *langoustines*. Since we receive *langoustines* without heads in the United States, bear in mind that they cook faster than those with heads still on. Please read the discussion on chicken (page 344) before purchasing the chicken legs.

Yield: 6 servings

Butter as needed
1 onion, *finely chopped*
1 *small carrot, finely chopped*
Small *bouquet garni*
18 *crawfish or small*
   langoustines
Salt
Pepper from the mill
1 *ounce cognac or Marc de*
   Savoie
6 *chicken legs, cut up into*
   drumsticks and thighs
1¼ *cups farm-style chicken*
   broth (page 183)
1¼ *cups heavy cream*
2 *tablespoons sour cream*
Dash of lemon juice
Chopped parsley

Heat 2 tablespoons of butter in a sauté pan. Sauté the onion and carrot until the onion is translucent. Add the *bouquet garni*. Devein the crawfish (See page 339) and add them to the pot immediately. Quickly toss into the hot vegetables; salt and pepper; heat the cognac or marc in a small pan, light it, and pour it flaming into the pan. Shake until the flames die, cover the pan and cook 8 to 10 minutes. Shell 12 of the crawfish; keep the remaining ones whole for decoration.

In another large sauté pan, brown the chicken pieces in 3 tablespoons of butter; salt and pepper well. Transfer the chicken to the pan in which the crawfish cooked. Discard the fat from the chicken browning skillet and deglaze it with half the chicken broth; pour that broth into the sauté pan, add 6 crawfish heads, cover, and cook 15 minutes. Turn the chicken pieces over, add the remaining broth, and finish cooking another 10 to 15 minutes.

When the meat is done, transfer it to a country-style serving dish. Add the crawfish tails and keep warm. Add the heavy cream to the sauté pan and on very high heat reduce until the sauce coats a spoon. Off the heat, add the sour cream and a dash of lemon juice. Correct the seasoning and strain the sauce over the meat and shellfish. Dot with chopped parsley and the reserved whole crawfish.

CAILLES EN GOURRES
Quail in Cabbage Leaves

When the camp director had her birthday, all the Madeleines of the community were coached in cooking her dinner, and this is how I caught terrible criticism from Mélanie for being careless in my wrapping of those little birds in cabbage leaves.

Yield: 6 servings

12 quail
12 cloves garlic
15 juniper berries
Salt
Pepper from the mill
Butter as needed
1 pound homemade sausage meat (page 317) or sweet Italian sausage
24 large cabbage leaves, ribs removed, blanched
2 cups farm-style chicken broth (page 183)

Put 1 garlic clove and 1 juniper berry, salt and pepper into the cavity of each quail. Truss the quail. Heat 2 tablespoons of butter in a large *cocotte* and brown the quail deeply. Remove the trussing.

Cool the birds. Crush the remaining 3 juniper berries and mix them into the sausage meat. Divide the sausage into 12 equal parts and wrap each bird into an even layer of sausage meat. Lay 2 overlapping cabbage leaves on the board and in it wrap the bird in its sausage wrapper. Tie with fine kitchen string.

In the same *cocotte*, adding another tablespoon of butter if needed, lightly brown the packages. Add one third of the broth, cover, and bake in a preheated 325°F oven 30 minutes. Turn the packages over, add another third of the broth, and finish baking another 30 minutes. When ready to serve, remove the packages to a serving dish; discard all the fat in the *cocotte* and add the remaining broth. Reduce it a minute and spoon it over the quail packages. Serve with potatoes and a good bottle of Pinot Noir.

PINTADE AUX CRATERELLES
Guinea Hen and Brown Chanterelles

The original of this dish was cooked for me, as I was the only guest in the house, way back in 1959 by Madame Schmidt, who was the owner of the Crèmerie du Bouchet in Les Praz de Chamonix. Her son Alain is now the chef and owner, much extended under its modern name, Hôtel de l'Arveyron. One of the best dining rooms in Northern Savoie for moderate prices and solid quality. Please read the discussion on chicken (page 344) before purchasing the birds.

Yield: 6 to 8 servings

2 guinea hens or free-range chickens
2 onions
2 bay leaves, crumbled
Salt
Pepper from the mill
Butter as needed
5 ounces slab bacon, cut into lardons 1 by ⅓ inch
1 pound brown chanterelles (Cratherellus lutescens), cleaned
3 cloves garlic, finely chopped
Chopped parsley

Stuff the cavity of each bird with 1 onion and 1 crumbled bay leaf, salt and pepper. Truss both birds. Heat 3 tablespoons of butter in a large *cocotte* and brown the birds on all sides, then remove them to a plate. In the same butter, add the lardons and brown them only lightly. Remove the lardons to a plate and discard all the fat in the *cocotte*.

Return the birds and the lardons to the *cocotte*; cover and cook on medium-low heat 45 minutes. Add the chanterelles and half the chopped garlic to the bottom of the pot and finish cooking another 15 minutes. Cut the birds into portions and serve them sprinkled with the remainder of the chopped garlic and the chopped parsley.

With these birds came steamed potatoes and a bottle of Gamay.

MODERN MEAT DISHES PREPARED WITH INGREDIENTS FROM SAVOIE MARKETS

Farmers bring to the Savoie markets some of the most succulent free-range birds as can ever be found; their only disadvantage is the chore of removing the pinfeathers. Even properly prepared, these birds can be a bit tough, since they have good muscles and are extremely well exercised. The toughness problem can be solved by letting the birds rest in the refrigerator for 2 to 3 days after purchasing to allow proper relaxation of the meat. In France, where birds are always half dressed, this does not present a problem; the upper respiratory organs keep the air from penetrating into the cavity, which prevents the development of bacteria. In the United States, however, the cavity is completely cleaned before the bird comes to market.

Since we are again able to find free-range birds in the United States, and since they taste considerably better than the common mass-produced animals, I have developed a method of aging them. With inexpensive vodka, I moisten a wad of paper towels large enough to almost fill the bird's cavity, then I push it into the cavity and let the birds sit 2 to 3 days in the refrigerator. There is absolutely no spoilage, and the toughness disappears. The vodka has nothing to do with the tenderization; it is only there to limit bacterial development in the cavity. I use this "sitting" method in combination with a slower roasting or baking temperature, which allows gradual softening of the meat and the production of a generous and delicious gravy. Be careful to note the day of production of the bird on its label and do not age the meat beyond 72 hours after that. Also, remember that plastic wrap is lethal for poultry, and keep your bird loosely wrapped in parchment paper. If you are worried that the skin will dry out too much, rub a little olive oil on it.

Fresh rabbits, like chicken, must rest in the refrigerator before being cooked or they will be tough even after proper cooking.

The recipes that follow are modern, since I established them all while I was working in Annecy. You must have noticed that in all the preceding recipes the meats were mostly stewed since one cooked mostly in a *cocotte*-type container. Now everyone has a *cuisinière* (stove); in old farms it is tucked under the hood of the old chimney. Awareness of diet and cholesterol have reached the Alps as they have spread across America. Everyone works as hard as we do, often harder, and speed has become essential. However, the same problem seems to be surfacing in the Savoie as it has in the United States—the younger the women, the less they know how to cook. It is not unusual nowadays to see young ladies buying prepared foods in supermarkets or charcuteries. The cost of our wonderful electric machines remains prohibitive for the average person, and as a result, there are not too many food processors, blenders, or microwaves used in the French Alps. Food is still cooked in good old-fashioned pots and pans; if I were to venture naming the most popular modern cooking implements, I think they would be the top-of-the-stove grill and the steamer, which are used quite extensively. One does roast quite a bit on Sunday, mostly what is called a *rosbif*, which, unless it is a filet, a piece of sirloin strip, or a rib of beef, is pretty tough by American standards; I would recommend avoiding the average roast beef in country inns and restaurants.

All recipes in this section yield 6 servings.

POULETS FUMÉS RÔTIS AUX RAVES CARAMELISÉS
Roasted Smoked Chickens with Caramelized Turnips

The baby purple turnips arrive in the markets in May and are no larger than an inch. If you have only larger turnips, quarter them and turn their angles to prevent breakage during cooking. Do not undercook the turnips; they must melt in the mouth.

2 chickens, 4½ pounds each, preferably free-range
Kosher salt as needed
1 cup brown sugar
Pepper from the mill
Butter as needed
1½ pounds small purple-topped turnips
½ teaspoon sugar
1 cup farm-style chicken broth (page 183)
Blanching water from the turnips as needed
Chopped chives

Truss the chickens. Pour a gallon of water into a large stainless steel bowl. Add enough kosher salt to make an egg float on its surface. Add the brown sugar and stir very well. Pepper the chickens' cavities and add the chickens to the pot. Let them soak in the brine 30 minutes. Smoke the chickens 1 hour (use whichever smoker you have, following the directions carefully). Brush the chickens with butter and roast in a preheated 325°F oven 45 minutes, or until the cavity juices run clear.

Meanwhile blanch the turnips in water for a few minutes; reserve a cup of the blanching water and drain the turnips into a colander. Pat them very dry. Heat 2 tablespoons of butter in a large sauté pan, add the turnips, and brown them well on medium heat; add the sugar, raise the heat, and caramelize it around the vegetables by shaking the pan back and forth. Add half the chicken broth and reduce, shaking the pan occasionally. Repeat the operation with the remainder of the broth.

When the chickens are done, remove them to a

platter and keep them in the turned-off oven. Place the roasting pan on high heat to caramelize the gravy. Using paper towels, dab the fat off. When all the fat has been removed, add the turnip blanching water to deglaze the roasting pan. Scrape well, correct the salt and pepper, and strain into a gravy boat.

Sprinkle the chicken with chopped chives, serve with the turnips and gravy and a good salad of escarole in a dressing made with walnut oil. A good Mondeuse, Gamay, or light Pinot will round out the meal.

POULARDE AUX SAVEURS DE SAVOIE
Steamed Chicken with Savoie Flavors

The plastic bag, of course, replaces the traditional use of the pig's bladder.

Two 4½-pound chickens
4 tablespoons butter
4 tablespoons chopped fresh dill weed
4 tablespoons chopped fresh coriander leaves
1 teaspoon powdered aniseeds
½ teaspoon ground cumin
Salt
Pepper from the mill
2 chicken cook-in bags
1 cup heavy cream
3 tablespoons sour cream
Cooked rice of your choice

Without breaking it, pass your finger under the skin of each chicken to separate it from the meat. Cream the butter with 3 tablespoons each of the chopped herbs, the spices, and salt and pepper. Slide 2 tablespoons of this aromatic butter under the skin of each chicken, spreading it well on the breasts and legs. Truss the chickens and put them into cook-in bags; tie well.

Place the cook-in bags in the basket of a lobster steamer, add half a gallon of water to the bottom container, bring to a boil, cover the steamer, and cook 50 minutes to 1 hour, until the juices accumulating into the angle of the bag are uniformly beige. If you prefer, you can cook the birds by immersing the bags in a bath of boiling water and simmering them 1 hour.

Pierce the bags and let the chicken juices escape

into a saucepan. Reduce the juices to a thick glaze. Add the heavy cream, cook a few minutes, then add the sour cream. Correct the seasoning, add the remaining herbs, and serve with the rice.

NOTE: This dish can be prepared without cream. Reduce the juices only by one half and add the herbs.

RÂBLES DE LAPIN GRILLÉS AUX TROIS MOUTARDES
Grilled Rabbit Loins with Tomato Mustards

Since rabbit loin does not stew very gracefully, here is a good way to cook it, with the wonderful three-colored tomatoes found in the market starting in September. The green tomatoes should not be dark green and hard as rock, but rather pale green.

*Loins of 6 rabbits, with their
    bones*
*Essence d'ail (garlic essence;
    page 336)*
Melted butter or oil
*1 pound each red, yellow, and
    green tomatoes*
3 cloves garlic, finely chopped
Salt
Pepper from the mill
1 tablespoon chopped parsley
4 tablespoons chopped chervil
3 tablespoons Dijon mustard

Brush the rabbit loin strips with garlic essence and let them dry at room temperature 1 hour. Brush the rabbit loins with melted butter.

Remove the stem ends of all the tomatoes, blanch and peel them. Cut them into wedges 1⅓ inches thick and seed them.

Heat 1 tablespoon of butter in a skillet, add 1 garlic clove and the parsley, toss them 1 minute in the butter, add the green tomato wedges, salt and pepper and toss well together, cover to extract their moisture, then finish cooking, uncovered, until the liquid has evaporated and the tomatoes form a compote. Repeat the process with the yellow and red tomatoes, cooking them each to the same consistency. To each tomato compote add chervil and Dijon mustard to taste, up to 1 tablespoon per type of tomato. Keep warm.

To serve the dish, you can either keep the compotes separated or mix them; I prefer mixing them.

Preheat a top-of-the-stove grill or barbecue very well and grill the rabbit loins 3 minutes on each side. Salt and pepper them well, slice the loins and serve them on a bed of tomato compote, sprinkled with the last tablespoon of chopped chervil. Serve with the *Fricasée de Coeurs de Pigeons et Petits Oignons* on page 275 and drink Mondeuse or Gamay.

POUSSINS AUX BAIES DE GENIÈVRE ET AUX CULS DE POULETS
Grilled Baby Chickens with Juniper Butter and Italian Plum Conserve

I have assumed a serving of one half Cornish hen per person, but you can use a whole one if you prefer. I used to make this conserve with fallen Lombardes I picked up along the road on my walks.

1 pound Italian prune plums, washed
⅓ cup brown sugar
2 cups dry red wine
Pinch of ground clove
10 juniper berries, powdered
¼ cup red wine vinegar
Salt to taste
Grated rind of 1 lemon
1 teaspoon coarsely ground black pepper
6 tablespoons butter
3 baby chickens or fresh Cornish hens

Put the plums, brown sugar, wine, clove, 5 of the powdered juniper berries, the vinegar, a pinch of salt, half the lemon rind, and ½ teaspoon of the cracked pepper in a large saucepan and bring to a boil. Simmer down until the mixture is thick and very little liquid is left. Put the compote in the blender with 3 tablespoons of the butter and puree very fine. Transfer to a small serving bowl.

With the remaining juniper berries, salt, remaining lemon rind, remaining butter and pepper, prepare a compound butter. Cut the chickens in half and slide an equal amount of the butter evenly under their skin. Broil the chicken halves, brushing them at regular intervals with the butter escaping into the broiler pan. The total broiling time is approximately 20 minutes.

Serve chicken and conserve together. The best

vegetable would be a plain *taillerin* on page 213. The same red wine as you used in the plum conserve would be fine.

BLANCS DE VOLAILLE GRILLÉS AUX COINGS
Grilled Chicken Cutlets with Quinces

Quinces are the last fruit of summer and arrive in reduced supply in the baskets of farm women. They must be ripened considerably before using them. Such is the case also in the United States, so do not hesitate to put quinces in a brown paper bag for several days in the company of a very ripe apple prior to cooking them.

6 quinces as ripe as possible
Juice of 1 lemon
2 tablespoons butter
Salt
Pepper from the mill
6 boneless chicken cutlets
    (white meat filets)
Oil of your choice as needed
½ cup farm-style chicken broth
    (page 183)
Chervil bouquets

Peel the quinces. Put the peels in a saucepan, cover them with water, and cook until they are soft and 1 cup of quince water remains. Drain the water into a bowl and discard the peels.

Meanwhile cut each fruit in half and core it. Transfer to a sauté pan large enough to hold the fruit in a single layer, add water to cover and lemon juice; bring to a boil and simmer until the fruit is almost done. Remove to a tea towel and dry well. Mix the peel water with the quince water and reduce again to 1 cup. Set aside.

Slice the quince halves horizontally; heat the butter and sauté the slices until light golden. Gradually add small amounts of the quince water to finish cooking the fruit until dark beige and as tender as quince will become; salt and pepper the fruit and keep warm.

Heat a top-of-the-stove grill; brush the cutlets with a thin film of oil and grill them 4 to 5 minutes on each side, pushing hard on them with a lid or spatula to force the heat rapidly to their center. Let them rest 2 minutes; salt and pepper them, and slice them horizontally.

On a large serving platter, alternate slices of quince with slices of chicken. Just before serving, pour the chicken broth into the grill and tilt the grill over the fruit and chicken to dribble the deglazing over them. The deglazing will have a slightly bitter taste; if you do not care for this, omit this last step. Decorate with chervil bouquets.

SALMIS DE PATTES DE CANARDS À L'ESSENCE D'AIL
Stewed Duck Legs with Garlic Essence

This was made both in the Savoie and in the United States with either the legs of domesticated duck or the very stringy legs of wild ones, which are so difficult to prepare otherwise. I used a mixture of mallards, black ducks, and widgeons; use as small duck legs as possible with as little fat as possible (Petaluma ducks for example).

12 small duck legs
1 tablespoon duck fat
6 cloves garlic, crushed in their skins
2 onions, peeled and sliced
4 shallots, peeled and sliced
1 quart farm-style chicken broth (page 183)
Bouquet garni
1 cup dry vermouth, preferably Boissière
3 tablespoons chopped lovage leaves
3 tablespoons butter
24 cloves garlic, peeled and blanched

Put the duck legs in a roasting pan; roast them in a preheated 400°F oven 30 to 40 minutes so as to discard as much fat as possible.

Meanwhile remove 1 tablespoon of duck fat from the roasting pan as soon as available and lightly brown the garlic cloves in their skins, the onions and shallots in a *cocotte*. As soon as the duck legs have browned, put them on the bed of vegetables and add the chicken broth, the *bouquet garni*, the vermouth, and 2 tablespoons of the chopped lovage. Bring to a boil, turn down to a simmer, cover with foil to form an upside-down lid and then the pot lid. Finish cooking in a 325°F oven approximately 1 to 1 hour and 15 minutes, until a skewer inserted into the thickest part of one of the legs comes out without resistance.

6 small zucchini, quartered
     lengthwise
Salt
Pepper from the mill

While the duck legs cook, heat 1½ tablespoons of the butter in a skillet and slowly brown the blanched garlic cloves until they turn nice and brown; do not let them burn or the whole dish will be bitter.

Cut the sticks of zucchini into triangles and brown them well in the remaining butter. Mix the garlic cloves and zucchini and season well. Keep warm.

Remove the duck legs from their sauce into a country-style serving dish, mix with the garlic and zucchini, and keep warm. Pour the sauce into a large measuring cup, let it settle, and, with a baster, remove all the fat-free gravy. Reheat very well and spoon over the duck and its garnish. Sprinkle with the remaining lovage.

Serve on very hot plates with a dish of plain buttered three-flour *taillerins* (page 213). The wine should be a Gamay.

CAILLES GRILLÉES AU POIVRE ET À L'ANIS
Grilled Quail with Pepper and Aniseeds

Since I like anise so much, and since there is so much of it in Savoie food, I developed this simple little recipe for quail, which can be made in a few minutes, even if you purchase whole quail.

12 quail, split open
3 tablespoons butter
1 teaspoon whole aniseeds
1 teaspoon coarsely cracked
     pepper
Salt
Oil of your choice as needed
⅔ cup farm-style chicken broth
     (page 183) (optional)

With scissors, remove the ribs of the quail and break the breastbone by bending it backward; this will allow the quail to lie flatter on the grill or broiler pan and to cook more evenly.

Mix well the butter, aniseeds, pepper, and salt and slide an equal amount of the mixture under the skin of each little bird.

Brush each bird with a thin layer of oil. Grill, skin side down, on a top-of-the-stove grill or under the broiler 5 minutes. Salt and pepper and turn the quail over. Finish grilling another 4 to 5 minutes on the skin side. If desired, deglaze the grill with the broth and use as a very short gravy. Serve with a nice salad of lamb's lettuce (page 283). Mondeuse would be best.

ESCALOPES DE DINDE AUX NOIX ET VIEUX REBLOCHON
Scallops of Turkey with Walnuts and Old Reblochon

1 side of a medium turkey breast, whole
½ cup clarified butter
½ cup chopped walnut meats
6 shallots, sliced
3 yellow onions, sliced
Salt
Pepper from the mill
2 cloves garlic, finely chopped
2 tablespoons chopped parsley
1 tablespoon finely chopped lovage or celery leaves
2 cups farm-style chicken broth (page 183)
Flour as needed
1 whole ripe Reblochon or 1 pound Italian Fontina cheese, skinned

Slice the turkey meat into small scallops ⅓ inch thick. Set them aside.

Heat half the clarified butter in a skillet and sauté the walnuts until they toast lightly. Remove them to a plate with a slotted spoon.

In the same butter, sauté the shallots and onions until very mellow and almost compote-like; season well; arrange these aromatics on the bottom of a 1-quart glass or porcelain baking dish. Sprinkle with the chopped walnuts, the garlic, chopped parsley, and the lovage or celery.

Meanwhile reduce the chicken stock to ¾ cup; correct its seasoning well.

Heat the remaining clarified butter in a skillet; flour the scaloppine, salt and pepper them, and quickly sauté them in the butter so they are colorless and still uncooked at the center. Sprinkle the chicken stock over the whole dish.

Slice the cheese; alternate layers of cheese slices with meat slices and bake in a preheated 425°F oven 6 to 7 minutes to finish cooking the meat and melt the cheese.

EPAULE D'AGNEAU SAUTÉE À LA VERVEINE ET AUX COEURS DE PIGEONS
Roasted Lamb Shoulder with Verbena Sauce and Baby Potatoes

Fresh verbena or lemon verbena is truly preferable for this dish, but if you do not have it, use some dried verbena tea (pure, please, not blended with other herbs) and simmer it in the stock before making the gravy. Verbena perfumes many stands of the Annecy market throughout the summer. *Coeurs de pigeons* are baby potatoes sold by the farmers, which one fries in butter without peeling.

1 boned shoulder of small lamb
⅓ cup fresh, very finely scissored verbena leaves
Salt
Pepper from the mill
1 pound baby potatoes, or larger potatoes recut but unpeeled
6 tablespoons butter
1½ cups bouillon (page 182)
Verbena or parsley bouquets

Flatten the meat on the table and sprinkle it inside with a tablespoon or two of scissored verbena leaves. Roll and tie the lamb to a uniform round shape. Place in a roasting pan and roast in a preheated 325°F oven 1 to 1½ hours to an internal temperature of 135 to 140°F. Salt and pepper the roast only after it has sealed well.

During the last 30 minutes of cooking the meat, fry the potatoes in 3 tablespoons of the butter until nice and golden. Keep warm. Mash the remainder of the butter with the remainder of the verbena. Reduce the bouillon by half.

When the meat is done, remove it from the oven and let it rest 5 minutes before slicing. Pat the fat from the juices in the roasting pan with paper towels. Pour the reduced bouillon into the roasting pan and deglaze well, scraping to obtain a good gravy; correct its seasonings. Strain it into the blender container, add the verbena butter, and homogenize well; strain again into a heated gravy boat.

Slice the meat and present it on a platter surrounded with the potatoes and decorated with bouquets of greens.

TOURNEDOS DE VEAU AU CHÈVRE ET AUX NOIX
Grilled Veal Steaks with Goat and Walnut Butter

Use an aged goat cheese that has a lot of taste; plenty are imported from France, and use the rib of veal, not any other cut, or you will have problems making the veal tournedos.

6 rib veal chops from milk-fed
    or Provimi veal, ¾ to 1
    inch thick
½ cup unsalted butter
3 tablespoons chopped
    walnuts, untoasted
1 large clove garlic, finely
    chopped
Pinch of ground cumin
Pinch of ground caraway seeds
2 tablespoons chopped parsley
Salt
Pepper from the mill
1 ounce very ripe goat cheese
Oil as needed

Carefully remove all the fat surrounding the rib veal chops, remove the chops from the bone, wrap the flap around the eye of the chop, and tie each chop into a tournedo. Cover and set aside.

Put the butter, walnuts, garlic, cumin, caraway seeds, parsley, salt, pepper, and goat cheese in a food processor and work into a compound butter. Shape into a stick 1 inch thick and store in plastic wrap; keep refrigerated.

Heat a top-of-the-stove grill. Brush the veal tournedos with a thin film of oil. Grill them 3 to 4 minutes on each side to medium rare, pushing on them with a pot lid or a spatula. Season the tournedos carefully. Top each one with a thick slice of compound butter.

Serve with the saladine on page 282 and a bottle of Chignin or Dézaley.

FRICANDEAU DE VEAU À LA LIVÈCHE ET À L'ANETH
Veal Fricandeau with Lovage and Dill

This very old-fashioned way to cook veal goes back at least to the eighteenth century. The veal in Annecy was so good that I did it for fun and fell in love with the dish all over again. The larding takes a bit of time but is a nice leftover from a slow past when one had time for everything.

1 large veal top round from
  Provimi or milk-fed veal,
  approximately 3 pounds
½ pound fatback
½ pound fresh pork rind in 1
  piece
2 yellow onions, sliced
1 large carrot, sliced
Bouquet garni
3 tablespoons each chopped
  lovage and dill
½ cup dry white wine
2 cups bouillon (page 182)
Salt
Pepper from the mill

Cut the veal into slices 1 inch thick *following the direction of the meat fibers*, not across. Cut the fatback into strips ¼ inch wide. Using a larding needle, pass the strips through each slice of meat as if you were sewing stitches in the meat in neat rows spaced ½ inch apart; lard each slice only on one side.

Place the pork rind at the bottom of a large *cocotte*. Sprinkle the sliced onions and carrot over it, add the *bouquet garni* and 1 tablespoon each of lovage and dill. Put on medium-high heat. Add the wine; let it evaporate completely. Add ½ cup of the bouillon and let it evaporate completely. Add the remainder of the bouillon so it just covers the meat. Salt and pepper lightly. Cover the meat with parchment paper and the pot lid, and bake in a preheated 325°F oven until a skewer goes in and out of the thickest slice of meat without difficulty. Remove the slices to a serving platter. Strain the cooking juices, which should be very concentrated; add the remainder of the lovage and dill, and serve with a dish of plain *fides* (page 212). You can chose a Chignin or a Mondeuse as you prefer.

LA GRILLADE DU PETIOU
Neil's Pork Grillade

Le Petiou is the name given within the family in Savoie to small and young boys. So Neil Kamman was, of course, my *petiou*, and each day this lucky mother had to cook his lunch because he refused to eat in the school cafeteria. This is one of those lunches, dedicated to Richard Weiss, who apparently would not have minded taking part in this teenage feast. Have the butcher slice the pork for you with his automatic slicer.

1 tablespoon currants
1 tablespoon red wine vinegar
3 tablespoons butter
1½ teaspoons tarragon
    mustard
Salt
Pepper from the mill
6 slices Boston butt, ⅓ inch
    thick

Soak the currants in the vinegar overnight, or until they have absorbed all the vinegar. Mix the currants, butter, and tarragon mustard. Salt and pepper to taste and shape into 6 equal patties.

Heat a top-of-the-stove grill until smoking. Grill the slices of pork until crisp on both sides. Top with the currant butter.

RIS DE VEAU AU SAFRAN ET À L'ANIS
Sweetbreads with Saffron and Anise

This is a mixture of new and old, as the sweetbread slices are lightly grilled and the short sauce is made by reduction as in the old days. It is perfect as a first course or as luncheon fare.

2 pairs veal sweetbreads,
    soaked in water overnight
Bouquet garni
2 cups bouillon (page 182)
Large pinch of saffron threads
⅓ teaspoon aniseeds
Salt
Pepper from the mill
3 tablespoons melted butter

Blanch the sweetbreads, starting the blanching in cold water. When the water comes to a boil, turn it down to a simmer, add the *bouquet garni*, and cook 10 to 12 minutes. Drain well and cool overnight in the refrigerator. Clean of all hard tissues.

Reduce the bouillon to ¾ cup; while it is still very hot add the saffron and aniseeds; add salt and pepper if needed and cool completely. Also refrigerate overnight.

The next day, slice the sweetbreads into scallops ⅓ inch thick. Brush them with melted butter. Heat a top-of-the-stove grill and grill them a few minutes on each side. Salt and pepper them well. Reheat the stock slowly without boiling it. Add whatever melted butter is left to the stock and spoon it over the sweetbread slices. Serve with Romaine and Seckel Pear Salad (page 285).

RIS DE VEAU AU CERFEUIL, CITRON, ET ASPERGES

Sweetbreads with Chervil, Lemon, and Asparagus

This is an old-fashioned recipe with the sweetbreads braised and well done.

2 pairs sweetbreads, blanched
   as in the preceding recipe
2 onions, sliced
1 carrot, sliced
2 tablespoons butter
Bouquet garni
Salt
Pepper from the mill
2 cups bouillon (page 182)
3 tablespoons green Chartreuse
Juice of 1 lemon
3 tablespoons chopped chervil
1½ tablespoons finely
   julienned lemon rind,
   blanched
3 tablespoons unsweetened
   whipped cream
18 jumbo asparagus, cooked
Chervil bouquets

Clean the blanched sweetbreads of all hard tissues. Sauté the onions and carrot in the butter and add the *bouquet garni*. Place the sweetbreads over the vegetables; salt and pepper them well. Add the bouillon, green Chartreuse, lemon juice, 1 tablespoon of the chopped chervil, and ½ tablespoon of the lemon rind. Cover with foil, forming an inverted lid, and the pot lid and bake in a preheated 325°F oven 45 minutes.

Remove the cooked sweetbreads to a serving dish. Strain the sauce into a skillet and quickly reduce it to ⅔ cup. Add the whipped cream, the remaining chervil and lemon rind, and correct the final seasoning. Spoon the sauce over the sweetbreads and garnish with the hot asparagus and the chervil bouquets.

Desserts

According to Jean Nicolas, desserts were relished by the upper classes and the sugar habit was well entrenched from the late 1600s through the eighteenth century. Besides being, as Nicolas puts it, a "physiological necessity," sugar was often used as a gift or exchange item. In daily life it was sprinkled directly on soft white cheese and used in large quantities to prepare all sorts of preserves—the famous confitures. Confitures are still in style; modern markets still display a whole array of elegant jars, sealing paraffin cakes and, nowadays, self-sealing jars. Even today, receiving a gift of homemade confitures is a sign that you are a true friend. The only thing one can do is to reciprocate, so the same old jar has been traveling back and forth between Georgette and me for the last six years; she gives me plum jam or quince jelly and, once it has fallen victim to my bunch of forever hungry fellows, I return the jar filled with marmalade in the Anglo-Saxon manner.

Confitures means, of course, fruit, of which there is a large quantity in the Savoie. A little ride between Tamié and Saint Pierre d'Albigny will be very revealing of the beautiful orchards that line the right-hand side of the lower Isère valley. The fruit trees have been there a very long time, and apricots, peaches, plums, melons, Reinette and Calville apples, as well as six different types of pears, seem to have graced the tables of seventeenth- and eighteenth-century Savoyards. The markets were also visited by Provençal *citronniers*, who came up the Rhône valley to sell their citrus fruit; one of their descendants still sells *citrons non traités* ("non-sprayed lemons") from a basket every Sunday morning at the Annecy market. The lower classes had nothing but fruit, and all their sweets revolved around its use in combination with flour, eggs, and milk.

The most rustic sweet preparation is cited by both Marie Thérèse Hermann and Constantin Desormaux's *Dictionnaire Savoyard* as being the RUTSA, a toast of oat or barley bread, covered with sweetened water cut with wine. Another rustic delicacy was LA MOUIRETTE, or toasted slices of bread moistened with a sweet composition of water, sugar, and wine. When I read this bit of information, I realized that I had finally found the origin of that mysterious wine sauce of Burgundy, La Meurette, that is used on everything from eggs to meats or fish. The variation MOUILLETTE is also found, describing basically the same dish.

As we have seen (page 108), wine and alcohol were consumed daily and without shyness at all levels of society, until tea, coffee, and chocolate arrived via Geneva around 1700. By the time of the French Revolution coffee had reached the farms and partly replaced *la goutte*, or morning brandy; what actually happened is that the *goutte* went into the black coffee, an inveterate French country habit that persists to this day. Café au lait was not solidly established until the last third of the nineteenth century, at least in the villages, as I have already mentioned in the Soups chapter.

It is very probable that some of the earliest sweet preparations to be enjoyed by all came at the time of bread baking, when one would prepare with the leftover bread dough a type of sweet pizza. It had different names, the most current being *Levèches* as I have mentioned in the Bread chapter. Arsène Bourgeaux, in his essay on food in Mont Saxonnex, calls those flat breads with fruit *Flamelles*. Two recipes follow here.

FLAMELLE À LA CRUTZE
Sweet Pizza with Butter Solids and Honey

If you combine bread baking with butter melting for winter storing you obtain this lovely flat bread, which could be done with a semi-sweet dough if you prefer it. To accumulate enough milk solids to prepare this *galette*, freeze whatever milk solids you obtain when you clarify butter and keep adding them to the jar.

Yield: 6 to 8 servings

½ recipe Pain Tout Blanc
   (page 135)
½ cup unsalted butter
1½ cups milk solids from
   skimming clarified butter
1 tablespoon honey
¼ cup sugar
Pinch of salt
1½ tablespoons marc

Roll out the bread dough into a 10-inch circle no more than ⅛ inch thick. Roll the edge slightly upward all around to make a rim.

Cream the butter, add the milk solids, honey, sugar, salt, and marc, and mix until homogenous. Spread over the bread; let stand at room temperature 15 minutes, then bake in a preheated 425°F oven until the sugar turns lightly brown. Cool slightly before serving with a good cup of café au lait.

FLAMELLE À LA RHUBARBE
Rhubarb Pizza

This fruit "pizza" can be executed with any fruit in season: apricots, Italian prune plums, peaches, or nectarines; pears and apples will be better if they are sautéed in butter first.

Yield: 6 to 8 servings

½ recipe Pain Tout Blanc
   (page 135)
2 cups peeled rhubarb, cut
   diagonally into ⅛-inch slices
Sugar as needed
1–2 tablespoons unsalted
   butter

Roll out the bread dough into a circle approximately 10 inches in diameter and no more than ⅛ inch thick.

Arrange the slices of rhubarb into one layer of concentric circles on the dough. Sprinkle with sugar to taste and dot with tiny pieces of butter. Bake in a preheated 425°F oven until the rhubarb starts developing black tips. Cool before enjoying with café au lait.

As life became easier in the Savoie, the use of brioche dough for many of the confections became more prevalent. As you can see in the Bread chapter, *riâmes* and *bescoins* were made out of brioche dough; as late as the beginning of this century, soldiers celebrated their release from the army, *la classe*, by donating a large brioche to the conscripts of the following year. Here is the *Brioche de Saint Genix*, a small community of the Petit Bugey, around the western part of the Montagne de l'Epine, which dominates the lake of Le Bourget (Aix les Bains).

BRIOCHE DE SAINT GENIX
Saint Genix Brioche

First you must prepare the red pralines unless you do not mind not having the red color sticking to the cake, in which case you can purchase some excellent French or British pralines (Crabtree and Evelyn) and use them in their light brown robe. The taste is identical.

Yield: 6 to 8 servings

FOR THE PRALINES:
18 almonds, peeled
3 tablespoons water
½ cup sugar
1 teaspoon pure vanilla extract
½ teaspoon red food coloring
½ tablespoon unsalted butter

FOR THE BRIOCHE DOUGH:
3 cups unsifted all-purpose flour
3 tablespoons cornstarch
1 envelope active dry yeast
3 tablespoons milk
2 tablespoons sugar
½ teaspoon salt or less, to taste
1 teaspoon orange flower water
3 eggs, beaten
½ cup soft unsalted butter plus
   1 tablespoon

Lightly toast the almonds in a preheated 325°F oven 10 minutes so they are very pale and very dry; cool them. In a superclean stainless steel skillet, combine the water, sugar, vanilla, and red food coloring. Bring to a boil and cook to the hard crack stage; add the almonds and toss them into the sugar very quickly to coat them as evenly as possible. The sugar syrup may crystallize; this is no problem. Remove the pralines to a lightly buttered cookie sheet and cool them completely.

Sift the flour and cornstarch together. Put one third into a bowl. Add the yeast and ¼ to ⅓ cup of lukewarm water. Gather the dough into a loose ball. Pour warm water around the ball of dough and let it come floating to the top of the water.

Meanwhile make a well in the remaining flour mixture, add the milk, sugar, salt, and orange flower water; add the eggs and gather into a batter. As soon as the starter floats on top of its bowl of water, lift it out with your hand, letting the water drip well;

deposit the starter into the basic egg dough and mix well together.

Soften the ½ cup of butter with your hand. Divide it into 4 equal pieces and place one at each corner of the dough. With your fingertips, work the butter into the the dough, emulsifying very well. The dough will turn whitish. Work the dough a few minutes by pulling it from the table top and flopping it back down. Transfer the ball of dough to a large glass mixing bowl; cover and let rise until doubled in bulk.

Pass your hand gently under the raised dough and deflate it. Smooth its top and refrigerate overnight.

To bake the brioche, bring the dough to room temperature. Butter a 10-inch cake pan with the remaining tablespoon of butter, smooth the ball of brioche, and set into the pan. Let rise until 1½ times as large. Bake in a preheated 375°F oven. After 10 minutes, cut a large cross into the top of the brioche and top it with at least 8 of the prepared pralines, more if you like. Finish baking another 15 minutes and cool completely.

Excellent with butter, café au lait, and a compote of fruit (page 377).

LE PAIN DE MODANE
Modane Sweet Bread

This is not bread, as the name seems to indicate, but a cake made with a different brioche dough. It is a specialty of Modane, the train station on the border between France and Italy and the entrance to the Upper Maurienne. This is my interpretation of the pastry sold in Modane:

Yield: 6 to 8 servings

FOR THE BRIOCHE-TYPE CAKE:

10 egg yolks

⅓ cup sugar

⅛ teaspoon salt

1 envelope active dry yeast

3 tablespoons warm milk

2 cups unsifted all-purpose flour

2 tablespoons cornstarch

¾ cup melted unsalted butter

FOR THE FILLING:

¾ cup diced candied melon

3 tablespoons Grand Marnier

6 ounces almond paste

1 egg yolk

To prepare the batter, beat the egg yolks, sugar, and salt until the mixture is very white and forms a ribbon falling from the beater. Meanwhile dissolve the yeast into the warm milk and let it bubble. Add the yeast mixture to the eggs, sift the flour and cornstarch mixed into the batter, and beat in the butter, using a spatula, *not an electric mixer, or a whisk*, until the dough acquires a slight amount of body. Let it rise until doubled in bulk, punch it down gently, and refrigerate at least 6 hours.

Macerate the melon overnight in 2 tablespoons of the Grand Marnier. Grate the almond paste, then mix it with the last tablespoon of Grand Marnier and the egg yolk. Cover with plastic wrap and set aside.

The next morning, flour the counter, your hands, and the rolling pin lightly. Roll the dough into a 10-inch circle ⅓ inch thick. Spread the almond paste evenly over the disk, leaving a ½-inch border all around. Spread the melon over the center of the disk. Roll into a large cigar 2 inches in diameter. Immediately put on a greased baking pan and allow the dough to almost double in bulk. Bake in a pre-heated 375°F oven until golden brown, approximately 30 minutes. Cool on a rack. Enjoy with Earl Grey tea.

ÉPOGNES

Épognes are the ancient local Savoie tarts, the crusts of which are made of brioche dough. Use the following ingredients and refer for the method to the *Brioche de Saint Genix* on page 361. Their filling will vary from a plain fruit to a mixture of pastry cream or almond cream and fruit. Feel free to vary the filling to your heart's content; there is so much variety in the Savoie that anything is possible. Here are the basic recipes and the method for putting the *épognes* together.

Each épogne will yield 6 to 8 servings.

BRIOCHE À ÉPOGNE
Brioche Dough for Savoie Country Tarts

2 cups unsifted all-purpose flour
2 tablespoons cornstarch
1 envelope active dry yeast
2 tablespoons sugar
1 teaspoon orange flower water
   or grated lemon rind
2 eggs
6 tablespoons unsalted butter

PASTRY CREAM FILLING FOR
TWO 8-INCH ÉPOGNES:
6 egg yolks
½ cup sugar
Pinch of salt
6 tablespoons flour
2 cups cold milk
1 teaspoon orange flower water
   or other flavoring of your
   choice

AMANDINE CREAM:
4 tablespoons softened unsalted
   butter
½ cup grated almond paste
1 egg, beaten
Tiny pinch of salt
¼ teaspoon almond extract
1 teaspoon cornstarch

Follow exactly the procedure indicated on pages 361–62. To shape the *épogne*, keep the dough cold, roll it out into 2 flat disks to fit into one 12- or two 8-inch buttered baking pans. Fill as you like, using the suggestions below or another of your choice.

Beat the egg yolks with the sugar and salt until they form a heavy ribbon when falling from the beaters. Sift in and gradually incorporate the flour. Dilute gradually with the cold milk and bring to a boil on medium heat. Stir with a blunt-ended wooden spatula until the mixture just begins to boil, then quickly switch to a whisk to prevent lumping. Continue boiling for a few minutes, until the custard has thickened completely. Add the flavoring of your choice. Spread over the pastry before adding the fruit.

Cream the butter, then add the grated almond paste, the egg, salt, almond extract, and the cornstarch. Beat well with a whisk and spread over the pastry before adding the fruit.

Pairing of the fruit and custard:
   The best combinations of fruit and custard are, for my personal taste, those that follow, but you may substitute any that you prefer.

Fruits to use without precooking:

> Apricots and pastry cream, flavored with 2 tablespoons Kirsch
>
> Blueberries and amandine
>
> Cherries and amandine
>
> Red currants remain best by themselves; they are cooked without any addition in the plain crust and heavily sugared when the *épogne* is cooked.
>
> Black currants and amandine plus 1 teaspoon grated lemon rind
>
> Cranberries (to replace lingonberries) and pastry cream; sugar the cranberries after cooking.
>
> Italian prune plums and pastry cream plus 1 teaspoon grated lemon rind
>
> Yellow peaches and pastry cream flavored with lemon rind
>
> Nectarines, same as peaches
>
> Rhubarb, on plain pastry or with pastry cream

Fruit requiring precooking:

> Pre-sauté apples and pears in butter before putting them into the *épogne* crust.
>
> Apples and pastry cream flavored with marc
>
> Pears and amandine flavored with ½ teaspoon ginger powder

MODERN TARTS WITH SWEET PASTRY CRUST

Many tarts now prepared at home or in pastry shops are made with the sweet pastry crust so much in favor all over France, a few in regular short pastry. The texture, taste, and color of the pastry will vary, depending on the area in which it is made.

To make the pastry, you can either use a food processor, which is the easiest way, or if you do not own one, a bowl and a spatula. Electric mixers, if used alone one second too long, can make the pastry very tough.

Using the food processor:

> Cream the butter, add the sugar, egg(s), and flavoring(s). Pour the flour through the opening of the processor until the dough forms a ball. Flatten the dough into a ½-inch cake and store between 2 layers of plastic wrap.

By hand:

With the mixer or by hand, cream the butter; beat in the sugar and egg(s). Using a rubber spatula, flatten the flour by hand into the creamed butter to prevent the development of gluten. Flatten the finished dough into a ½-inch-thick cake and store between 2 layers of plastic wrap.

Do not let the dough stay in the refrigerator so long that it hardens too much and will not roll out. Should it harden too much, let the dough stand at room temperature until manageable enough to be rolled out.

All tart recipes yield 6 to 8 servings.

TARTE AUX POMMES DE COURMAYEUR À LA FARINE JAUNE
Apple Tart Courmayeur Style

This tart is a specialty of Courmayeur and is sold there in most shops. Our friend Jean Lantermoz, who was born in Saint Vincent d'Aosta, used to prepare it this way, in a large oval earthenware dish, which was not the best choice. Use a 10-inch springform cake pan.

FOR THE PASTRY:
½ cup unsalted butter plus 1
  tablespoon
¼ cup sugar
Pinch of salt
1 egg
1 tablespoon marc
½ cup superfine corn flour
1½ cups all-purpose flour

FOR THE FILLING:
2 tablespoons unsalted butter
8 apples, preferably
  Gravenstein, Rome Beauty,
  or Cortland, peeled, cored,

Prepare the pastry as described on page 365 using ½ cup of butter.

Butter the cake pan with the remaining tablespoon of butter. Roll the pastry between the layers of plastic into a ⅙-inch-thick circle that fits into the pan. Remove the top layer of plastic and invert the pastry into the pan. With the plastic still on, fit the pastry well into the pan. Remove the plastic and build a small edge. If you have too much pastry, make a few cookies with the remainder. Should the pastry stick to the plastic, your dough is too warm; put the pan in the refrigerator a few minutes.

To prepare the filling; heat the butter in a large skillet. Sauté the apples just a few minutes in the hot butter, cool them completely and transfer to the

and cut into ¼-inch-thick
   slices
1 egg
1 egg yolk
1 cup heavy cream
3 tablespoons honey
2–3 tablespoons marc
Pinch of salt

pastry. Bake in a preheated 350°F oven approximately 1 hour and 15 minutes, until the apples are deeply cooked and start collapsing into the pastry. Beat the egg, egg yolk, heavy cream, and honey, dilute with the marc, and slowly pour over the apples, forcing the custard to flow between the apples with the tip of a parer. Finish baking until the custard is set, or another 15 to 20 minutes. Cool and serve the same day. Should you have access to true unpasteurized *crème fraîche*, not the fabricated product, serve a dish of it with the pie. Cappuccino is in order.

TARTE AUX POIRES RENVERSÉE
Upside-down Pear Tart

The sauce must be made with light cream; heavy cream will break when you deglaze the caramel from the pear-baking pan.

FOR THE PASTRY:
6 tablespoons unsalted butter
2 tablespoons sugar
2 egg yolks
1 tablespoon pear brandy
⅓ cup ground walnuts
1 cup sifted all-purpose flour
Pinch of salt

FOR THE FILLING:
2 tablespoons unsalted butter
4 Bosc pears, peeled, cored,
   and cut in half
½ cup sugar
1 cup light cream
2 tablespoons pear brandy
12 walnut halves

Prepare the pastry as described on page 365.

To make the filling, spread 1 tablespoon of the butter into a 1-quart baking dish, add the pears rounded side up, cover them with the sugar, and bake in a preheated 350°F oven until the sugar has caramelized lightly. Turn the pears over and finish baking until the caramel is brown but not black, or the sauce will be bitter. Remove the pear halves to a buttered plate and cool enough to be able to handle them. Deglaze the pan with the light cream and reduce well to make a sauce. Add the brandy.

Butter a 9-inch pie plate with the second tablespoon of butter. Cut the pear halves crosswise into ¼-inch-thick slices. Slightly fan the pear halves and arrange them, rounded side down, and the walnut meats, crinkly side down, in the pan.

Roll the pastry into a 10-inch circle. Place it over the pears, fold the edge over, and pleat it to strengthen the edge of the pie. Cut openings into the pastry with the tip of a scissor and bake in a 375°F oven 15 to 20 minutes, or until the pastry is done. Invert onto a plate and serve with the pear cream.

TARTE À LA RHUBARBE ET AUX FRAISES
Rhubarb and Strawberry Tart

Fresh rhubarb and strawberry tart glazed with raspberry jelly for sweetness; a good way to use those huge strawberries that may look better than they taste.

FOR THE PASTRY:
6 tablespoons unsalted butter
2 tablespoons sugar
Pinch of salt
1 teaspoon grated lemon rind
1 egg
¼ cup finely ground almonds
1 cup sifted all-purpose flour

FOR THE FILLING:
1 tablespoon unsalted butter
1½ cups rhubarb, cut on a
    slant into ¼-inch thick slices
1½ cups large strawberries,
    sliced lengthwise ¼ inch
    thick
½ cup strained raspberry jam
2 tablespoons black currant
    liqueur (cassis)

Prepare the pastry as described on page 365. For the filling, butter an unbendable cookie sheet with the tablespoon of butter. Trace on it a circle approximately 10 inches in diameter. Roll the pastry into a circle approximately ⅙ inch thick and put it on the tracing. Raise and crimp the edge all around to form a ⅓-inch-thick container for the fruit.

Arrange the rhubarb and strawberries in concentric circles, alternating the slices of fruit. Bake in a preheated 375°F oven until the tips of the rhubarb start to brown. Cool to lukewarm. Heat the jam to a flowing texture, add the liqueur, and brush carefully over the fruit.

LA VIEILLE TARTE AUX NOIX DE LA CHARTREUSE
Old-fashioned Walnut Tart

This old-fashioned tart is common to the Savoie and Dauphiné parts of the Chartreuse mountains. The recipe that follows is my version of one served by Mr. and Mrs. Mahaut at their charming Hôtel du Col du Cucheron. In France, to replace the brown sugar, I use *vergeoise*.

FOR THE PASTRY:

½ cup unsalted butter

3 tablespoons brown sugar

Pinch of salt

1 tablespoon dark rum

1 egg

1 egg yolk

1–1¼ cups sifted all-purpose flour

FOR THE FILLING:

½ cup unsalted butter at room temperature

1⅓ cups chopped walnuts

¾ cup brown sugar

2 eggs

2 tablespoons espresso-strength coffee

1 tablespoon dark rum

FOR THE ICING:

½ teaspoon walnut oil (very fresh!)

3½ ounces bittersweet chocolate, preferably Valrhona 61% cocoa or the equivalent

Prepare the pastry as described on page 365 using 7 tablespoons of the butter. With the remaining tablespoon of butter, grease a 10-inch springform pan very well. Roll the pastry ⅙ inch thick between 2 sheets of plastic wrap, fit it into the pan, and build a small edge.

In the food processor, mix all the ingredients for the filling and process until homogenous. Pour into the prepared shell. Bake on the lowest shelf of a preheated 350°F oven 20 minutes, and another 35 minutes on the top shelf. Remove from the oven and cool completely.

To ice, mix the walnut oil and chocolate and melt in a double boiler, cool slightly, and brush evenly on the top of the tart. Serve in 1-inch portions since it is very rich, with an excellent cup of double-strength café au lait.

TARTE AUX CROQUEMOLLES
Hazelnut Tart

In Savoie patois, the name *croquemolles* is applied to filberts, an aptly descriptive word since it means "soft chewing." This tart, which has some of the same components as the *Linzer Torte* of Austria, has been commercialized under the name *Régal Savoyard* and varies greatly in texture and quality from one pastry shop to the next. This is my personal version.

FOR THE PASTRY:
6 ounces unsalted butter plus
   1 tablespoon
3 tablespoons sugar
Pinch of salt
1 teaspoon pure vanilla extract
1 egg
⅓ cup finely ground hazelnuts
1 cup sifted all-purpose flour

FOR THE FILLING:
4 tablespoons unsalted butter
⅓ cup sugar
⅔ cup finely ground hazelnuts
1 egg
⅔ cup raspberry jam

FOR THE TOPPING:
3 egg whites
⅓ cup sugar
1⅓ cups finely ground
   hazelnuts

Prepare the pastry as described on page 365 using 6 ounces of butter. With the remaining tablespoon of butter, grease an unbendable cookie sheet and a 9-inch pastry ring. Roll the cooled pastry to a thickness of ⅙ inch, fit it into the pastry ring on the cookie sheet, and build a small pretty edge. Put all the ingredients for the filling except the jam into the food processor and process them all at once for no more than 30 seconds. Pour the filling into the pastry shell; it will not fill it. Bake in a preheated 350°F oven 20 minutes or so, until the filling is set. Remove the tart from the oven and spread the jam over the filling. Cool to barely lukewarm.

Beat the egg whites until they form stiff peaks, mix the sugar and hazelnut powder and fold into the egg whites. Spread over the jam in an even layer well anchored to the edge of the tart. Bake in a 325°F oven about 20 minutes, or until the meringue is nice and crusty. Serve on the second day after baking in 1-inch portions.

TARTE AUX DEUX FRAMBOISES OU AUX MYRTILLES
Tart with Two Kinds of Raspberries or with Bilberries or Blueberries

Toward the end of summer Savoie markets offer the most delightful white raspberries, not unlike cloudberries. In the United States, do not hesitate to use those wonderful salmonberries from the West Coast if you can get them. If you use blueberries, choose wild huckleberries.

FOR THE PASTRY:

1 cup sifted all-purpose flour

6 tablespoons unsalted butter cut into 1-tablespoon portions, very cold, plus ⅓ tablespoon

2–3 tablespoons water

Pinch of salt

Pinch of sugar plus 3 tablespoons

FOR THE FILLING

1½ cups each white and red raspberries, or

2–3 cups huckleberries

1 cup pure raspberry puree from fresh red raspberries

3 tablespoons melted currant jelly

2–3 tablespoons black currant liqueur (cassis)

Sugar or honey if needed, to taste

Tiny pinch of salt

To prepare the pastry, put the flour on a tabletop or board. Add the pieces of butter and mix together with your fingertips until the butter is the size of small peas. Mix together the water, salt, and the pinch of sugar and gradually add to the pastry without kneading. Fraise once only (see Quick Puff Pastry, following recipe, page 372.) Refrigerate, covered, 15 minutes.

Give the pastry 4 turns, as you would for puff pastry, 2 at a time with a 30-minute interval between (see page 372). Keep the pastry refrigerated 1 hour before using it.

Butter an unbendable cookie sheet lightly with the ⅓ tablespoon of butter. Sprinkle evenly with 1½ tablespoons of sugar. Trace a 9-inch circle into the sugar. Roll out the pastry ⅙ inch thick into a 9½-inch circle. Put it on the traced circle on the sheet. Turn the uneven edge under and flatten with the tines of a fork. Sprinkle the top of the pastry with the remainder of the sugar and prick every quarter inch with a fork. Refrigerate 30 minutes, then freeze. Preheat the oven to 425°F. Remove the sheet from the freezer, cover the pastry with a sheet of parchment paper, and top with a second baking sheet. Bake 20 minutes. Remove the sheet and parchment, turn the oven down to 350°F, and finish baking until nice and dry, another 15 minutes or so. Cool completely.

Arrange the two kinds of raspberries in an alternating pattern on top of the crust. Mix the red raspberry puree with the melted currant jelly and the cassis. Taste, and add sugar or honey if desired. Serve each pie wedge in a pool of berry puree.

Since the penetration into the countryside of the classic pastries of France after the annexation, there has been a widespread use of puff pastry throughout the Savoie. Here is a simple recipe for it that will make the next two recipes accessible to all cooks:

QUICK PUFF PASTRY

2 cups less 1 tablespoon all-
  purpose flour
1 tablespoon cornstarch
1 cup (½ pound) unsalted
  butter, chilled
½ teaspoon salt
¼–⅓ cup ice cold water

Mix the flour and cornstarch. Divide the butter into 2-tablespoon portions. Sprinkle with the salt. With your fingertips, break up the butter and mash it into the flour until it is the size of large macadamia nuts.

Gradually mix in the ice cold water, using your fingertips. The pastry will make a large ball. With the heel of your hand, lightly push the ball of dough forward into large flat pieces (this is called the fraisage). Gather into a ball again, shape into a rectangle 6½ by 4½ inches, and refrigerate 1 hour in the vegetable crisper.

Now give 6 turns, 2 at a time, at 30- to 40-minute intervals. Proceed as follows: Roll the dough 6 inches away from you and 6 inches toward you, keeping it 6½ inches wide and ⅓ inch thick. With the rolling pin, tap the edges of the pastry to keep them neat. Fold the dough in thirds lengthwise. Now turn the obtained dough package by 90°, so that it looks like a book ready to be opened; apply a bit of pressure with the rolling pin at the top and bottom of the package to seal the ends well. Roll and fold again exactly as described.

This procedure will be repeated 3 times. Refrigerate the finished pastry at least 2 hours before using. It is advisable to prepare it way ahead of time, keep it frozen, and slowly defrost in the refrigerator.

BICHONS
Lemon Cream Turnovers

These delightful pastries are prepared by two shops in Annecy; those of Monsieur Nivon at La Gâterie in the rue Sainte Claire are the very best. This is my interpretation of his irresistible little turnovers.

FOR THE FILLING AND THE PASTRY:

4 egg yolks

½ cup sugar

Pinch of salt

2 tablespoons cornstarch

1 cup cold water

¼ cup very finely ground almonds

3–6 tablespoons lemon juice, to taste

1 teaspoon grated lemon rind

1 recipe puff pastry (page 372)

Instant superfine sugar as needed

Beat the egg yolks with the sugar and salt until they form a ribbon when falling from the beater. Dilute the cornstarch in the water. Gradually whisk the water into the ribboned yolks. Bring to a boil on medium heat, stirring very well to prevent lumping. Off the heat, add the almonds and the lemon juice and rind. Cool completely.

Roll the pastry out into a circle ⅛ inch thick. Refrigerate after rolling. Dust the counter lightly with flour. Cut 6 circles, each 5 inches in diameter out of the pastry. With a touch of the rolling pin, elongate the circles into ovals. Brush the outer edge with water. Put a large tablespoon of lemon cream on the pastry and fold it over into a turnover. Crimp the edge of each turnover with a fork or by rolling the side of a crinkled cutter over it.

Lightly butter an unbendable cookie sheet. Sprinkle superfine sugar very evenly on the underside of the turnovers. Set them on the sheet so they do not touch one another. Brush or spray the tops of the turnovers very lightly with water and sprinkle them with superfine sugar. Refrigerate at least 1 hour.

Bake in a preheated 425°F oven 20 to 25 minutes, or until deep golden and starting to caramelize. Remove from the sheet with a spatula as soon as they are done. Cool on a rack—and do not eat all 6 at once!

PÂTÉ DE VOGUE
Pear Torte

This specialty of the Lyon area has penetrated some of the villages of the Savoie, in the area of the Chautagne vineyards, where I bought one (made with lard) quite a few years back during the yearly village celebration. Here is my own version.

8 large Bosc pears, not too ripe, unpeeled
2 tablespoons butter
½ cup sugar
Pinch of salt
1½ cups Gamay, Mondeuse, Pinot Noir, or any other dry red wine
½ cup tawny port
Crushed heads of 6 cloves
1 recipe puff pastry (page 372)
Instant superfine sugar
Crème fraîche (optional)

Cut the pears in half, core them, and slice them lengthwise ¼ inch thick. Heat the butter in a sauté pan; sauté the pears until they start browning. Add the sugar, the pinch of salt, and the wines mixed in successive small additions until the pears are well coated with a nice sugar glaze. Add the cloves.

Cut the pastry in half. Butter a 9-inch porcelain quiche pan. Roll out half the pastry ⅛ inch thick and fit it into the pan. Let the pastry hang about ½ inch over the edge of the pan. Fill with the pears, trim the edge evenly with scissors, and flip the pastry back over the pears. Moisten the edge with water. Roll the second piece of pastry and center it well over the dish. Pass the rolling pin over the pastry to cut off the edge. Push the edge of the pastry well into the dish to seal well. Trace a crisscross pattern with a fork to decorate the top. Cut a few small openings to form steam vents. Brush or spray a very fine layer of water over the top of the torte and sprinkle with superfine sugar. Refrigerate at least 1 hour before baking in a preheated 425°F oven 30 to 35 minutes. Cool completely before enjoying it plain, or serve it lukewarm with a bowl of true unsweetened *crème fraîche*.

TWO TRADITIONAL PASTRIES

BUGNES

Bugnes are carnival fare and nothing but the best fried dough, hailing from Lyon again, and from times probably as ancient as the Roman colonization. The styles vary *ad vitam aeternam*, some like them thin, some like them fat. This is Georgette's recipe. She likes them fat. The baking powder is a modern addition to make them fatter!

Bugnes appear with regularity each winter in Savoie cities. What a pleasure, in the middle of a cold afternoon, to stop at the Fidèle Berger in Annecy to enjoy one of the very best *Bugnes* in town with a cup of double-strength café au lait.

This recipe yields 15 to 20 bugnes.

2⅓ cups sifted all-purpose flour
1 tablespoon cornstarch
1½ teaspoons baking powder
5 tablespoons sugar
¼ teaspoon salt
¼ cup water
2 eggs, well beaten
1 teaspoon lemon rind
1 tablespoon dark rum
Corn oil for deep frying
Confectioners sugar

Mix the flour, cornstarch, and baking powder. Make a well in the mixture. Dilute the sugar and salt in the water; mix with the beaten eggs, lemon rind, and rum. Gradually add the liquid ingredients to the dry ones and mix well to form a smooth dough. Allow the dough to rest 1 hour at room temperature under a clean towel.

Roll the dough out no thicker than ⅛ inch. Cut it into rectangular pieces 5 by 2 inches. Cut a slit in the center of each piece, leaving 1 inch of dough uncut at each end. Slip one end of each pastry into the cut to obtain twisted sides. Heat oil for deep frying until it starts smoking and deep-fry the *Bugnes* 3 or 4 at a time, no more, until they are golden. Drain on paper towels and sprinkle with confectioners sugar.

REZULS

Rezuls, in French *rissoles*, were the holiday dessert. Prepared by the hundreds, they invaded houses and farmhouses around Christmas and one ate them for the next two months. In many areas nothing has changed. Around Christmas, Savoie markets offer the dried Lombardes prunes, home-dried in the fall with the preparation of Christmas *rezuls* in mind. A Christmas without *rezuls* is so unthinkable that there is always an older farm woman or two at the market who sells them, knowing that the majority of younger women have no time to prepare them. Also, small cafés in some of the intra-Alpine valleys sell them around Christmas time, and often way into Lent. Modern refrigerators allow one to keep them frozen, to be fried as needed, so that they are always fresh instead of dried out as when I was young! A good *rezul* has a thin crust, always nice and leafy, but I tested mine with a somewhat richer dough that did not thin as well as the crust below, and Georgette went into all kinds of diplomatic rhetoric before it came out, finally, that they were a bit too thick—so I removed half the butter, and there it is. More important even than the crust is the filling—in patois *L'prin*—which should be plentiful and tasty.

There are thousands of recipes for *rezuls*; this one received Georgette's approval on the second try. I found the first try—made with a full half pound of butter—better and mellower, but I was not born in Annecy-le-Vieux. The pears used in the Savoie are called Jandet, and they are always a bit hard. I suspect this is because they are St. Michel d'Hiver pears (a type of Doyenné for those of you versed in fruit trees), which do not come to full maturity in the harsh climate of some Alpine valleys. They turn a beautiful red when they cook in wine, red or white.

This recipe yields 18 rezuls.

FOR THE CRUST:
2 cups sifted all-purpose flour
10 tablespoons unsalted butter,
  cut into 1 tablespoon pieces
1 tablespoon sugar
⅓ teaspoon salt

Reread the techniques for preparing puff pastry on page 372. Mix the flour and butter. Stir the sugar and salt into 3 tablespoons of the cold milk; mix until completely melted. With your fingertips, mix together the flour and butter until the butter is in ⅓-inch lumps. Then add the milk mixture and the marc, until the dough forms a ball. If more liquid is needed, add the remaining milk. Cool the ball of

4–5 tablespoons cold milk
1 tablespoon marc

FOR L'PRIN:
12 large, not too ripe Bosc
    pears, peeled and cored
1 cup port or sherry
1/3 cup honey of your choice
Pinch of ground clove
3 tablespoons marc
1 tablespoon unsalted butter
1 egg, beaten
Corn oil for deep frying
Confectioners sugar

dough 15 minutes.

Give the dough 4 turns, one at a time, refrigerating it 15 minutes between each turn. Keep the dough refrigerated at least 1 hour before rolling it out.

Meanwhile prepare the *prin*: Cut the pears into small chunks and put them in a sauté pan. Add the wine, honey, and clove and cook to a very very thick puree. Do not be impatient; it is essential that you reduce and reduce the way things reduced over the hearth in the old days. Don't try to rush things by putting the compote in the microwave, because it will never thicken properly and, what is worse, it will not have *le bon goût*, which means that it will not taste right. When it is very thick, lighten it a bit by adding the marc and the butter.

Roll the pastry out into a sheet 15 by 21 inches. Cut into 3-by 5-inch rectangles. Divide the filling among the 21 rectangles obtained. Brush the edge of half of each rectangle lightly with beaten egg and fold the rectangles into 2½-inch cushions, which will enclose the filling. Seal well with the tines of a fork. Deep-fry just a few minutes until golden. Sprinkle with confectioners sugar. If you prefer, you can brush the top of each *rissole* with egg and bake it in a preheated 375°F oven, but it does not compare to that sinful bath of oil.

COMPOTES

I have chosen to put the compotes immediately after the *rezuls* because most of them can be very reduced to become a delicious filling. What is called a compote in the Savoie—and in many other parts of the French countryside —has nothing to do with the fruit, carefully poached in syrup and still retaining its shape, of the Classic cuisine. A compote, some people say "*une marmelade,*" is a shapeless composition in which the fruit has fallen apart and the texture is that of our jam. In essence, a low sugar jam that one enjoys with cake or plain for breakfast or dessert. Mélanie always gave it to us with clabbered milk or fresh white cheese. It can be made with white or brown sugar or, as in the ancient Savoie, with the wonderful honey that comes from local hives. Use at least 2 pounds of fruit and sweetener to your taste. Compotes are excellent sources of fiber; leave the skins on.

Apricots: sweeten with evergreen or other honey

Ambrezales: Ambrezales are lingonberries; use some if you have them up there in Alaska; otherwise use cranberries and keep them unstrained

Cherries: Here is a different way: Pit 1 pound *each* of sour and dark sweet cherries. Mix with ⅓ cup of honey and pour into a baking dish. Bake until three quarters of the juices have evaporated. Deep-chill before enjoying

Pears: Same as in the preceding *rezul* recipe, but add raisins and a dash of clove

Apples: Make as you would applesauce, but reduce twice as much; flavor with lemon rind and a dash of cinnamon. Add a tablespoon of butter

Wrinkled apples: Mélanie used to take old wrinkled apples and call them "*demi-cruchons.*" She cut them in chunks *unpeeled* and let them sweat in a sauté pan until they fell apart; then she added some honey. An excellent source of fiber and a good cholesterol fighter for those who are afflicted

Plums: Locally, the purple plums are called by all kinds of names, including *chouesques*, variation of the Alsatian *quetsch*. Cook them with sugar to taste until they fall apart and enjoy them with white cheese or grilled chicken.

POIRES DE CURE À L'EAU DE NOIX
Pear and Walnut Wine Compote

Here is a true recipe for a true compote in the Classic manner. It came about in my own Annecy kitchen, after I failed to drink the walnut wine of one year and had to make room for the new one.

1 pound unpeeled Seckel
  pears, whole
2 cups walnut wine (page
  409)
⅓ cup sugar
1 ounce marc
Whipped cream, unsweetened

Mix the pears, wine, and sugar in a saucepan. Bring to a boil and simmer until the pears are tender. Put the pears into a compote dish, reduce the cooking juices by half and add the marc. Serve deep-chilled topped with whipped cream. Spoon the syrup over the cream.

CAKES AND PUDDINGS

Until the arrival of Classic French pastries in Savoie bakeries at the end of the nineteenth century, the number of true cakes and prepared desserts presented on Savoie tables was limited. Many, such as the *Pouding de Megève* on page 383 must have been made with a base of bread. Among the prepared desserts, rice pudding was first a favorite of the bourgeoisie and then, when rice from Piemonte became available sometime after the middle of the eighteenth century, a bravura dessert for farm women as well. What the Classic European pastry lore calls *Biscuit de Savoie* is called in the Savoie itself *Gâteau de Savoie* and has a very uncertain history. Historian Jacques Lovie cites several possible origins. The most ancient recipe might come from Pierre de Yenne, the illegimate son and kitchen master to Amadeus V in 1343. Another possibility is that the cake may have been prepared in 1416 by Morel one of the "*queux*" to Amadeus VIII, for the famous banquet presented to Sigismund, Emperor of Germany; baked in the shape of the County of Savoie, it was one of the delicacies served by Amadeus VIII, and may have played a part in making the count a duke (see page 41). Another possibility is that the Green Count, Amadeus VI, might already have presented the cake to the Emperor sometime between 1373 and 1383. Whatever the date, the cake has a long history, and it is certain that it was baked along with the bread, since it requires a very slow heat. From historian Lovie one learns that "one would never use orange flower water as a flavoring since it would keep the batter from raising properly." The flavorings did, indeed, vary, and could be grated orange or lemon rind, or precisely orange flower water and chopped praline. At the end of the nineteenth century, one started using vanilla, sugar, and anise from Italy. In a more modern, slightly Americanized version, I have successfully added tiny chocolate chips.

All recipes in this section yield 8 to 12 servings.

GÂTEAU DE SAVOIE

The cake must be enjoyed the day it is prepared if it is to be mellow and moist. It tends to become dry and brittle after a day. The ladyfingers from Italy known as *Savoiardi* are made out of the same batter; they dry remarkably well and absorb a maximum of liqueur when used in a charlotte.

7 eggs, separated
1 cup sugar
Pinch of salt
1 teaspoon each pure vanilla extract and grated lemon rind
¾ cup potato starch or cornstarch
⅔ cup sifted all-purpose flour
1 tablespoon butter

Beat the egg yolks with the sugar and salt until they form a heavy ribbon when falling from the beater, *but do not beat to soft peaks or the cake will be dry.* Add the vanilla and lemon rind. Sift the starch and flour together twice; set aside.

Beat the egg whites until a raw egg in its shell will not fall into the egg mass by more than ¼ inch. Mix one quarter of the whites into the yolk foam. Slide the remainder of the whites over the yolk foam, sift the mixture of starch and flour a second time over the whites, and fold all three layers of ingredients until homogenous.

Butter a large Bundt pan lightly with the tablespoon of butter. Turn the batter into the pan and bake on the lowest shelf of a preheated 325°F oven 35 to 40 minutes. Unmold immediately onto a rack and cool completely.

The best way to enjoy a *Gâteau de Savoie* is with a rich *crème anglaise* made with heavy cream (see page 388) or with the pears baked in cream on page 391.

QUATRE QUARTS AUX POIRES CARAMÉLISÉES
Pound Cake with Caramelized Pears

All my friends in the Savoie make the best pound cake, probably because of the wonderful cream and butter. Here is the Savoie version of the pound cake batter, poured over the very special pears of the Savoie in their caramel coating.

1 tablespoon butter plus ¾ cup
½ cup sugar plus ¾ cup
3 Bosc pears, peeled, halved, and cored
3 eggs, separated
Large pinch of salt
⅓ cup heavy cream
2 tablespoons marc
1½ cups sifted all-purpose flour
⅓ cup potato or corn starch

Lightly grease a 1-quart fireproof baking dish with 1 tablespoon of butter. Sprinkle with ¼ cup of sugar. Add the Bosc pear halves, rounded side down, and sprinkle them with another ¼ cup of sugar. Bake in a preheated 350°F oven until the pears are well caramelized. Remove the pears to a board, cool completely, and slice them crosswise ¼ inch thick. Add 1 cup of water to the caramel in the pan and reduce it until it becomes thickish again. Brush the caramel on the bottom of a 10-inch non-stick cake pan. Arrange the sliced pears, rounded side down, over the caramel to cover the bottom of the pan completely.

Cream the remaining ¾ cup of butter; add the remaining ¾ cup of sugar and the salt, and beat until fluffy and white; add the egg yolks one after another, beating heavily after each addition. Beat in the heavy cream and the marc. Remove the bowl from the electric mixer. Mix the flour and starch together and gradually sift them into the batter. Flatten it into the creamy mixture with the flat side of a large rubber spatula without stirring, to minimize gluten formation. Beat the egg whites until they can carry the weight of a raw egg in its shell, and fold into the cake batter. Spoon the batter over the pears, even the surface well with a rubber spatula, and bake in a preheated 325°F oven 45 to 55 minutes. When the cake is done, immediately unmold onto a platter.

LE PAIN D'ÉPICES DES APICULTEURS
Beekeeper's Spice Cake

Bees all over the Savoie produce some of the very best honeys ever. Their tastes range from mild acacia to that of Alpine flowers strong with sage or gentian, or even the very strong evergreen, which flows from the frames dark brown and gives cakes and creams the slightly resinous flavor I dearly love, but which is an acquired taste. Here is my version of a cake that all the beekeepers sell at the Savoie markets; I have used an American cake batter because the French one is made with a simple mixture of flour, hot water, and honey that is a bit too dry for my taste.

½ cup unsalted butter plus 1 tablespoon
1 cup honey of your choice, evergreen being the best
½ cup whole milk yogurt
½ cup sour cream
1 tablespoon lemon juice
1 cup each unsifted all-purpose and rye flours
½ teaspoon salt
1 teaspoon baking soda
⅛ teaspoon ground clove
⅔ cup coarsely chopped walnuts

Cream the ½ cup butter, then gradually whisk in the honey, yogurt, sour cream, and lemon juice. Mix the flours, salt, baking soda, clove, and walnuts. Gently combine the liquid ingredients with the dry ones until just mixed. To prevent gluten development, *positively do not beat or whisk.* Butter an 8-inch square cake pan with the remaining tablespoon of butter, turn the batter into the pan, and bake immediately in a preheated 350°F oven 40 to 45 minutes, or until a skewer inserted at the center of the cake comes out clean. Cool completely in the pan and unmold onto a cake rack.

PAIN DE PISTACHES
Pistachio Cake

On the afternoon of the 15th of August, in that beautiful property in Veyrier-du-Lac that I mentioned in the Fish chapter on page 286, we were given for an afternoon snack the most delicious pistachio cake together with a glass of orange juice, which in those pre–World War II days was still a luxury. Years later, after formally learning pastry work, I realized that the pastry chef who baked this beauty for us used half almonds and half pistachio nuts, combined into a simple *Pain de Gênes* as described by Lacam.* I have modernized the recipe considerably, using electric equipment and giving the proportions in weight rather than volume, because flour varies so much from one part of the United States to another. The cake is so rich that it easily yields sixteen 1-inch portions.

1 tablespoon unsalted butter plus 5½ ounces

5 ounces pistachios, shelled, peeled, and chopped

3 ounces almonds, peeled and chopped

½ pound sugar

Pinch of salt

4 eggs

1 ounce Kirschwasser

1¼ ounces each sifted all-purpose flour and corn or potato starch

½ teaspoon baking powder

Butter a 9-inch round cake pan with the tablespoon of butter. Cut a circle of parchment paper and fit it into the bottom of the pan.

Put the pistachios, almonds, sugar, and salt in the food processor.

Process until a very fine powder is obtained and the mixture almost turns into a paste. Add the eggs and process until very thick and foamy.

In the electric mixer, cream the remaining butter until white; gradually add the nut-sugar mixture and continue beating until well emulsified. Beat in the Kirschwasser. Remove the beaters; mix the flour and starch with the baking powder, sift them over the batter, and gradually fold them in.

Turn into the prepared pan and bake in a preheated 325°F oven 35 to 40 minutes, or until a skewer inserted at the center of the cake and removed burns the top of the hand. Unmold immediately onto a cake rack and remove the paper. Serve cold, with a Kirsch *crème anglaise* if you desire (see page 388).

POUDING DE MEGÈVE
Megève Pudding

Arsène Bourgeaux, in his text on food in Mont Saxonnex, mentions that the *farcement* for Christmas was made with chocolate. I have not made chocolate

*Lacam is the author of the late nineteenth-century pastry bible.

farcement, but I did enjoy the description of the *Pouding de Megève*, so here is a version of it, direct from my Annecy kitchen; the light cream replaces the very rich Savoie milk.

⅓ cup dark raisins
18 soft pitted prunes
½ cup dark rum
16 slices of French bread,
    crust removed and air-dried
½ cup clarified butter
½ cup sugar
½ cup liquid honey of your
    choice
1 quart scalding light cream
4 eggs
Pinch of salt
Pinch of saffron threads

Soak the raisins and prunes overnight in the rum. Sauté the slices of French bread in the clarified butter until golden.

Put the sugar in a skillet and cook it to a dark caramel. Pour it evenly into the bottom of a 1-quart baking dish. Arrange one layer of bread over the caramel, cover it with the mixed fruit and any rum left with it, then top the fruit with a second layer of bread. Melt the honey into the scalding cream; beat the eggs with the salt and gradually add the sweetened cream. Add the saffron. Bake in a hot water bath in a preheated 325°F oven 35 to 40 minutes and serve lukewarm or cold.

LES PETITES BÉCHAMELLES CHEZ MONSIEUR L'ABBÉ
Béchamelle Custards as Made in Thônes

Very few young girls who have been raised as Catholics fail to remember the terror of going to confession on Fridays. Our Monsieur l'Abbé, who lived in Thônes, one day invited our group to tea, probably because he knew we were so scared of him. This is the lovely little dessert that we were given by his housekeeper, whose name I never knew.

½ cup sugar plus ⅔ cup
2½ tablespoons all-purpose flour
2 tablespoon butter
2 cups scalding milk
1 egg

To prepare the *béchamelles*, melt the ½ cup sugar and cook it to a dark caramel. Pour evenly into six ½-cup molds to coat their bottoms well.

Cook the flour in the hot butter for a few minutes; meanwhile dissolve the ⅔ cup sugar in the scalding

1 egg yolk
¼ teaspoon each *ground cinnamon, nutmeg, cardamom, and allspice*
Large pinch of ground clove

SAUCE:
4 egg yolks
¼ cup sugar
Pinch of salt
1 cup light cream, heated
2 ounces chocolate, at least 50 percent cocoa content, finely grated

milk. Bind the butter and flour mixture with the sweet milk and bring to a boil. Off the heat, add the egg and egg yolk one at a time, beating well. Season with all the spices, pour into the prepared molds, and bake in a hot water bath in a preheated 325°F oven 25 to 30 minutes, or until a skewer inserted at the center of a cream comes out clean and hot. Cool in the molds and refrigerate. Unmold when ready to serve.

To prepare the custard, mix the egg yolks, sugar, and salt very well; dilute with the hot cream and thicken on medium-high heat, stirring constantly until the custard coats the spatula. Add the chocolate and stir well. Strain into a sauceboat. Serve over the little *béchamelles*.

PAIN DE CHÂTAIGNES AU CHOCOLAT
Chocolate Chestnut Loaf

Mélanie made for us a classic chocolate and chestnut loaf with the chestnuts we had gathered at La Grande Jeanne in Annecy on a Sunday afternoon excursion. I have often made this chocolate loaf and served it with what in Savoie would be called a *sambayon*, or zabaglione. In researching which wine could be used in the Savoie to make the *sabayon*, I realized that Jean Nicolas, in his text on food in the eighteenth century, mentions that just about every fortified wine except Marsala was served with the chestnuts. All was not lost, however, since, still according to Nicolas, the 1781 inventory of wines belonging to Baron de Villette showed four bottles of "Petroguimenes." Nicolas puts a (?) after the funny name. I deducted that Pedro Jimenez was already in existence at the time, so here is my *sambayon* with my version of Mélanie's chestnut chocolate loaf.

CHESTNUT LOAF:

1 pound hot peeled chestnuts,
 fresh or canned
1⅓ cups confectioners sugar
1½ teaspoons vanilla extract
Pinch of salt
½ cup unsalted butter
4 ounces bittersweet chocolate,
 preferably Valrhona 61%
 cocoa, melted

SAMBAYON:

3 egg yolks
⅓ cup sugar
Pinch of salt
1 cup Fino sherry

Put the chestnuts, sugar, vanilla, salt, butter, and chocolate in a food processor and process until homogenous and smooth. Line a 1-pound loaf pan with parchment paper and pour the mixture into it. Cover with plastic wrap and refrigerate overnight.

When ready to serve, beat the egg yolks with the sugar and salt heavily. Put the beaten yolks directly over medium heat and gradually add the dry sherry. Cook, whisking quickly, until you can see the bottom of the pan for a few seconds.

Unmold the loaf onto a serving dish and serve topped with the *sambayon*.

PUDDING DE RIZ AU SAFRAN
Saffron Rice Pudding

This is mentioned in Arsène Bourgeaux's essay (see Selected Bibliography) as being a star item in the country kitchen of the Arve valley, but Mélanie served it often, and it is really nothing more than one of the many versions of the *bourre chrétien*–type dessert found in the Savoie countryside and in all other provinces of France. This was the true delight of all children of my generation. Saffron and anise are special to the Savoie.

1 cup Italian Arborio rice
2 cups cold water
3 cups scalding milk
1 cup sugar
¼ cup raisins, soaked in water
1 teaspoon aniseeds
½ teaspoon grated orange rind
⅛ teaspoon saffron threads

Wash the rice. Add the cold water, bring to a boil, and cook 10 to 15 minutes until the rice starts swelling, at which point it should have absorbed all the water. Add the scalding milk, ½ cup of the sugar, the raisins, aniseeds, and orange rind. Cook until most of the milk has been absorbed. Cool to lukewarm, then add the saffron. When the rice is almost cold, fold in the whipped cream.

1 cup heavy cream, lightly
  whipped

Put the remaining ½ cup of sugar into a skillet and quickly cook to a dark caramel. Pour it onto a lightly buttered cookie sheet. Let it harden; when it is hard, chop the caramel and sprinkle it all over the top of the pudding.

BAVAROISE CHOCOLAT CHARTREUSE
Chocolate Chartreuse Bavarian Cream

In my personal passion for green Chartreuse, I have put it in almost any dessert I could. This Bavarian cream dessert met with great success on one of my American tours. Bavarians in the Savoie repertory of desserts would be classified as tourist fare. I use very little gelatin and serve the dessert in champagne cups rather than molding it stiffly in the old-fashioned way. If you prefer to unmold it, use a whole envelope of gelatin. The chocolate bits should be no smaller than ⅙ inch, or else they will melt and color the cream.

4 egg yolks
½ cup sugar
Pinch of salt
1 cup scalding milk
½ envelope of gelatin
¼ cup green Chartreuse plus 6
  teaspoons
1 cup heavy cream
2 ounces bittersweet chocolate,
  as close as possible to 70
  percent cocoa content,
  coarsely chopped
Another ounce of chocolate,
  finely shaved

In a sauté pan, mix the egg yolks, sugar, and salt very well until a light white foam forms, but not to the point where they ribbon heavily. Using a blunt-ended wooden spatula, gradually dilute the egg and sugar mixture with the scalding milk. Put directly on medium-high heat and stir constantly, scraping the bottom of the pan and keeping the mixture always in movement. As soon as the white layer of foam disappears into larger bubbles that go to the edge of the pan, remove the pan from the heat and whisk with a stainless whisk until a heavy foam forms. Add the gelatin directly to the hot custard and stir well to dissolve. Strain the custard into a stainless bowl.

Whip the cream until it foams well and barely holds its shape. Place the bowl of custard in a larger bowl containing ice, water, and salt and stir the custard until it thickens visibly. It will not set at this point since there is not enough gelatin. Remove the bowl of custard from the ice, whisk in the liqueur, then the heavy cream until completely blended with visible variation in color. During the last few strokes, add the chocolate bits. Ladle the cream into 6 champagne glasses and chill until semi-solid, approximately 4 hours.

Just before serving, pour a teaspoon of Chartreuse on the top of each cup and sprinkle with shaved chocolate.

LES GLACES (Ice Creams)

Most Savoie tourist centers boast a proliferation of ice cream parlors; most of them have discovered the ice cream cone made of a delicious wafer of the *bricelet* type (see page 393). Otherwise, they still serve a whole array of *coupes* inspired by all the possible combinations of fruit and ices. The following recipes are my favorites made with Savoie ingredients, and have been the pleasure of many guests in Annecy and in my restaurants. The technique used to cook the ice cream custard in all the following recipes is that of the Basic *Crème Anglaise*; only the proportions will vary.

BASIC CRÈME ANGLAISE FOR VANILLA ICE CREAM

This is the recipe to use in all Savoie desserts calling for *crème anglaise*, and as a companion to the *Gâteau de Savoie* on page 380. It makes 3 cups of custard, which would serve 12 people; in addition to the vanilla, you may add any liqueur of your choice or any other flavoring such as grated citrus rind or infused herbs. Do not use a double boiler; this custard is very easy to make and cooks in a matter of minutes provided you follow the directions carefully.

8 egg yolks
½ cup sugar
Pinch of salt
2 cups scalding light cream
1 tablespoon pure vanilla
  extract

Mix the egg yolks, sugar, and the salt well until a fine layer of foam appears on the surface. Very gradually add the scalding cream, using a wooden spoon. Cook on direct medium-high heat, stirring constantly and scraping the bottom and angle of the pan until the foam disappears and turns into large air bubbles at the sides of the pan. Remove from the heat and whisk very heavily 2 minutes. Add the vanilla and any other flavoring. Let stand 5 to 10 minutes, then strain into a clean bowl.

GLACE AUX ALOGNES ET AU MIEL
Hazelnut and Honey Ice Cream

If you use the large filberts, skip the garnish of toasted nuts or the custard will be too strong.

5 cups scalding light cream
2 cups wild hazelnuts, chopped
  and deeply toasted, or
1½ cups regular filberts,
  toasted
12 egg yolks
½ cup honey
Pinch of salt
½ cup peeled, coarsely
  chopped, and toasted
  hazelnuts (optional)

Pour the cream into the blender container and add the nuts. Liquefy completely. Let stand at least 6 hours to allow the taste of the nut oil to permeate the cream.

Break the egg yolks into a sauté pan and reheat the hazelnut cream with the honey. Very gradually dilute the yolks with the cream mixture; add the salt. Cook over medium-high heat until the custard coats the spatula or wooden spoon well. Remove from the heat and cool by whisking. Strain to discard all traces of hazelnut powder.

Refrigerate overnight and churn the next day, according to the directions on your ice cream maker. If adding chopped nuts, sprinkle them onto the almost finished ice cream during the last few turns of the churning. Serve topped with a tablespoon or so of hazelnut liqueur.

GLACE AUX NOIX
Walnut Ice Cream

This is a direct descendant of the walnut custard recipe that appears in my book *When French Women Cook*.

5 cups scalding light cream
2 cups chopped, lightly toasted English walnuts
½ cup sugar
¼ cups honey of your choice
12 egg yolks
Pinch of salt
Walnut wine (page 409) as needed

To the scalding cream add the toasted walnuts. Liquefy in the blender and let steep 4 hours.

Meanwhile put the sugar in a skillet and quickly cook it to a deep caramel. Reheat the walnut milk and in it dissolve the caramel. Add the honey and stir until melted. Mix the egg yolks very well and very gradually dilute them with the walnut and caramel milk. Add the salt. Thicken, stirring on medium-high heat and strain through several layers of cheesecloth rinsed under cold water and squeezed dry. Refrigerate the mixture several hours before churning, according to the directions on your ice cream maker.

Serve the ice cream in cups and top each portion with a tablespoon or so of walnut wine.

CRÈME GLACÉE AU MIEL DE SAPIN ET À L'ORANGE
Evergreen Honey and Orange Ice Cream

If you cannot find Alpine evergreen honey, the Greek Attiki honey will do very well.

1 quart scalding light cream
Rinds of 3 oranges peeled in large pithless strips
⅔ cup evergreen honey
12 egg yolks
Pinch of salt

Infuse the large strips of orange rind in the scalding cream at least 2 hours. Reheat the cream and in it dissolve the honey. Mix the egg yolks very well and gradually add the hot orange milk to the pan. Thicken on medium-high heat as described on page 389. Strain and refrigerate overnight. Just before churn-

2 teaspoons orange flower water
Rinds of 3 more oranges cut
    into 1/8-inch-thick julienne
1 cup each sugar and water

ing, stir in 1 teaspoon of the orange flower water.

Blanch the julienne of orange rind 2 to 3 minutes. Mix the sugar and water, add the julienne of rinds, and bring slowly to a boil. Simmer until the rinds are candied and translucent. Cool slightly and add the second teaspoon of orange flower water.

Serve the ice cream in cups and top each cup with some of the candied rinds. Any remaining syrup will make kids' pancakes turn into a feast.

CRÈME À LA VERGEOISE BRÛLÉE
Crème Brûlée Ice Cream

This is nothing but *crème brûlée* served *chez* Thomas Jefferson, but I have chopped the *brûlée* into the cream. The pears, prepared in the Savoie manner with a bit of Marsala, make this dessert the perfect blend of Savoie and USA.

FOR THE PEARS:
1½ tablespoons butter
6 Bosc pears, peeled, cored,
    and halved
½ cup dark brown sugar
1½ cups Marsala, as dry as
    possible
Water as needed

FOR THE ICE CREAM:
1/3 cup sugar
Pinch of salt
8 egg yolks
1 quart scalding heavy cream
½ tablespoon butter
2/3 cup dark brown sugar

Grease a large baking dish with 1 tablespoon of the butter. Add the pears, sprinkle them with the brown sugar, add the Marsala, and bake in a preheated 375°F oven 30 minutes, or until brown. Turn the pears over and continue to bake them until well caramelized. Remove the pears to a plate lightly greased with the remainder of the butter. Dissolve the caramel in the dish with a bit of water to make a very thick sauce. Set both aside.

To prepare the ice cream, mix the sugar, salt, and egg yolks and stir until foamy but not ribboning. Gradually add the scalding cream and cook over medium-high heat, stirring constantly. When the foam has receded, remove from the heat and whisk 2 minutes. Strain, cool completely, and refrigerate several hours.

Butter a piece of heavy foil with the ½ tablespoon of butter; sprinkle the brown sugar evenly over it to make a layer no more than ⅙ inch thick. Broil 4 inches from the source of heat until the sugar melts and turns liquid. Remove to room temperature and let harden. Break into lumps ¼-inch square.

Churn the ice cream according to the directions on your ice cream maker, and during the last few turns add the lumps of hard brown sugar.

To serve, place half a pear, rounded side down, on each dessert plate. Fill the pear cavity with ice cream and top with a small spoonful of the deglazing syrup.

SAVOIE COOKIES FOR ICE CREAM OR AS PLAIN DESSERT

There are not many fancy cookies in the Savoie; most of those prepared now come from the Classic French repertory. The most popular are, by all means, those huge meringues shaped with large spoons that, in the village of Grésy, are still given the traditional antique shape of women's breasts. Otherwise, Marie Thérèse Hermann mentions some *jembelles* made with polenta that are amazingly identical to those cornmeal *sables* that my stepgrandmother used to make. Mique Grandchamp has a good recipe for what he spells *brisselets*. Here they are:

GROSSES MERINGUES AUX NOISETTES
Large Hazelnut Meringues

In several pastry shops in both departments of the Savoie I have seen these meringues laced with nuts. The best, of course, are those glorious *croquemolles*, or filberts identical to those produced in Oregon.

6 egg whites
Pinch of salt
⅓ cup confectioners sugar
1½ cups granulated sugar
⅔ cup peeled, toasted
   hazelnuts, halved

Beat the egg whites to soft peaks with the salt; gradually beat in the confectioners sugar until the whites form stiff peaks. Fold in the granulated sugar and the hazelnuts. Line an unbendable cookie sheet with parchment paper. Shape 12 meringues with 2 large spoons. Deposit them onto the parchment and let

FOR THE GARNISH:
2 cups heavy cream
Hazelnut liqueur of your choice, to taste

them dry 4 hours in a preheated 175°F oven. The meringues should be ivory colored. Cool completely.

Beat the cream almost stiff, add the hazelnut liqueur to taste, and finish beating until stiff. Cut each meringue open through its center and pipe the cream into the opening. Sweet, but delicious.

SABLÉS À LA FARINE JAUNE
Cornmeal Shortbread

This rustic shortbread would indeed have been a treat for country children used only to dark bread. The unpasteurized butter of the Northern Alps makes the *sablés* absolutely splendid. They are very well liked by young visitors at our home.

½ cup butter
¼ cup white sugar
¼ cup brown sugar
Pinch of salt
1 cup fine cornmeal (not corn flour)
1 cup sifted all-purpose flour
1 egg
1 teaspoon orange flower water
1 teaspoon pure vanilla extract
1 teaspoon finely grated lemon rind

Put the butter, sugars, and salt into a food processor and process until the mixture is smooth; add the cornmeal and flour and process 15 seconds; add the egg and the three flavorings. Gather the dough into a ball and flatten between two sheets of plastic wrap to a thickness of ¼ inch. Cut into your favorite shapes and bake in a preheated 375°F oven 10 minutes. Remove to a cooling rack. The shortbreads harden as they cool and keep very well in a tin away from greedy little hands.

BRICELETS

This is an adaptation of the recipe given by Mique Grandchamp. Still very popular, *bricelets* remain a great specialty of Geneva and the surrounding countryside. They are first cousins to the *anis pizelle* of Italy. Great munching fare with coffee or tea, they also make super ice cream cones. *Pizelle* irons can be found in all Italian neighborhoods and a Teflon version—electric at that—can be found in department stores.

3 cups sifted all-purpose flour
1 tablespoon cornstarch
1¼ cups butter at room
    temperature
1¼ cups light brown sugar
1 cup heavy cream
1 ounce Kirschwasser or marc
1 teaspoon finely grated lemon
    rind
Pinch of salt
1 jumbo egg or 2 medium
    eggs, well beaten

Mix the flour and cornstarch with the butter and brown sugar, sanding it well with your fingertips. Gradually add the heavy cream, the Kirsch, lemon rind, salt, and, finally, at least 1 well beaten-egg. Work the dough so it is very smooth and light.

Heat the *pizelle* iron very, very hot, place a ball of dough as large as a walnut in the center of the iron, and cook until it is golden and comes off the iron by itself. I must insist on the iron being very hot or there will be problems removing the *bricelets*. Cool them on a rack and store them in a tin.

To make ice cream cones, roll the wafers into cornucopias while they are still hot.

A TASTE FOR CHOCOLATE

Many Savoie cities, particularly Annecy, Chambéry, Evian, Aix les Bains, and others dedicated to the tourist trade, have developed their own chocolate specialties. All you have to do is stroll through the streets and look. I bet it will not be long before you enter a specialty shop and come out with one of those lovely little cellophane bags with a lacy edge filled with some insidious and lovely delicacy. Here are a few recipes for Savoie-style chocolates; enjoy them, they are easy to prepare. Since all good shops in the Savoie now use the excellent Valrhona chocolate to prepare their candy, you may want to try finding some for the recipes that follow. I know it is sold in the United States. Any good American chocolate, however, will do very well.

TRUFFONS À LA CROQUANTE DE NOISETTES
Truffles with Hazelnut Brittle

These chocolate candies are square and flavored with Chartreuse because it is my favorite liqueur. Keep the basic candies well refrigerated and do not coat them with the brittle too long before serving.

9 ounces bittersweet chocolate
as high in cocoa content as
possible
½ cup unsalted butter
¼ cup warmed heavy cream
2 cups sugar
3 tablespoons water plus ⅓
cup
2 tablespoons green Chartreuse
3 drops lemon juice
1½ cups coarsely chopped
peeled hazelnuts
½ tablespoon butter

Melt the chocolate and butter together, stir in the warm cream, and homogenize well. Mix ½ cup of the sugar with 3 tablespoons of water and cook to the thread stage (215°F). Gradually stir the sugar syrup into the chocolate mixture. When cool but still semi-liquid, add the Chartreuse. Refrigerate until solid.

Put the remaining sugar in a sauté pan, add the lemon juice and the remaining water. Cook to a light caramel. Add the chopped hazelnuts and finish cooking to a dark caramel. Pour onto a cookie sheet greased with the butter and harden completely into a brittle. Chop the brittle into ⅛-inch pieces.

Sprinkle half the chopped brittle onto the counter. Remove the chocolate candy from its bowl and, using a spatula, knead the brittle into the chocolate paste. Cut pieces of the paste and shape them into 1-inch square pieces; refrigerate again.

About 1 hour before serving, spread the remaining brittle onto parchment paper and coat each candy with it. Put in candy paper cups. Keep cool.

ABRICOTS À LA GANACHE
Ganache-filled Apricots

These little beauties were given to me by Aileen Martin, who is my neighbor in Annecy. Unfortunately, I never took note of the name of the confectioner's shop they came from.

10 Australian candied (not
dried) apricots
½ pound bittersweet chocolate
as high in cocoa content as
possible
1 cup scalding heavy cream

Cut the apricots in half lengthwise. Open the apricot halves into pockets and shape them as round as you can.

Put chocolate in the bowl of an electric mixer. Melt it over a double boiler. Remove from the heat. Beat it on medium-low heat, gradually adding the

FOR THE COUVERTURE:

*6 ounces bittersweet chocolate
  as above*

1 teaspoon hazelnut oil

hot cream. Continue beating until the cream hardens into a *ganache*. While the *ganache* is still malleable, put it into a pastry bag fitted with a star tip. Pipe a large rosette of *ganache* into each prepared apricot container. Cool completely and refrigerate to harden.

Melt the chocolate for the *couverture* with the hazelnut oil and stir well. Cool until semi-solid. Dip the hardened apricots into the *couverture* so the fruit is covered by at least ⅛ inch. Let the candies harden in small paper cups.

PÂTES DE NOIX DIVERSES
Chocolate Nut Candies

These candies can be prepared with whatever kind of nut you prefer. The proportions remain the same. My favorites are hazelnuts, walnuts, and pistachios. Use green Chartreuse with hazelnuts, marc or rum with walnuts, and Kirschwasser with pistachios.

1 cup ground almonds

*1 cup ground hazelnuts,
  walnuts, or pistachios*

1⅓ cups confectioners sugar

*2 tablespoons liqueur (see
  above)*

Egg white as needed

FOR THE COUVERTURE:

6 ounces bittersweet chocolate

*1 teaspoon hazelnut or walnut
  oil*

*24 peeled hazelnuts or walnut
  halves or peeled pistachios*

Put both ground nuts, the confectioners sugar, and liqueur in a food processor and process 15 seconds. From the top of the processor, add egg white 1 teaspoon at a time until a solid ball forms; remove from the processor and shape into 1- by ⅔-inch ovals. Refrigerate 2 hours.

Melt the chocolate and chosen oil together, cool to coating texture and dip the nut pastes into the *couverture*. Top each chocolate with a nut; let harden on a lightly buttered sheet. If you like, you can coat the decoration nuts with caramel.

LES PETITS FOURS GÂTERIE
"Bermuda Triangle" Cakes

La Gâterie is, in my opinion, the best pastry shop in Annecy. Monsieur Nivon in his rue Sainte Claire shop uses only the best chocolate and makes chocolate candies only during the winter season. This is my interpretation of a dessert cake he sells under the name Bermuda Triangle. I have made the cakes smaller as it is always easy to have several pieces if one wishes.

FOR THE TORTE BATTER:

6 egg whites

1 cup each powdered almonds and hazelnuts

⅔ cup sugar

Pinch of salt

1 tablespoon each butter and all-purpose flour

FOR THE FILLING:

½ pound semisweet chocolate as high in cocoa content as possible

1 cup scalding heavy cream

FOR THE ICING:

½ pound semisweet chocolate as above

1 teaspoon hazelnut oil

To prepare the batter, beat the egg whites until they can carry the weight of a raw egg in its shell. Mix the nuts, sugar, and salt and fold into the egg whites. Butter and flour a jelly roll pan and spread the nut mixture to an even ⅙-inch thickness on the bottom of the pan. Bake in a preheated 325°F oven approximately 15 minutes. Cut into 1½-inch squares and cool completely on a rack.

To prepare the filling, melt the chocolate directly in the stainless bowl of an electric mixer placed over a double boiler. Remove from the heat. Start the mixer on medium-low speed and add the scalding cream. Continue beating until the chocolate *ganache* thickens and becomes spreadable. Put two squares of torte together with a layer of filling ½ inch thick and harden completely in a very cold place.

Melt the chocolate for the icing, add the hazelnut oil, cool until it spreads properly, and coat the small cakes with it as evenly as you can. Cool on a rack until completely cold. This deserves the best cup of espresso.

CONFITURES (Jams)

The markets of the Savoie all have their wonderful tiny farmstands selling not only garden vegetables but also some home-cooked products, among them *rezuls* (page 376) and, of course, jams. They come in those wonderful *pots à confitures*, which I have known all my life and which William Sonoma a few years back started to sell across the United States as water glasses. The dome lid has not yet arrived in France and one still must cover the "pots" with a neat square of cellophane that stretches, nice and concave, over the smooth layer of jam. Bags of paraffin are also sold, which one melts and pours over the top of the jam if one thinks the supply will last over the winter; most of the time, it does not.

My mother, now in her eighties, still makes jam with just about every fruit she can lay her hands on, and my afternoon snack for all my growing years was a piece of bread, some 6 inches long, filled with a ¼-inch layer of butter and a ½-inch layer of jam so my intake of "iron" would be assured. One of my extremely wellborn classmates, with a name all too well known in France, did not bat an eye at exchanging her snack of *biscottes*, meagerly spread with store-bought jam by her governess, for my thick bourgeois fare, while each of us felt guilty at the thought of our mothers, one who would have been absolutely horrified, the other terribly hurt. This was, of course, during the war when everything—jam, butter, and bread—was at a premium.

All the time I was in Annecy, I simply followed the season and made two or three "pots" with a pound or so of whatever the market had to offer starting in June and ending in September. I astonished Georgette and a few of my other friends by making those wonderful fresh American jams with pectin and a reduced amount of sugar that I would keep in my freezer, a habit I got from my good friend Ann Palmer in my Philadelphia days. The tendency in the Savoie is to make jams the old-fashioned way, by reduction with the same weight of sugar and fruit. While this is necessary for such fruits as pears, apples, rhubarb, and apricots, the results for berry jams are disastrous; the original fresh tang of the berries is lost in the reduction and the dark confections of my youth have stopped being attractive to my taste buds. So you will see here two styles, the old-fashioned way and the new pectin way. And always there will be a solid addition of spirit, simply because it tastes good and also because the jam keeps better. When I say net weight in a recipe, I mean that the fruit has been peeled, cored, and prepared for cooking before being weighed.

Personally, I prefer to pour my jams into baby food jars that have been sterilized in the dishwasher and I do pour some paraffin over the top in a vain hope that the jams will be around for some time, which they never are. And, with the small jars, it is easier to change the fruit more often.

To make jam in such small quantities all you need is a very clean, large, stainless steel sauté pan.

Here is my Annecy collection of jams:

RSENO
Pear Butter

Rseno, or *Vin cuit*, is a second cousin to our apple butter, only it is made with pears. It is, according to two different sources, a very ancient preparation of pears cooked in cider, which, as we have seen earlier, is made of half pear and half apple juice in the Savoie. On Savoie farms around the lower Arve valley this would cook in huge quantities and over a very long period of time using exclusively the natural sugar of the pears and cider. I have adapted the recipe to our modern kitchens:

3 pounds very ripe pears, peeled, cored, and halved, net weight
¼ pound honey
Juice of 1 lemon
6 cups sweet fresh apple cider

Puree 1 pound of the pears in the blender. Pour them into a large sauté pan and add the other 2 pounds of pears cut into ¼-inch slivers. Add the honey, lemon juice, and apple cider. Bring to a boil, turn down to a simmer, and cook, stirring occasionally with a wooden spoon, until the mixture is dark brown and reduced to approximately the texture of apple butter with a few remaining slivers of pear here and there. Ladle it into 6 or 7 sterilized baby food jars. Top with paraffin and the jar lid.

CONFITURE D'ABRICOTS AUX NOYAUX
Apricot Jam

Savoic apricots are not plentiful and most of the time this jam is made with the Bergeron apricots of Provence at the end of their season, when they are plentiful, super-ripe, and inexpensive. *Be careful* of the number of almonds of apricots added to the jam; more is not better. You will need a hammer to break the pits and extract the almonds. Try also shortbread made with a few finely chopped apricot almonds added to the dough. But again, *only* a few.

Yield: 10 baby food jars

2½ pounds apricots, pitted and halved, net weight
12 almonds of apricots, separated into their natural halves
Juice of 1 lemon
2½ pounds sugar
1 ounce cognac or marc
½ ounce Amaretto di Sarrono

Put the apricots, apricot almonds, lemon juice, and sugar in a large sauté pan. Toss well together and let stand 2 hours. Bring slowly to a boil. Turn down to a simmer and cook until it is very reduced and the color has changed to a translucent deep orange. Let the jam attach and caramelize a bit on the bottom of the pan; stir well, scraping this caramel into the mass of the jam. Cool slightly, add both liqueurs and mix well. Put into jars, cover with paraffin and the jar lids.

CONFITURE DE POIRES, POMMES, ET NOIX
Pear, Apple, and Walnut Jam

This should be made in the fall, when the pears are super-ripe and the apples inexpensive and crisply fresh. The walnuts and Calvados do a lot for the final taste.

Yield: 10 baby food jars

1½ pounds Gravenstein apples, peeled, cored, and slivered, net weight
1½ pounds Bartlett pears, peeled, cored, and slivered, net weight
Juice of 1 lemon
3 pounds sugar
1 cup water
24 walnut halves
1½ ounces Calvados or marc

Put the apples and pears in a large sauté pan, add the lemon juice and sugar, and mix well. Let stand only 30 minutes. Add the water. Bring to a boil and turn down to a slow simmer. Cook until thick, approximately 45 minutes to 1 hour. Add the walnut halves as soon as you turn the heat off. Immediately ladle into sterilized baby food jars; seal with paraffin and the jar lids.

CONFITURE DE RHUBARBE ET CROQUEMOLLES
Rhubarb and Filbert Jam

Like the apricot jam, this one must attach ever so slightly to the bottom of the pan for perfect taste. The hazelnuts should be barely toasted so the heat of the jam extracts their natural oil and finishes toasting them.

Yield: 10 baby food jars

2½ pounds fresh rhubarb, peeled and slivered
Juice of 1 lemon
2½ pounds sugar
24 lightly toasted hazelnuts, halved

Put the rhubarb, lemon juice, and sugar in a large sauté pan. Let stand 3 hours. Bring to a boil, turn down to a simmer, and cook until the jam starts to attach at the bottom of the pan. Scrape well to dissolve the caramel. Remove from the heat and add the hazelnuts. Immediately pour into sterilized baby food jars; cover with paraffin and the jar lids.

CONFITURE DE FLEURIVES
Sour Cherry Jam

Fleurives or *grefions* is the name given in various parts of the Savoie to what is known in French as a *griotte*, the sour cherry. There is as much of a rush in France for sour cherries as there is in the United States; news of their arrival spreads quickly and, come the middle of June, Georgette never fails to ring my bell announcing that they are here. I make only a few jars, for I have no control over my greed when it come to this jam.

You have two choices: Either you can use the cherries when they are red-orange and your jam will be frankly sour, or you can spread the cherries on a clean sheet and let them turn as dark crimson as they will become without turning brown. There will then be less acid and more cherry flavor in the jam. Take your pick; I like both. When you taste this jam, you will realize that most sour cherry jams sold under fancy labels contain some sour cherries but also quite a few dark sweet cherries.

It is essential to use pectin, usually 1½ ounces per 2½ pounds each of cherries and sugar. If you do not like the sour taste, add 2 ounces of sugar. I find it unnecessary.

Yield: 10 baby food jars

12 cherry pits broken
2½ pounds pitted sour
* cherries, net weight*
1½ ounces powdered pectin
2½ pounds sugar
1½ ounces Kirschwasser

Wrap and tie the broken cherry pits in a cheese-cloth, put them and the cherries into a sauté pan and slowly bring to a boil. In a small bowl, mix the pectin powder with 1 cup of the sugar. Sprinkle this mixture over the fruit. Bring to a full boil and boil hard 2 minutes.

Gradually add all the remaining sugar and bring back to the boil. From now on, you are on your own. I usually reduce the jam approximately 35 minutes in spite of the pectin; you may, however, stop cooking it after just a few minutes of boiling. The fresh fruit taste will be even more vivid. When it has cooled for a minute or so, remove the pits, add the Kirsch and store in sterilized jars.

NOTE: You can prepare this jam with only two thirds of the sugar indicated here and keep it in the re-frigerator or freezer.

CONFITURE DU FAUBOURG DES BALMETTES
Blackberry Jam

Walking our dog each morning, I soon found just behind my apartment building a large supply of blackberries, which I turned into this Americano-Savoisienne jam. For once, volume measurements work better than weights.

Yield: 10 baby food jars

4 cups blackberries
3 cups sugar
2 tablespoons very finely
* julienned lemon rind*
1 ounce Jack Daniels

Puree the blackberries in a blender and strain the pulp to discard all seeds. Mix with the sugar and slowly bring to a boil. Meanwhile blanch the ju-lienned lemon rind, drain and pat dry. When the jam boils, turn the heat down to a simmer and add the lemon julienne; continue cooking until a drop tipped over a plate holds its round shape. Turn the heat off and add the Jack Daniels. Mix well and pour immediately into sterilized baby food jars.

NOTE: You can use only two thirds of the sugar and

no liquor and keep the jam in the refrigerator or freezer.

CONFITURE AUX QUATRE BAIES
Four-berry Jam

If you can still find some sour cherries in addition to the berries indicated here, you may add ½ pound of them and the same amount of sugar, plus 2 teaspoons powdered pectin; it does not always happen, since the overlapping of the seasons depends so much on the weather. For those of you who are able to find red currants, by all means let them replace the blackberries.

Yield: 10 baby food jars

½ pound sliced strawberries
½ pound raspberries
½ pound black currants or wild blueberries
½ pound blackberries, salmonberries, or cloudberries
2 pounds sugar
1¼ ounces powdered pectin

Wash your hands well. Crush the fruit with your hands. Bring the berries to a boil. Add all but 1 cup of the sugar. Mix the pectin with the remaining sugar and stir it into the berries. Bring to a full boil and boil hard 2 minutes. You may stop cooking right now and jar the jam if you please. I prefer to cook it another 20 minutes, or until the jam dripped onto a plate from the tip of a spoon forms a ball that does not collapse.

NOTE: You may use only two thirds of the sugar and the pectin. It will allow you to have a less sweet jam that must be kept refrigerated or frozen.

CONFITURE DES CITRONNIERS
Citrus Marmalade

When the summer jams run out toward February, I prepare this marmalade, which is always a pleasure for my Savoie friends, for whom it remains a bit exotic. The marmalade is very different depending on whether it is made with American or European citrus. Calamondin oranges are those cut little ones produced by the dwarf decorative orange trees; they make the most wonderful jam.

Yield: 10 baby food jars

1 large pink grapefruit
2 juice oranges
1 lemon
1 lime, 4 calamondin oranges,
    or 6 kumquats
6 cups water
2½ pounds sugar
1 teaspoon angostura bitters
1 ounce dark rum

Scrub the fruit and dry it perfectly. On a board with an indentation to collect the liquids, slice the fruit; chop the slices of fruit, remove all pits, and put the chopped fruit and its juice into a sauté pan. Add the water and allow the fruit to soak 12 hours.

Bring the mixture to a boil. Turn the heat down and simmer 20 minutes. Remove from the heat and let stand another 12 hours. Reheat the mixture, add the sugar, bring to a boil, and simmer approximately 55 minutes to 1 hour, until a drop of the marmalade makes a ball when dropped on a plate. Add the angostura bitters and the rum and immediately store in sterilized baby food jars.

CONFITURE DE PRUNES LOMBARDES
Italian Plum Jam

Lombardes are the Italian prune plums indigenous to the Savoie. They have other curious names such as *culs de poulets, chouesques,* or *proumes.* They lie on the ground, abandoned, and all one has to do is pick them up and start making jam. If you use prune plums bought in a supermarket, spread them in the sunshine for a few hours before making the jam. Then wash and dry them and proceed.

Yield: 10 baby food jars

2 pounds pitted prune plums,
    net weight
1 lemon, thinly sliced, pits
    removed
1½ cups dry red wine
2 pounds sugar
1 ounce marc

Bring the plums to a boil. Meanwhile simmer the lemon in the wine until only ½ cup of wine is left. Add the reduction to the plums. Add the sugar and cook until thickened, approximately 45 minutes. Add the marc, mix well, and immediately pour into sterilized baby food jars.

CONFITURE DE GRATA-CU
Rose Hip Jelly

Come October, all the rosebushes that line the shores of the Annecy lake are full of hips that can be transformed into a wonderful jelly. Do not use pectin or the jelly becomes hard and does not spread properly. This recipe is for only a small quantity since rose hips that have not been sprayed are not always easy to find.

Yield: 4 baby food jars

1½ pounds rose hips
⅔ cup water
1 cup dry vermouth
Sugar as needed

Mix the rose hips, water, and vermouth. Bring to a boil and simmer until soft. Drain and puree in the blender, then pour into a bowl. Weigh the puree and add an equal amount of sugar. Bring to a boil and simmer until well reduced, approximately 45 minutes. Pour into sterilized baby food jars.

CONFITURE DE COURGE JAUNE
Pumpkin Jam

Savoie markets do not offer quite the same abundance or variety of pumpkins as in the northeastern United States, but still there is quite a choice. Here is a wonderful jam, made with honey rather than sugar, which must be kept refrigerated. The American sweet pumpkin pie spices are pleasant in this jam if you prefer them to the lemon

Yield: 8 baby food jars

4 pounds pumpkin in a large
wedge
Juice of 1 lemon
Rind of 1 lemon, finely
julienned and blanched
Honey as needed

Preheat the oven to 350°F. Put the wedge of pumpkin on a jelly roll pan and bake until all the juices have run out and the meat is tender. Gather the juices into a sauté pan. Puree the pumpkin meat in the food processor, add it to the juices, and weigh the pumpkin meat. Add the lemon juice and rind and honey to equal the weight of the pumpkin. Cook until very thick and store in jars. Keep refrigerated and spread on fresh home-baked bread.

HOMEMADE WINES AND LIQUEURS

Since very ancient times, homemade alcoholic beverages have presented the same fascination for the Savoie people as for the rest of the French population. Every area has its favorite, such as the Vespetro, which was so popular in the Poitou, and the Pineau des Charentes, which sends a whole group over the line from happiness to slight folly, in the Saintonges and the Aunis.

After inspecting a whole volume dedicated to the preparation of homemade wines and cordials, I discovered why they were considered so extremely luxurious by country people and made regularly in bourgeois and upper-class households only. Their sugar content was so outrageous that no peasant household could ever have spent the money just for the sugar needed to produce a good bottle of *tonique*. I use the word *tonique*, of course, in the old French manner, because these wines were supposed to pep up the consumer and have special curative effects. The mere fact that a slice of toasted bread soaked in a mixture of half wine, half water could have been considered a comforting potion for postpartum mothers and sick old people alike, can be taken as an indication of the pharmaceutical properties attributed to flavored wines.

Mountain meadows and home gardens were full of all kinds of plants and berries that could be put to use. The most common were the argousier (*Hippophaë rhamnoides*), which nowadays has been completely forgotten, and all the different types of genepis, called in French *armoises*. Among the *armoises*, the best was artemisia genepi, the black genepi that is still used both in the Italian Val d'Aosta and in the French Tarentaise to produce a spirit that is highly analgesic. There are three other minor types of artemisia, which nowadays are often blended with the true genepi.

All through the Alps, one can to this day find the most delightful wild strawberries, which I have picked at the edge of the back road between Annecy and Sevrier and used to make a splendid wine. This little *Fragaria vesca* is ever so splendid, but must be very ripe. Since we have a lot of its cousins in the United States, the recipe for the wine will follow.

With the wild juniper berries that are easy to find all the way up to 7500 feet and plain pure pharmaceutical alcohol, I have made a wonderful gin, and if you go to Thônes, at the Nouvel Hôtel du Commerce, Monsieur and Madame

Bastard Rosset will be pleased to serve you a tiny but potent glass of yellow gentian root liqueur. If you decide to produce such a liquor, be very careful not to dig a root of *Veratrum album* instead of the true yellow *Gentiana lutea*. You can recognize the true gentian by its leaves, which always grow with two facing each other, while the leaves of the *Veratrum* always sit alone on one side of the stem. One of my friends never drinks anyone else's gentian for fear of a good bellyache or even worse. And then there was *Sorbus aria*—a type of mountain ash—the red berries of which went into alcohol to make a liqueur or were dried and added, as we do now with dried cranberries, into solid country bread as a source of vitamin C.

And last but not least, there were also the sloe tree's little plums, which we were taught to respect and not to pick until the frost had passed over them so as to tame their astringency. I remember a trip up a certain path on a clear freezing November afternoon to pick a bucket of prunelles, which disappeared into Mélanie's domain and were never seen again! From *Prunus spinosa*'s tiny plums comes that wonderful spirit sold in half bottles because of its cost. If you find some—it is not that difficult—do not miss buying it. A drop in a champagne flute topped with a crackling champagne will do much to relieve the monotony of Kir Royal.

Here is a small collection of wines that I have prepared in Annecy; Georgette is also a homemade wine addict, and we love to compare tastes and alcoholic potency. Her favorite concoction of mine is the wild strawberry wine.

The wines used as a base for these recipes are generally the red Mondeuse or a tingling little white Crépy. In the United States, use mellow wines, not great ones such as Pinot Noirs, Cabernet Sauvignons, or Chardonnay.

VIN DE FRAISES DES BOIS
Wild Strawberry Wine

Use, if you can, the tiny berries that grow along roadsides. If these are not available, you can use the cultivated *fraises des bois*. The vodka is an essential preservative because of the small amount of sugar in the beverage.

1 pound wild strawberries
1 cup sugar
1 bottle dry white wine
2/3 cup vodka

Blend the strawberries to a puree. Mix with the sugar and wine. Bring to a boil and simmer a good 10 minutes. Cool slightly and add the vodka. Store in a sterilized wide-mouthed jar at least 1 week, then strain through a coffee filter. Do not push on the filter, just let the wine drip into a sterilized bottle until the filter contains no more than a dry extract of strawberries. Store in a dark cupboard at least 3 months before enjoying. Do not cut with water, just pour over ice cubes.

FRUIT WINES

The favorite fruit wines in the Savoie are raspberry, black currant, blueberry, and lingonberry. They are all prepared as above with slight variations in the amount of sugar. Follow the instructions in the recipe for wild strawberry wine and use the following proportions:

RASPBERRY WINE:
1 pound raspberries
1 cup sugar
1 bottle dry white wine
2/3 cup Framboise brandy

BLACK CURRANT, RED CURRANT, OR BLUEBERRY WINE:
1 pound of any berry
1 cup sugar
1 bottle dry red wine
1/2 cup marc

CRANBERRY OR LINGONBERRY WINE:
1 pound lingonberries or cranberries
2 1/2 cups sugar
1 bottle dry white wine
1/2 cup gin

VIN DES CITRONNIERS
Citrus Fruit Wine

Marie Thérèse Hermann describes a less elaborate version of this as a tonic for people approaching their fifties.

1 bottle dry white wine
4 tablespoons sugar

Bring the wine to a boil, add the sugar and citrus rinds and cool to lukewarm. Add the saffron and

1 strip each *orange and lemon rind*
½ teaspoon *saffron threads*

let it steep a whole week. Strain into a clean bottle. Keep refrigerated; it tastes best chilled anyhow.

VIN DE NOIX
Walnut Wine

My book *In Madeleine's Kitchen* includes a recipe for walnut wine prepared with Chartreuse. Here is another version, a bit more potent in walnut taste; you must use walnuts that show no trace of wood inside the green shell; the time for picking in France is usually around June 24, but it is at least three weeks earlier in California.

6 soft *walnuts, crushed*
1 bottle *dry red wine*
¾ cup *sugar*
½ cup *marc*
2 tablespoons *pure vanilla extract*

Mix all the ingredients together, stir well to dissolve the sugar, and cover. Steep at least 6 months before sipping or using in pastries. If you do not like it "that much," try it over a super vanilla ice cream.

SATAGNES AU VIN DE NOIX
Candied Chestnuts in Walnut Wine

When I read in Jean and Renée Nicholas's *La vie quotidienne en Savoie aux 17ème et 18ème siecles* that the Duchesse de Mazarin, the beautiful Hortense, niece of the powerful cardinal, visited Chambéry in 1673 and consumed half a dozen *carafines* of chestnuts cooked in Italian wine, it gave me an idea that left the Kamman clan, who consumed it, rather happy. A tiny bit expensive but very nice.

12 candied *chestnuts*
Enough walnut wine to cover *them*

Put the chestnuts and walnut wine into a small jar, making sure that the nuts are very generously covered. Seal the jar and keep refrigerated at least 6 weeks. Have a nice evening!

LIQUEUR DE CASSIS
Black Currant Liqueur

This liqueur is not French in origin; the spicing suggests that it is most probably Germanic. The recipe appeared in one of the many local newspapers that I always find in my mailbox in Annecy. There was no author's name on the article. After trying it, I adopted it because it is delicious and so easy to prepare; it makes the best Kirs I ever had.

1 pound black currant berries, net weight
⅔ cup fresh raspberries
2 tablespoons crushed black currant leaves
1 clove
¼ teaspoon cinnamon
1 bottle vodka
1¼ cups sugar

Break up the berries coarsely in a food processor. Put the berries in a wide-mouthed jar, add the currant leaves and the spices. Add the vodka and mix well. Close the jar with several layers of cheesecloth and infuse 1 month in a dark place. Strain through a coffee filter. Add the sugar and stir every so often to dissolve it. Pour into a bottle and keep covered. May be served as soon as the sugar has fully melted.

NOTE: Using the very same proportions of fruit and sugar, but not the spices, you can prepare the following liqueurs: pure raspberry, strawberry, blackberry, cherry, salmonberry and cloudberry. If you cannot find plum liqueur, make it, with or without sugar, by steeping 1 cup of slivered Italian prune plums in a bottle of vodka. The same applies to pear; for use in pastries and pastry creams, a pear brandy made by steeping 2 slivered ripe pears, unpeeled, in a bottle of vodka is very good and less expensive than the distilled brandy.

When making brandies with red berries, you can expect to see the color of the fruit change considerably after a few months, but the flavor is very intense.

Here is one of my favorite brandied fruits:

DOUBLE KIRSCH

Use a small wide-mouthed jar that seals well with a rubber ring. This is nothing more than a refined version of *cerises à l'eau de vie*.

1 pound sour cherries
1 cup sugar
2 cups Kirschwasser

Wash and dry the cherries. Cut each stem ½ inch above the berry. Put the cherries into the jar and add the sugar. Pour the Kirschwasser over the fruit. For the next 15 days, shake the jar back and forth to allow the sugar to melt. Steep at least 6 months. NOTE: These cherries can be eaten out of a brandy glass, but they make the best Black Forest Cake ever, and wrapped into fondant, they can be coated with bitter chocolate.

HERB LIQUEURS

Herb liqueurs are as easy to prepare as the preceding cassis. Remove ½ cup of vodka from a full bottle and add enough of any herb to fill the bottle again. Add sugar to taste and steep until the herbs fall apart. Then strain through a coffee filter. The following herbs can be used: tarragon; a combination of dill and crushed caraway to obtain a homemade Kümmel; a combination of thyme and wild oregano, of which there is plenty in the Savoie; 1½ ounces of crushed juniper berries.

LIQUEUR DE NOYAUX
Apricot Almond Liqueur

This is a form of amaretto. Keep adding the pits all through the summer as you consume the peaches and apricots. To know how many pits you have added, attach a small piece of cardboard around the neck of the jar and punch a hole in it with a pin each time you add a pit. Make certain you use no more than one third apricot pits. This liqueur is a first-rate flavoring for fresh fruit salad.

1 bottle vodka
50 peach pits
25 apricot pits
¾ cup sugar

In a wide-mouthed glass jar, add the pits to the vodka as they come along. Let them steep in the spirit a whole month. Remove the pits and add the sugar. Stir every so often to dissolve the sugar. When the sugar has melted completely, strain the liqueur through a coffee filter into a bottle. Keep well-sealed between consumptions.

LE CHOCOLAT DES SKIEURS
Skiers' Chocolate

As a fitting recipe to close this collection, here is our family's favorite after-ski drink. For us it means good times, the joy of having played in God's wonderful snowy acres and below his wonderfully blue sky; may it bring you all the happiness that is ours when we sit around our family table. The amount of Chartreuse is for an inveterate Chartreuse lover; if it seems too much for your personal taste, do not hesitate to increase the sugar and decrease the Chartreuse. I can see that some people might want to garnish their chocolate with whipped cream. Now, *that* I would find totally decadent!

Yield: 6 mugs of chocolate

6 heaping tablespoons cocoa
¾ cup water
6 teaspoons sugar
5½ cups whole milk
6 ounces green Chartreuse

In a large saucepan, dilute the cocoa with the water and bring to a boil. As soon as the mixture boils, add the sugar and the cold milk. Slowly bring the milk to the boiling point. Pour the mixture into 6 mugs and add 1 ounce of green Chartreuse per portion.

SELECTED BIBLIOGRAPHY

To write this book I have read and studied the texts listed below. Although they appear under different headings, many of these small or large volumes contained information on all four of the listed subjects. The names of the authors come first when the book was authored by one or two persons only; the names of the volumes, booklets, or pamphlets come first when they constitute a joint publication of several writers. All texts but a few have been published in French and to my knowledge have not yet been translated into any other language. I have indicated the original language of publication for the few volumes that were translations from either English or German. All titles and names of cities of publication are spelled in their French form.

The books listed below are all in my personal library; I have also consulted the vast collections of books in the "Fonds Savoyard" of the Annecy Public Library and the Archives de la Haute Savoie. Most of the texts I consulted there, if not on this list will be mentioned in the book.

Bibliography for the geographical, geological and historical information, and the modern development of the Savoie:

Books written by one or two authors:

Blanchard, Raoul. *Naissance et développement d'Annecy.* Annecy: Société des Amis du Viel Annecy, 1978–79.

Braudel, Fernand. *L'identité de la France.* 2 vol. Paris: Arthaud, 1986–1987.

Chapoutot, Pierre and Lovie, Claude. *Voyage à travers la Savoie.* Colmar: SAEP, 1974.

Fritsch, Robert. *Fleurs de Savoie.* Colmar: SAEP, 1973.

Glauser, Michel, and Hutter, Pierre. *Les Chamois et les Bouquetins.* Paris: Payot, 1981.

Jeudy, Jean-Marie. *Chambéry, Aix-les-Bains autrefois, au Pays de la Sasson.* Horvath, 1984.

Menabrea, Henri. *Histoire de la Savoie.* Grenoble, 1976.

Nicolas, Jean. *La Savoie au dix-huitième Siecle, Noblesse et Bourgeoisie.* 2 vol. Paris: Maloine, 1978.

Nicolas, Jean and Renee. *La vie quotidienne en Savoie aux 17ème et 18ème siecles.* Paris: Hachette, 1979.

Rachel, Jacques. *Les Juifs en Savoie*. Atra, 1984.

Regat, Christian. *Annecy au long du Temps*. Menthon Saint-Bernard: Les Sillons du Temps, 1987.

Books and pamphlets written by teams of authors:

Actes des Congrès des Sociétés Savantes de Savoie. *La sociabilité des Savoyards*. 1982.

———. *La Savoie, identités et influences*. 1984.

Glières. Genève: Chevalier, 1983. This book is a memento of the Résistance at the Plateau des Glières during World War II.

Histoire et Civilisations des Alpes. 2 vol. Privat Toulouse et Payot Lausanne, 1980.

La Forêt de Savoie. Chambéry: Association pour le developpement de l'Université de Savoie, 1983.

La Savoie: des origines à l'an mil; de l'An Mil à la Réforme; de la Réforme à la Révolution Française; de la Révolution Française à nos jours. 4 vol. Rennes: Ouest France Université, 1983.

La Savoie sous l'Occupation. Rennes: Ouest France, 1885.

Les Sources Régionales de la Savoie. Paris: Fayard, 1979.

Pays de Savoie. Paris: Christine Bonneton, 1982.

Réalités des Pays de Savoie. Chambéry: Association pour le développement de l'Université de Savoie, 1984.

Savoie. Paris: Christine Bonneton, 1985.

The following booklets, each 25 to 75 pages long, are sold on library stands and look somewhat like "tourist" books; they are not. On the contrary, they are extremely well researched and historically very accurate:

> *l'Alpinisme*
> *Défense et illustration du Parc National de La Vanoise*
> *La Maison de Savoie et l'Europe*
> *Le Thermalisme en Savoie*
> *Les Anglais en Savoie*
> *Les Comtes qui en 400 ans firent la Savoie*
> *Les Patois Témoins de l'Histoire*
> *Migrants et Emigrés*
> *Préhistoire en Savoie*
> (9 booklets. Chambéry: Société Savoisienne d'Histoire et d'Archéologie, 1970s through 1980s)

Bibliography for the place of art and religion in everyday life:

Books written by one or two authors:

Alléra, Jacques. *Art Polupaire Savoyard*. Allera, 1980.

De Maistre, Joseph and Xavier, diverse extracts from their respective works.

Dufournet, Paul. *l'Art Populaire en Savoie*. Paris: Christine Bonneton, 1981.

Germain, Félix. *Hommes et Montagnes de Savoie*. Paris: Arthaud, 1961. Lovely photographs of costumes and religious jewelry as they were still worn in the late 1950s. This book has been translated into English.

Milleret, Abbé René. *Termignon*. Curendera, 1987. Abbé René Milleret is the priest of the parish of Termignon.

Olivier, Lucille. *Mobiliers Savoyard and Dauphinois*. Charles Massin, n.d.

Rousseau, Jean-Jacques. *Les Confessions*. Paris: Classic French Éditions de la Pléiade, Paris.

Sales, Saint François de. *Introduction à la Vie Dévote*. Annecy: Édition du Couvent de la Visitation, n.d.

Samivel et Norande, C. *Monastères de Montagne*. Paris: Arthaud, 1982.

Sonkin, J. and M. *l'Objet Paysan, sa Beauté, son Mystère*. Charles Massin, n.d.

Booklets and books published by teams of authors:

Pèlerinages et Chapelles du Val d'Abondance. Booklet. Cooperative text of the priests from the valley, n.d.

Thônes, L'Église Saint Maurice. Booklet. Lyon: Lescuyer, n.d.

Un Sanctuaire Marial dans les Alpes: Notre Dame de la Vie à Saint Martin de Belleville. Booklet. Lyon: Lescuyer, n.d.

The following booklets each 25 to 75 pages are sold on library stands and look like "tourist" books; they are not. On the contrary, they are extremely well researched and historically very accurate:

L'Art Baroque en Savoie
La Savoie Baroque
La Vie Musicale en Savoie
Noëls Savoyards
Pierres à Cupules et Roches Gravées en Savoie

Bibliography for the ethnology:

Books written by one or two authors:

Billard, Thérèse. *Thérèse Billard raconte ses jeunes années*. Chambéry: Collection Gens de Savoie, 1987.

Boyer, Roland. *Les noms de lieux de la Région du Mont Blanc*. Imprimerie Fot, 1987.

Bravard, Y., and Chavoutier, L. *La Tarentaise, Déclin et Renouveau Contemporain*. Chambéry: l'Histoire en Savoie, 1985.

Canziani, Estella. *Costumes et Légendes de Savoie*. Chambéry: Imprimeries Réunies, 1978. Remarkable drawings and paintings by English painter Estella Canziani during the first two decades of the twentieth century. Since this book was adapted from the English edition by A. Van Gennep, the original edition in English, which was published in London between 1915 and 1920, must be available in British libraries.

Charvin, Abbé Marcel. *Histoires de la Val d'Isère*. Several editions, Val d'Isère, through the 1980s.

Chavoutier, Abbé Lucien. *Saint Bon Courchevel*. Chambéry: Trésors de la Savoie, 1978.

Dequier, D., and Viallet, J. H. *Un Village en Maurienne: Jarrier*. Chambéry: l'Histoire en Savoie, 1982.

Desormeaux, Constantin. *Dictionnaire Savoyard*. Marseilles: Jeanne Lafitte, 1977.

Dompnier, P., and Amourous, C. *La Haute Maurienne*. Chambéry: Société Savoisienne d'Histoire et d'Archéologie, 1986.

Dubois, Yvonne. *La Vallée des Cyclamens*. Cerf, 1983.

Freppaz, Celestin, and Hudry, Maurice. *La Vie traditionnelle en Haute Tarentaise*. Curendera, 1987.

Gay, Maurice, and Balmat, Marie-France. *Les Pellarins*. Chamonix, 1986.

Goldstern, Émilie. *Bessans*. Curendera, 1987. Translated from the original German text published in 1922 in Vienna, Austria, and probably still easy to locate in Austrian libraries.

Hermann, Marie-Thérèse. *Le Genevois*. Chambéry: Société Savoisienne d'histoire et d'archéologie, 1987.

Hudry, Maurice. *La Tarentaise*. Colmar: SAEP, n.d., probably in the 1970s.

Justin, Albert. *En Savoie, Vie, Moeurs et Coutumes du Haut Chablais*. Alléra, 1979.

Lévy-Pinard, Germaine. *La Vie quotidienne à Vallorcine au 18ème siecle*. Annecy: Académie Salésienne, 1983.

Marnezy, Alain. *Maurienne Terre Humaine*. Chambéry: Société Savoisienne d'Histoire et d'Archéologie, 1984.

Paluel-Guillard, André. *Le Beaufortain*. Pamphlet. Chambéry: Société Savoisienne d'Histoire et Archéologie, 1970. This thin and inconspicuous booklet should not be missed; it contains a wealth of information on traditional life in the valleys around Beaufort.

Perrier, J. G. *Le Petiou*. Chambéry: Collection Gens de Savoie, 1981.

Soquet, Dr. Charles. *Megève et son passé*. Megève: 1980.

Souvy, Cyriel. *Morzine au fil des Siècles*. Jean Vuarnet, 1978.

Van Gennep, A. *Culte populaire des Saints en Savoie*. Maisonneuve et Laroze, 1973.

————. *En Savoie du Berceau à la Tombe*. Marseilles: Jeanne Lafitte, 1977.

Van Gennep's works cover in details every angle of life in the traditional Savoie and should be considered the primary source for any ethnological study. His works cover all regions of the Savoie and are based on personal interviews with villagers, priests, trade and professional people.

Books and pamphlets written by teams of authors:

Châlets, Maisons, Momunents, Villages. Booklet. Thônes: Amis du Val de Thônes, 1981

École et Montagne en Savoie. Pamphlet. Chambéry: l'Histoire en Savoie, 1981.

Habundantia, La Vie au Val d'Abondance à travers les temps. Abondance, 1983

Histoire Locale et Traditions. Booklet. Thônes: Amis du Val de Thônes, n.d.

La Montagne Face au Changement. Grenoble: Centre Alpin et Rhôdanien d'ethnologie, 1984.

Le Val de Thônes. Booklet. Thônes Les Amis du Val de Thônes, undated):

Yvoire, Village mediéval. Syndicat d'initiative d'Yvoire, n.d. Tourist pamphlet with good historical interest.

Bibliography for the study of foods, wines, culinary habits, and techniques:

Books written by one or two authors:

Alléra, Jacques. *La Cuisine Traditionnelle Savoyarde.* Alléra, 1980. Besides very informal traditional recipes this book contains lists of modern ideas, the source of which is not mentioned.

Arnaud, Chantal. *Angeltine, La Cuisine à Quatre Mains de mes Grand-Mères aux Pays des Alpes.* Nonette Puy de Dôme: Creer, 1981.

Carnacina, L., and Buonassissi. *Il Libro Della Polenta.* Firenze: Martello-Giunti, 1974.

Chavoutier, Abbé Lucien. *L'histoire millénaire des Alpages.* Chambéry: Société Savoisienne d'Histoire et d'Archéologie, 1985.

Delacretaz, Pierre. *Les Vieux Fours à Pain, Valais, Savoie, Vallée d'Aoste.* Genève: Delpast Romanel, 1982.

Fritsch, Robert. *Les Plantes Médicinales de la Savoie.* Colmar: Delta 2000, SAAEP, 1982.

Girel, Roger. *Le Vignoble Savoyard et ses Vins.* Glénat: Polénat Lucon, 1985.

Grandchamp, Dominique, aka "Mique." *Le Cuisinier à la Bonne Franquette.* Genève, 1883.

Hermann, Marie-Thérèse. *La Cuisine Paysanne de Savoie, La Vie des Fermes et des Châlets racontée par une enfant du Pays.* Sers, 1981. This book is the major work and the major source of information for an understanding of Savoie cuisine between 1880 and 1950.

Julie, Eugénie. *Cuisine Savoyarde.* booklet. Guide RJ, 1980. This name is a pseudonym; the real name of the author is unknown to me, the information is basically accurate and some drawings are enlightening.

La Grande Chartreuse, par un chartreux. Sadag, Bellegarde, 1976. This book is the anonymous work of a Carthusian father.

Lansard, Monique. *Recueil de la Gastronomie Savoyarde.* Colmar: Delta 2000 SAEP, 1982.

Liqueurs et Sirops à Faire Soi-Même. pamphlet. Lure: La Lanterne, 1979.

Noble, N. and Borille, F. *Les dossiers de la Chasse: Le Petit Gibier.* Jacques Gaucher, 1979.

Vanel, Charlotte. *La Bonne Cuisine des Montagnes, Savoie-Dauphiné.* Paris: Solar, 1981.

Books written by teams of authors:

La Chartreuse, Un site, un Lieu. Booklet. Paris: Encyclopédie Intégrale, Nathan, 1984. Contains a historical overview of the monastery and recipes to use the liqueurs.

Le Reblochon de la Vallée de Thônes, le Chevrotin, le Persillé des Aravis. Thônes: Revue Annuelle des Amis du Val de Thônes, 1987.

Museums to visit in Savoie, Dauphiné, Switzerland, and Italy (several of the museums give very interesting series of lectures).

Musée Château d'Annecy, Annecy, Haute Savoie

Musée d'Arts et Traditions Populaires du Val d'Arly, Château du Crest Cherel, Ugine, Savoie

Musée Régional de Thônes, Thônes, Haute Savoie

Musée Savoisien, Square Lannoy de Bissy, Chambéry, Savoie

Musée de Conflans, Conflans, Savoie

Musée Régional de Thonon, Thonon les Bains, Haute Savoie

Musée de Moutiers, Moûtiers, Savoie

Musée Dauphinois, 30 rue Maurice Gignoux, 38031, Grenoble Isère 38031

Musée d'Ethnographie de la Ville de Genève, collection of Monsieur Amoudruz, Annexe de Conches, 7 chemin Calendrini, 12310 Conches, Switzerland

Musée d'Ethnographie de Neuchâtel, 4 rue Saint Nicolas 2006, Neuchâtel, Switzerland

Museo Nazionale della Montagna, Via Gaetano Giardino 39, 10131 Torino, Piemonte, Italy

Private collections:

Pottery: Musée de la Poterie, Monsieur Jean Christophe Hermann, Evires, Haute Savoie

Tools and Vehicles: Musée de l'Outil et des Techniques, Madame Marie Thérèse Hermann and her family, Evires, Haute Savoie

Musée Paysan d'Eloise, Eloise, Haute Savoie, Monsieur Fillon

Musée Paysan de Fessy Lully, Haute Savoie, Monsieur Bernard Lacroix; the pieces are mixed, some ancient some recent

Chapelle Saint Antoine de Bessans, Savoie, for the fresco paintings

Chapelle Saint Sébastien de Lanslebourg, Savoie, for the collection of wooden hand-carved statues

Churches Not to Be Missed:

Some of the churches in remote intra-Alpine valleys are closed due to the absence of proper supervision during the week. If you want to visit or photograph, call the priest whose name is always listed under *Eglise* or *Centre Paroissial* or *Curé* or *Abbé*; there is no uniformity of listing.

Eglises of the small towns and villages of:

Peisey-Nancroix, Tarentaise
Doucy, Tarentaise
Avrieux, Maurienne
Termignon, Maurienne
Valloire, Maurienne
Saint Gervais, Faucigny
Thônes, Genevois is always opened
Saint Bon (Close to Courchevel), Tarentaise
Champagny, Tarentaise
Lanslevillard, Maurienne
Séez, Haute Tarentaise
Sainte Foy, Haute Tarentaise, is brand new, but the altars and statues of the old church decorate the new church, which can be seen from the outside through large glass panels.

This is just a short list. Do try to see the church in any village; it is always very beautiful and well worth seeing. No admission is charged; just drop a coin or two in the special renovation fund box. If you request a special opening of the church to take photographs, please leave an envelope with a donation for the church renovation fund.

INDEX